THE GUINNESS
BOOK OF
IRISH
FACTS & FEATS

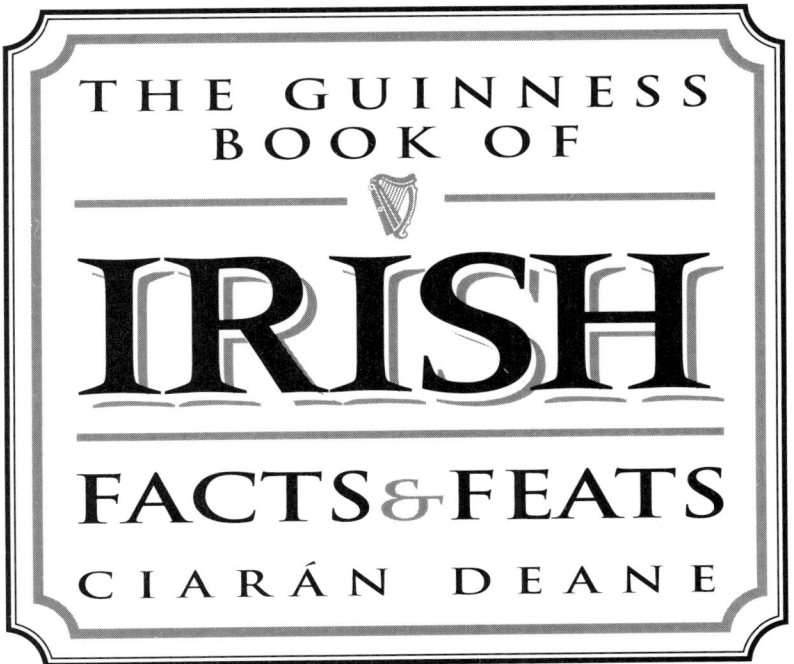

THE GUINNESS BOOK OF

IRISH

FACTS & FEATS

CIARÁN DEANE

In association with the
Irish Tourist Board

GUINNESS PUBLISHING

The author would like to thank the following for their assistance in
compiling this book:
The Argentine Embassy (Dublin), The Canadian Embassy (Dublin), Mark
Cohen, John de Courcy Ireland, Conor Deane, Cormac Deane, Emer Deane,
Marion Deane, Seamus Deane, The Gaelic Athletic Association, The Irish
Rugby Football Union, Louis MacManus, Cathal O'Farrell, Dara O'Leary
and David Odlum.

Editor: Richard Milbank
Assistant Editor: Roselle Le Sauteur

Design and Layout: John Rivers

Typeset in Century Old Style by Ace Filmsetting Ltd., Frome, Somerset.
Printed and bound in Great Britain by The Bath Press, Bath

A catalogue record for this book is available from the British Library.

ISBN 0–85112–793–2

contents

contents

íntroöuctíon

To list all the achievements and records of Ireland and its people would be the function of an encyclopedia of Ireland. *The Guinness Book of Irish Facts and Feats* makes no claim to be comprehensive. Some people and places in this book will be already well known, others will not. The places have all achieved renown because they are distinctive in themselves or because of their relation to men or women of historic importance. Some of the people may be worthy of praise and adulation, others are less than lovable. Particular attention has been paid to people and places throughout the world that are not traditionally associated with Ireland. The diversity of human achievement represented here goes beyond the boundaries imposed by received notions of the Irish national stereotype.

Irishness is not limited to the island of Ireland in much the same way that Jewishness is not confined to Israel. There are just over five million people living in Ireland (including Northern Ireland), while there are over sixty million people worldwide who consider themselves Irish by heritage. Today in the United States, where over forty-three million people claim Irish descent, Irish-Americans are the second most influential ethnic group.

Ireland has always played a role in Western civilisation disproportionate to its size. This is largely an accident of history and it cannot be claimed that the merit of such a role has always coincided with its prominence. However, the far-reaching importance of so many people highlighted here is undisputed. Their diverse contributions date from the Dark Ages, when Ireland was the last preserve of Western Christianity and learning, to the era of European dominance during which Irish people made a huge contribution to the Spanish, French (Napoleonic) and, most of all, British Empires. The Irish were also prominent in the history of dissent from the dominant political and religious cultures. For instance, the Irish Church in the Dark Ages was perceived as a radical threat to the influence of Rome, while in the 19th century and earlier the Irish were always renowned for their opposition to colonialism and imperialism whether they were in Melbourne, Mexico or Mitchelstown.

This book hopes to make the reader more aware of the full range of Irish facts and feats and to give a wider than usual view of the Irish contribution to history. Omissions have been made, some dictated by the restrictions of time and space, others by oversight. The author welcomes any suggestions by readers for people or places that they believe should be included.

Guinness Publishing gratefully
acknowledges the support of the
Irish Tourist Board,
150–151 New Bond Street,
London, W1Y 0AR

A cross-section of the Fenian Ram, *the first successful submarine, designed by J.P. Holland of Liscannor, Co. Clare. It was launched in New York in 1881 and was intended for the revolutionary republican group, the Fenians, for use against the British Navy.*

science, technology and medicine

INVENTORS, ENGINEERS AND SCIENTISTS

✤**The submarine** was invented by **John Philip Holland** (1841–1914) of Liscannor, Co. Clare. In 1872, after 14 years of teaching with the Christian Brothers, Holland was dispensed of his vows and went to the United States. He first put forward his plan of a submarine boat to the US Navy in 1875 but it was dismissed by the Secretary of the Navy as a 'fantastic scheme of a civilian landsman'. He persevered and developed a small submarine after years of experiment with the funding of Irish friends and Clan na Gael, the Fenian movement, who hoped that the vessel could be used against the British Navy. The *Fenian Ram* was launched in 1881 in New York City,

built by the Delamater Iron Company. The vessel measured 31 × 6 × 6 ft (9.45 × 1.83 × 1.83 m) and displaced 19 tons (19.31 tonnes). It was driven by a 15 hp engine and was armed with an underwater cannon fired by compressed air.

Holland won competitions for submarine designs launched by the US government in 1888, 1889 and 1893. He received a contract from the US Navy Secretary, Theodore Roosevelt, to build a submarine in 1895. The first model, completed in 1898, was unsuccessful, but the second model, *The Holland*, passed all tests and was accepted. The decision to accept had been spurred on by news of successful trials being conducted by the French navy on their own prototype designed by Laubeuf. (Spain and Italy had also just produced successful prototypes.) Six of Holland's original prototype were ordered. Britain, Russia and Japan had models built in the run-up to World War I.

The *Fenian Ram* was never used for its intended purpose and spent most of its time in storage. In 1916 it was publicly displayed to raise funds for the victims of the British Army shelling of Dublin. Today it is on permanent display in Paterson, New Jersey.

Britain's first Holland submarine was salvaged intact from the English Channel in 1983 after 70 years on the seabed. It is now on display at the submarine museum at Gosport. The periscopes for Britain's submarines in World War I were built by the Grubb factory in Rathmines, Dublin (see p. 17).

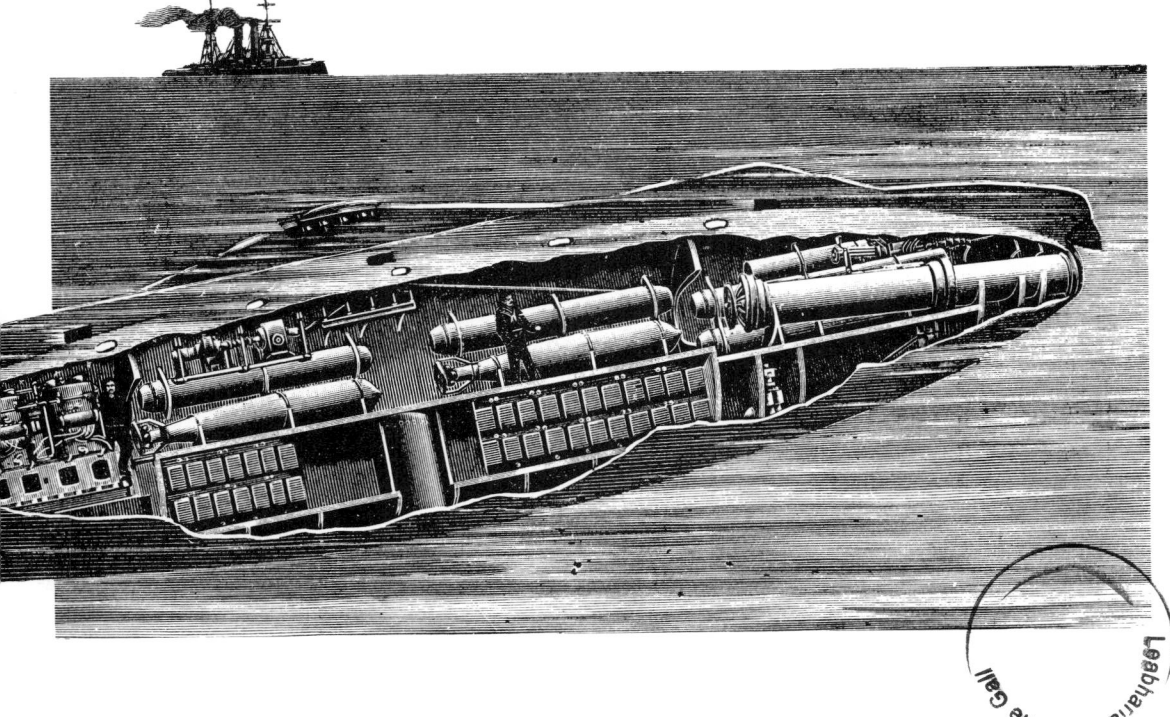

The submarine designed by William Garrett of Trinity College, Dublin and constructed at Birkenhead, Liverpool in 1879. The vessel carried no compressed air. When the submarine was submerged the air in it was cleaned chemically.

Although Holland's submarine is recognised as **the first commercially successful underwater craft**, his was not the first to be built. The development of the submarine was the result of technology and experiment accumulated since the 18th century.

The submarine built by the **Reverend George William Garrett** of Trinity College, Dublin, and launched at Birkenhead, England in 1879, was very nearly successful. Garrett's craft measured 45ft (13.7m) in length and 8ft 10in (2.7m) in beam. It descended by means of pistons which varied the displacement of water and it did not require to take water on board (the stumbling block of so many early submarine designs). The Swedish engineer Thorston Nordenfelt was sufficiently impressed to employ Garrett in the construction of *Nordenfelt I, II, III* and *IV* in Stockholm from 1885. The submarines operated successfully when they were partially submerged but proved to be unsafe when fully under water.

♣ **James J. Wood**, born in Kinsale, Co. Cork in 1856, was probably **Ireland's most prolific inventor** of all with over 240 patents. As a boy he went to America with his family and was raised in Connecticut. An accomplished electrical engineer, in 1880 he patented his first invention, the arc-light dynamo. In 1885 he installed the first floodlight system at the Statue of Liberty in New York. He designed the electrics of the internal combustion engine for Holland's submarine and the machines that constructed the cables for Brooklyn Bridge. He became Chief Engineer of Gen-

eral Electric in 1885 and made numerous innovations in the designs of a/c generators, electric motors and transformers. He died in North Carolina in 1928.

♣ The **underwater mine** was invented by the Irish-American **Robert Fulton** (1765–1815), son of Robert Fulton Snr of Kilkenny. A gifted engineer, he was responsible for the construction of many canals and bridges in the United States. (He was also a talented painter of miniatures and was a pupil of Benjamin West.)

In 1807 Fulton designed a steamboat, the *Clermont*, which was **the first steam-powered vessel to prove that steam travel was both technically and commercially feasible**. It plied a successful route between New York and Albany, covering the distance of 150 miles (93.75 km) in 32 hours. He also invented a submarine which he launched in 1801. The *Nautilus*, although fully operational, proved ineffective in battle and was turned down by both the British and French navies, who had initially expressed interest during the Napoleonic Wars. In 1814 he designed *Fulton the First*, **the world's first steam-powered warship**.

His inventiveness was recalled in 1955 when the United States Navy launched its first nuclear-powered submarine, and named it *Nautilus* after Fulton's earlier model.

♣ **The dirigible torpedo, monorail, and first unmanned helicopter** were all the creations of

Louis Brennan (1852–1932). Born in Castlebar, Co. Mayo, he emigrated to Melbourne, Australia at an early age. He was working as a watchmaker in Melbourne when he developed the first internally-driven dirigible torpedo. Intending it initially for Australian coastal defence (the project was partly funded by the government of Victoria), he sold the rights to the British government in 1886. The £100,000 paid by the British government for the exclusive rights caused uproar at the time. There were many opponents of the scheme who considered it too expensive and who doubted its effectiveness.

From 1887 to 1907 Brennan worked at the British government factory in Gillingham, Kent on torpedo design and coastal defence systems. He also invented a monorail system that was balanced and propelled by a high-speed gyrostat rotating in a vacuum. He showed a model of his design to the Royal Society in 1907. He worked for the British Ministry of Munitions 1914–18 and with the Air Ministry 1919–26. It was with the Air Ministry that he was engaged in the development of helicopters and succeeded in achieving **the first unmanned helicopter flight** – reaching an altitude of 2000ft (609.6m) and a speed of 20mph (32km/h).

🍀 **The pneumatic tyre** was invented in Ireland by **John Dunlop** (1840–1921), who was born in Ayrshire, Scotland. As a child Dunlop moved to Belfast, where he later set up a successful veterinary practice. In 1887 he developed an inflatable rubber tube for his son's bicycle. After a number of successful test runs, he applied for a patent which was duly granted in 1888. Although the idea of a pneumatic tyre had been put forward by another Scot, Robert Thompson, as early as 1845, Dunlop succeeded in manufacturing the first practical form of the tyre. On 18 May 1889 the cycle race at Queen's College Sport's Day in Belfast was won by a rider using fitted Dunlop tyres. It was an event that heralded a revolution in the history of transport.

🍀 **The first transatlantic cable*** was designed in 1865 and then laid using instruments designed by **William Thompson (Lord Kelvin)** (1824–1907). He was born in College Square East, Belfast and matriculated to the University of Glasgow at the age of 11. After a spell at Cambridge, he accepted the post of professor of natural history at Glasgow when only 22 years old. He held this post for 53 years, during which time he established himself as one of the leading scientists of the 19th century. He was a prolific inventor who devised numerous instruments for measuring electricity as well as tide-gauges and predictors and depth-sounding apparatus. His principal achievement was his **discovery of the second law of thermodynamics**. He is particularly remembered in the Kelvin absolute scale of temperature used for low-temperature studies.

🍀 **Wireless telegraphy and radio transmission** were revolutionised by **Marchese Guglielmo Marconi** (1874–1937), the engineer and inventor born in Bologna of an Italian father and an Irish mother. His father was a wealthy landowner and his mother was Anne Jameson of the famous whiskey-distilling family. He made his first successful experiments in wireless telegraphy in Bologna in 1895 before travelling to England to make further research. He made **the first international transmission** in 1899 between France and England.

A dramatic demonstration of Robert Fulton's submarine Nautilus *given in the presence of the British Prime Minister William Pitt on 15 October 1805. The ship destroyed was the Danish brig* Dorothée.

---

* *The transatlantic cable was laid by Wicklow navigator Robert Halpin (see p. 33) and promoted by Cyrus Field and John Mackay, an Irish-born American mining tycoon (see p. 44).*

On 12 December 1901 it was believed that radio waves could 'bend' around the earth when Marconi transmitted the first transatlantic radio signals from Poldhu, Cornwall in England to St John's, Newfoundland (a province of Canada since 1949). Later discoveries proved that the radio waves were, in fact, reflected from the earth's ionosphere.

Marconi was **awarded the Nobel Prize for Physics** with the German physicist Karl Braun in 1909.

As is the case with most scientific developments, Marconi was only one in a series of scientists who worked on radio transmission. However, it was Marconi who was the first to perfect radio and to take it out of experimental science and into commercial use.

✽ **The first sporting event ever reported on radio** was the Dún Laoghaire yacht race in 1898. Marconi sent messages from the tug *Flying Huntress* to the Kingstown (now Dún Laoghaire) harbourmaster's house.

✽ One of Ireland's leading scientists was **George Francis Fitzgerald** (1851–1901), without whom the work of Marconi (see p. 11) and also of Einstein might never have borne fruit. Fitzgerald, who was professor of physics at Trinity College, Dublin, is best remembered for the Fitzgerald-Lorentz contraction theory which states that a moving body will contract in the direction of its motion. (Lorentz was a Dutch physicist who worked with Fitzgerald.) The mathematical principle of this hypothesis was an essential factor in Einstein's development of the theory of relativity in 1905.

Fitzgerald was a pioneer in the electro-magnetic theory of radiation and in 1883 he proposed a practical procedure to achieve the high-frequency currents required to produce VHF radio waves. This was an important step toward the transmission of radio waves and was soon improved upon by Hertz and Marconi. Fitzgerald was a polymath whose discoveries and theories were relevant to many different fields of science. He was **the first scientist ever to suggest that the tail of a comet is formed by the pressure of solar radiation.** Fitzgerald took an active interest in the science of flight. In 1895 he constructed a glider which he flew in the grounds of Trinity College. A special ramp was constructed for him to run down with helpers towing the glider like a kite. The glider would only carry Fitzgerald for a few yards, but flew well without a passenger.

✽ **The harpoon gun** was invented by **Thomas Nesbitt** of Kilmacredon, Co. Donegal for the whaling industry that was established in Killybegs in 1737. Nesbitt designed his swivel-gun around 1759–60. Although there is evidence that harpoon guns were being unsuccessfully experimented with elsewhere in Europe in the latter half of the 18th century, it was Nesbitt who produced the first workable weapon.

✽ **Hydraulically controlled farm machinery** was developed by **Harry Ferguson** during World War I in response to British government calls to grow more food and increase productivity. Ferguson was born Henry George at Gromwell near Hillsborough, Co. Down in 1884. He left home at 16 to become a mechanic and soon showed his aptitude for invention. He **built the first Irish aeroplane**, flying it for the first time in a force 9 gale on 31 December 1909. It was the first plane to have a tricycle undercarriage and the design was adapted for passenger jets fifty years later.

John Dunlop with his pneumatic tyred bicycle. Patented in 1888, the pneumatic tyre was used – with great effect – in the Belfast bicycle race of 1889.

The Belfast scientist, William Thompson (later Lord Kelvin), gives his last lecture at Glasgow University in 1899. Thompson developed the Kelvin absolute scale of temperature by which he is eponymously remembered.

At this time, mechanised ploughs were dragged between two cumbersome steam engines at either end of a field. Ferguson resolved to invent a plough that could be mounted on a tractor with the implements hydraulically controlled. In 1935 the prototype was built and in 1939 he became Henry Ford's one and only partner in a handshake agreement that had him selling 306,000 Fordson tractors and a million pieces of equipment over the war years. In 1947, following the death of Henry Ford, the Ford company was taken over by Ford's grandson, who promptly broke the agreement. Ferguson's response was to set up his own factory, the Ferguson Tractor Company, in Detroit which recorded sales of $33 million by 1949. After lengthy compensation suits Ferguson was eventually awarded $9.25 million in 1952. He always insisted that the law suit was not for the money but to protect the rights of the small inventor against the big corporations.

The Ferguson Tractor Company merged with the Canadian Massey Company in 1953. Massey-Ferguson came into being in 1958 and operated until 1987, when it was renamed the Variety Corporation.

🍀 **The first practical system of colour photography** was patented by the engineer, geologist and physicist **John Joly** (1857–1933), aptly born in Hollywood, Co. Offaly. He was professor of geology at Trinity College, Dublin 1897–1933 and produced a constant flow of inventions. In 1894 he invented a system of colour photography by taking and viewing photographs on plates scored with numerous thin lines in three colours. The method produced excellent transparencies. Joly also invented a meldometer to measure the melting and sublimation of materials, a steam calorimeter to measure specific heats and a photometer to compare the intensities of two light sources, thus calculating the intensity of an unknown from a known source. In 1899 he measured the age of the oceans by estimating the rate of deposit of sodium and also devised a method for the dating of rocks. With Dr Walter Clegg Stevenson of Dr Steevens' Hospital in Dublin he developed a technique of treating cancer growths using radon gas, thus pioneering the radium method (see p. 26).

🍀 The **hypodermic syringe** was invented by **Francis Rynd** (1801–61), an accomplished doctor and a member of the so-called 'Dublin School' of medicine that achieved so much in the last century. It was developed specifically for the injection of morphine as an anaesthetic rather than administering it by mouth as had been the practice.

🍀 **Shorthand writing** was first invented by **John R. Gregg** (1876–1948) of Rockcorry, Co. Monaghan. He based his system on the natural movement of the hand and published his first pamphlet in Liverpool in 1893 before travelling to the United States, where he revised his system and published the Gregg Shorthand Method. It has been adapted to 13 different languages and is still widely used. The method has continued to be revised and updated over the years.*

🍀 **The cup anemometer,** which is used to measure exact wind speeds, was invented by the Dublin-born astronomer and physicist **Thomas Romney Robinson** (1792–1882). In 1823 Robinson was appointed Chief Astronomer at the Armagh Observatory where he made invaluable contributions to contemporary astronomical research. The anemometer was developed at Trinity College in 1843 and was first put into use on Dún Laoghaire pier in 1852. The anemometer consists of three or four cups mounted symmetrically on a vertical axis. The cups rotate at a rate determined by the speed of the wind. The speed of individual gusts and an overall average speed can thus be calculated.

🍀 **John Wigham** of Booterstown, Co. Dublin patented the **first illuminated harbour buoy** in 1869. In 1895 the buoy was successfully employed in Southampton harbour, burning for a month without stopping against all the elements.

Wigham made other developments in coastal navigation that have been put into use worldwide. In 1865 he fitted Howth Baily lighthouse in Dublin Bay with the **world's first gas light.** As well as being less likely to break, the new gas light gave out 3000 candle-power as opposed to an average 240 for the oil lamps then in general use. In 1872 he fitted a new gas light in Wicklow Head lighthouse and attached a clockwork valve to produce an intermittent flash. This idea was developed further in 1872 at Howth Baily. The gas light was increased in intensity to 9000 candle-power and an intermittent gas light with a revolving lens produced flashes in groups. This was eventually recognised as the most efficient and effective way of warning and directing shipping traffic and has been employed internationally. Wigham set up his own company, Barrett & Co of Schoolhouse Lane, Dublin, which continues to export lighthouse equipment today.

🍀 **The 'Mitchell Screw Pile'** was invented by Dublin-born civil engineer **Alexander Mitchell** (1780–1868). It was patented in 1842 and was a simple but effective method of constructing lighthouses in deep water or on shifting or unstable sands. Many

Harry Ferguson photographed on his Gloucestershire estate. Ferguson's greatest innovation, a tractor with a hydraulically powered plough, revolutionised agricultural production worldwide.

lighthouses throughout Ireland and Britain are built using the device. It is also used on the viaducts and bridges of the Bombay and Baroda railway and the entire Indian telegraph system.

🍀 **Ultra-rapid cinematography and the electrocardiograph** were both inventions of Dublin-born **Lucien Bull** (1876–1972). He pioneered and developed the first ultra-rapid cinematography pictures and had recorded 500 images per second as early as 1902. For the first time slow-motion photography could reveal the passage of a bullet through a glass screen or the movement of a drop of milk falling into a bowl. In 1952 he recorded one million images per second. The electrocardiograph (ECG) was developed in 1908 and greatly advanced the monitoring of heart illnesses. Bull was director of the Institut Marey, Paris in 1914, in charge of research at the National Office of Research and Invention 1933, Director of the School of Higher Studies 1937 and President of The Institute of Scientific Cinematography 1948.

✿ **The first commercial use of refrigeration** was made by **Michael Cudahy** (1841–1910) of Callan, Co. Kilkenny. In 1849 he and his family emigrated to the United States, where they settled in Milwaukee, Wisconsin. Cudahy worked as a meatpacker and worked his way into management before establishing his own firm, the Cudahy Packing Company, in 1890.

During the 1870s refrigeration technology was developed enough for Cudahy to explore new possibilities for the meat industry. As a partner in the Chicago company Armour & Co from 1875, he built the first cold storage warehouses and commissioned the construction of refrigerated railroad cars. Many businesses took advantage of the new technology, but Cudahy is recognised as its foremost proponent and financier. Refrigeration revolutionised food making and consumption by making fresh food available to the public all year round for the first time. Cudahy made a vast fortune and eventually bought Armour's share in the partnership.

✿ **The armoured tank**, or the first workable version of a tank, was designed by **Walter Gordon Wilson** (1874–1957) of Blackrock, Co. Dublin and the London-born engineer William Tritton.

Wilson worked with the naval engineer Percy Pilcher and together they formed Wilson, Pilcher & Co which in 1899 designed **the world's first internal combustion aero-engine**. Unfortunately Pilcher was killed in a gliding accident before a working engine was ever put to the test in flight. Wilson, more suited to engine than aviation design, turned to the manufacture of automobile engines and created the Wilson-Pilcher motor car with epicyclic gears – a cluster of gears made up of a central gear wheel, a coaxial gear wheel of greater diameter and one or more planetary gears engaging with both of them to provide the greatest gear ratio in a small space.

In 1904 he joined Armstrong-Whitworth & Co and designed the successful Armstrong-Whitworth automobile. In 1908, with J&E Hall of Dartford, Wilson designed the Hallford lorry which was used by the British Army in World War I.

In 1915 Winston Churchill set up a committee to investigate the possibility of building an armoured vehicle capable of resisting bullets and shrapnel, crossing trenches, flattening barbed wire and negotiating the mud of no-man's land. Wilson was put in charge of the first experiments at Burton-on-Trent. Tritton and Wilson designed and built the first tank within the year. However, in August 1915 the machine was given a new set of mobility requirements that took the engineers back to the drawing board. Wilson developed the idea of caterpillar tracks* surrounding the vehicle on both sides and the new version, tested before Lloyd George, Balfour and Kitchener in early 1916, was accepted. The Mark I Tank was used for the first time at the Battle of the Somme in September 1916. Wilson later designed a self-changing gearbox and developed epicyclic gears for the Mark I tank. He also founded the Self-Changing Gear Company in Coventry.

✿ **The aircraft ejector seat** was invented by **James Martin** (1893–1981) of Crossgar, Co. Down. Martin moved to England in 1924 to pursue a career in engineering. In 1929 he joined what is now the Martin Aircraft Works in Middlesex. With his colleague James Val Baker, he designed the MB2 and MB3 RAF fighter planes. Baker was killed during a test flight of the MB3, an event that prompted Martin to concentrate on safety design in military aircraft.

The final impetus for a design that allowed pilots to escape from their planes came after the Battle of Britain. Martin devised a canopy with an explosive release mechanism and an ejector seat that would catapult the pilot safely away from the aeroplane. The design process progressed steadily during the war years and the **first successful ejection from a moving aircraft** was made in July 1946. The tests were so successful that MB ejector seats were being fitted to all new military jet aircraft by 1947. Martin was awarded a knighthood and an OBE.

✿ **The ophthalmoscope,** a device for inspecting the interior of the eye and the retina in particular, was invented by the surgeon and antiquarian **William Robert Wilde** (1815–76). He ran a highly successful practice as an eye and ear specialist on Molesworth Street, Dublin, but is perhaps better remembered as the father of Oscar Wilde (see p. 137).

✿ **The heat exchanger** is an important energy-saving device that remains today an apparatus crucial to the success of many industrial chemical plants and is the standard method of production of industrial spirit. The first heat exchanger was invented in 1830 for use in the distillation of whiskey by Dublin-born **Aeneas Coffey** (1780–1852) and was known as Coffey's Patent Still.

* *Caterpillar tracks were patented in 1899 and first successfully demonstrated in 1904 by John Walker of Castlecomer, Co. Kilkenny.*

🍀 **The turbine** was invented in 1884 by **Charles Parsons** (1884–1931), son of the 3rd Earl of Rosse of Birr Castle, Co. Offaly. When first demonstrated in 1897 for Queen Victoria's diamond jubilee, the vessel, *Turbinia*, steamed through the rest of the fleet on display at 34.5 knots (63.9 km/h), establishing a new world water-speed record for a mechanically propelled ship. The mercantile marine adopted the new turbines and the Cunard Line vessel *Mauritania* subsequently held the Blue Riband for crossing the Atlantic for nearly 25 years. (The Hales Trophy or 'Blue Riband' is awarded to the vessel that attains the highest average speed on a transatlantic voyage.) The *Turbinia* was built at Wallsend-on-Tyne, Tyne & Wear, England in 1894. It was 98 ft (30 m) in length and displaced 45.2 tonnes. The engine consisted of three steam turbines providing a total power of about 2000hp. The ship is preserved today in Newcastle-upon-Tyne, England.

Parsons' turbines were employed in the construction of the 17,900-tonne battleship *Dreadnought* in 1906 and took it to a top speed of 22.4 knots (41.5km/h). *Dreadnought's* size, power and speed were superior to anything built previously and rendered the battleships of the rest of the world obsolete. From the day of its launch, *Dreadnought* changed the face of naval construction. The turbines enabled propeller blades to rotate much faster, more efficiently and more cleanly than before. The engine rooms of ships fitted with turbines were quieter, cleaner, safer and filled with fewer noxious fumes than the steamships.

By the time of Parsons' death all the navies of the world, military and mercantile, had installed his turbines in their best ships. (His company, NEI Parsons of Newcastle-upon-Tyne, is still in business.)

🍀 **The induction coil** was invented by **Nicholas Joseph Callan** (1799–1864), of Dundalk, Co. Louth.

A diagram of Coffey's Patent Still or heat exchanger. Dubliner Aeneas Coffey designed the still in 1830 with the intention of making the production of whiskey more efficient. The still was, in fact, too successful, producing a 95% pure spirit that eleminated most of the elements that give malt whiskey its taste.

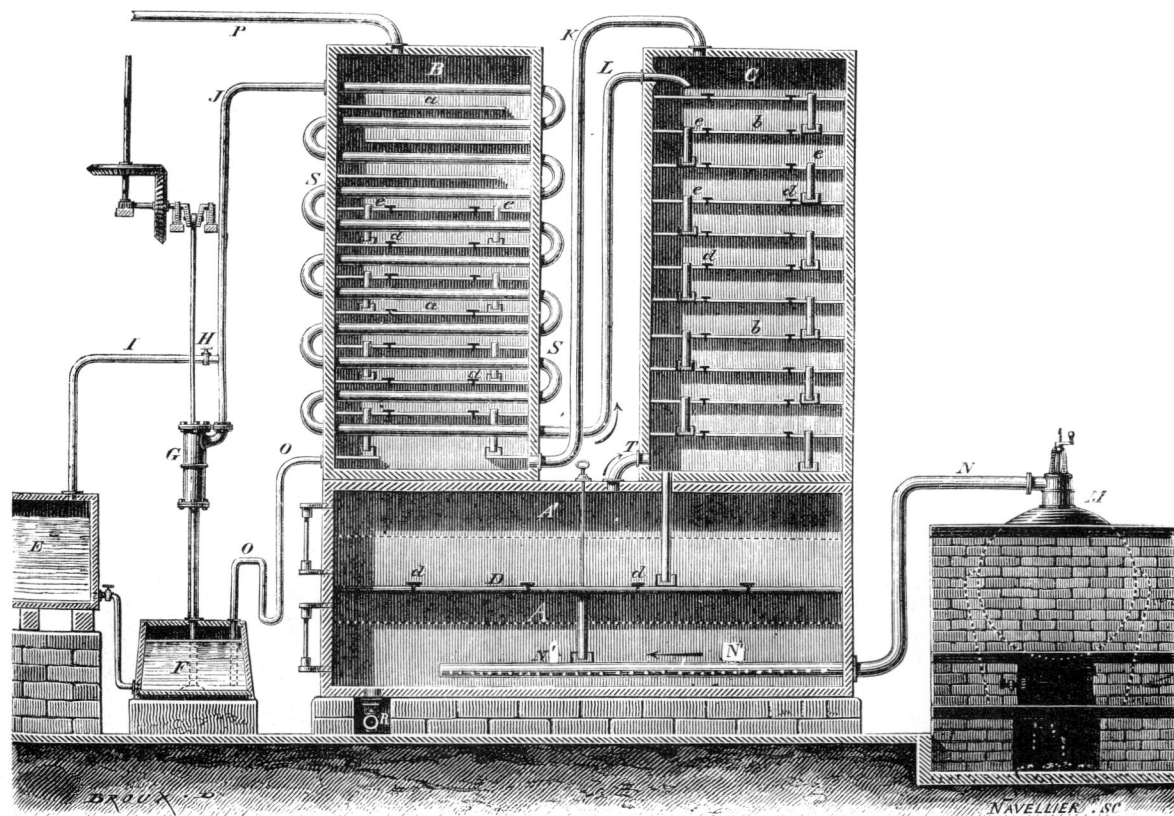

A priest and professor of natural philosophy at Maynooth College, Callan was a pioneer in the development of electrical science. The induction coil, predecessor of the modern transformer, generated very high voltages for the first time. The invention made it possible to produce X-rays and provided the means of studying electrical discharges in rarefied gases, thus contributing to our knowledge of atomic structure.

❧ **Soda water** was first artificially produced by **Robert Percival** (1756–1839) in 1800, professor of chemistry at Trinity College, Dublin.

❧ **Irish coffee** was first made, it is claimed, at Foynes, Co. Limerick by Dublin chef **Joe Sheridan** in 1943. He made the drink to lift the spirits of the earliest transatlantic travellers on the Boeing B314 flying boat service that was often forced to turn back owing to strong headwinds and ice.

❧ **Telescopes: Thomas Grubb** (1800–78), born in Kilkenny, was a self-taught mechanic and engineer who devised a machine for engraving, printing and numbering banknotes for the Bank of Ireland. But, as a practising optician, his main subject interest lay in optics and, from the 1830s, he designed and built telescopes. His most famous construction was the 48-inch (122-cm) reflecting telescope for Melbourne, Australia. The Grubb engineering shop in Dublin expanded to become internationally famous. Grubb's son, Howard (1844–1931), continued and developed the business. In 1877 he completed a 27-inch (68.6-cm) equatorial refracting telescope and four domes for the Royal Observatory in Vienna. Grubb telescopes were exported to Russia, South America, Australia, India and elsewhere. Howard Grubb also devised smaller instruments, including the celostat, a clockwork instrument which revolves to follow heavenly bodies. It was this instrument that was first used to test and

Charles Parsons' vessel Turbinia. *Parsons' triumphant demonstration of the steam turbine in 1897 revolutionised marine propulsion. The turbine rapidly supplanted the reciprocating steam engine in naval craft and other ships.*

The Birr Castle telescope at Birr, Co. Offaly was the largest in the world between 1845 and 1917. It was designed by William Parsons, the third Earl of Rosse, and built by local craftsmen and labourers. Through the telescope, William Parsons discovered the spiral shape of distant galaxies.

verify Einstein's theory of relativity in Sobra, Brazil in 1919.

During World War I the Grubb firm, taken over by the sons of Howard Grubb, made gunsights, periscopes and various instruments for the British Army. The firm moved to St Albans in England in 1922. In 1925 the Grubb and Parsons Company was founded in Newcastle-upon-Tyne in a joint venture with Charles Parsons (see p. 16), inventor of the turbine. The company remained in operation until 1984.

❦ **The largest telescope in the world from 1845 to 1917** was located at Birr Castle, Co. Offaly, home to the Parsons family since 1620 and seat of the Earl of Rosse from 1807. William Parsons, 3rd Earl of Rosse and MP for King's County (Offaly) 1831, resigned his seat in 1834 in order to dedicate his time to scientific study. Parsons devised and built the telescope *Leviathan* with local workmen on the estate, where they made their own tools, furnaces and ovens. The construction of the 72-inch (182.8-cm) speculum was begun in 1842. By 1845 it was completed and

mounted. The tube in which it was mounted is 58ft (17.5m) long and 7ft (2.1m) in diameter, slung in chains between two piers of masonry 50ft (15.2m) high and all built at an estimated cost of £20,000. When completed the telescope could see further into space than ever before. Parsons' main discovery was the spiral shape of many of the distant galaxies. His findings were extensively published and he was honoured by many societies. He was President of the Royal Society 1849–54 and awarded membership of the Royal Academy of St Petersburg in 1853. In 1862 he became Chancellor of Dublin University. The visitor's book at Birr Castle records a long list of renowned scientists and astronomers from all over the world who came to view the enormous telescope that remained the world's largest until the commissioning of the Hooker Reflector at the Mount Wilson Observatory in California in 1917. The telescope is now in the Science Museum, London.

❦ The **temperature of the surface of the moon** was first estimated by **Laurence Parsons** (1840–

1908). He built an instrument that measured lunar radiation through the 72-inch (182.8-cm) telescope and produced temperature graphs whose accuracy was only recognised long after his death in 1908. (Laurence Parsons was the son of the 3rd Earl of Rosse and brother of Charles Parsons (see p. 16), inventor of the turbine.)

❧ The **'father of chemistry'** and Ireland's most famous chemist, **Robert Boyle** (1627–91), was born in Lismore Castle, Co. Waterford, the son of the Earl of Cork. He was chiefly responsible for transforming Western chemistry from a mystical subject (alchemy)

Robert Boyle, Earl of Cork and 'the father of chemistry', in an engraving by George Vertue after a painting by Isaac Kerseboom. Boyle established chemistry as a modern science based on demonstration by experimentation.

to an experimental science. Alchemists had sought a mythical 'philosopher's stone' that would turn a base metal to gold. Contemporaries of Boyle such as Huygens and Leibniz rejected the notion of demonstrating by experiment and preferred to prove theories through logical argument. Boyle's great achievement, 'Boyle's Law', states that the volume of a gas is inversely proportional to its pressure at constant temperature. He also experimented in the transmission of sound through air, specific gravities, refractivity, electricity and colour. He proved the existence of a vacuum and that atmospheric pressure was responsible for the phenomenon. Boyle was fluent in French, Italian, Hebrew, Greek and Syriac, studied the writings of Galileo in Florence when only 15 and was a founder member of the Royal Society in London in 1660 following the restoration of Charles II to the throne. He donated the then huge sum of £700 to Bishop Bedell in order to have the Bible translated into Irish.

❧ **The splitting of the atom** was first achieved by **Ernest Walton**, born in Dungarvan, Co. Waterford in 1903. Walton, a graduate of Trinity College, Dublin, split the atom for the first time in history in a room in the Cavendish Laboratory, Cambridge in 1931. From the safety of a rudimentary shelter to protect himself from high voltages, he observed scintillations on a lithium target caused by a stream of protons accelerated to 700,000 volts. (The accelerator, **the world's first nuclear particle generator**, was built to his own design.) Walton, together with his colleague John Cockcroft (1897–1968), received the Nobel Prize for Physics in 1951.

❧ **Quaternions** are important mathematical devices that make use of imaginary numbers. They are the basis for today's quantum mechanics and nuclear physics. The quaternion formula was carved into Brougham Bridge over the Royal Canal in Dublin by **Sir William Rowan Hamilton** (1805–65) in October 1843 in a burst of inspiration. While out walking with his wife, the solution to the algebraic problem that had obsessed him for 10 years suddenly came to mind and he carved his formula on Brougham Bridge lest he forget it. Hamilton was born in Dominic Street, Dublin in 1805 and proved to be a child prodigy. He spoke nine languages at the age of seven and had added a further five by his twelfth birthday. He had mastered Newton's *Principia* while a teenager and in 1827, while still an undergraduate at Trinity College, Dublin, he was appointed professor of astronomy and superintendent of Dunsink Observatory. He was made

Astronomer Royal in the same year. In 1834 his *General Method in Dynamics* proved immensely influential in Europe and won him honorary membership of the Academy of St Petersburg. He was twice honoured with a gold medal by the Royal Society and became president of the Royal Irish Academy in 1837. *The Elements of Quarternions*, his best-known work, was published in 1866, the year after his death. (He also devised a geometrical game from which it is said Rubik's Cube later derived.)

♣ **'The founder of pure mathematics', George Boole** (1815–64), who was born in Lincoln, England, spent his career in Ireland and made his revolutionary discoveries as the first professor of mathematics at Queen's College, Cork (now University College, Cork). He invented a whole new field of mathematics – invariant theory – and made huge advances in operator theory, differential equations, probability and mathematical logic. He also devised a new form of algebra, 'Boolean algebra', which modern scientists and engineers have found ideal for use in the design and operation of computers. Much of the 'new mathematics' taught in today's schools, such as set theory, binary numbers and probability, originated in Boole's work.

♣ **Austrian Nobel Prize Winner in Physics 1933, Ernest Schrödinger** (1887–1961) was expelled from the University of Graz when Austria was occupied by Nazi Germany and settled in Dublin in 1944. He was the first senior professor of Eamon de Valera's Dublin Institute of Advanced Studies after its foundation in 1940 and he became an Irish citizen. In the 1920s, Schrödinger helped to explain the structure of the atom with the theory of wave mechanics, calculated using the mathematics developed by Sir William Rowan Hamilton, Ireland's leading mathematician (see p. 19).

♣ **The Beaufort Scale**, by which the velocity and force of winds are measured, is named after **Francis Beaufort** (1774–1857) of Navan, Co. Meath. Beaufort, the grandson of a Huguenot refugee, joined the British Navy in 1787 and served in the Napoleonic Wars. Wounded in 1800, he returned to Ireland to help his brother-in-law, Richard Lovell Edgeworth, to establish a semaphore system that could transmit messages from Galway to Dublin in eight minutes. He returned to service and was wounded again in Turkey in 1812. He was Hydrographer to the Navy 1829–55 and devoted his life to producing accurate navigational charts and the standardised meteoro-logical notation still used today. Under his supervision, the British Admiralty Chart won worldwide recognition for reliability – a reputation it continues to hold.

Beaufort was troubled by the lack of standardised measurement of the velocity of the wind. Terms such as 'light airs', 'stiff breezes' and 'half gales' used at the time had no universally accepted meaning and were unscientific and impractical. Beaufort decided that the problem could be solved by measuring the wind against a well-known standard. He chose the full-rigged man-o'-war of the British Navy. The effects of the wind on the vessel thus determined the number on the Beaufort Scale. For example, a 'light air' was described as the minimum wind necessary 'to give steering way' and was called 'force 1'. In a 'whole gale', the same ship could only show 'close-reefed main topsails and a reefed foresail' – this was called 'force 8'. The highest number on the scale, 'force 12', is a hurricane wind when a man-o'-war could show no sails and was in serious danger of being wrecked.

The Beaufort Scale is used in international shipping forecasts today. It was modified in 1906 to describe the effects of the wind on the sea rather than on a ship and was extended to 13 forces of strength.

Francis Beaufort was elected a Fellow of the Royal Society and served on the royal commission on pilotage (1835) and on the harbours and rivers of the UK. He was an accomplished explorer of uncharted territories. The Beaufort Sea near the Alaskan oilfields is named in his honour and the Beaufort Prize is awarded annually to the best student of navigation in the Royal Naval College in Dartmouth, England.

The fame of Charles Darwin and his evolutionary theory rested on his being recommended by Francis Beaufort (in his position as Hydrographer to the Navy) as the official naturalist on the celebrated HMS *Beagle* expedition (1831–36). The **first official use of the Beaufort Wind Scale** was in the ship's log of HMS *Beagle* on 22 December 1831.

♣ **Seismology**, the study and measurement of earthquakes, was 'invented' as a modern scientific discipline by **Robert Mallet** (1810–81) on Killiney Beach, Dublin in October 1849. Dublin-born Mallet exploded 25lb (11.3kg) of gunpowder buried in the sand and measured the transit times of the shockwaves through various types of deposit exposed at the earth's surface. His experiments culminated in a detonation of 12,000lb (5443.2kg) of gunpowder on Holyhead mountain in Wales. He was fortunate to experience a very rare occurrence – an earth tremor in Dublin on 9 November 1852. In 1857 he was **the first person to**

Thomas Andrews, appointed first professor of chemistry at Queen's College, Belfast in 1849, was the first person to establish the composition of ozone.

measure the epicentre, or focus, of an earthquake during the catastrophe that befell Naples in that year. He compiled **the first seismic map of the world** and coined the terminology for his new science. He was also an accomplished engineer who built bridges and viaducts and sank coalmines. In 1852 he patented the 'buckled plate' used to strengthen flooring on bridges by combining maximum strength with minimum weight. The swivel bridge over the River Shannon Navigation in Athlone is one of his major works.

✿ **The first scientist to prove the existence of the earth's core** was Dublin-born seismologist **Richard Dixon-Oldham** (1858–1936). He made his discovery by observing that the arrival of primary, or compressional, waves was delayed at places opposite the focal point of an earthquake and from this he deduced that the earth contains a central core which is less dense. His system of analysis of seismic waves continues to be used today, and has provided most of the information we have about the internal structure of the earth.

✿ **Cross stratification**, a means of ageing and identifying different layers of rock and the forces that the earth has put upon them over time, was first discovered by the geologist **Patrick Ganly** (1809–99) of Dublin who was working with Richard Griffith on the Valuation of Ireland. He first observed cross stratification near Cardonagh in Co. Donegal and later tested and proved his theory at Fahan on the Dingle Peninsula in June 1838. He did not publicise his discovery until 1856, when he revealed his findings to the Dublin Geographical Society. Unfortunately the significance of his findings was not realised and was forgotten for nearly 70 years before its rediscovery by American geologists.

✿ **The composition of ozone** was originally determined by **Thomas Andrews** (1813–83), the first professor of chemistry at Queen's University, Belfast. He proved that ozone was an allotrope (different form of the same substance) of oxygen. He also devised heavy glass tubes to contain gases in experiments involving extremes of pressure. In this way he became the **first to discover the liquification of gases** – that each gas has a 'critical point' at which it liquefies. This proved that Boyle's Law (see p. 19) did not work under extreme conditions.

✿ **John Tyndall** (1820–93) of Leighlinbridge, Co. Carlow was **the first scientist to discover why the sky is blue**. In 1859 he discovered the eponymous 'Tyndall effect' which describes the scattering of light by fine particles in the air and in liquids, an effect which makes a beam of light visible. From this he studied light frequencies and explained why the sky is blue: atmospheric dust particles (and density differences in the air) scatter the shorter (blue) wavelength components of sunlight to a greater degree than the longer (red) wavelength components, giving the sky its overall blue appearance.

Tyndall also worked on experiments in thermal conductivity and was a pioneer of glacial studies. He was professor of natural philosophy at the Royal Institution from 1853 to 1867. He was a close friend and colleague of Faraday and wrote his authoritative biography *Faraday as a Discoverer* in 1868. Tyndall was one of the first people to climb the Matterhorn in the Swiss Alps and was the first to ascend the Weisshorn in 1861. His achievement is commemorated by a monument erected by his widow in 1911 at Alp Lusgen in the Swiss Alps.

🍀 **The existence and composition of the ionosphere** were first determined by **Arthur Edwin Kennelly** (1861–1939), born at Colaba, near Bombay in India, the son of an Irish naval officer from Cork who was working as a sea captain with the British East India Company. Kennelly left school in Britain at 13 and worked with several telegraph companies before emigrating to the United States. From 1887 to 1894 he was the principal assistant to Thomas Edison, the American inventor and scientist.

Kennelly set himself up as a consulting engineer and in 1902 he began an academic career as professor of electrical engineering at Harvard University. Kennelly made many invaluable contributions to the theory of alternating currents and to the accurate measurement and standardisation of electrical units. In 1902 he suggested that a layer of electrically charged particles, capable of reflecting radio waves back to earth, existed in the upper atmosphere. This helped to explain how Marconi was able to make the first radio transmission across the Atlantic Ocean on 12 December 1901 (see p. 12). The ionosphere was thus determined and was initially known as the Heaviside-Kennelly layer after the two scientists who had independently and simultaneously determined its existence. The existence of the ionosphere was eventually confirmed in 1924 by Sir Edward Appleton.

🍀 **Acetylene gas was first discovered and isolated** in Dublin by **Edmund Davy** (1785–1857) of Penzance, Cornwall, who was professor of chemistry at the Royal Cork Institution. He presented his new compound to the Royal Dublin Society in 1837. He was a cousin of the famous British inventor Sir Humphry Davy. He spent his career in Ireland and concentrated on the possible applications of chemistry to agriculture.

🍀 **The discovery of the atom** is almost exclusively attributed to the English meteorologist John Dalton. However, **William Higgins** (1763–1825) of Collooney, Co. Sligo published a book entitled *The Comparative View of the Phlogistic and Antiphlogistic Theories* (1789) in which he suggested the existence of atoms and the attractions between them, refuting the then current phlogiston theory. Higgins practised as a chemist in Dublin and was professor of chemistry at the Royal Dublin Society.

🍀 **The existence of electrons** was first suggested by **George Johnstone Stoney** (1826–1911) of Oakley Park, Co. Offaly, in a paper in the 'Scientific Transactions of the Royal Dublin Society' in 1891, in

which he coined the term 'electron'. (The electron was first observed physically by Sir J.J. Thompson at Cambridge University in 1897.) Stoney was one of the first advocates of women's right to higher education and was largely responsible for their obtaining medical qualifications in Ireland ahead of Scotland and England.

The quark, or sub-atomic particle of which protons and neutrons are composed, was named by US physicist Murray Gellman who took the word from James Joyce's *Finnegans Wake*.

🍀 In 1945 the crystallographer **(Dame) Kathleen Yardley Lonsdale became the first woman to be admitted as a Fellow of the Royal Society** in Britain. Born in Newbridge, Co. Kildare in 1903, her brilliance became evident at an early age. In 1922 she graduated from Bedford College, London, taking first place in maths and physics, and was employed by the Royal Institute. She made many crucial discoveries in crystallography, solving the problems of organic crystal structures. Her major publication was the first description of the structure of benzene in 1929.

In 1949 Lonsdale was appointed professor of chemistry at University College London. She received the Davy Medal from the Royal Society in 1957 and was Vice-President of the Royal Society 1960–61.

The Lartigue Monorail, opened in 1888, was the first passenger-carrying commercial monorail in the world and ran between Listowel and Ballybunion, Co. Kerry until the line was closed in 1924.

✿ **The landing craft and floating 'Mulberry' Harbours used in the D-Day invasion of Europe**, 6 June 1944, were designed by **John Desmond Bernal** (1901–71), a farmer's son from Nenagh, Co. Tipperary. He was appointed scientific adviser to Lord Mountbatten in 1942 and his work was later acknowledged as crucial to the success of the Normandy Landings (although as an active member of the Communist Party, his position caused concern to British security forces). He was a graduate of Emmanuel College, Cambridge and a Fellow of the Royal Society. In 1948 he was appointed professor of physics at Birkbeck College, London. Bernal's studies in X-ray crystallography at the Cavendish Laboratory in Cambridge laid the foundation for the discoveries of his pupils, Dorothy Hodgkin and Max Perutz, who revolutionised the subject of microbiology through the determination of the three-dimensional structure of complex biological molecules such as proteins.

✿ **The first railway in Ireland** was constructed between Dublin and Dún Laoghaire (Kingstown) in 1831 by **William Dargan** (1799–1867). Dargan was born in Carlow and studied in Britain under the great Scottish engineer Thomas Telford. He returned to Ireland to set up his own contracting company and by 1853 had constructed over 600 miles (965 km) of railway as well as the Ulster Canal connecting Lough Erne to Belfast. He amassed a great fortune and was able to spend £20,000 on the Great Dublin Exhibition of 1853 that followed London's Great Exhibition of 1851. He supplied the money for the building of the National Gallery in Dublin and is commemorated there. Dargan refused a baronetcy from Queen Victoria, who visited his house at Mt. Anville in Dublin. His later business pursuits were less successful and he died in financial ruin.

✿ The engineer-in-chief of Ireland's first railway, **Charles Blacker Vignoles** (1793–1875), of Woodbrook, Co. Wexford, acquired an international reputation for his work on the construction of railways in France, Switzerland, Germany, Spain, Russia and Brazil. He was elected **the first professor of civil engineering at University College**

London in 1841 and a Fellow of the Royal Society in 1855.

🍀 The Lartigue Monorail ran 9 miles (15 km) from Listowel to Ballybunion, Co. Kerry. Opened in March 1888, it cost £30,000 to construct. It was **the first commercial passenger-carrying monorail in the world** and was devised by the scientist Alphonse Lartigue. The train ran on a single elevated line about one metre high with lower guide rails on each side. Speeds of 18.6 mph (30 km/h) were achieved. The line fell into disuse owing to a lack of passengers and was finally closed in October 1924. However, the Listowel–Ballybunion monorail system proved to be an invaluable prototype for similar projects elsewhere.

🍀 **The world's first hydro-electric powered tramway** operated from the Salmon Leap Power Station near Bushmills, Co. Antrim. The tram ran the 6 miles (9.5 km) between Portrush and the Giant's Causeway from 1883 to 1950. It was engineered by William Acheson Traill (1844–1933).

🍀 **New York City's first subway** was built between 1900 and 1910 by **John B. McDonald** (1844–1911) who was born in Fermoy, Co. Cork. His parents emigrated in 1847, when he was still a child. His father ran a successful contracting business and gained political influence in Tammany Hall (headquarters of New York's Democratic party where Irish-Americans held sway). McDonald started out as a clerk and worked on many large construction projects, was promoted to inspector and took over his father's business when he died. He became one of America's most successful railway contractors and gained fame with the completion in 1894 of the Baltimore belt-line railroad that involved digging a two-mile tunnel under Baltimore. He made a successful bid for the $35m New York subway contract in 1900. He was also the contractor for the Jerome Park reservoir in New York City which was, on completion, **the largest artificial reservoir in the world**. The power in the city's subways was shut off for two minutes as a mark of respect for his achievements following his death in 1911.

🍀 **John Daniel Crimmins** (1844–1917) was born in New York City, the son of Thomas Crimmins and Johanna O'Keefe. He took over his father's construction firm and became one of the leading construction contractors in New York's history. The Crimmins

firm built over 400 buildings, laid down miles of streets and gas lines, dug miles of tunnels for the underground cables that gave New York electricity for the first time, paved Broadway and built most of the city's elevated railway network.

Crimmins' ancestry was never verified, probably to conceal the poverty of his family origins, but he was an ardent Irish-American in public life, a member of the Irish-American Historical Society and the Friendly Sons of St Patrick. Pope Leo XIII made him a Knight of the Order of St Gregory in recognition of his charitable works.

🍀 **Ireland's first canal and the first in the British Isles** ran 18 miles (29 km) from Lough Neagh to Newry and into the sea at Carlingford Lough. Completed in 1741, 20 years before James Brindley finished the Bridgewater canal in Manchester, the Newry canal used 14 locks to climb and descend from the 250ft (76.2m) summit-point near Poyntzpass. The canal was begun in 1731 by Meath-born architect **Edward Lovett Pearce** (1699–1733), who then passed on the work to his German-born draughtsman and assistant Richard Castle (Cassels). Although completed in 1741, it was another year before the canal was opened to transport coal from the coalstrips of Co. Tyrone to the fast-growing population of Dublin.

🍀 **The Pitt Kennedy/Great Himalayan Highway** from the plains of Simla towards Tibet was built by the engineer and agriculturalist **John Pitt Kennedy** (1796–1879) of Carndonagh, Co. Donegal. Educated at Foyle College, Derry and the Royal Military Academy, Woolwich, he was commissioned in the Corps of Engineers 1815–31. He settled in Tyrone and in 1837 was appointed Inspector-General of National Education and concentrated on instruction in agricultural techniques. He rejoined the army in 1849 at the invitation of Sir Charles Napier, Commander-in-Chief in India, and constructed the military highway that bears his name to this day. He was a founder and managing director of the Bombay, Baroda and Central Indian Railway.

🍀 **Charles Yelverton O'Connor** (1843–1902) of Gravelmount, Co. Meath was two years old when the Famine hit Ireland. His family sold their home and moved to Waterford, where Charles received an education at an endowed school. He trained in engineering as an assistant on the construction of the Kilkenny–Waterford Railway before emigrating to New Zealand in 1865. By 1890 he was Marine Engineer for all New

Zealand and in 1891 he was invited to Western Australia as Engineer-in-Chief.

He designed and supervised the construction of Perth harbour between 1892 and 1899 and extended the railway network in Western Australia by several hundred miles. By 1897, with the railway reaching the booming Kalgoorlie goldfields, the demand for water was exceeding the supply. O'Connor designed a system to pump 5,000,000 gallons per day from Perth to Coolgardie and the reservoir at Kalgoorlie. At the time it was **the largest public works development in the world and today remains the world's longest water pipeline** at 350 miles (563 km). Branches from the main line have since increased the system's overall length fivefold. Overworked, under pressure and severely criticised by sceptics, O'Connor committed suicide in 1902, less than a year before the completion of his scheme.

❧ **Michael Maurice O'Shaughnessy** (1864–1934), born in Limerick, was City Engineer of San Francisco 1912–34, during which time he rebuilt much of the city's infrastructure that had been destroyed in the earthquake of 1906. His biggest project was the construction of the Hetch Hetchy Water Supply System that took 400,000,000 gallons (1,818,440 litres) of water per day from Yosemite Park in the Sierra Nevada mountains to San Francisco.

❧ **The founder of the British Museum**, physician and naturalist **Sir Hans Sloane** (1660–1753), was born in Killyleagh, Co. Down. He studied medicine at Paris and Montpellier and graduated from the University of Orange in 1683. He was elected a Fellow of the Royal Society in 1687 and left for Jamaica the same year to work as physician to the governor. In two years he collected a herbarium of 800 new specimens of plants. He returned to London to a successful medical practice in Bloomsbury in 1689. He attended Queen Anne on her deathbed and was appointed King's Physician to George II in 1727. His major work, *The Natural History of Jamaica*, was published in two volumes in 1707 and 1727. He was visited in London by the great Swedish botanist Linnaeus and by Benjamin Franklin. He built up a collection of some 50,000 books and 3500 manuscripts. He bequeathed the latter, along with numerous cabinets of specimens and curiosities, to the British nation on the condition that £20,000 be awarded to his family. His great collection formed the nucleus of the British Museum, which opened near his Bloomsbury home in 1759, six years after his death.

❧ Dublin-born inventor **John Howard Kyan** (1774–1850) patented a method of preserving wood in 1832. 'Kyanised' wood was used in the construction of the British Museum, the Royal College of Surgeons in London, Temple Church and Ramsgate harbour. The process was eventually superseded by the distillation of creosote. Kyan also patented a method of ship propulsion by a jet of water ejected at the stern and was planning the filtering of New York's water supply when he died there in 1850.

❧ **The world's first commercial fertiliser factory** was opened in Dublin in 1817 by **James Murray**. At a time when the nutritional requirements of crops had begun to be scientifically investigated, Murray discovered that the fertilising properties of phosphorus, found naturally in bones, could be greatly enhanced by dissolving it in sulphuric acid to make a superphosphate solution. His Dublin venture was moderately successful, but it was at the Lawes Superphosphate Factory, which opened in London in 1843, that large-scale production began.

MEDICINE

Irish medicine in the last century produced several figures of international prominence who transformed the practice of Western medicine not only through their revolutionary methods of treatment but also through their diagnoses and innovations. They are remembered eponymously in some cases for their descriptions of previously undiagnosed ailments.

❧ **Graves Disease**, or hyperthyroidism, was first diagnosed by **Robert James Graves** (1796–1853), born in Dublin and the earliest member of what became known as the 'Dublin School'. He graduated from Trinity College, Dublin in 1818 and continued his studies in Europe before returning to Dublin, where he was appointed physician to the Meath Hospital. Together with William Stokes (see p. 26), he began to reform clinical practice in the Meath Hospital by putting emphasis on bedside clinical teaching for the benefit of students and patients alike. He made further revolutionary reforms in the treatment of fever through 'supportive therapy'. Previous techniques of starvation, bleeding and blistering were abandoned and the benefits of his treatment, once observed, were quickly adopted worldwide. He reputedly told his students one day on his rounds, after noticing the healthy appearance of a patient recently recovered from severe typhus fever, 'lest when I am gone you may be at a loss for an epitaph for me, let me give you one in three words, "He fed fevers".'

❦ **William Stokes** (1804–78), born in Dublin, was junior partner to Robert Graves (see above). With Graves, he established a new school of teaching in the Meath Hospital, Dublin. While still a student he published a book on the use of the stethoscope, the first in English explaining the benefits of the newly invented device. In 1837 he published a treatise on *Diseases of the Chest* and in 1854 *Diseases of the Heart and Aorta,* both long regarded in their field as models of medical exposition. He is remembered today for his descriptions of the condition now known as **Cheyne-Stokes breathing** or **Stokes-Adams syndrome**. He was elected a Fellow of the Royal Society in 1861 and physician-in-ordinary to Queen Victoria in the same year. He was made President of the Royal Irish Academy in 1874.

❦ **Arthur Jacob** (1790–1874), born in Knockfin, Portlaoise, studied in Dublin, Edinburgh, London and Paris before becoming demonstrator of anatomy at Trinity College, Dublin in 1819. He discovered a previously unknown membrane in the eye which was named after him – **membrana Jacobi**. He was professor of anatomy at the Royal College of Surgeons of Ireland 1826–69 and was President three times of the College. He was a leading founder of the City of Dublin (Baggot Street) Hospital in 1832.

❦ **Dominic John Corrigan** (1802–80) was born in Thomas Street, Dublin. After qualifying from Edinburgh University in 1825, he returned to Dublin as physician to Jervis Street Infirmary. He was the first of the new Catholic middle class to rise to fame in medicine, filling his position the year after Catholic emancipation (1829). He discovered a disease of the valves of the heart now known as **Corrigan's Pulse.** He was a leading member of the Central Board of Health during the Great Famine and was President of the Royal College of Physicians of Ireland for an unprecedented five years 1859–63. He was made honorary physician in Ireland to Queen Victoria in 1847 and was elected Liberal MP for the City of Dublin in 1870. He canvassed vigorously for a non-denominational university in Ireland whilst building an enormously successful practice which purportedly earned him in excess of £9000 per year.

❦ **Samuel Haughton** (1821–97), the Carlow-born scientist, mathematician and doctor, graduated in mathematics from Trinity College, Dublin before turning his attentions first to geology and then, at the age of 38, to medicine. On graduating from the medical school at Trinity in 1862, he was appointed registrar. He is remembered amongst many achievements for **Haughton's Drop** – a calculation that determined the length of drop needed to dislocate the cervical spine of a hanged man and so cause instantaneous death rather than slow strangulation as had been the case previously. His most humane combination of mathematics and medicine was quickly adopted and remained in use for as long as the death penalty itself.

❦ **Colles Fracture** was named after its original diagnosis by **Abraham Colles** (1773–1843) of Millmount, Kilkenny. He was educated at Kilkenny Grammar School and Trinity College, Dublin, studying medicine at the College of Surgeons in Dublin, Edinburgh and London. He was surgeon to Dr Steevens' Hospital 1799–1841 and professor of anatomy and surgery at the Royal College of Surgeons, Dublin 1804–36, where he was also elected President in 1802 and 1830.

❦ **The pioneer of subcutaneous or hypodermic therapy**, **Francis Rynd** (1811–61) was born in Dublin and received his education at the Meath Hospital. In June 1844 he became the first doctor to inject medicine beneath the skin of a patient when he inserted a pain-killing solution of morphia into the region of the nerves on the patient's face. The instrument developed by Rynd did not have a plunger and the fluid entered the tissues by the force of gravity alone. His revolutionary technique was readily adopted worldwide and modifications on his instrument culminated in the syringe design of Charles-Gabriel Pravaz of Lyons.

❦ **The electrocardiograph** was invented by Dubliner **Lucien Bull** (see p. 14).

❦ **John Joly** (1857–1933; see p. 13), born in Hollywood, Co. Offaly, **pioneered the treatment of cancer using radioactivity**. In 1914, he persuaded the Royal Dublin Society to buy a supply of radium salts and to set up the Radium Institute. The radon gas produced during the radioactive decay of radium was collected in sealed glass capillary tubes which were loaded into serum needles and could then be surgically implanted in tumours to destroy them. This was the prototype of the modern radium needle. The new method was first tried in 1914 at Dr Steevens'

Hospital in Dublin by Dr Walter Clegg Stevenson who successfully treated a patient for skin cancer.

🍀 **Bennett's fracture** describes a form of fracture at the base of the metacarpal bone of the thumb, first diagnosed in 1880 by **Edward Hallaran Bennett** (1837–1907), born at Charlotte Quay, Cork City. Bennett was an authority on bone fractures and dislocations and assembled a collection of cases for the pathological museum of Trinity College, Dublin, where he was a professor of surgery. He was President of the Royal College of Surgeons of Ireland 1884–86 and President of the Royal Academy of Medicine 1894–97.

🍀 In the treatment of leprosy, **Vincent Barry** (1908–75), a graduate of University College, Dublin and later

---

Dr Thomas John Barnardo, the Dublin-born philanthropist who opened his first home for destitute boys in Stepney, London in 1870. The organisation continues to care for thousands of children today.

professor of chemistry at the University of Galway, made great advances while researching into the treatment of tuberculosis. He synthesised and tested hundreds of new compounds against mycobacteria and discovered that phenazine B663 was most effective against leprosy. It is now established as one of the three first-line drugs in the treatment of the disease.

🍀 **Doctor Barnardo's Homes** were founded at Stepney Causeway, East London in 1870 by **Thomas John Barnardo**, born in Dublin in 1845. In 1862 he became an evangelical Protestant and moved to London four years later to train as a medical missionary for China. While studying he decided to devote himself to the thousands of homeless children who were starving and destitute in the slums of Victorian London. Working on the principle of 'no destitute child ever refused admission', Dr Barnardo's Homes had up to 8000 children in their daily care by 1900. Dr Barnardo died in Surbiton, London in 1905. It is estimated that in his lifetime alone as many as 250,000 children were rescued. The work of the organisation continues today.

🍀 The **surgeon to Napoleon on St Helena** was **Barry Edward O'Meara**, who was born in Ireland in 1786. He joined the British Army as an assistant surgeon in 1804 and served in Sicily and Egypt before transferring to the Navy in 1808. He was serving on HMS *Bellerophon* when Napoleon surrendered on that vessel on 14 July 1815. Napoleon was impressed by his personality and his knowledge of Italian and requested that O'Meara accompany him to St Helena as his personal physician. O'Meara remained with Napoleon until 1818 when he was dismissed by the Irish governor of the island Sir Hudson Lowe after O'Meara expressed reluctance to report on private conversations with the ex-emperor. He returned to England, where he published *Napoleon in Exile, or A Voice from St Helena*. The book caused a sensation and went to five editions. He was a founder member of the Reform Club in London and it is said that his death in 1836 was a result of catching a cold at one of Daniel O'Connell's outdoor meetings (see p. 54).

🍀 **Founder of the first medical institution in Buenos Aires, Michael O'Gorman** was born in Ennis, Co. Clare in 1749. Barred from being educated in Ireland by the anti-Catholic penal laws, he travelled to France to pursue his medical training. He later moved to Spain and was appointed head of medicine to the first viceroy of the River Plate region (present-day Argentina), Pedro de Ceballos. As the senior medical officer in Buenos Aires, he founded the city's first medical institution, the Protomedicato, which became the School of Medicine in 1799. O'Gorman died in Buenos Aires in 1819.

🍀 **Court physician to Jan Sobieski, King of Poland, Bernard Connor** was born in Co. Kerry c. 1666. Compelled to leave Ireland to receive an education, he studied medicine at the University of Montpellier and at Reims, where he graduated in 1691. He was employed to care for the sons of the High Chancellor of Poland in Paris and later travelled with them to Italy. He stayed with the Emperor Leopold of Austria and in 1694 was appointed personal physician to Jan Sobieski. He moved to England in 1695 and lectured at Oxford in anatomy and physiology. A Fellow of the Royal Society and a member of the Académie française, Connor wrote treatises on medicine and philosophy. He also wrote a two-volume *History of Poland* (1698). He died of fever in 1698.

🍀 **Physician to King Philip V of Spain, John Higgins** (1670–1729) was born in Limerick and studied medicine in Montpellier after the defeat of the Jacobite cause in Ireland. In 1700 he was invited by the Duke of Berwick, general of the allied Spanish and French forces, to become chief medical officer of his army. In 1718 he was appointed chief physician by Philip V in recognition of ten years' service in the War of the Spanish Succession. In 1719 Philip V grew seriously ill, but recovered under the care of Higgins. Consequently, he was made a royal councillor and was elected President of the Royal Academy of Medicine. In 1721 the French ambassador to Spain recovered from smallpox under Higgins' supervision and his fame spread throughout Europe. Higgins died in Madrid.

🍀 **Europe's first purpose-built maternity hospital,** the Rotunda, was founded by **Bartholomew Mosse** (1712–59). Mosse rented a large house in George's Lane, Dublin and opened it in 1745 as the 'lying-in hospital' for poor, expectant mothers – the first of its kind in Ireland or Britain. Encouraged by his success, Mosse leased a larger plot on Dublin's north side and began the building of the Rotunda Maternity Hospital. Mosse personally laid out the magnificent gardens adjacent to the site, which became a fashionable resort and concert venue. He also provided funds for the building. Further funds were raised through grants, lotteries and subscriptions. (Three of Dublin's leading architects, Cassels, Gandon

and Ensor, worked on the construction of the hospital at various stages, making it an architectural as well as a medical landmark.)

The Rotunda was opened on 8 December 1757 and marked the beginning of a revolution in maternity care services that brought doctors and students from all over Europe to Dublin. The cleanliness and efficiency of the Rotunda reduced the number of maternity deaths dramatically and the hospital remains in use today.

In 1993, UNICEF's annual report, *The State of the World's Children,* revealed Ireland to be **the safest country in the world for women giving birth and for children under five**. The mortality rate for children under five in Ireland in 1992 was six per 1000 (equalled only in Japan). Maternal mortality rate in Ireland in 1992 was only two per 1000, the lowest of any of the 145 countries included in the UNICEF survey.

explores, Discoverers and frontiersmen

EXPLORERS

🍀 **The discovery of America** has widely been attributed to **St Brendan***, son of Finnlug and Cara, who was born near Fenit, Co. Kerry c. AD 484. Brendan was apparently of noble birth and was a member of one of the earliest Christian communities in Ireland, founded by Bishop Erc (who had been sent to Kerry by St Patrick). Brendan was tutored by Erc in the Old and New Testaments, Latin, Hebrew, Greek, the sciences, mathematics and astronomy. He received holy orders in 510 and went to Ardfert in Co. Kerry, where he founded his first monastery.

Between 535 and 553 Brendan made the voyages that were later recounted in the 11th-century work *Navigationis Brendani* ('Brendan's Voyage'), which was translated into several European languages. The work tells of how Brendan, with the intention of bringing the gospel to foreign lands, selected 14 monks to search with him for the 'Land of Promise'. They sailed from Kerry in a vessel with wicker sides and ribs covered with cow-hide and tanned in oak-bark. They first landed on Sheep Island (in the Hebrides) and then sailed on to the Paradise of the Birds (the Faroes), before drifting southward to St Ailbe (Madeira). Prevailing winds brought them back to the Faroes from where they set out westward to the Island of Smiths (Iceland) and then to the Crystal Pillar (Greenland). From there, it is said that they sailed to the Region of Fog (Newfoundland) and then further again to the Land of Promise (America) as had been foretold to Brendan in his dreams. Although we cannot be sure that each of Brendan's landing points as described in *Navigationis Brendani* actually corresponds to these places, and although no physical evidence exists that St Brendan did discover America, it is certain that Irish monks did travel as far as Iceland and Greenland at this time. The island of Westmannayaer off the southern coast of Iceland

literally translates as 'Irishman's island', suggesting that it was settled by Irish monks before the arrival of the Vikings. There is now archaeological evidence that Irish monks settled in Iceland (then uninhabited) in the 8th century.

In an attempt to prove the feasibility of Brendan's voyage, the English explorer Tim Severin set out from Co. Kerry in May 1977 in a small craft reconstructed exactly as that of St Brendan and successfully retraced his possible route to America via Iceland, Greenland and Nova Scotia. The boat was frequently pierced by ice *en route* and the holes had to be stitched with one man inside the boat and another outside submerged in the freezing water. The adventure is recounted by Severin in *The Brendan Voyage* (1979) and the craft is preserved and on display at the Craggaunowen Project site in Co. Clare.

St Brendan founded many monasteries and also visited Wales and Brittany. The monastery in Clonfert, Co. Galway became his largest and most renowned settlement, attracting students and clerics from around the world. Up to 3000 monks are said to have resided here. Brendan died on 16 May 578 at 94 years of age and was buried in Clonfert.*

🍀 **The first European to sight Antarctica, Edward Bransfield,** was born in Cork c. 1783. As a merchant seaman, he was pressed into the British Navy and took part in the blockade of Brest (1813–14) during the Napoleonic Wars. By 1815 he had risen to be a master, the highest rank available to him. From 1819 to 1821 he explored and charted the South Shetland Islands (as named by him). In 1819 he discovered Trinity Land, the northwestern tip of the Antarctic peninsula. Bransfield Island, Bransfield Strait, Bransfield Rocks and Mount Bransfield are named after him. He returned to the merchant navy in later years and commanded several cargo ships. He died in 1852.

🍀 **Ireland's leading Antarctic explorer** was **Sir Ernest Henry Shackleton** (1874–1922), who was born in Kilkea, Co. Kildare on 15 February 1874. He was educated at Dulwich College, London and qualified as a master mariner. In 1901 he joined Captain Scott's Antarctic expedition on board the *Discovery*. He led his own expedition in 1907 on the *Nimrod* and

A strong cult of St Brendan grew up in northern Europe in the years after his death. In 1106 Lothair, Duke of Saxony, took over the northeastern part of Germany from the Slavs and named it Brandenburg after the saint. Thus the town of Brandenburg and, more famously, the Brandenburg Gate in Berlin is named after him.

came within 97 miles (156 km) of the South Pole. At 88° 23′ south, this was 366 miles (589 km) closer to the pole than had previously been reached. His ambition of being the first to reach the South Pole was thwarted in 1912 by the Norwegian Roald Amundsen, and then by Captain Scott (who perished on the return journey). In 1914 he set out once more on the *Endurance* with the aim of crossing the Antarctic from the Weddell Sea to the Ross Sea. However, in January 1915 *Endurance* became icebound. After nine months the ship was finally crushed and Shackleton led his crew across the ice floes, with two small craft salvaged from the ship, to Elephant Island. He then undertook an incredible journey of 800 miles (1287 km) with five companions (including two other Irishmen – Timothy Macarty and Tom Crean* of Annascaul, Co. Kerry), in their 22 ft (6.7 m) boat through some of the world's most treacherous seas to the island of South Georgia, then a Norwegian whaling station. The journey took from 24 April (the day of the Easter Rising in Dublin) to 10 May 1916. The rest of his crew on Elephant Island were eventually rescued after three attempts.

Shackleton's third journey to Antarctica in 1921 ended prematurely when he died suddenly in South Georgia on 5 January 1922. He published two books on his explorations, discoveries and scientific research: *The Heart of the Antarctic* (1909) and *South* (1919). Many geographical features in Antarctica, including a glacier, an ice-shelf, an inlet and a section of coastline, now bear his name.

❀ **Francis Rawdon Crozier** (1796–1848), born in Banbridge, Co. Down, joined the British Navy in 1810. He accompanied Captain Parry on three Arctic voyages (1821–27), and was promoted to the rank of lieutenant. He explored the Antarctic between 1839 and 1843, as second in command to Sir James Ross, and was promoted to captain on his return. Crozier was captain of the *Terror* in Sir John Franklin's ill-fated expedition to the Arctic in 1845. His fate was unknown until 1859 when McClintock (see p. 31) discovered his records. These showed that the expedition had reached the Northwest Passage in 1846, only to become ice-bound. Franklin died in June 1847, leaving Crozier in command. With minimal provisions, he managed to lead the surviving crew of 105

* *Tom Crean of Annascaul, Co. Kerry, was a member of Scott's expedition to Antarctica in 1902. He then joined Shackleton in 1914. Crean accompanied Shackleton on the desperate journey from Antarctica to South Georgia described above. In 1920 he returned to Annascaul where he opened the South Pole Inn, still open today.*

to land and headed for Back/Great Fish River estuary on the Canadian mainland in April 1848. Unfortunately, all perished on the way. Cape Crozier on King William Island, Canada, is named after him.

In all, 39 expeditions were sent to discover the fate of Franklin and his crew. Small pieces of information were gradually pieced together until McClintock's discovery of Crozier's documents solved the mystery. Each expedition was a voyage of discovery in its own right and the discovery of Franklin became secondary in importance as the chances of his survival became slimmer. At the Royal Society in London, forensic research on the remains of those who perished has revealed evidence of cannibalism. Those who died last were probably reduced to eating the remains of their dead colleagues in a vain attempt to avoid starvation.

❀ **The discoverer of the Northwest Passage** was **Robert John Le Mesurier McClure** (1807–73), born on Main Street, Wexford. He was adopted and educated by General Le Mesurier, who sent him to Eton and Sandhurst, entering the British Navy in 1824 and serving in the Arctic expeditions of 1836 and 1848. He was first lieutenant in Sir John Ross's expedition in search of Franklin.

In the search for Franklin mounted in 1850, McClure was second-in-command (to Richard Collinson) of the expedition. Francis Beaufort (see p. 20), believing in the existence of a Northwest Passage, directed the party through the Magellan Straits and then north up the east Pacific to the Bering Straits, where McClure's ship, the *Investigator*, was separated from its companion and ice-bound until the following spring. McClure had advanced further than Collinson and he moved on by sledge across the ice in 1851 to discover Baring's Island and then reached Winter Harbour, Melville Island – the furthest point that Edward Parry had reached from the east on his expedition of 1819. The final link in the sea route along the northern coast of Canada was thus discovered, connecting the Atlantic and Pacific via the Arctic Ocean. McClure Strait is now the name of this final link of the Northwest Passage.

McClure's difficulties continued as he became ice-bound once again, on this occasion for over two years. McClure and his crew were forced to abandon their ship and walk across the ice before they were eventually rescued by Captain Henry Kellett. McClure was knighted in 1854 and awarded £10,000 by Parliament. He was made an admiral after further service in Chinese waters. He published his adventures in *Voyages* (1884).

✤ **Sir Francis Leopold McClintock** (1819–1907), born in Dundalk, entered the British Navy in 1831 and was a lieutenant by 1845. Between 1848 and 1852 he made his first voyages of discovery in the Arctic (in 1852 as captain of the *Intrepid*). In each journey he made unsuccessful attempts to discover the fate of Sir John Franklin. His several long journeys by sledge across the Arctic gave him the practical experience to make the many improvements in that method of transport that were adopted in future explorations.

In 1855 Lady Franklin commissioned him to make a further search for her husband following the British government's refusal to finance another venture. He set out in the *Fox* and eventually found the graves, belongings and remains of the ships of Franklin's expedition, together with Franklin's written records that continued to 25 April 1848. On McClintock's return to Britain in 1859, he published his findings and these were added to the Franklin memorial at Westminster Abbey.

✤ **Sir Henry Kellett** (1806–75), vice admiral in the Royal Navy, was born at Clonacody, Co. Tipperary. He took part in four separate voyages between 1848 and 1853 in cooperation with the expeditions in search of Franklin. In 1849 he was **the first European to sight and chart Ostrov Vrangelya (Wrangel Island)** in the Chukchi Sea north of eastern Siberia. Cape Kellett, on the easternmost point of Banks Island in Canada, is named after him. He was Superintendent of the Maltese naval base (1864–67) and Commander-in-Chief in China (1869–71). He died at Clonacody.

✤ **Sir Edward Sabine** (1788–1883) was born in Great Britain Street (now Parnell Street), Dublin and educated at Marlow and the Royal Military Academy, Woolwich. He served in Gibraltar and Canada before returning to London in 1816 to devote himself to scientific studies in terrestrial magnetism, astronomy and ornithology. He was appointed astronomer to the

An incident from Robert McClure's Arctic expedition of 1850–54. Despite being ice-bound twice, the Wexford-born explorer succeeded in discovering the Northwest Passage.

Arctic expeditions of Ross (1818) and Parry (1819–20) in search of the Northwest Passage. He made **the first pendulum and magnetic experiments** in the Arctic and on the coasts of Africa and America. He superintended the establishment of magnetic observatories in territories throughout the British Empire.

♣ **Molesworth Phillips** (1755–1832), companion to Captain James Cook on his last voyage, was born in Swords, Co. Dublin. He joined the Royal Marines in 1776 as second lieutenant and sailed from Plymouth for the Pacific with Cook in July of that year. They landed at Hawaii with an escort of marines in February 1779, but were attacked by the natives, who killed Cook and all but two of the marines. Phillips was wounded, but managed to escape and swim to a boat. He was promoted captain on his return and later inherited an estate in Ballycotton, Co. Cork, where he lived from 1796 to 1799.

Francis McClintock receives proof of the grim fate of John Franklin and his party from Inuit in northern Canada. McClintock brought the Inuit's knowledge of travel and survival techniques back from the Arctic, making subsequent explorations more effective.

♣ **'The father of the Suez Canal', Francis Rawdon Chesney** (1789–1872) was born at Ballyvea, near Annalong, Co. Down. He won a cadetship to the Royal Military Academy, Woolwich and was appointed to the artillery in 1805. Despite constantly volunteering, he was fortunate never to see military action. In 1829 he was commissioned to make a comparative survey of various overland routes through Ottoman territory to India. He travelled in Egypt and Syria and sailed the length of the Euphrates River by raft. In his report on his journey, he described the possibility of digging a canal from the Mediterranean to the Red Sea. The French engineer Ferdinand de Lesseps, who later undertook the task, dubbed Chesney 'the father of the Suez Canal'. Chesney was awarded £20,000 by the British government to explore a new route to India through Syria and the Persian Gulf. He was accompanied by two Irish brothers, Richard and Henry Blosse Lynch (see p. 33). Hastings F. Murphy, who had completed the Great Triangulation of Ireland, was appointed to undertake the triangulation of the Bay of Iskenderun (on the southeastern Mediterranean coast of Turkey). The expedition landed at Antioch in 1835 and transported two steamboats across the desert to the Euphrates.

One vessel was sunk with the loss of 20 lives, but the venture continued and Chesney successfully charted the Euphrates, the Tigris and the Karum rivers before completing the passage to India. In 1843 he was appointed Commandant of Hong Kong. He retired to the family estate of Packolet near Kilkeel, Co. Down in 1851. He kept his commission and became a general in 1868.

🍀 Second-in-command to Chesney on his expedition to explore the Euphrates route to India was **Henry Blosse Lynch** (1807–73), who was born at Partry House, Ballinrobe, Co. Mayo. He had been a midshipman in the Indian Navy since the age of 16 and worked on the survey of the Persian Gulf. He learned Persian and Arabic and, on promotion to lieutenant in 1829, was made interpreter to the Gulf Squadron. On Chesney's return home in 1837 Lynch was placed in command and became **the first man to ascend the Tigris to Baghdad**. From 1851 to 1853 he commanded a squadron of the Indian Navy during the Second Anglo-Burmese War. He retired to Paris in 1856. The Shah of Persia nominated him to the highest class of the Order of the Lion and the Sun. Lynch died in Paris on 14 April 1873.

🍀 **Thomas Kerr Lynch** (1818–91) was the younger brother of Henry Blosse Lynch and accompanied him on the Euphrates Expedition of 1837–42. He established **the first steamer service on the Tigris**, linking Baghdad with India. He was appointed consul-general for Persia in London. The Shah accorded him the same honour as his brother, making him a Knight of the Lion and the Sun.

🍀 One of the **greatest navigators of the 19th century** was **Captain Robert Charles Halpin** (1836–94), born in the Bridge Hotel in Wicklow Town. He first went to sea at the age of 10 and rose to officer rank as a young man. In 1855 he worked on his first steamship and was soon in command of Atlantic mail routes. By 1866 he was master navigator on the *Great Eastern,* then **the world's largest ship**. At 692 ft (211 m) in length and 18,000 tons (18,288.8 tonnes), the *Great Eastern* was four times the size of its nearest rival. It was designed by Isambard Kingdom Brunel and launched in 1858.

Halpin left Valentia Island, off the Kerry coast, on 23 July 1865 to lay the first transatlantic cable. The *Great Eastern* was carrying 2615 miles (4184 km) of cable that was made up of 25,145 miles (40,232 km) of copper wire, 35,203 miles (56,325 km) of iron wire and 402,325 miles (643,720 km) of hempen strands. How-

ever, 1068 miles (1709 km) out to sea the cable broke and the project was called off.

One year later Halpin took the *Great Eastern* back to the exact spot, raised the broken cable and repaired it. On 27 July 1866 he arrived at Heart's Content, Newfoundland, 1844 miles (2951 km) from Valentia Island, and successfully completed the laying of **the first transatlantic cable**. In 1869, as captain of the *Great Eastern*, he laid an even longer cable, from Brest, France to Newfoundland, Canada.

Halpin spent many years laying the first international cable networks, linking Bombay to Aden and Suez, and Madras to Singapore and Penang in 1869–70. In 1871 he connected Australia to Indonesia and in 1874 joined Madeira to St Vincent, Cape Verde and Recife. He was made a Knight of the Order of the Rose by Emperor Pedro II of Brazil for his services. In all, he laid over 26,000 miles (41,600 km) of cable in his career, a distance equal to the circumference of the earth. He died of gangrene following an injury in 1894 and is commemorated by a monument in Wicklow Town.

🍀 **Europe's first lifeboat service (and possibly also the first in the world)** was set up by Dublin Port Authority in 1801 at Dún Laoghaire Harbour, Co. Dublin. Dublin Bay was a notoriously dangerous harbour to approach and many lives were lost even with the new service in operation. Stations were set up in Clontarf, Sutton, Sandycove, Bulloch Harbour and Pigeon House. A Howth station was added in 1816. Only in the early years of the present century, when motor engines were fixed to lifeboats, did rescue at sea become more certain in the event of shipwreck. The lifeboat service was set up following the first hydrographical survey of Dublin Bay by Admiral William Bligh (1754–1817), better remembered as Captain Bligh of the *Bounty*.

🍀 The leader of **the first European expedition to traverse the Australian continent** was **Robert O'Hara Burke** (1820–61) – who was born at St Cleran's, Co. Galway. Burke was educated in Belgium before joining the Austrian army at the age of 19. In 1848 he returned to Ireland to work as a police officer, but emigrated five years later to Australia to become an inspector of police in Victoria. In 1860 he volunteered to lead an overland expedition from Melbourne to the Gulf of Carpentaria. The trip was sponsored by an Australian-Irish tycoon, Ambrose Kyte. Burke left Melbourne on 20 August 1860 with three

Robert Burke, ex-soldier and policeman from Co. Galway, sets out from Royal Park, Melbourne to explore the interior of the Australian subcontinent in 1860.

companions: Wills, Gray and King. John King (1838–72) was born in Moy, Co. Tyrone.

On 11 November they reached the half-way point at Cooper's Creek only to find that vital provisions needed to allow them to continue were not there for them to pick up. On 16 December Burke decided to go ahead and complete the journey, leaving behind an assistant named Brahe who was instructed to wait for up to four months for their return. On 12 February 1861 they reached the Gulf of Carpentaria and became the first white people to traverse the continent. However, Gray died on the return journey. When Burke, Wills and King reached Cooper's Creek on 21 April 1861, they discovered that Brahe had given up hope of their survival and had left earlier that very same day, leaving only meagre provisions behind. Burke died of starvation on 28 June 1861 and Wills suffered the same fate shortly afterward. King was rescued by aborigines and reached by a relief expedition on 21 September.

❀ **The first Irishman to traverse the African continent** was **Surgeon-Major Thomas Heazle Parke** (1857–93) of Drumsna, near Carrick-on-Shannon, Co. Leitrim, who joined the Great Congo Expedition of 1887, led by the Welsh explorer Henry Morton Stanley. Before joining the British Army, Heazle Parke worked as a dispensary doctor in Ballybay, Co. Monaghan, as a graduate of the Royal College of Surgeons of Ireland. Posted to Egypt in 1882, he served with the desert column sent to Khartoum to rescue General Gordon from the Mahdists. In 1887 he volunteered for Stanley's expedition to relieve Emin Pasha, governor of the Upper Nile area of Equatoria. The journey involved travelling over 1000 miles (1600 km) up the Congo River before penetrating deep into the Congo rainforests to reach the east coast of Africa. In the jungle Stanley contracted a severe fever and was cured by Parke, who was thus credited with saving the mission. There was little left to save in the end: the expedition took two and a half years and cost hundreds of lives, particularly among the African natives, who were treated abominably by the explorers. Of their own group, there were 44 deaths in the first 50 days and many were eaten by cannibals. Less than a quarter of the 800 who set out survived, and ultimately the Emin Pasha decided not to back the expansion of the British Empire and transferred his allegiance to the Kaiser. On his return to Britain in May 1890, Parke was presented with gold medals from many learned societies, including the British Medical Association and the Royal Geographical Society. His health, however, had been permanently damaged in the tropics and he died prematurely in 1893. He is buried in Drumsna, Co. Leitrim (in a tiny graveyard measuring 7 × 18 yards (6.4 × 16.46 m), claimed by locals to be **the smallest graveyard in Ireland**). His statue stands in front of the Natural History Museum in Dublin and he is commemorated by a bust in the Royal College of Surgeons.

♣ **The first British Everest expedition** in 1921 was under the command of **Colonel Charles Howard Bury** (1881–1963), who was a native of Mullingar, Co. Westmeath. That year the Tibetan side of the mountain was surveyed for the first time in preparation for an ascent. A route was discovered by expedition members Mallory, Bullock and Wheeler, who climbed to 23,000 ft (7000 m) up the north col at the head of the Kharte Valley. They mapped 13,000 sq. miles (33,667 sq. km) of new territory.

♣ **The first Irish expedition to climb Mount Everest** reached the summit on 27 May 1993. Team leader **Dawson Stelfox** (1959–), an architect from Belfast, became the first Irish person to reach the mountain top 29,078 ft (8863 m) (average) above sea level. The other members of the climbing team on the 72-day expedition were deputy leader Frank Nugent and team members Dermot Somers, Mike Barry, Richard O'Neill-Dean, Robbie Fenlon, Tony Burke and Mick Murphy. The Irish team was only the eighth successful team to conquer the mountain by the notorious North Ridge. Three of those expeditions took place in 1993. As a native of Belfast, Dawson Stelfox can claim to have made **the first British and Irish ascent of the North Ridge**.

Dawson Stelfox, the Belfast architect who headed the first Irish expedition to climb Mount Everest in May 1993, photographed with members of his support team.

Transatlantic crossings

Ireland's geographical position has made it an inevitable starting – and finishing – point for pioneering transatlantic voyages and communications.

♣ **The first steamship to cross the Atlantic solely under steam power**, the *Sirius,* was built for the St George Steam Packet Company by Robert Menzies and Son of Leith, Scotland. On 3 April 1838 the vessel, under the command of Lt Richard Roberts of Passage West, left Cobh for New York. The 703-ton (714-tonne) ship carried 38 crew, 40 passengers, 457 tons (464 tonnes) of coal, 19.67 tons (20 tonnes) of water and 58 casks of resin. *Sirius* arrived in New York on 22 April, covering the 2897 miles (4635 km) in 18 days and 10 hours at an average speed of 161 knots (298 km) per day. There was less than 16 tonnes of coal left when *Sirius* docked at New York.

♣ **The first turbine-engined vessel to cross the Atlantic** took just 8 days in 1905. The Belfast-built *Victorian,* propelled with the turbine engines of Charles Parsons (see p. 16), journeyed from Moville, Co. Donegal to New York.

♣ **The first east–west transatlantic crossing by air** was made by Dubliner **Colonel James C. Fitzmaurice** (1898–1965) with two German companions, Captain Köhl and Baron von Hünefeld, on board the *Bremen.* The 2300-mile (3680-km) flight

SS Sirius – *visible behind the bowsprit of the SS* Great Western – *was the first steam-powered ship to cross the Atlantic. The ship is shown here arriving in New York 18 days after leaving Cork.*

from Baldonnel, Co. Dublin to Greenly Island off Labrador, Newfoundland took 36.5 hours on 12–13 April 1928.

Fitzmaurice, a veteran of World War I, joined the Royal Flying Corps in 1917 and flew **the first night mail service** between Folkestone and Cologne in 1919. He resigned from the Royal Air Force after the Anglo-Irish Treaty of 1921 and returned to Ireland to join the Army Air Corps. He first attempted to cross the Atlantic from east to west in September 1927 as co-pilot to Captain R.H. McIntosh on the *Princess Xenia,* but the mission was abandoned when engine trouble developed 500 miles (800 km) into the flight. However, the following year Baron von Hünefeld, publicity manager of Lloyd's Shipping Company in Germany, realising that such a venture in a German plane would contribute to restoring Germany's image in the aftermath of the war, invited Fitzmaurice to join him in what proved to be a successful second attempt.

♣ **The first British-sponsored east–west trans-atlantic crossing by air** was made by Charles Kingsford-Smith (pilot) and Captain Patrick J. Saul (navigator) on board the *Southern Cross,* from Portmarnock, Co. Dublin to Harbor Grace, Newfoundland in June 1930. **Captain Patrick J. Saul** was born in Dublin in 1894 and was an accomplished seaman. He made several voyages around Cape Horn and served in World War I on gunboats on the River Tigris before being posted to the Royal Engineers in Basra in Mesopotamia. He returned to the sea after the war, but the ship under his command was sunk in a storm off the French coast. He managed to swim ashore to safety with his infant daughter, but his wife was drowned. Thereafter Saul returned to Dublin, where he ran the family coal business and was instrumental in the development of private flying in Ireland. He worked as a civilian navigation instructor with the RAF in 1937 and was drafted as a wing-commander during World War II. In 1941 he returned to Ireland, at the request of the Irish government, to supervise air-traffic control at the new Foynes airstrip in Co. Limerick. He was chief of air-traffic services in the Department of Industry and Commerce 1950–59.

🍀 **The first non-stop transatlantic flight** was made on 15 June 1919 by Captain John Alcock (1892–1919) as pilot, with Lieutenant Arthur W. Brown (1886–1948) as his navigator, in a Vickers Vimy biplane bomber. They took 16 hours and 12 minutes to fly the 1900 miles (3040 km) from St John's, Newfoundland to Derrigimlagh Bog, near Clifden in Co. Galway, at an average speed of 120mph (190 km/h). They landed by the Marconi telegraph station at Clifden (see p. 11) at 8.40am GMT on what they incorrectly assumed was 'dry' land. They survived the landing and news of their arrival was telegraphed immediately to London. Alcock and Brown received the £10,000 prize put up by the *Daily Mail* for the first pilots to complete the journey. The plane is now exhibited at the Science Museum in London.

🍀 **The first woman to fly the Atlantic solo** was Amelia Earhart (1898–1937) of Kansas, USA. On 20 May 1932 she left Harbor Grace, Newfoundland and 13 hours and 15 minutes later landed at Ballyarnet near Derry City. Her true destination had been Paris but she was taken off course and forced to make an emergency landing.

🍀 **The first transatlantic crossing in a hot-air balloon** was made by Richard Branson and his pilot, Per Linstrand, both of Great Britain, 2–3 July 1987. They ascended from Sugarloaf, Maine, USA and covered the distance of 3075 miles (4947 km) to Limavady, Co Derry, Ireland in 31 hours and 41 minutes.

🍀 **Douglas Corrigan**, an Irish-American amateur pilot from New York, set off from Floyd Bennet Airfield, New York on 16 July 1938 to make a non-stop flight to Los Angeles. Leaving at 5.00am in thick fog, he first noticed something was wrong two hours into the flight when the fog persisted and the temperature began to drop dramatically. After 26 hours of flying

Amelia Earhart photographed at Hanworth aerodrome on 22 May 1932, two days after her celebrated transatlantic flight.

through fog and cloud, he reached a clearing where, to his horror, all he could see were miles and miles of ocean. He was unsure of his bearings and now believed that he might have overflown Los Angeles and was over the Pacific Ocean. In his uncertainty, he continued in the same direction and was surprised to reach land one hour later. Below he saw green hills and fields and realised that he had flown in the wrong direction and had crossed the Atlantic to Ireland. Eventually he reached Dublin, which he was able to recognise from maps he had studied before.

In Ireland he was welcomed by the Taoiseach, Eamon de Valera (see p. 66) and enthusiastic crowds. On his return to New York, he was given another hero's welcome and was christened 'Wrong-way Corrigan' by New Yorkers.

Many were not convinced that he had made an honest mistake. As a 20-year-old mechanic, Corrigan worked on Colonel Charles A. Lindbergh's plane, *Spirit of St Louis*, for its historic solo transatlantic flight in 1927. Always wishing to emulate the colonel, he managed to acquire an aged Curtiss Robin monoplane, but was refused permission to make the 3000-mile (4800-km) Atlantic crossing by the US Bureau of Air Commerce. Permission was granted in 1938 for an attempted non-stop solo flight to Los Angeles. Corrigan took up this challenge, but misread his compass and set off in the wrong direction – or did he? He was closely questioned by police and aviation authorities and even underwent a lie detector test, but there was no proof his mistake had been deliberate.

❦ **The world's first transatlantic passenger service by air** operated from Foynes in Co. Limerick. The first such crossing by the Boeing B314 flying-boats was made in 1937 and by 1939 a regular service was in operation. The 4-engined aeroplanes took 12 hours to cross between Foynes and St John's, Newfoundland, which was at the limit of their range. The flight offered a combination of luxury, considerable danger and minimum reliability. Passengers were served seven-course meals and a honeymoon suite was built in the back of the plane. However, storms, strong headwinds and ice frequently forced the planes to turn back or kept them grounded for days. It was to cheer up disheartened travellers that the airport barman Jim Sheridan invented Irish coffee in 1943 (see p. 17).

After World War II Foynes was moved to Shannon across the estuary. Shannon International Airport remains an important refuelling stop for transatlantic flights today.

OUTLAWS, COWBOYS, BUSHRANGERS AND FRONTIERSMEN

❦ **David (Davy) Crockett** (1786–1836) was born in Hawkins, Tennessee, the son of John Crockett, an Irish-born American revolutionary soldier. Crockett grew to be one of America's legendary frontiersmen, establishing outposts further and further into the American continent. An uneducated magistrate who 'relied on natural born sense rather than law learning', Crockett epitomised the rough-and-ready character of the 'Wild West'. He was a scout for Andrew Jackson (see p. 80) in the Creek War of 1813–14 and was twice a US Congressman (1827–33 and 1833–35). He died at the Alamo, a chapel fort in San Antonio, Texas, where he was holding out with Jim Bowie, William Travis and 180 Texans against several thousand Mexican troops under General Santa Anna during the Texan Revolution of 1836. Although the defenders were killed, the cry 'Remember the Alamo!' rallied the Texans to defeat Santa Anna six weeks later. At the memorial shrine, now in San Antonio, Texas, 12 Irish-born Texan defenders are remembered.

❦ **George Croghan** (d. 1782) was born near Dublin and emigrated to Pennsylvania in 1741, where he established a home on the frontier. He learned the languages of the Delaware and Iroquois Indians and established trading posts in upper Ohio. He was a representative of Britain in councils and treaties with the American Indians and his journals and correspondence constitute one of the chief sources of the history of the American West between 1745 and 1775. In 1756 William Johnson appointed Croghan his Deputy Superintendent of Indian Affairs. In this capacity Croghan opened Illinois to English occupation, removing the French and concluding a treaty with the Ottawa Indian chief Pontiac in 1766.

❦ **Jesse Woodson James** (1847–82) was the son of an emigrant from Astee, Co. Kerry who settled in Missouri, where Jesse was born. The family supported the Southern cause during the American Civil War and was ruined following the North's defeat of the Confederacy in 1865. After the war Jesse assumed a bandit lifestyle and joined a guerrilla force, making his name as a marksman. He was soon leading his own gang robbing banks and trains. His gang members, the Ford brothers (who were also Irish), eventually shot him dead and collected the $10,000 reward. A pub in Astee bears his name today.

❧ **Billy the Kid** (1859–81) was born Henry McCarty in New York City, son of Michael and Catherine McCarty, both immigrants from Ireland. In 1862 the family moved to the Irish settlement of Coffeyville in Kansas, where Henry's father died. They moved on to Colorado and then in 1865 to Santa Fe, before finally settling in Silver City, New Mexico in 1868. Mary McCarty died of TB in 1874 and Henry was left to fend for himself at 14. At 17 years of age he killed an army blacksmith (an Irishman called Frank Cahill) in a fight and was forced to flee a lynch* mob on a stolen horse. He changed his name to William Bonney and in 1877 went to work for J.H. Tunstall, an English cattleman in the Pecos Valley.

On 12 February 1878 he witnessed the beginning of the Lincoln County cattle war when his employer was killed by a posse of the Murphy faction – a gang of three Irishmen, Murphy, Dolan and Riley – who ran the locality. Tunstall had been working with John Chisum, a Texas cattle baron who was interested in buying up the local land. Billy became the fighting leader of the McSween faction (also in the employ of Chisum) and was involved in several battles. He was one of a party of six who killed Sheriff James A. Brady and a deputy, and in July of 1878 he figured prominently in the continuing Lincoln County cattle war. Billy was present when McSween was shot by the Murphy–Dolan–Riley gang.

General Lew Wallace, appointed by President Rutherford B. Hayes to resolve the war, urged Billy to surrender and offered him a pardon for indictment. The war ended but, fearing instant death, Billy did not put down his gun. Chisum the rancher and Dolan of the Murphy faction – former adversaries – were now united in seeking the death of the Kid, who had been witness to the murder of McSween. With 12 companions, the Kid began a spree of wholesale cattle stealing from Chisum in lieu of the payment he had never received, despite having fought in Chisum's interests. In 1880 Chisum and other cattlemen induced Pat Garrett (another Irishman) to accept nomination for sheriff. In March 1881 the Kid was captured and convicted of killing Sheriff Brady and sentenced to hang. In April, shackled and handcuffed, he killed two deputies guarding him and escaped. By 15 July he had been tracked again by Pat Garrett to Fort Sumner and was shot dead at the age of 21.

The story of the life of Billy the Kid is a mixture of known fact and popular lore. Either way, the story reads like an ancient Irish tale. A local hero with a price on his head is caught between two rival clans in a power struggle. There are cattle raids and terrible oaths of vengeance after which martyrdom and unarmed death is the inevitable, almost desired, result. The list of names involved in the story is almost exclusively Irish and reflects the ethnicity of this remote part of the Wild West. It is known that many settlers in Lincoln County, New Mexico were Irish soldiers who had come west during the Civil War and, having no roots elsewhere in America, decided to stay after the war ended. This is, to a great extent, the story of the Wild West in general.

❧ **James Butler ('Wild Bill') Hickok** (1837–76) was the grandson of Otis Hickok who emigrated from Ireland and fought in the Anglo-American War of 1812. Hickok operated a stage coach from Kansas over the Santa Fe and Oregon Trails 1855–60. He became famous throughout the West for surviving many gunfights unscathed while leaving a trail of dead bodies behind him. Tradition has it that he was never the aggressor, but was lethal if provoked. His knowledge of remote territories and his tough image were enhanced by his years of service as a Union Army scout during the Civil War. His term as Marshal at Fort Riley, Kansas in 1866 was followed by one at Hays City, Kansas 1867–69 and Abilene, Kansas in 1871. He was a ruthless enforcer of the law in the toughest towns in the remotest reaches of the American Wild West. His area of jurisdiction at Fort Riley covered an area of 400 × 500 miles (640 × 800 km) and had to be controlled by force. Cattle and horse thieves were shot on sight.

In 1872–73 he toured with Buffalo Bill (see below) and worked with Union Army generals in driving the Plains Indians from their lands. He settled at Deadwood, Dakota Territory with his companion Calamity Jane in 1876, but was murdered by a vagrant called Jack McCall in the same year. The wonder is that he survived so long.

❧ **William Frederick ('Buffalo Bill') Cody** (1846–1917) was born in Davenport, Iowa, the son of an Irish immigrant father. He worked as an army scout and then as a pony express rider. His nickname was earned by the slaughter of over 5000 buffalo in 18 months in order to feed the workers on the Kansas–Pacific Railroad.

---

* *The expression 'to lynch' originates with Colonel Charles Lynch (1736–96) who was a commander of irregular forces during the American War of Independence and whose brutal treatment of Loyalists gave rise to the term 'lynch laws'. His father was John Lynch of Co. Galway, who settled in Virginia in 1760, and his son, Charles Lynch Jnr, later became governor of Louisiana.*

Cody became a popular folk hero by exaggerating his own exploits in *Buffalo Bill's Wild West Show*, which he organised in 1883. The show toured the United States, went to London's Earls Court and then to Spain, Italy, France and Germany. Sitting Bull or 'Tatanka Iyotake' (1834–90), Chief of the Dakota Sioux during the Sioux War 1876–77, which saw the defeat of General Custer and M.W. Keogh (see p. 79) at the Battle of Little Big Horn, joined the Wild West Show in 1885. Always reluctant to perform and ever rebellious, he was shot dead by the police in the Ghost Dance* uprising of 1890.

Buffalo Bill was largely responsible for the mythical image of the Wild West which prevailed until recently. Irving Berlin's musical, *Annie Get Your Gun***, enhanced his reputation, built on the slaughter of native Indians and the shooting for sport of thousands of buffalo on which the Indians depended. So long a schoolboy hero, his reputation has now been dramatically revised.

✤ **Ned Kelly** (1854–80), born at Wallan, Victoria, was the son of John 'Red' Kelly of Tipperary, who was deported to Tasmania for the theft of two pigs. Ned Kelly began as a small-time horse thief and cattle rustler, for which he spent some time in jail. In April 1848 he shot a police constable in the wrist to prevent him arresting his brother Dan. They were consequently on the run in the Australian outback, where they were joined by Joe Byrne and Steve Hart. In October 1878 they shot three policemen in a gunfight and the gang was outlawed, with a reward of £8000 raised for their capture (or death). However, many of the inhabitants of the Australian outback, by their very presence there, had reason enough to distrust the authorities. Ned Kelly and his gang had many sympathisers who sheltered them and advised them of police movements. In 1879 they held up the bank at Euroa and later the same year they pillaged the town of Jerilderie in New South Wales. A former associate of Kelly, Aaron Sherritt, was called in to track the gang. Sherritt was shot dead by the gang in June 1880. An entire trainload of police was sent to take the gang

James Butler 'Wild Bill' Hickok, the grandson of an Irish soldier of the American War of Independence, photographed in 1875. A frontiersman and US marshal, he gained legendary status as a marksman. He was murdered at Deadwood, South Dakota in 1876.

– dead or alive. But for the warning of a local schoolmaster at Glenrowan, the train would have been derailed by the gang who had wrecked the tracks. The police were then able to surround the hotel at Glenrowan where the gang held out. In the course of the ensuing gunfight, three bushrangers were shot dead. Kelly, wearing a suit of rough armour, came out shooting. He was shot in the legs, captured, tried in Melbourne on 29 October and hanged on 11 November 1880.

The very first feature film ever made (according to the Cinémathèque Française's definition of a feature being a commercially made film of over one hour's duration) was Charles Tait's *The Story of the Kelly Gang* (Australia 1906). The film had a running time of over 60 minutes and was produced by the J &

---

* *The ghost dance was a ritual central to the messianic religion instituted c. 1870 among the Paiute Indians by their prophet Wovoka. The religion prophesied an end to the westward expansion of the Europeans in North America and the return of their land to the Indians. (The ritual was danced for five successive days. The Sioux performed it prior to being massacred at Wounded Knee.)*

** *Annie Oakley (1860–1926) joined Buffalo Bill's Wild West Show in 1885 with her husband and double-act partner Frank Butler, who was born in Ireland.*

Ned Kelly, Australian bushranger and son of 'Red' Kelly who was transported from Co. Tipperary for pig-stealing. Kelly's legendary exploits ended with his arrest and execution in November 1880.

Tait Theatrical Co. of Melbourne, Victoria. The actual armour which had belonged to Ned Kelly was borrowed from the Victorian Museum and worn by the starring actor.

Many Irish convicts transported to Australia did not adapt easily to their new environment. Most were petty offenders driven to theft by poverty and hunger. British policy was to transport offenders to reduce the population in Ireland and thus lessen the risk of rebellion. While most Irish settlers in Australia did not re-offend, there was a disproportionate number of Irish among the bushrangers of the Australian outback. Men like **Martin Cash**, born in Enniscorthy in 1808, or **Jack Donohue, the 'wild colonial boy'**, born in 1809 in Castlemaine, Co. Kerry, were outlaws who were admired by the labourers of Australia – Irish and British alike.

Martin Cash, always generous with his takings, achieved Robin Hood status in rural Australia for his escapades against the military and police. In a new nation of settlers, many of whom had been victims of injustice, there was always the sense that the old regime could not rule with the same efficiency as in Britain.

❧ Thief of the Crown Jewels from the Tower of London, Colonel Thomas Blood (1618–80) was a Galway-born soldier who fought for the Parliamentarians in the English Civil War (1642–48). He was awarded lands in Ireland for his services, but these were then taken away at the Restoration of the monarchy in 1660. Colonel Blood led an attempt to storm Dublin Castle and kill the Lord Lieutenant, Ormond, with a force of Cromwellians in 1663, but he was betrayed and forced to flee to Holland. In 1666 he was in Scotland fighting with the Covenanters at Pentland Hills. Four years later, in 1670, he made a second unsuccessful attempt to kill Ormond in London. In May 1671 he managed to steal the Crown Jewels from the Tower of London, but he was caught red-handed in a nearby tavern trying to buy credit with his loot. Charles II, at the colonel's insistence, gave him an audience and was so impressed by his daring that he gave him a full pardon and restored his Irish estates. Thomas Blood died at Bowling Alley in Westminster in August 1680.

❧ Pirate of the Caribbean, **Anne Bonny** (1700–?) was born near Cork and was taken to Charleston, South Carolina as a child. She rebelled against her genteel upbringing and eloped with a seaman called James Bonny while still in her teens.

She moved to Providence Island, then a haven for pirates and smugglers, and became involved with the pirate Jack 'Calico' Rackham. She abandoned her husband and, with her new partner, set out to sea, where she is reported to have taken centre stage in a series of raids on ships and ports on the eastern seaboard of the United States and in the Caribbean. Her crimes were theft and piracy – she was never accused of murder. There was no evidence to prove otherwise when she and the rest of Rackham's crew were captured and put on trial in Jamaica on 28 November 1721. All were executed except Anne Bonny, who was apparently spared because she was pregnant at the time.

There was much speculation as to her fate after the trial. Rumours circulated that she had been sold into slavery on a sugar plantation and had escaped. However, reliable records of her life end in 1721.

commerce, finance, economics and industry

MILLIONAIRES, BANKERS, ECONOMISTS AND INDUSTRIALISTS

❧ **The richest person in Ireland** is **Tony O'Reilly**, whose total estimated wealth is over IR£350 million. He is chairman and chief executive officer at the Heinz Corporation, Pittsburgh, USA, where he holds stock options worth about $240 million (IR£165 million) and earns a salary of IR£1.6 million. In Ireland he holds a 28% stake in Independent Newspapers worth about IR£100 million and has combined interests in Arcon and Fitzwilton worth £10 million. He owns properties in Cork, Kildare, Pittsburgh and Barbados and has stakes in Ashford and Dromoland Castles, together with a family stake in the Australian-based newspaper group APN worth IR£50 million. Born in Dublin in 1936, O'Reilly was an accomplished international rugby union player for Ireland and a record-breaking try scorer for the British Lions (see p. 196). O'Reilly's wife, shipping heiress Chryss Goulandris, is worth an estimated IR£292 million.

In 1991 Tony O'Reilly became **the world's highest-paid executive**, if unexercised stock incentives are not included, when he received a salary of $75,085,000. This total includes a 1991 salary of $1.1 million, bonuses and stock options of $71.5 million (granted in 1983 but only exercised in 1991 and therefore considered income for that year by the IRS).

❧ The **Dunne family**, owners of the Dunnes Stores supermarket chain (see box, p. 43), is **the richest in Ireland** with an estimated minimum value of IR£600 million.

❧ **'The father of political economy'**, **Richard Cantillon** (1680–1734), was born in Ballyheige, Co. Kerry. He worked as a merchant in London before moving to Paris, where he founded a banking house. The English original of his book, *Essai sur la Nature*

du Commerce en Générale, Traduit de l'Anglais (published in Paris, 1755), was never found. The French translation contains an introduction to political economy and treatises on currency, foreign commerce and exchange. He was widely quoted by Adam Smith, Condillac and Quesnay.

❧ **The first bank in Ireland** was founded by **William George La Touche** (1747–1803), grandson of a Huguenot refugee. Born in Dublin, William was educated at St Paul's, London. He was appointed British resident in Basra, Iraq in 1764 and won fame by paying the ransom demanded for the freedom of Zohier, captured by the Persians. He returned to Dublin in 1784 and married into the Pugets, a family of London bankers. He entered the family business and established a successful banking house. He built the family mansion on St Stephen's Green in Dublin.

❧ **An outstanding mathematical economist** of the late 19th century was **Francis Ysidro Edgeworth** (1845–1926) of Edgeworthstown (Mostrim), Co. Longford. He was educated at Trinity College, Dublin and then at Oxford. He was called to the bar in 1877 but never practised law. In 1888 he was appointed professor of political economy and in 1891 he took up the same post at Oxford.

Edgeworth was the first editor of the *Economic Journal* and later worked as its co-editor with J.M. Keynes. His economic theory was modelled mathematically, determining economic equilibrium and measuring probability and statistics. *Mathematical Psychics* (1881) introduced the indifference curve and the contract curve which he used in the 'Edgeworth Box' diagram. The latter is widely used to illustrate the most efficient allocation of resources between two producers, or of two goods between two consumers. *Theory of Monopoly* (1897) introduced another new concept by describing a model of duopolistic competition, eponymously known as 'the Edgeworth Duopoly'.

❧ **'The Richest Commoner in England'**, **Sir Peter Warren** (c. 1703–52), was born in Warrenstown, Co. Meath. He joined the British Navy and served in North America. He captured his first booty in 1745 following a successful attack on the French-held port of Louisburg, Cape Breton Island and was promoted to rear-admiral shortly afterwards. He was knighted in 1747 for further actions against the French. Warren married a Dutch heiress from New York and increased his fortunes through shrewd investment in the American property market. On his return to London he served as MP for Westminster and is commemorated in Westminster Abbey by an ornate monument. He was reputedly worth over $2m when he died in 1752, whilst on a visit to his family estates in Ireland.

✿ **The oldest investment bank in the United States** was founded by **Alexander Brown** (1764– 1834) of Ballymena, Co. Antrim. He emigrated to the USA in 1800 and began importing linen from Ulster to Baltimore. He soon had enough money to send for his sons, whom he took into partnership and then sent out to establish branches in Liverpool, Philadelphia and New York. The business prospered and ex- panded into the export of tobacco and cotton, eventually establishing its own fleet of ships. In the 1820s the company was trading in a wide variety of goods and Brown took the inevitable step of forming a banking house. Alexander Brown and Sons, surviv- ing today under the name of Brown Brothers Harriman, is **the oldest investment banking firm in the US**. Brown was worth an estimated $2 million at the time of his death and was one of the nation's first millionaires.

✿ A shipping magnate and **the first Catholic mayor of New York City, William Russell Grace** (1832–1904), of Riverstown, Co. Cork, ran away to New York at the age of 14. Four years later he moved to Peru, where he joined the shipping firm of Bryce and Company as a clerk. By 1854 he was a partner of Bryce, Grace and Company and the firm grew to control most of the trade on the coasts of Chile and Peru. Leaving the firm in the hands of his brother in 1865, he returned to New York to set up his own shipping company, W.R. Grace and Company. The new company grew to become a large multinational firm that controlled most of the trade between the United States and South America. Grace was elected mayor of New York 1880–84, the first Catholic and Irish-born holder of that office. In 1892 he established **the first direct steamship service between New York and Peru**.

✿ **The world's first billionaire, Andrew W. Mellon** (1855–1933) joined the Pittsburgh Bank, founded by his Irish immigrant father, and rose to the top in ten years. He was an astute backer of the companies that were soon to rank amongst America's most successful, including Gulf Oil, The Aluminum Company of America and Union Steel. He financed and went into partnership with H. McClintic and C.D. Marshall, whose firm constructed the Panama Canal

IRELAND'S TOP COMPANIES

The top five companies in Ireland entering the year 1993 as described in the annual report of Dublin-based *Business & Finance Magazine*:

1. **The company with the largest turnover in Ireland** was the **Jefferson Smurfit Group** of Beech Hill, Clonskeagh, Dublin, which re- corded an annual turnover of IR£1,259.57 million. Pre-tax profits in the same year amounted to IR£95.525 million. A print and packaging company, they are **the largest manufacturing firm and the largest employers in the country** with 17,341 em- ployees.

2. **An Bord Bainne (The Milk Company)** re- corded a turnover of IR£1,231 million with profits of IR£16.16 million in 1992. Em- ploying 2300 staff, Bord Bainne exports Irish dairy products worldwide. They are **the largest agribusiness company in Ire- land.**

3. Manufacturers of building materials, **CRH** of Clondalkin in Dublin recorded a turn- over of IR£1,113.93 million in 1992, with profits of IR£62.6 million. They employ 10,552 staff.

4. **The Electricity Supply Board** recorded a turn-over of IR£915.3 million with pre-tax profits of IR£1.187 million in 1992. The ESB employs 10,946 people.

5. **Dunnes Stores,** the supermarket chain, recorded an estimated turnover of IR£875 million with pre-tax profits of £70 million in 1992. Dunnes Stores employ 7000 staff.

✿ **Allied Irish Bank** became **Ireland's first company with over IR£2 billion** in assets in 1993. On 3 November AIB assets were val- ued at £2.009 billion on the Irish Stock Exchange (ISEQ).

　Peter Sutherland (1946–) left his chair- manship of Allied Irish Bank in June 1993 to become director-general of the General Agreement on Tariffs and Trade (GATT).

locks, Hell Gate Bridge, the George Washington Bridge and the Waldorf-Astoria Hotel. In all he was involved as a director, partner or board member in over 60 companies.

Mellon became publicly known following his appointment in 1921 as Treasury Secretary to President Warren G. Harding. He was appointed Ambassador to Great Britain in 1932.

Prior to his death, Mellon donated his huge art collection to the nation, together with a major endowment, making possible **the foundation of the National Gallery in Washington**. The collection, worth an estimated £35 million, included works by Rembrandt, Vermeer, Titian, Velázquez, Goya, El Greco, Holbein, Dürer, Constable and Reynolds. Mellon purchased 21 pieces of art for $10million from the Hermitage in Leningrad after the Russian Revolution. The $1,166,000 paid for Raphael's 'Alba Madonna' was then **the highest sum ever paid for a painting**. The ancestral home of the Mellons can be seen at the site of the Ulster-American Folk Park near Newtownstewart in Co. Tyrone.

♣ **The first department store** was conceived and built by **Alexander Turney Stewart** (1803–76) of Lisburn, Co. Antrim, who emigrated to New York in 1820. By 1850 his dry goods store had become the biggest in the city and he constructed a new store on Broadway that was **the largest store in the world** when it was opened in 1862. Stewart was at one time the **richest man in the US** and left $40m in his will. He spent some of his fortune in the construction of Garden City, New York, one of the nation's first planned communities.

♣ **Henry Ford** (1863–1947; see also p. 52), **founder of the Ford Corporation of America**, was born in Dearborn, Michigan, the son of John Ford (who had been evicted from a small-holding in Ballinascarty, Co. Cork in 1847). Ford's first Model T car was produced in 1909 and over 10,000 were sold before the year was out. The 'tin lizzies', or Model Ts, were made affordable to the average American when Ford pioneered the technique of mass-production that enabled him to produce and sell in excess of one million cars per year by 1919. In 1922, having sold over 1.3 million cars, he became **the richest man in the world.** The Ford Company expanded to produce a wide variety of automotive vehicles and survives today as one of the world's largest.

♣ **The richest man in the world** during his lifetime, oil billionaire **John Paul Getty** (1892–1976) was the son of an Irish lawyer, George Franklin Getty (1855–1929), who entered the oil business in 1914 and laid the foundations for his son. John Paul Getty was president of the Getty Oil Company from 1947.

♣ **Founder of the Bank of Nevada and millionaire miner of the California goldrush of 1849, James Graham Fair** (1831–94) was born near Belfast and was brought to Illinois by his family at the age of 12. With his associates Mackay (see below), Flood and O'Brien, he discovered and extracted huge deposits of gold and silver, amassing $100 million in six years. Fair was elected senator for Nevada 1881–87.

♣ **John William Mackay**, born in Dublin in 1831, made his fortune through the discovery of the 'Big Bonanza' in the Comstock Lode in California/Nevada in 1873. His find was the most spectacular of that of the four investors at Comstock and yielded $120 million over five years. Mackay invested in real

Henry Ford, whose father emigrated from Ballinacarty, Co. Cork in 1847, instigated the greatest transport revolution of all time. 'There was, it was true, some personal sentiment in it', he said when he chose Cork as his first European production site.

estate, banking and railways, founding the Commercial Cable Company in 1883 and the Postal Telegraph Company in 1886.

❧ **William Shoney O'Brien** (c. 1825–78) of Co. Laois was another of the so-called 'Bonanza Princes' who made a fortune from the Comstock Lode. The $10,000 investment for rights to the mine was paid off when over $500 million-worth of silver was ultimately produced.

❧ **The 'Copper King', Marcus Daly** (1841–1900), was born in Ballyjamesduff, Co. Cavan, to Luke and Mary Daly, who landed impoverished in New York with their family in 1856. Marcus left for California, where he worked as a labourer in the mines and gradually gained expertise in prospecting. He worked with Fair and Mackay (see p. 44) in Nevada before moving to Butte, Montana. He sold his interest in Alice Silver Mine in Butte for $30,000 and raised the funds to buy the Anaconda Silver Mine, which revealed a rich vein of copper underneath a thin silver surface. Daly was renowned for donating lavishly to whatever cause appealed to him, for paying wages in excess of the norm and for the successful racehorses bred on his ranch. His last achievement was the amalgamation of a number of mining and lumber companies into the Amalgamated Copper Company, with a capitalisation of $75 million.

❧ **Patrick Hannan** (c. 1843–1925) emigrated in 1863 to Melbourne from Quin, Co. Clare, spending many years prospecting for gold in Australia and New Zealand. In 1889 he moved to Western Australia to dig at the Coolgardie goldfield. In 1893, in search of a lost horse, Hannan and two companions became separated from his band of miners. It was then that they discovered gold at Kalgoorlie. The amount of gold extracted from 1893 to 1983 totalled over 39 million fine ounces, valued at AUS$18,308,149,820.

❧ **'The Sheep King', Sir Samuel McCaughey** (1835–1919), one of the richest men in Australia in his lifetime, was born near Ballymena, Co. Antrim in 1835. He emigrated to Australia in 1856 and worked as a 'jackeroo' or apprentice on a sheep station in Victoria. Within two years he became manager and in 1860 bought his own station in New South Wales, where he founded the famous Merino stud. His business flourished and he bought up numerous stations, spending large sums of money on new methods of irrigation and schemes to increase his yields of wool. At one stage his stations were shearing one million

sheep a year. He was a member of the Legislative Council 1899–1919 and was knighted in 1905. He presented twenty warplanes to the Australian government in World War I and bequeathed £2m to education and charity. When he died his lands covered over 4 million acres (1620 million ha), greater than the total area of Northern Ireland.

❧ **The Durack ranchers of Western Australia, one of the nation's greatest and wealthiest dynasties**, were established by **Patrick Durack** (1834–98), who was born in Galway. He travelled to Australia with his parents and family in 1853. He had to face the challenge of raising the whole family when his father died soon after their arrival in New South Wales. Durack made a modest fortune on the Ovens River goldfield and invested his earnings in a farm. In 1867 the family transferred their growing herds deep into the Queensland outback and established Thylungra station at Cooper's Creek. Although extremely successful in his business, Durack decided that greater fortunes were to be made in the great unsettled lands in the Kimberley district of Western Australia. In 1882 he took up land on the Ord River and began **the greatest cattle drive in Australian history** by moving 7000 cattle and 200 horses over 3000 miles (4800 km) between 1883 and 1885. Despite losing many of his livestock, the rich pastoral lands of Kimberley quickly rewarded him for his trouble. The Durack ranches were the first in northwestern Australia and opened the region for subsequent economic development.

❧ Mining engineer, philanthropist, art collector and **the first honorary citizen of Ireland, Sir Alfred Chester Beatty** (1875–1968) was born in New York of Irish parentage, and educated at the Columbia School of Mines and Princeton University. He began his career in Denver, Colorado and devised a new method of extracting copper from low-grade ore. He built his immense fortune with mining interests in Mexico, Congo, Sierra Leone, the Gold Coast (now Ghana) and Russia.

Visiting Egypt in 1913, Beatty was impressed by the oriental manuscripts and copies of the Qur'an (Koran) on view in the bazaars. He began to build what is now **the world's largest private collection of oriental manuscripts** and copies of the Qur'an, which he brought to his home in Shrewsbury Road, Dublin in 1953. The collection was left in trust to the Irish nation and is now named the Chester Beatty Library. He also bequeathed to the National

Gallery paintings to the value of £1 million and his collection of oriental weapons to the Military College, Curragh Camp, Kildare.

❦ **Founder of the Argentine stock exchange and Buenos Aires Bank, Thomas St George Armstrong**, emigrated from his home in Garrycastle, near Athlone around 1817. He married into a wealthy Spanish family in 1829, thereby gaining the means to build his business empire. He was also a major financier of the Buenos Aires and Western railways and had interests in insurance and the beef trade. Armstrong's banking contacts allowed him to gain the credit to build a network of schools, hospitals, parish churches and orphanages for the growing Irish community in 19th-century Buenos Aires.

❦ **Alfred Harmsworth**, founder of the *Daily Mail* and *Daily Mirror* newspapers (see p. 131).

❦ In 1823 a Scottish settler, **John Barbour**, established at Hilden, Co. Down **a linen-thread works that was at one point the largest in the world**. Linen and synthetic threads are still produced for export at the Barbour Campbell factory. The linen industry is one of Ireland's oldest and is concentrated in Ulster. French Huguenots fleeing from France following the revocation of the Edict of Nantes in 1685 settled in Ulster in large numbers, bringing their expertise in linen manufacture with them. William Coulson of Co. Down became **the first manufacturer in Ireland to produce damask** in 1764 and became a supplier to the British, Swedish and Russian royal families.

❦ **The founder of the British alkali industry**, **James Muspratt** (1793–1886), was born in Dublin and apprenticed to a wholesale druggist and chemist at 14. In 1818 he began manufacturing chemicals on a small scale but, following the removal of a £30/ton government duty on salt in 1823, he took the opportunity to introduce the manufacture of soda into the Mersey Valley, where the proximity of coalfields, saltmines and sea ports offered great advantages. The soda-ash he produced **revolutionised the soap-making industry** and the business expanded rapidly as demand also grew from glass makers and the dyeing industry. Muspratt joined forces with Josias Gamble, a Scottish industrialist who had founded a bleaching factory in Dublin, and in 1828 they founded the alkali industry in St Helens. The by-product of the Leblanc process, used in the processing of the alkalis, was hydrochloric gas, which caused serious pollution. Muspratt was always reluctant to co-operate in minimising pollution and was prosecuted on a number of occasions. He eventually moved the business permanently to Widnes and Flint, where his sons took over after his retirement in 1857.

❦ **The world's first pneumatic tyre company** was founded in Dublin by **Sir Arthur Philip Du Cros** (1871–1955). In 1892 he joined his father and brother in a company formed to develop John B. Dunlop's invention (see p. 11). He founded his own Dunlop Rubber Company in 1901 and the business expanded worldwide over 25 years. The Great Depression hit the company hard and Du Cros lost much of his personal wealth. He wrote a history of the industry in *Wheels of Fortune: a Salute to Pioneers* (1938).

❦ **Thomas Lipton** (1850–1931) was born in Glasgow, Scotland, the son of Thomas Lipton and Frances Johnstone of Clones, Co. Monaghan, who escaped the worst of the Famine in Ireland. Thomas Lipton Jr was born soon after their arrival and was working in his father's shop by the age of nine. At 15 he went to America and laboured for five years before returning to Glasgow, where he opened his own goods store. By importing foodstuffs directly from Ireland, he was able to cut out the middleman and sell his goods at cut price. Lipton spent several years travelling between Ireland and Scotland and amassed a fortune. He opened many new stores and was a millionaire by the age of 30. He moved his headquarters to London and in 1889 expanded into the American market. In the same year he bought his first tea plantations in India. Today Liptons Teas are the enduring legacy of his business empire.

In 1899 Lipton made his first challenge for the America's Cup yacht race in *Shamrock I*. In 1930 he failed to secure the cup for the fifth time, in *Shamrock V*, but was given a special award as 'The World's Best Loser' by the New York Yacht Club.

❦ **Longest Working Career: Susan O'Hagan** (1802–1909) worked for 97 years in domestic service, with three generations of the Hall family of Lisburn, Co. Down, from the age of ten until her death at the age

---

Harland & Wolff shipyards, Belfast, once the world's largest, also produced some of the world's largest ships. This photograph was taken in 1910, at the time of the construction of the Titanic.

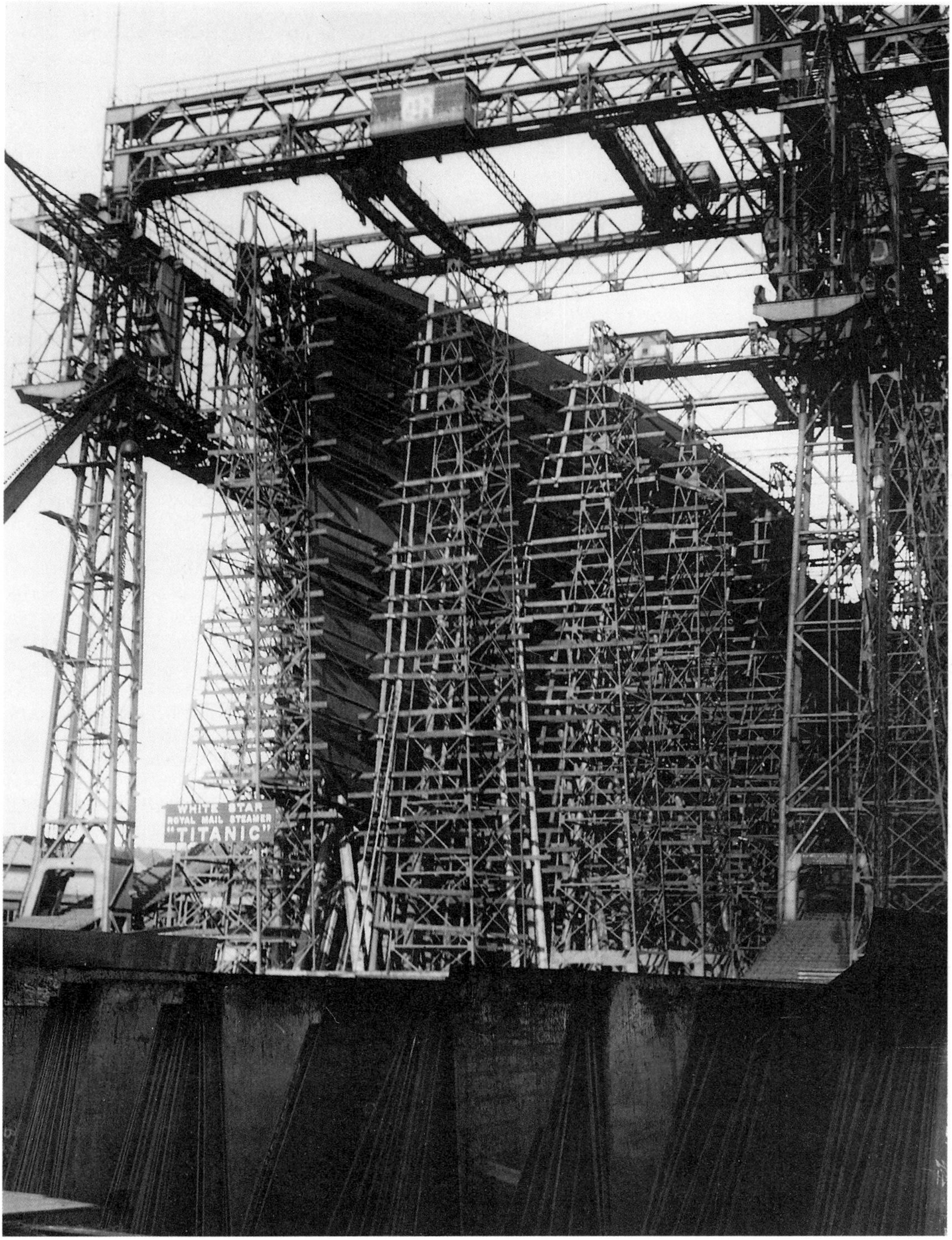
WHITE STAR
ROYAL MAIL STEAMER
"TITANIC"

of 107. (This is only one year short of the world record for the longest working life held by Mr Izumi of Japan, who worked for 98 years at a sugar mill at Isen, Tokunoshima 1872–1970.)

♣ **The world's largest hand-cut crystal factory**, with a turnover of IR£273.6 million in 1992, is **Waterford Crystal Ltd**, part of the Waterford Wedgwood Group. First established in 1783 by George and William Penrose, the company flourished for 68 years and won several awards at the Great Exhibition in London in 1851. The business crashed, however, and was not re-established until 1947. From small beginnings, the company expanded rapidly to become the largest of its kind.

♣ **'Shipbuilders to the world', Harland & Wolff** of Belfast, were **the largest shipbuilding firm in the world** at the turn of the century. The success of the company was mostly due to **William Pirrie** (1847–1924) who was born in Quebec, Canada, where his father settled from Conlig, Co. Down to work in the timber industry. When his father died in 1849 he returned to Co. Down to live with his grandfather, attending the Royal Belfast Academical Institute. He joined Harland & Wolff as an apprentice when the company was formed in 1862. (Edward Harland was a Yorkshire businessman and Gustav Wolff was a marine draughtsman from Hamburg.) By 1874 Pirrie was chief draughtsman and a partner in the firm. During the 1880s he gradually took control of the company and oversaw the construction of the *Teutonic*, which was **the largest ship in the world** at 10,000 tons (10,161 tonnes) when it was completed in 1889. Ten years later the *Oceanic* was completed for the White Star Line and was **the world's largest ship** at 17,000 tons (17,272 tonnes). By 1904 Pirrie was chairman of the company and in sole control. Harland & Wolff's status as the world's leading shipbuilders was confirmed with the completion of the ill-fated *Titanic* in 1911 which displaced an unprecedented 76,500 tons (77,732 tonnes). Pirrie pioneered the idea of ocean liners as floating hotels and was quick to recognize oil as the fuel of the future. He manufactured diesel engines in Glasgow and had shipyards in Govan, Liverpool, Southampton and London. He was a director of White Star and other shipping lines and became a millionaire.

Harland & Wolff also built the great P&O cruise ship *Canberra* and the oil tanker *Myrina,* which at 186,999 tons (190,000 tonnes) was **the largest vessel ever built in Europe when it was launched in 1967.** Built for Deutsche Shell AG of Hamburg,

Myrina was launched on 6 September 1967. Today the shipyard has been greatly reduced by recession and increased competition. Nevertheless, its repair dock can cater for vessels of up to 200,000 tons (203,220 tonnes).

Pirrie enjoyed a troubled political career, becoming in turn a Unionist, a Liberal Unionist and a Liberal. He was mayor of Belfast 1896–97 and became **the first Freeman of the City**. He failed to win a seat at Westminster chiefly because his politics were too liberal. He became a viscount and a member of the new Northern Ireland Senate following partition in 1922.

♣ **The chief designer of the Titanic, Thomas Andrews** (1873–1912), was born in Comber, Co. Down and was a nephew of the chairman of Harland & Wolff, William Pirrie (see above). He became a managing director of the company in 1907, but perished on his own ship when she sank on her maiden voyage to New York in April 1912. A memorial hall in Comber is named in his honour.

♣ Once **the largest rope-manufacturing company in the world**, the Belfast Ropeworks Company was founded in 1873. The development of the ropeworks ran parallel with the expansion of the Belfast shipyards. From their humble beginnings in 1873, when 50 people were employed, the ropeyards grew to employ 3500 by 1920 in three separate mills on a 40-acre (16.2 ha) site. The company had over 100,000 customers worldwide in the inter-war years, producing 16,000 tons (16,258 tonnes) of products per annum.

The factories were completely destroyed by the German Luftwaffe in 1941, but were rebuilt and updated to produce new synthetic yarns bought from ICI and Courtaulds. However, the industry could not compete with cheaper competitors in the 1950s and 60s and was eventually destroyed by the advent of the new plastic products.

BREWING, DISTILLING AND WINE-MAKING

♣ **The oldest distillery in the world is the Old Bushmills Distillery in the village of Bushmills, Co. Antrim**. Situated on the banks of the River Bush, it was granted a licence in 1608 by James I to a local planter landlord, Sir Thomas Phillips. Local records show that soldiers were fortified on the same site as early as 1276 with draughts of 'aqua vitae' – 'the water of life'. The word 'whiskey' derives from the Irish *uisce beatha*, also meaning 'water of life'. The 'e' in Irish whiskey distinguishes it from Scotch whisky. Irish whiskey was widely exported and consumed. Queen Elizabeth I and Tsar Peter the Great of Russia are known to have had a particular taste for Irish blends. The water from the River Bush tributary, St Columb's Rill, is still used today to make the whiskey.

♥ **The Guinness Brewery at St James' Gate in Dublin was the largest in the world at the turn of the century.** The brewery was founded by **Arthur Guinness** (1725–1803), who was born in Celbridge, Co. Kildare. He bought the disused brewery in 1759 and started making traditional Irish ale. He soon changed to a new drink made from roasted barley that was popular in London at the time. The new drink was called 'porter' after the porters in Covent Garden who were particularly fond of it. By 1799 Guinness was producing only porter and the drink was selling well in Britain. Initially the drink was unpopular with Dubliners who resented Guinness's opposition to the radical United Irishmen. The protest, however, did not last since the attraction of the new drink overcame political considerations. During the recession that followed the Napoleonic Wars, when other beers were being watered down, Guinness produced a stronger, 'extra stout' porter, shortened over the years to 'stout'. By the beginning of the present century St James' Gate in Dublin was the largest brewery in the world. Today Guinness is sold in 130 countries worldwide and brewed in 46 of them. St James' Gate can currently produce some 4 million pints (2.27m litres) of Guinness per day and is **Ireland's largest brewery**. It still uses the same strain of yeast pioneered by Arthur Guinness and the brewing process – involving roasted Irish-grown barley, soft water, hops and yeast – remains the same.

♣ **Hennessy Brandy** was first distilled by **Richard Hennessy** (1720–1800), who was born in Ballymoy, Killavullen, Co. Cork where his ancestors still live. He went to France in 1740 and became an officer in Dillon's Irish Regiment of the French Army, fighting at Dettingen (1743), Fontenoy (1745) and other battles in the War of the Austrian Succession. He retired after being wounded and later married his cousin Ellen, widow of James Hennessy of Brussels and a cousin in turn of Edmund Burke (see p. 135). He settled in Cognac in 1765 in the département of Charente and established the distillery that produces Hennessy Brandy. His son James continued the business after his death and the world-famous drink survives today.

Ireland and the Bordeaux Vineyards

'For two centuries a small group of wine merchants originally from Germany, Britain and Ireland, but living in Bordeaux, dominated the sale of clarets and sauternes for which the Bordeaux region is famous.' (N. Faith, *The Winemasters*).

The prevalence of Irish names among the 'Chartronnais', as the wine producers of Bordeaux were known, is not surprising when put into historical context. Most were Catholic – for example the McCarthys who followed James II into exile – but a few were Protestants from Ulster. The English Parliament had destroyed the prosperous Irish wool trade with the Irish Wool Prohibition Act of 1699 in order to protect English interests in that area. Subsequently many previously wealthy farming and merchant families in Ulster, unable to trade under pain of death, found themselves impoverished, and left Ireland to make their living abroad. Bordeaux, at the time, was a long-established partner in trade for Irish wool and beef in return for wine, and many Irish families went to settle there. The Bartons and the Johnstons were the most successful of these and their names continue to adorn the labels of Bordeaux wines today. **William Johnston** came to France as a boy in 1716 to learn French, worked for Pierre Germe and inherited a portion of his estates. From this he built his trade and made his fortune.

♣ **Thomas Barton** or 'French Tom' was working as a factor in Marseilles and Montpellier by 1712 and set up his own business in Bordeaux in 1715 at the age of 30. By the 1740s he was wealthy enough to buy Grove estate in Fethard, Co. Tipperary for the enormous sum of £30,000. He also bought the Château le Boscq in St Estephe and a country house in Médoc. He was **the biggest single purchaser of fine claret during the second half of the 18th century.**

In the early 18th century more wine was consumed in Britain, Ireland, Germany or Holland than in France, where it was, in fact, relatively rare. Dublin and Leith in Scotland were importing more wine at this time than London, although it tended to be of inferior quality. The thirst for wine in Ireland at the time is evident in widely used round-bottom glasses that did not allow the drinker to rest his glass on the table. Ireland was importing more wine at the beginning of the 18th century than England and Scotland put together. The drinking habits of Dean Swift, a known connoisseur of fine clarets, were not unique to himself. Many contemporary visitors to Dublin remarked on the sheer volume of wine consumed by the citizens of all social classes. Many Irish families settled in Bordeaux and became involved in the wine trade through ownership, marriage and commerce – so much so that there is hardly a wine produced in Bordeaux that does not have an Irish connection. The main families involved are Johnston, McCarthy, Barton, Lynch, Kirwan, Morgan, Phelan, Clarke, Dillon, Boyd, Burke, Roche, Lawton and Murphy. Their descendants continue to live and produce wine today as the French citizens of Bordeaux.

Leading Irish vineyards in Bordeaux

🍀 **Château Leoville Barton/Château Langoa Barton:** Today the vineyards are managed by Anthony Barton, who is an eighth-generation descendant of the Barton family. **Thomas Barton** was born near Enniskillen, Co. Fermanagh in 1695.

🍀 **Château Ducru-Beaucaillou** was first acquired in 1795 by Bertrand Ducru. In 1866 the Johnston family bought it out. William Johnston (see p. 49) left for France in 1716, but later returned to Ireland to marry, finally moving back to France to live in 1729.

Like Barton, he was an Ulster Protestant. He set up his own trading company and was prospering by 1734. His son, Nathaniel, joined him in 1765. The Johnstons took French citizenship and converted to Catholicism. Today their descendants are no longer vineyard owners, but they still trade in wine in Bordeaux under the name of Nathaniel Johnston.

🍀 **Château Lynch-Bages** was inherited by Mme Lynch (née Drouillard) who was the wife of Thomas Michel Lynch, eldest son of John Lynch, born in Galway in 1699. John Lynch was a veteran of the Battle of the Boyne who fled to France after the Jacobite defeat and set up a trading company. In 1710 the family adopted French citizenship.

🍀 **Château Dauzac** was built in the early 1700s and was then given as a dowry on the marriage of Elizabeth Drouillard to Thomas Michel Lynch in 1740.

🍀 **Château Latour** is one of the oldest estates in Bordeaux, producing one of the world's finest wines. In 1841 Barton & Guestier, together with Nathaniel Johnston, bought out the estate.

🍀 **Château Boyd-Cantenac** was bought in 1754 by Jacques Boyd whose family were prominent Bel-

fast wool traders in the earlier part of the century. In later years the Irish Lawton family earned an interest through marriage.

🍀 **Château Kirwan** was bought by an English merchant, Sir John Collingwood, in 1751. His daughter married Mark Kirwan from Galway who inherited the castle and vineyards in 1781 and changed the name. Kirwan was beheaded in the French Revolution, but his family managed to retain their property.

🍀 **Château Léoville Poyferré** was inherited by the Lawton family through marriage. The Lawtons ran a shipping company, Tastet and Lawton, in Bordeaux which is still active. Today's family are the sixth generation in direct line from Abraham Lawton, who emigrated from Cork in 1739. **Daniel Lawton is the leading wine broker in Bordeaux today**, operating from the same office as his ancestor at 60 Quai des Chartrons.

🍀 **Château Clarke** was bought in 1973 by Baron Edmond de Rothschild. The château and vineyard were developed by Luc Tobie Clarke, a great grandson of James Clarke, who was born to Thomas and Marie Clarke of Killaly, Co. Louth. James Clark was an alderman of Dublin City in 1688.

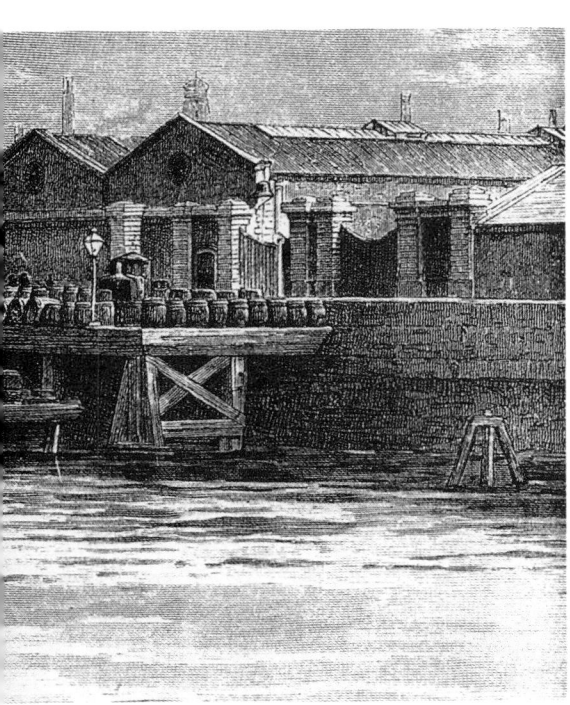

🍀 **Château Dillon,** Cru Bourgeois, Haut Médoc is today the Lycée Agricole de Bordeaux-Blanquefort. It was acquired by General Robert Dillon whose father had fled Dublin after his bank had failed. In 1764 the father died and the Dillon family came under the protection of Monsignor Dillon, Archbishop of Nantes. Robert Dillon was a page at the court of Louis XV and later rose through the ranks to become Maréchal de Camp.

🍀 **Château MacCarthy.** The MacCarthy family originated from Castle Cloghan near Skibbereen, Co. Cork. Denis MacCarthy supported James II in 1690 and sought refuge in France following the failure of the Jacobite cause. The MacCarthys were admitted to the ranks of the French nobility. Denis set up a trading company, MacCarthy Frères, which traded successfully for more than 100 years. He was a first Consul of the Bourse in 1768. His three nephews were members of the States General, having been ennobled in 1785. The MacCarthys intermarried with other Irish families: the O'Byrnes, Lawtons and the Cognac Exshaws. The Exshaw Company was founded in 1802 by John Exshaw from Dublin and still bears his name today.

🍀 **Château Phélan-Ségur**, Cru Grand Bourgeois Exceptionnel. This vineyard owes its name to Bernard Phelan, born in Clonmel in 1770. The Phelans were prosperous landowners and neighbours of Thomas Barton who had purchased Grove House from the proceeds of his wine trade in France (see p. 49). Phelan was invited to France by Barton and he managed the wine business very well.

🍀 **Château Haut-Brion.** This is *not* a corruption of Château O'Brien as has been suggested. This wine has an Irish connection that is remote but worthy of mention. The property was bought in 1935 by Clarence Dillon of Far Hills, New Jersey. Dillon was originally a Pole who had changed his name by deed poll. However, T.P. Whelehan in his book, *The Irish Wines of Bordeaux,* describes his correspondence with a Mrs Christine Allen of Athenry, Co. Galway, through the *Irish Times* newspaper. In their correspondence, Mrs Allen, granddaughter of the American Clarence Dillon, revealed that Clarence's grandmother, Pauline

---

A view of the Guinness Brewery fronting onto the River Liffey at Victoria Quay in Dublin in 1894. Founded by Arthur Guinness in 1759, the brewery was the world's largest in 1900. Today it is still Guinness's – and Ireland's – largest brewery, producing up to 4 million pints per day.

Dillon, had emigrated to the USA from Poland via France. It transpired that this Polish-Irish woman got her name from the Dillon Regiment of Napoleon's Army which must have been popular with local women. A village by the name of Dillon exists in Poland today.

IRELAND AND THE MOTOR CAR INDUSTRY

The importance of Irish-developed technology in the transport revolution of the 20th century is not widely recognised.

🍀 **Richard Lovell Edgeworth**, inventor, scientist and father of the novelist Maria Edgeworth (see p. 136), was an outstanding road engineer whose road improvements in Ireland were quickly taken up and applied in Britain.

🍀 **Professor John Shaw Brown** of Dunmurray, near Belfast **imported the first car to Ireland on 6 March 1896** – a steam-engined Serpollet Steamer. Brown, a Fellow of the Royal Society, was the **inventor of the viagraph,** an instrument which enabled an accurate profile of a road surface to be drawn, leading to smoother and safer road construction.

🍀 **The first internal combustion car in Ireland** was imported at Easter 1896 by the Reverend Ralph Harvey, headmaster of Cork Grammar School. In an effort to raise funds for his school, he managed to secure the loan of a Benz Velo from London. The citizens of Cork came in their hundreds to see the new machine and continued to pay for rides well into the night.

🍀 **The first owner-driver of an internal combustion car in Ireland** was Dr Colohan of Blackrock, who first drove his car on the streets of Dublin in November 1896.

🍀 When **Willie Hume** won the cycle race in Belfast in 1889 using the pneumatic tyres designed by John Dunlop (see p. 11), he caught the attention of a Dublin champion boxer, fencer and paper manufacturer, Sir Arthur Du Cros (see p. 46). Du Cros had seven sons who had dominated Irish cycling contests hitherto. The consequence of this was the founding of the **world's first pneumatic tyre factory on Stephen Street, Dublin**, which was opened within the same year. Once patented and manufactured, the pneumatic tyre became the vital catalyst of the greatest transport revolution of all time. Motor-driven vehicles immediately became faster, more practical and more comfortable. Du Cros was knighted in Britain and awarded the French Légion d'Honneur. (His Huguenot ancestors had fled religious persecution in France in 1704.)

🍀 **Henry Ford** (see also p. 44), the pioneering car manufacturer, son of John Ford from Ballinascarty, Co. Cork, greatly influenced the development of modern transport with his Ford Model T, first produced in 1909. In 1917 he set up the **first Ford assembly line in Europe** in Cork City. The plant closed down in 1984.

🍀 **The first Volkswagen Beetle assembled outside Germany** was built in a tramway depot on Shelbourne Road, Dublin in 1950 and was imported by **Stephen O'Flaherty**, who subsequently acquired the import franchises for Britain and Canada.

Labour and protest

♣ **Theobald Wolfe Tone (1763–98),** born at 44 Stafford Street (now Wolfe Tone Street), Dublin, was called to the bar in 1789 but chose to pursue a political career. With Thomas Russell and Napper Tandy he founded the Society of United Irishmen in 1791. His aims were 'to break the connection with England, the never-failing source of all our political evils'. Disappointed by the limited rights conceded by the Catholic Relief Act of 1793, Tone decided to enlist help for his cause from France. When the Dublin clergyman William Jackson was sent by the French government to meet with the United Irishmen, Tone convinced him that Ireland was ripe for a French invasion. Jackson was arrested, however, in April 1795 and Tone was implicated in the conspiracy and was banished to America. In 1795 he met the French foreign minister, Delacroix, in Paris and persuaded him to send an expeditionary force to Ireland. On 15 December 1796 13 ships and 15,000 men set sail from Brest under the command of General Hoche, only to be scattered by winter storms off the western coast of Ireland days later. The expedition was aborted and Tone and Hoche returned to the continent to plan a second sttempt. Hoche died suddenly in September 1797 and Tone's plans were impeded once more. However, when he heard news of the United Irishmen's rising in Ireland in May 1798, Tone organised

The capture of Wolfe Tone, Irish Protestant and nationalist. Tone was arrested by the British in the abortive rebellion of 1797–98 and condemned to hang, but he cut his throat before he could be executed.

another French fleet. On 12 October 1798 the fleet was confronted and captured by a powerful English force in Lough Swilly, Co. Donegal. Tone was court-martialled in Dublin, found guilty of treason and sentenced to be hanged. His pleas for a soldier's death by firing squad went unheeded and, on the morning planned for his execution, he committed suicide by slitting his throat with a pen-knife.

❀ **Daniel O'Connell** (1775–1847), 'The Liberator', was **the leading political figure of modern Irish history**. Born near Cahirciveen, Co. Kerry, he was educated locally and then in Douai, France from 1791 to 1794. He was called to the bar in 1798. The rising in Ireland that year, and the slaughter that followed, confirmed in his mind a lifelong abhorrence of violence.

In 1823 O'Connell founded the Catholic Association with the aim of using all constitutional means available to secure Catholic emancipation. The Catholic Association became a formidable political force. In 1828 O'Connell was elected in Clare (illegally) by an overwhelming majority with the support of the forty-shilling freeholders against the government candidate. Fearing popular revolt, Wellington and Peel conceded Catholic emancipation in April 1829. On 4 February 1830 O'Connell became **the first Catholic to sit in the House of Commons**.

O'Connell now turned to the repeal of the Act of Union (1801). British hostility to repeal was strong and the parties in Westminster closed ranks. In Ireland the repeal movement gained momentum and O'Connell declared that the Year of Repeal would be 1843. A series of 'monster meetings' were held nationwide. 150,000 attended at Mullingar, 400,000 at Mallow, 400,000 at Lismore and 800,000 to 1,000,000 at Tara to hear O'Connell's speeches. However, the penultimate and largest meeting of all, to be held at Clontarf in Dublin, was declared illegal. O'Connell called it off rather than risk a violent confrontation. He was put on trial In London by a carefully chosen jury and sentenced to one year in jail for conspiracy. He entered the Richmond Bridewell Prison in Dublin in May 1844 but emerged in September that year after the trial had been condemned by the House of Lords who ordered his release. His mental and physical health had been seriously impaired, however, and his confidence in the Repeal Party had gone. The party split in 1844 and the differences between O'Connell and the increasingly revolutionary Young Ireland movement grew. With the demise of the repeal movement and the trauma of the Famine of 1845–49, O'Connell saw his aspirations would not be realised. In January 1847 he

(above) *Daniel O'Connell, founder of the Catholic Association which mobilised support for Catholic emancipation.*

(right) *Charles Stewart Parnell addresses an anti-rent meeting in Limerick. His resignation of the Irish Party leadership in 1890, after being cited in the O'Shea divorce case, arguably changed the course of Irish – and British – history.*

left Ireland for the last time and made an impassioned plea in the House of Commons for the alleviation of Famine victims in Ireland. In February he left for Rome, but did not survive the journey. He died in Genoa on 15 May 1847.

❀ **Charles Stewart Parnell** (1846–91), 'the Uncrowned King of Ireland', born at Avondale, Co. Wicklow, was **the leading figure of Irish nationalism in the late 19th century**. The son of a Protestant landowner of nationalist sympathies, in 1875 Parnell joined the Home Rule party of Isaac Butt and headed the movement himself by 1879. That same year he was chosen as President of the National Land League, founded by Michael Davitt. The land war that followed (1879–82) initiated a succession of land acts that allowed the Irish peasantry to buy the land on which they lived and worked. However, under a new Coercion Act the Land League was suppressed and Parnell and other leaders were arrested. In the

Kilmainham Treaty of 1882, Prime Minister Gladstone introduced a programme of land reform in return for an end to agitation.

In the general election of 1885 the Irish Party pledged to pursue legislative independence by constitutional means and won every seat outside of northeast Ulster and Dublin University. The 1886 Home Rule bill was defeated by opposition from Conservatives in alliance with Ulster Unionists. A general election was called once again and the Conservatives, who were returned to government, embarked on a policy of 'killing Home Rule by kindness'. (By continuing with land reforms they hoped to maintain the Union.)

In 1887 *The Times* published a series of letters entitled 'Parnellism and Crime' which were intended to discredit Parnell by accusing him of complicity in murder. The letters were later revealed to be forgeries. Parnell was cleared at a special commission of the High Court in February 1890. In November of that year, however, a former member of the Home Rule Party, Captain O'Shea, divorced his wife Katharine on the grounds of an affair between her and Parnell. Nonconformist opinion in the British Liberal Party was shocked and no longer considered Parnell fit to lead the Home Rule cause. When he married Katharine O'Shea in June 1891, the Catholic hierarchy in Ireland withdrew their support and his fall was complete. He died suddenly in Brighton in October 1891.

🍀 The verb 'boycott' – to refuse to have dealings or to trade with a person or an organisation as a means of protest – was first used by the *Daily Mail* newspaper to describe the techniques employed by the Land League against **Captain Charles Cunningham Boycott** (1832–97), who was working as a land agent for Lord Erne's estate at Lough Mask, Co. Mayo in 1873. In protest against his refusal to reduce their rents, the tenants refused to work the land and allowed the crops to start to decay in the soil. Over 1000 government troops were employed to transport a workforce of 50 Orangemen from Cavan to save the crops.

🍀 **The Easter Rising** of 1916 was organised by radical Irish separatists who were convinced that Britain would not honour her commitment to grant Home Rule. The Rising had been planned in secret by the Military Council of the Irish Republican Brotherhood and was intended for Easter Sunday, 23 April 1916. After a series of mishaps, a meeting of IRB leaders decided to proceed with a rising the following day. Defeat was inevitable but it was hoped that the 'blood sacrifice' would motivate the populace. On Easter Monday a rebel force of 1558 volunteers led by **Padraic Pearse** and 219 of James Connolly's Irish Citizen Army occupied strategic positions across Dublin City. Taking the General Post Office on Sackville Street (O'Connell Street) as the rebel headquarters, Pearse stood outside and proclaimed the Irish Republic (see p. 58). By 29 April, with much of central Dublin reduced to rubble by British artillery fire, Pearse surrendered.

In all 64 rebels were killed. Twenty thousand British troops were called in, of whom 103 were killed. Seventeen policemen and an estimated 300 civilians also died. Martial law was declared on 25 April and between 3 May and 12 May 15 Republican leaders were executed, including all the signatories of the Proclamation.

In Ireland the initial reaction to the rebels was hostile. However, the imposition of martial law and the execution of the leaders antagonised popular opinion. A government attempt to introduce conscription in 1917 alienated the populace still further. As it became obvious that Home Rule was no longer an option, the country moved towards violent insurgency. In the 1918 general election Sinn Féin won 73 seats against 25 Unionist, six Home Rule Party and one Independent Unionist. The first Dáil Eireann was formed in Dublin on 21 January 1919. The Anglo-Irish War raged until July 1921. On 7 January 1922 Dáil Eireann ratified the Anglo-Irish Treaty which partitioned Ireland and split the Republican movement.

❦ **Michael Collins** (1890–1922), born at Woodfield, near Clonakilty, Co. Cork, was **the leading strategist of the Anglo-Irish War of 1919–21**.

In 1906 he moved to London, where he worked as a post office clerk and later as a stockbroker. He joined the Irish Republican Brotherhood there and returned to Ireland in 1916 to take part in the Easter Rising. He escaped a death sentence and was interned in Frongoch

---

Michael Collins as commander of the army of the Free State during the Irish Civil War, August 1922. After signing the Anglo-Irish Treaty of 1921 Collins presciently remarked that he had signed his own death warrant. His brief spell as head of the provisional Free State government was cut short by an IRA bullet on 22 August 1922.

Prison in Wales until December 1916. He stood for election for Sinn Féin in 1918 having stood down from the party executive in order to form an intelligence system with Harry Boland. He was elected to the first Dáil Eireann and became Minister for Home Affairs and then Minister for Finance from April 1919 to August 1922. With the foundation of Dáil Eireann on 21 January 1919, the official army of the new government became the Irish Republican Army. Collins became President of the Supreme Council and gathered around him an elite staff known as the 'Squad'. With this group Collins made a series of attacks on British military intelligence. On the morning of 'Bloody Sunday', 21 November 1920, an IRA 'squad' entered houses and hotels across Dublin and shot dead 14 British secret service agents. That afternoon the British Army retaliated by opening fire on a Gaelic football crowd at Croke Park in Dublin, killing 12 civilians and one player.

Following negotiations for a truce, Collins reluctantly chose to accept the Anglo-Irish Treaty on 6 December 1921. The Treaty provided for the partition of Ireland and was ratified by 64 votes to 57 in Dáil Eireann. In the Civil War that ensued, Collins resigned his position as Minister for Finance and became Commander-in-Chief of the National Army. On 20 August 1922 he was shot dead by anti-Treaty Republicans in an ambush at Béal na mBláth, Co. Cork, only a few miles from his birthplace.

🍀 Irish-born **Terence Vincent Powderly** joined **America's first nationwide union movement**, the Knights of Labor, in 1874. Within five years he rose to the head of the organisation as Grand Master Workman. He presided over its development during the 1880s, when its membership grew to over 700,000. He was the nation's **most powerful union leader**, served as mayor of Scranton, Pennsylvania, was a member of Clan na Gael, and in 1897 was appointed Commissioner General of Immigration by President McKinley.

🍀 **'The father of Labor Day'**, **Peter James McGuire** (1852–1906), was born in New York to Irish immigrant parents. McGuire worked for the Social Democratic Party in the 1870s and campaigned for the unionisation of carpenters. His efforts led to the foundation of the United Brotherhood of Carpenters and Joiners (UBC). He also campaigned for the eight-hour day and led the May Day demonstrations of 1886 and 1890. After 12 years of campaigning, McGuire succeeded in creating Labor Day as a national holiday in 1894. McGuire was also a leading founder of the

American Federation of Labor (AFL) in 1886 and served as its first secretary and vice-president.

🍀 **Founding member of the Transport Workers Union of America** in 1934, **Michael Joseph Quill** (1905–66) of Kilgarvan, Co. Kerry dominated America's labour movement for three decades. An IRA veteran of the Anglo-Irish War and the Civil War, he emigrated to the USA in 1926. As president of the TWUA in 1935, he was elected president of the new International Transport Workers Union in 1937. Quill was imprisoned in 1965 for refusing to call an end to a transport strike that had paralysed New York for 12 days.

🍀 **The first woman to head the US Communist Party**, **Elizabeth Gurley Flynn** (1890–1964) was born in New Hampshire of a long line of Irish socialists. At 15 she was making speeches on street corners, and in 1906 joined the Industrial Workers of the World ('Wobblies'). She was a co-founder of the American Civil Liberties Union in 1920 and joined the Communist Party in 1937. She became party leader or First National Woman Chairman in 1961. She died in Moscow and was given a state funeral in Red Square despite her lifelong opposition to Soviet domination of American Communist Party politics.

🍀 **Kate Kennedy** (1827–90) formed **America's first union of schoolteachers** in Oakland, California. She was born in Gaskinstown, Co. Meath into a prosperous farming family. Following the death of her father in 1841 and the Famine, the family were forced to flee to America, where Kennedy began working in the needle trade. In 1856 she followed her sisters to San Francisco and took up teaching. By 1867 she was principal of North Cosmopolitan Grammar School but, as a woman, was only entitled to primary school wages. Her tireless campaigning on behalf of California's women teachers paid off when equal pay legislation was introduced in 1874.

🍀 The labour leader **Leonora Barry** was born in Co. Cork in 1849, emigrating with her family to the US in 1852. She joined the Knights of Labor in 1884 and between 1887 and 1889 delivered reports on the working conditions of women and children in America's sweathouses. Her campaigning resulted in **the first Pennsylvania Factory Inspection Act** of 1889. She became a figure of national prominence and a hero of the working classes. Barry was a leading figure in the successful campaign for women's suffrage in Colorado State in 1893. (She married Obadiah

The Provisional Government
of the
IRISH REPUBLIC
To the People of Ireland.

IRISHMEN AND IRISHWOMEN:: In the name of God · and of the dead generations from which she receives her old tradition of nationhood, Ireland, through us, summons her children to her flag · and strikes for her freedom.

Having organised and trained her manhood through her secret revolutionary organisation, the Irish Republican Brotherhood, and through her open military organisations, the Irish Volunteers and the Irish Citizen Army, having patiently perfected her discipline, having resolutely waited for the right moment to reveal itself, she now seizes that moment, and, supported by her exiled children in America · and by gallant allies in Europe but relying in the first on her own strength, she strikes in full confidence of victory.

We declare the right of the people of Ireland to the ownership of Ireland, and to the unfettered control of Irish destinies, to be sovereign and indefeasible. The long usurpation of that right by a foreign people and government has not extinguished the right, nor can it ever be extinguished except by the destruction of the Irish people. In every generation the Irish people have asserted their right to national freedom and sovereignty; six times during the past three hundred years they have asserted it in arms. Standing on that fundamental right and again asserting it in arms in the face of the world we hereby proclaim the Irish Republic as a Sovereign Independent State, and we pledge our lives and the lives of our comrades-in-arms to the cause of its freedom, of its welfare and of its exaltation among the nations.

The Irish Republic is entitled to, and hereby claims, the allegiance of every Irishman and Irishwoman. The Republic guarantees religious and civil liberty, equal rights and equal opportunities to all its citizens, and declares its resolve to pursue the happiness and prosperity of the whole nation and of all its parts, cherishing all the children of the nation equally, and oblivious of the differences carefully fostered by an alien government, which have divided a minority from the majority in the past.

Until our arms have brought the opportune moment for the establishment of a permanent National Government, representative of the whole people of Ireland, and elected by the suffrages of all her men and women, the Provisional Government, hereby constituted, will administer the civil and military affairs of the Republic in trust for the people.

We place the cause of the Irish Republic under the protection of the Most High God, Whose blessing we invoke upon our arms, and we pray that no one who serves that cause will dishonour it by cowardice, inhumanity or rapine. In this supreme hour the Irish nation must, by its valour and discipline, and by the readiness of its children to sacrifice themselves for the common good, prove itself worthy of the august destiny to which it is called.

Signed · on behalf of the Provisional Government :

✣ Thomas J. Clarke. Sean MacDiarmada.
Thomas MacDonagh. P. H. Pearse. Eamonn Ceannt
✣ James Connolly ✣ Joseph Plunkett. ✣

The 'proclamation of independence' read out on the steps of Dublin's General Post Office by Padraic Pearse during the Easter Rising, 24 April 1916.

Read Lake in St Louis, Missouri in 1890 – hence her nickname 'Mother Lake'. This was her second marriage. Her first husband, William Barry, also Irish-born, died in 1871. Her maiden name was Kearney.)

🍀 **Mary Harris Jones, or 'Mother Jones',** was born in Cork in 1830, emigrating to America with her parents in 1835. Her involvement with the trade union movement began with her marriage to a member of the Iron Molders' Union in 1861. Her husband and four children died of yellow fever in 1867 and she moved to Chicago to work as a dressmaker. Disaster struck again in 1871 when she lost everything in the Great Fire of Chicago.

From then on she devoted her time to union activity and campaigned for the improvement of working conditions and wages throughout the United States. Jones was a co-founder of the American Social Democratic Party in 1898 and of the Industrial Workers of the World ('Wobblies') in 1905. She lobbied in Washington for the rights of workers and for Mexican revolutionaries. She made her last public address in 1924 at the age of 94.

🍀 **The first woman to be elected to the British Parliament** and member of the first Dáil Eireann, **Countess Constance Markievicz** (1868–1927), née Gore-Booth, was elected as Sinn Féin candidate for the St Patrick's division of Dublin in December 1918. Born in London, she was educated in Lissadel in Co. Sligo, where her father, Henry Gore-Booth, held the family estates. Having lived in Paris and the Ukraine, she settled in Dublin in 1903 and became involved in the Gaelic League and Abbey Theatre circles. In 1906 she rented a cottage in Ballally, Co. Dublin. It was there that she came across back issues of *The Peasant* and Sinn Féin publications left behind by the previous tenant, poet and writer Padraic Colum (see p. 145), and her interest in the cause of Irish independence was aroused. She joined Sinn Féin and Inghinidhe na hEireann (Daughters of Ireland) in 1908. In 1909 she founded Na Fianna for the drilling of boys in the use of arms. She served with Michael Mallin at the College of Surgeons during the 1916 Easter Rising, for which she was sentenced to death though later released in the general amnesty of June 1917. Elected as an MP in the general election the following year, Markievicz refused to take her seat in Parliament, in keeping with Sinn Féin policy. As Minister for Labour, she was a member of the first Dáil Eireann that met on 21 January 1919. She was jailed twice during the Anglo-Irish War of 1919–21 and opposed the Anglo-Irish Treaty in 1921. She was defeated in the 1922 election,

but re-elected in 1923 in Dublin South. She joined de Valera's Fianna Fáil party at its inception in 1926 and was elected once more in 1927.

🍀 **Founder of the revolutionary woman's society Inghinidhe na hEireann** (Daughters of Ireland), on Easter Sunday 1908, **Maud Gonne MacBride** (1865–1953) was born in Aldershot, England, the daughter of an army officer of Irish descent and an English mother. Her father was posted to Dublin in 1882 and she acted as his hostess until his death. Whilst recuperating in France from tuberculosis, she met Lucien Millevoye, a journalist and politician, who encouraged her to act on her sympathies for the cause of Irish independence. She spent the 1890s touring France, England, Scotland and America, promoting the cause and collecting funds. It was in Dublin in 1900 that she founded the revolutionary women's movement Inghinidhe na hEireann.

MacBride took the leading role in the 1902 play *Cathleen ni Houlihan* by W.B. Yeats (whose marriage proposal she had rejected in 1891). Her beauty and ability as an actress created a sensation. In 1903 in Paris she married John MacBride, a leader in the 1916 Easter Rising, and remained there until 1917.

She was arrested in Dublin in 1918 and imprisoned in Holloway prison for six months. She worked with the White Cross for the relief of the victims of the Anglo-Irish War 1919–21 and opposed the Anglo-Irish Treaty of 1921.

🍀 **Leading founder of the Irishwomen's Suffrage Federation** in 1911, **Louie Bennett** (1870–1956), born in Temple Hill, Dublin, also helped to found the Irish Women's Reform League which allied itself to the Suffrage Federation and worked to improve the economic plight of women workers. She represented Ireland on the International Executive of the Women's League for Peace and Freedom during World War I. In 1932 she became **the first woman president of the Irish Trade Union Congress**.

🍀 **The youngest woman MP ever elected to British Parliament** was **Bernadette McAliskey** (née Devlin; 1947–), who was elected for Mid-Ulster as an Independent Unity candidate on 17 April 1969 at the age of 21 years 359 days.

🍀 **Helen Blackburn** (1842–1903), **pioneer of the women's suffrage movement**, was born on Valentia Island, Co. Kerry. Her parents moved to London in 1859 and she involved herself in the movement for women's suffrage, becoming the Secretary

(above) *Countess Markievicz (born Constance Gore-Booth) was sentenced to death for her role in the Easter Rising, but was reprieved. The following year (1917) she became the first woman MP to be elected to the British parliament.*

(below) *Bernadette Devlin, the youngest woman MP ever elected to the British parliament, arrives in London to take her seat in the House of Commons, April 1969. She and her husband survived a gun attack by Loyalist paramilitaries in 1981.*

for the National Society for Women's Suffrage in 1874.

✤ **India's first woman magistrate** and a leading worker for women's rights, **Margaret Cousins** (née Gillespie; 1878–1954), born at Belmont, Boyle, Co. Roscommon, was appointed Treasurer of the Irish Women's Franchise League in 1908. She was one of six Irish delegates to the Parliament of Women in London in November 1910 and was sentenced to six months' imprisonment for throwing stones at 10 Downing Street. She moved to India in 1915 and became the first non-Indian member of the Indian Women's University at Poona in 1916. Cousins was a founding member of the Women's Indian Association in 1917 and the founding head-mistress of the National Girls' School in Mangalore 1919–20. She was imprisoned for a year in 1932 for protesting against emergency powers then in force and was compensated in 1949 by the Indian government in recognition of her sufferings on behalf of Indian freedom.

✤ **Britain's first woman factory inspector**, appointed in 1893 by the then Home Secretary, H.H.

Asquith, was **Margaret Mary Tennant** (née Abraham; 1869–1946), born in Rathgar, Dublin. She was treasurer of the Women's Trade Union League and dealt with the problems of illegal overtime, bad sanitation and safety conditions. She was Chairman of the Industrial Law Committee and a member of the Royal Commission for Divorce, and subsequently appointed chief adviser on women's welfare to the Ministry of Munitions during World War I.

🍀 **Ireland's first prominent socialist** was **William Thompson** (1775–1833) of Rosscarbery, Co. Cork. Born into a wealthy Protestant family, he inherited a 1500-acre (3706.6 ha) estate at Rosscarbery. He travelled in France and the Netherlands as a young man and was influenced by the writings of Saint-Simon and Sismondi. He supported the movement for Catholic emancipation in Ireland and abhorred the contrast between his own wealth and the conditions of his tenants. He was a friend of Bentham and a supporter of Robert Owen's self-supporting 'villages of cooperation'. Thompson regarded the unearned income of the idle classes as the leading social injustice and sought his own redemption by devoting himself to the welfare of others. In 1824 he published *An Enquiry into the Principles of the Distribution of Wealth Most Conducive to Human Happiness*, where he set out his theories. Thompson was also a pioneer of sexual equality and expounded his views in *Appeal to One Half of the Human Race, Women, against the Pretensions of the other Half, Men, to Retain them in Political, and thence in Civil and Domestic Slavery* (1825). He died in 1833, leaving his estate to aid the poor through the operation of schemes based on the principles of Robert Owen.

🍀 **The leader of the British Chartist movement**, **Feargus Edward O'Connor** (1794–1855), born in Connorville, Co. Cork, was educated at Trinity College, Dublin and called to the bar, but decided to turn to politics. He became Repeal MP for Co. Cork as a follower of O'Connell, but quarrelled with him and lost his seat in 1835. He moved to England, where his radical politics drew large crowds. In 1837 O'Connor founded the *Northern Star* newspaper, which found immediate success. In 1838 the 'People's Charter' of the Working Men's Association was adopted and O'Connor became the movement's most effective leader. Chartism was **the first example in the world of a national political working-class movement**. It preceded the writings of Marx and Engels, who were later to draw inspiration from it. O'Connor was arrested for seditious libel following the Newport Rising in 1839, despite his lack of involvement, but emerged from jail a year later as undisputed leader of Chartism. He was elected MP for Nottingham in 1847 and devoted his energies to his National Land Company, which unsuccessfully attempted to resettle urban workers in small rural holdings. He presided at the great Chartist meeting in London in 1848 and presented the petition to Parliament. His mental health steadily deteriorated and he was committed to an asylum in 1852.

🍀 The outstanding trade union organiser in early 19th-century Britain was **John Doherty** (c. 1798–1854) of Buncrana, Co. Donegal. Rather than local unions that were the norm at the time, Doherty wanted unions spanning the entire country, organised along the lines of O'Connell's Catholic Association – 'united as the Catholics of Ireland you will be blessed with similar success'. In Manchester in 1829 he founded the Grand General Union of Operative Spinners of Great Britain and Ireland and in 1830 the National Association of United Trades for the Protection of Labour. This central union soon had 150 local unions affiliated to it, and Doherty edited and published its hugely popular newspaper, *The Voice of the People*. The National Association was a precursor of the present-day British Trades Union Congress (TUC).

🍀 **The first activist for animal rights, Richard 'Humanity Dick' Martin** (1754–1834) was born in Dublin and educated at Harrow and Trinity College, Cambridge. His estates in Connemara, Co. Galway extended over 200,000 acres (80,939 ha), stretched 30 miles (48 km) from his front door and were said to provide him with **the longest avenue in Europe**. He sat in the Irish Parliament 1776–1800 as MP for Galway and was a supporter of the Act of Union. Known for his love of animals, in 1822 he succeeded in having passed the **first enactment in Great Britain for the protection of the rights of animals**. (Specifically, the act made the ill-treatment of cattle illegal.) He was one of the founders of the Royal Society for the Protection of Animals in 1824. Nicknamed 'Humanity Dick' by King George IV, he was in favour of Catholic Emancipation and campaigned for the abolition of the death penalty for forgery.

politics, military and government

REPUBLIC OF IRELAND

The Republic of Ireland is a mixed economy democracy and a member of the EEC since 1973. The country is a neutral state outside the North Atlantic Treaty Alliance (NATO). The Republic has been an independent state since 1922, when the union with Great Britain was broken after the Anglo-Irish War of 1919–21.

Northern Ireland remains part of the United Kingdom and is directly ruled through Westminster. As such, it has been part of the EEC since 1973 and of NATO since its foundation in 1949. Northern Ireland remains a more mixed economy than the rest of the UK which has been moving toward the free market since 1979. Its citizens are British subjects, although a large minority reject this status. Northern Ireland was partitioned from the rest of the island by the Anglo-Irish Treaty (6 December 1921) following the Anglo-Irish War of 1919–21.

Political Parties

The following are the political parties involved in the government and politics of the Republic of Ireland:

✤ **Fianna Fáil** ('Soldiers of Destiny') was founded on 16 May 1926 by Eamon de Valera (see p. 67) and was originally made up of the anti-Treaty faction of the Civil War. Sub-titled 'the Republican Party', their aims were the unification of Ireland, the preservation of the Irish language, the distribution of large farms among small farmers and a policy of self-sufficiency and protectionism. The party broke away from the Sinn Féin abstentionists and entered Dáil Eireann on 11 August 1927. Fianna Fáil first came to power in 1932 and has been the largest political party in Ireland since.

Today Fianna Fáil is a centre-right, populist party. It is pro-European and supports the expansion of the European Union. It continues to follow a traditional policy of neutrality in international affairs, albeit with less conviction than before. Its supporters, although coming from all sections of society, are less likely to be middle class and urban. On social issues, Fianna Fáil tends to be conservative. Economically, the party has been pushed to the right, in keeping with the trend of the 1980s, and encourages free trade, privatisation of national industry and reduced government spending.

The party leaders of Fianna Fáil have been: Eamon de Valera (1926–59), Seán Lemass (1959–66), John (Jack) Lynch (1966–79), Charles Haughey (1979–92) and Albert Reynolds (1992–). De Valera was also Taoiseach (1932–48), 1951–54 and 1957–59, as were Lemass 1959–66, Lynch 1966–73 and 1977–79, Haughey 1979–81, 1982 and 1987–92, and Reynolds 1992– .

✤ **Fine Gael** ('Family/Tribe of the Gaels') was founded in 1933 to merge Cumann na nGaedhal (which had been the party of government since 1922 and originated among supporters of the Anglo-Irish Treaty of 1921), the National Guard and the National Centre. Originally Fine Gael drew its support from industry, business, large farmers and the professions, and in the 1990s its core of support remains essentially the same. Today Fine Gael is a centre-right party with few ideological differences to Fianna Fáil. As the politics of the Civil War fade, so do the differences between Fianna Fáil and Fine Gael, and the latter has been struggling to maintain its support in recent years. Economically, Fine Gael is right-of-centre and pursues free trade, reduced government spending, privatisation of national industries and the curtailment of the power of trade unions.

Party leaders include: General Eoin O'Duffy (1933–34; not an elected TD, he led the party as head of the 'Blueshirts', a short-lived, quasi-fascist movement motivated by pro-Catholic, anti-socialist/IRA sentiment, that had no real direction); W.T. Cosgrave (1935–44); Richard Mulcahy (1944–59); James Dillon (1959–65); Liam Cosgrave (1965–77); Garret Fitzgerald (1977–87); Alan Dukes (1987–90); John Bruton (1990–). W.T. Cosgrave was Executive President 1922–32. Costello was Taoiseach 1948–51 and 1954–57, as were Liam Cosgrave 1973–77 and Garret Fitzgerald 1981–82 and 1982–87.

✤ **The Labour Party** was founded in 1912 by James Connolly and James Larkin, in Clonmel, Co. Tipperary. In 1918 the party developed into the Irish Labour Party and Irish Trade Union Congress until the latter became an independent body in 1930. The party supported the nationalist independence movement 1916–21 and abstained from the General Election in 1918 to avoid splitting the nationalist vote and to allow Sinn Féin's overwhelming victory. Consequently party members were not involved in the first Dáil Eireann and only joined the Dáil in opposition in 1922. Today the Labour Party is a centre-left party in the social democratic tradition, whose main body of public support is in Dublin City. Recent electoral success has widened the party's influence nationwide.

Party Leaders: James Larkin (1912–14); James Connolly (1914–16); Thomas Johnson (1916–27); T.J. O' Connell (1927–32); William Norton (1932–60); Brendan Corish (1960–77); Frank Cluskey (1977–81); Michael O'Leary (1981–82); Dick Spring (1982–).

🍀 **The Progressive Democrats.** The leader of the Progressive Democrats, Mary Harney (1953–), is currently the only woman to head an Irish political party. She also holds the distinction of becoming **the youngest-ever member of the Seanad** (Senate or Upper House), when she was elected in 1977 at the age of 24. The Progressive Democrats, founded by Desmond O'Malley and Mary Harney, split from Fianna Fáil in 1985. The party follows a right-of-centre political line in its economic policies, but has a liberal agenda on various social issues.

🍀 **Sinn Féin** was founded in 1905 by Arthur Griffith, who initially put forward the idea of a dual monarchy as a concept of Irish independence. Following the 1916 Easter Rising, Sinn Féin was reorganised under the leadership of Eamon de Valera and was built into a nationwide independence party. It won a sweeping victory with 73 seats in the 1918 election.

Following the Anglo-Irish War of 1919–21 and the Anglo-Irish Treaty, Sinn Féin split. Those who supported the Treaty formed the first Cumann na nGaedhal government in 1921, while those who refused to accept it continued to call themselves Sinn Féin. When de Valera formed Fianna Fáil in 1926 and joined the Dáil, he took most of Sinn Féin with him. Since then it has operated as a fringe republican army in the 26 counties of Southern Ireland. The movement split again in 1970, when Official Sinn Féin – the Workers' Party (see below) – moved away from Provisional Sinn Féin. The latter has since become a political force in Northern Ireland (see p. 73).

🍀 **The Workers' Party of Ireland** split from Sinn Féin in January 1970 led by Tomás MacGiolla. Its aims were the overthrow of the remnants of British rule in Ireland and the establishment of a 32-county socialist republic. It has since distanced itself from violent insurrection. The Workers' Party split again

in 1992. Most of its leaders went to form Democratic Left (see below). Party leader Tomás MacGiolla lost his Dáil seat in 1992. He was Lord Mayor of Dublin 1993–94.

Democratic Left split from the Workers' Party in 1992 led by party leader Pronsias de Rossa who took five elected members of the Workers' Party with him. Democratic Left's representatives in the Dáil are among the most vociferous of all the parties. They are a democratic socialist party.

🍀 **The Green Party (An Comhaontas Glas) of Ireland** was founded in 1982 as the Ecological Party. It changed its name to the Green Alliance before it became the Green Party and won its first seat in the Dáil in 1989 when Roger Garland was returned for Dublin South. Garland lost his seat in 1992 but the Greens maintained their representation with the election of Trevor Sargent in Dublin North. John Gormley became the first Green Party Lord Mayor of Dublin in 1994. In common with the Green Parties of other European nations, the Irish Green Party seeks to secure the ecological future of the earth and the redistribution of its resources.

Presidents of Ireland

The presidency is largely a symbolic office with little or no say in the government of the nation. The President is a member of the Oireachtas* and acts on the authority of the government. The primary function of the office is to sign bills into law. However, it has several other essential functions.

The President is guardian of the Constitution and holds the following powers: He/she may send any bills to the Supreme Court, except those that are money bills or those proposing to amend the Constitution. The President may call a referendum on a bill if the majority of the Senate and at least one third of the Dáil request him/her not to sign it. The President has 'absolute discretion' to refuse dissolution of the Dáil to a Taoiseach who has lost a majority or who interprets a defeat in a Dáil vote as a loss of confidence. The President formally appoints the Taoiseach and, on the Taoiseach's advice, he/she appoints the members of the government. (The termination of office also requires presidential approval.) The President is Commander-in-Chief of the Irish Army and all military officers hold their commissions from him/her.

* *The Oireachtas is the legislature of the Republic of Ireland. This includes the presidency, Dáil Eireann and Seanad Eireann. The President cannot be a member of either house.*

PRESIDENTS OF IRELAND

1) Douglas Hyde (1860–1949), **the first President of Ireland**, was born in Castlerea, Co. Roscommon. He was a graduate of Trinity College, Dublin and learned to speak French, German, Irish, Hebrew, Greek and Latin fluently, as well as winning awards for English verse and prose. He was a co-founder of the Gaelic League in 1893 and was its first president. The League was formed to stop the rapid demise of the Irish language and traditional Gaelic culture, and it had organised over 550 branches by 1905. Hyde was successful in making Irish a compulsory subject for matriculation to the new National University of Ireland, founded in 1908. He was elected the **first professor of modern Irish at University College, Dublin** in 1909. Hyde consistently but unsuccessfully tried to keep the Gaelic League from becoming a political movement but, as an organisation founded to revive the nation's spirit and culture, it inevitably played a crucial part in the nationalist revolution 1916–21.

When the office of President of Ireland was created under the Constitution of 1937, Hyde, as a non-political patriot and esteemed scholar, was selected by all parties and held office for the full seven-year term until 1945. He was the author of many works and his revitalisation of Irish literature and folklore inspired much of the literary revival. His play *Casadh an tSúgain,* produced by the Irish Literary Theatre in October 1901, was **the first play in Irish to be performed professionally on the stage.**

2) Sean T. O'Ceallaigh (O'Kelly) (1882–1966), born in Dublin, was a member of the Gaelic League, the Celtic Literary Society, a founding member of Sinn Féin in 1905, and was staff captain to Padraic Pearse during the 1916 Rising (see pp. 55 and 58). He was interned in England but was returned as Sinn Féin MP for the College Green division of Dublin in the General Election of 1918. He was *Ceann Comhairle* (chairman) of the first Dáil in the Mansion House in January 1919 and was sent to the Peace Conference at Versailles, as an envoy of the Republican government, in an attempt to secure international recognition for the new state.

O'Ceallaigh opposed the Anglo-Irish Treaty of 1921 and was a founding member of the Fianna Fáil party in 1926, holding various ministerial posts when Fianna Fáil was in power 1932–45. He was elected second President of Ireland in 1945 and was returned unopposed for a second term 1952–59.

3) Eamon de Valera (1882–1975) became the third President of Ireland in 1959 and was re-elected for a second term 1966–73. He received many distinguished visitors, including Presidents Charles de Gaulle of France and John F. Kennedy of the US. He served for 14 years as President of Ireland, the longest period allowed under the 1937 Constitution, which he himself had drafted. De Valera also holds the distinction of being **the only person to hold all the offices of President since the foundation of the state: of Dáil Eireann, the Republic, the Executive Council and Ireland.** (See also p. 66.)

4) Erskine Hamilton Childers (1905–74) was born in London, the son of Robert Erskine Childers, the patriot and author. Erskine Hamilton moved permanently to Ireland in 1932 and settled at Glendalough House, Annamoe, Co. Wicklow, the home of his paternal grandmother, Anna Barton. He was first elected in 1938 as a Fianna Fáil TD for Athlone-Longford. He was a TD for 35 years without losing his seat and held several ministerial positions. As Minister for Posts and Telegraphs 1951, he was a liberalising influence in the organisation of the national radio and television network, RTE. He was *Tánaiste* (assistant Prime Minister) and Minister for Health in the Fianna Fáil government 1969–73. Childers was elected President in May 1973, defeating the Government candidate, T.F. O'Higgins.

5) Cearbhall O'Dálaigh (1911–78) was born in Bray, Co. Wicklow. He began his distinguished legal career in 1934, when he was called to the bar. He was Senior Counsel in 1945 and then Attorney-General 1946–48 and again 1951–53. He was appointed judge at the Supreme Court in 1953 and became Chief Justice in 1961. In 1972 he became the Irish member of the EEC Court of Justice. His appointment as President of Ireland was agreed upon by all political parties in the Dáil after the death of Erskine Childers and he was inaugurated on 19 December 1974. In September 1976, when an Emergency Powers Bill was presented to him for signature, he referred it to the Supreme Court to verify its constitutionality. The court ruled that it was not unconstitutional and the bill was passed. However, the Minister for Defence, Patrick Donegan, called his action a 'thundering disgrace'. On 22 October 1976 O'Dálaigh resigned in order to 'assert publicly my personal integrity and independence as the President of Ireland and to protect the dignity and independence of the presidency as an institution'.

As Chief Justice, O'Dálaigh allowed greater freedom of interpretation of the laws laid out in the constitution and developed the Supreme Court as a guardian of the rights of Ireland's citizens.

6) **Patrick Hillery** (1923–) was born in Miltown Malbay, Co. Clare. A graduate of University College, Dublin, he qualified in science and continued in his studies to qualify as a surgeon and obstetrician. He was awarded a diploma of public health in 1952 and in 1955 became a member of the Health Council. He was coroner for West Clare 1958–59 before taking his position as Minister for Education in the Fianna Fáil government of 1959–65. He was Minister for Industry and Commerce 1965–66, Minister for Labour 1966–69 and Minister for Foreign Affairs 1969–73. He served two full presidential terms 1976–83 and 1983–90.

7) **Mary Robinson** (1944–), **the first woman President of Ireland** (1990–), born in Ballina, Co. Mayo, began her distinguished legal career at Trinity College, Dublin, where she won the Henry Hamilton Hunter Memorial Prize in 1965. In 1967 she was awarded a Moderatorship in legal science (1st class), an LLB degree (1st class), the degree of Barrister-at-Law (1st class) and a fellowship to Harvard University. She graduated from Harvard with an LLM (1st class) in 1968 and in 1969 was appointed Reid Professor of Law at Trinity College, Dublin: at 25 years of age she was **the youngest ever professor of law at TCD**. She was elected to the Irish Senate in 1969. She is an acknowledged expert in European Law and served on the Joint Committee on EC Legislation. She has played an important role in several civil and human rights cases in Irish and European courts. She was nominated for the Presidency in 1990 by the Labour Party, supported by the Workers Party and the Green Party. Her public appeal spread across the political spectrum and she defeated a number of more experienced opponents.

Mary Robinson, Ireland's first woman President – and the youngest person to hold that office – photographed at the John F. Kennedy Presidential Library in Boston, Massachusetts, 11 March 1994.

The term of office of the presidency is seven years. The President is directly elected and cannot hold office for more than two terms.

History of the presidency

The presidency has taken various forms since the foundation of the Irish State, and clarification of the ambiguities that arose in the earlier years is necessary.

At the first Dáil Eireann, called in April 1919, Eamon de Valera was appointed the President of Dáil Eireann, an office which gave him the authority of Prime Minister. On his visit to the United States 1919–20 he was welcomed as the President of the Irish Republic. His followers chose to keep that title when they re-elected him, after refusing to recognise the Anglo-Irish Treaty in January 1922. (De Valera resigned his position as President of Dáil Eireann in January 1921 and lost the election to Arthur Griffith.)

When the Irish Free State officially came into existence in December 1922, the head of government became known as President of the Executive Council, with the role of Prime Minister.

When de Valera was elected in March 1932, he set about dismantling the Anglo-Irish Treaty and began drafting the Constitution of 1937, which was approved by referendum and replaced the 1922 Constitution.

From 1937 to 1949 the President was known as President of Eire. Since the Republic of Ireland Act in 1949, the President has been officially known as the President of the Republic of Ireland, but is usually referred to simply as the President of Ireland.

Taosaigh na hEireann
(Prime Ministers of Ireland)

Taoiseach, the title of the leader or Prime Minister of the Irish government, was a word chosen by Eamon de Valera in the Constitution of 1937. It is the Irish word for the chief or head of the tribe in the Gaelic clan

---

William Cosgrave, President of the Executive Council of the Irish Free State (left foreground) in February 1923. Kevin O'Higgins is standing to his left. Cosgrave and O'Higgins made uncompromising use of their 'emergency powers' to break the republican war of attrition 1922–23.

system. From 6 December 1922 to 29 December 1937, during the lifetime of the Irish Free State, the leader of the government was called the President of the Executive Council.

🦢 **William T. Cosgrave** (1880–1965), born in Dublin, was **the first President of the Executive Council of the Irish Free State.** His first term of office was from 6 December 1922 to 21 September 1923. He joined the Irish Volunteers in 1913 and fought in the 1916 Rising under Eamonn Ceannt. He was elected Sinn Féin MP for Kilkenny in 1918. A supporter of the 1921 Anglo-Irish Treaty, he became leader of the Cumann na nGaedhal government (which split from Sinn Féin after accepting the Treaty) following the deaths of Arthur Griffith and Michael Collins (see p. 56). He remained in office until 1932.

🦢 **Eamon de Valera** (1882–1975) (Fianna Fáil) was born in Manhattan, New York in 1882 to Catherine Coll from Bruree, Co. Limerick and Vivion Juan de Valera, a Spanish sugar-trader. De Valera was sent to Ireland to be educated from the age of two, when his father died. An excellent scholar and an accomplished mathematician, he graduated from the Royal University in 1904. In 1908 he joined the Gaelic League and his lifelong devotion to the restoration of the Irish language began. He joined the Irish Volunteers in 1913 and soon became commandant of the Third Battalion. He took part in the landing of guns from the *Asgard* in July 1914.

During the Easter Rising, 24 April 1916, de Valera occupied Boland's Bakery to cover the southeastern approach to Dublin City. Sentenced to death after the surrender of the rebels, he received a reprieve for unknown reasons, but it is believed his American birth certificate was an important factor. He was elected as a declared Republican in East Clare and was chosen as President of the new Sinn Féin in 1917. In the General Election of 1918 Sinn Féin won 73 seats although 45 candidates were in jail. De Valera was returned for Mayo East whilst interned in England in Lincoln Prison. He escaped from Lincoln and returned to Dublin to be unanimously elected President of the first Dáil Eireann.

Failing to achieve recognition at the Peace Conference at Versailles, de Valera decided to travel to the United States in June 1919 to seek public and financial support. Returning with $6m in December 1920, he found Ireland in the grip of war with the regular British Army and the infamous 'Black and Tans' (the auxiliary force of the Royal Irish Constabulary). The Anglo-Irish Treaty of 6 December 1921 was negoti-

Eamon de Valera, the most celebrated Irish politician of the 20th century, photographed in 1932. A veteran of the 1916 Easter Rising – 'Dev' went on to become Ireland's longest serving Prime Minister and President.

ated by the British Prime Minister Lloyd George and an Irish delegation including Michael Collins and Arthur Griffith. The Treaty did not provide for an independent republic but partitioned Ireland, creating a 26-county state with dominion status whose representatives were required to swear to 'be faithful' to the British king, and allowing six mainly Protestant counties in the northeast of Ireland to remain within the UK as a self-governing province. The Treaty was accepted by the Dáil on 7 January 1922 (by 64 votes to 57) and subsequently in June of that year in an election by the war-weary Irish nation. A significant minority, however – 35 Dáil seats – stood against it. De Valera was foremost in opposition to the Treaty, although he never ranked as a military leader in the bitter Civil War that followed (June 1922–May 1923), fought between Irish Free State forces and anti-Treaty republicans.

De Valera was re-elected in August 1923 in Clare, but was arrested and imprisoned until July 1924 by the Free State government. In April 1926 he formed a new party, Fianna Fáil. Having won 44 seats out of 155 in the 1927 General Election, de Valera decided to sign the oath of allegiance as a formality, without officially recognising its validity, and joined Dáil Eireann. At the 1932 General Election Fianna Fáil became the largest party in the Dáil, with 72 seats, and de Valera became president of the Executive Council. He then set about dismantling the Treaty of 1921. He withheld payment of land annuities to Britain, which retaliated with trade sanctions. De Valera enacted the Constitution of 1937, which was passed by referendum, and secured the return of the Treaty Ports, naval ports of strategic importance held by Britain under the terms of the Treaty.

In September 1938 de Valera was elected as the 19th president of the Assembly of the League of Nations. It was an international recognition of his independent stance in international affairs and of Ireland's own national integrity, and placed de Valera in a position of unassailable authority at home.

De Valera was voted out of office in 1948 after 16 years of government. Although Fianna Fáil were returned again in 1951, they found themselves incapable of dealing with the country's serious economic problems and were once again removed from office in 1954. De Valera was Taoiseach for a final period 1957–59 before resigning. He appointed Seán Lemass as his successor.

In 1959 he was elected for the first of his two terms as President of Ireland. Prior to his retirement from office in 1973, he was **the world's oldest head of state** at 91 years of age.

Jack Lynch, former hurling and Gaelic football star, arriving at Heathrow Airport for talks with British Prime Minister Edward Heath at the height of the 'Troubles' in Northern Ireland in 1971.

✿ **John A. Costello** (1891–1976) (Fine Gael) was born in Dublin and educated at University College, Dublin. He pursued a legal career and was attorney-general 1926–32. In this capacity, he represented the government at Imperial conferences and at the League of Nations. He was approached to become Taoiseach in 1948 as a candidate for Dublin Southeast on behalf of the Fine Gael Party. His political career up to then had been unassuming, but he was chosen as someone who could unite the diverse interests of the first inter-party coalition government. At a press conference in Canada on 7 September 1949, Costello declared that the External Relations Act would be repealed and that Ireland was to become a republic. The Republic of Ireland was formally inaugurated on Easter Monday 1949. (See also p. 98.)

✿ **Seán Lemass** (1899–1971) is associated with modern industrialisation and the rapid growth of the Irish economy in the 1960s. He was a volunteer in the Easter Rising of 1916 but escaped execution because of his youth and low rank. He was a veteran of the Anglo-Irish War of 1919–21 and opposed the Anglo-Irish Treaty in 1922. He fought with the anti-Treaty side in the Civil War and was arrested and interned 1922–23. He was elected as Sinn Féin member for Dublin in 1925, but did not take his seat. The following year he joined the Fianna Fáil Party and became its secretary. He was appointed Minister for Industry and Commerce in 1932 and held this office until 1959, with two periods as opposition spokesman. In 1945 he became Tánaiste (Deputy Prime Minister). Lemass was responsible for setting up Aer Lingus (the national airline), Bord na Móna (the turf board for the production and supply of peat fuel) and Irish Shipping, the country's first indigenous shipping company.

Lemass succeeded de Valera as Taoiseach in 1959 and vigorously pursued foreign investment and economic expansion. Free trade with Britain was re-established in 1965 in preparation for joining the EEC. The results of his policies were reflected in a 30% reduction in unemployment between 1958 and 1963. In the same period, population decline owing to emigration was halted for the first time in over 120 years and national output increased by 25%. These levels of positive growth in the Irish economy were maintained until the 1980s.

✿ **John 'Jack' Lynch** (1917–) was born in Cork city. He worked in the Department of Justice from 1936 and was called to the bar in 1945. He was returned as Fianna Fáil TD for Cork City in 1948. In 1952 he ended a successful sporting career (see p. 181) in order to devote his time to politics. He served as Minister for Lands (1951–54), Minister for the Gaeltacht (1957), Minister for Education (1957–59), Minister for Industry and Commerce (1959–65) and Minister for Finance (1965–66). He succeeded Seán Lemass as leader of Fianna Fáil and Taoiseach of Ireland in 1966.

Re-elected in 1969, he was faced with the growing crisis in Northern Ireland as civil rights demonstrators clashed with the police and paramilitary forces. He consistently emphasised the importance of consent and constitutional action in the resolution of the Northern Ireland conflict and kept open diplomatic channels with Britain after the British Army's 'Bloody Sunday' massacre in Derry in January 1972.

Lynch legislated against the IRA with the Offences Against the State Act in 1972. His first government fell in 1973 to a Fine Gael/Labour coalition pact. Four years later he led Fianna Fáil back into government with a record 84 Dáil seats. The honeymoon with the public was short-lived, however, and opposition to his leadership grew within his own party. He resigned from office in December 1979.

🍀 **Liam Cosgrave** (1920–) was born in Dublin. He was educated in law at the King's Inns and in 1958 became a Senior Counsel. He was elected to the Dáil in 1943 and served as Parliamentary Secretary to the Taoiseach and the Department of Trade and Industry in 1948. He was Minister for External Affairs in the 1954–57 coalition government and chairman of the

PRIME MINISTERS OF IRELAND

21 September 1923–23 June 1927	W.T. Cosgrave (Cumann na nGaedheal)
23 June–12 October 1927	W.T. Cosgrave (Cumann na nGaedheal)
12 October 1927–9 March 1932	W.T. Cosgrave (Cumann na nGaedheal)
8 February 1933–21 July 1937	Eamon de Valera (Fianna Fáil)
21 July 1937–30 June 1938	Eamon de Valera (Fianna Fáil)
30 June 1938–2 July 1943	Eamon de Valera (Fianna Fáil)
2 July 1943–9 June 1944	Eamon de Valera (Fianna Fáil)
9 June 1944–18 February 1948	Eamon de Valera (Fianna Fáil)
14 June 1951–2 June 1954	Eamon de Valera (Fianna Fáil)
2 June 1954–12 February 1957	John A. Costello (Fine Gael–Labour, Clann na Poblachta, Clann na Talmhan coalition government)
20 March 1957–23 June 1959	Eamon de Valera (Fianna Fáil)
23 June 1959–12 October 1961	Seán Lemass (Fianna Fáil)
12 October 1961–21 April 1965	Seán Lemass (Fianna Fáil)
21 April 1965–10 November 1966	Seán Lemass (Fianna Fáil)
10 November 1966–2 July 1969	Jack Lynch (Fianna Fáil)
2 July 1969–14 March 1973	Jack Lynch (Fianna Fáil)
14 March 1973–5 July 1977	Liam Cosgrave (Fine Gael/Labour coalition government)
5 July 1977–11 December 1979	Jack Lynch (Fianna Fáil)
11 December 1979–30 June 1981	Charles Haughey (Fianna Fáil)
30 June 1981–9 March 1982	Garret Fitzgerald (Fine Gael–Labour coalition government)
9 March 1982–24 November 1982	Charles Haughey (Fianna Fáil)
24 November 1982–10 March 1987	Garret Fitzgerald (Fine Gael–Labour coalition government)
10 March 1987–12 July 1989	Charles Haughey (Fianna Fáil)
12 July 1989–November 1992	Charles Haughey (Fianna Fáil–Progressive Democrat coalition government).
February 1992–	Albert Reynolds (Fianna Fáil–Labour coalition government).

first Irish delegation to the United Nations General Assembly in 1956. He succeeded James Dillon as leader of Fine Gael in 1966 and became Taoiseach of the National Coalition Government 1973–77.

♣ **Charles Haughey** (1925–) was born in Castlebar, Co. Mayo. He went to school in Dublin and later attended University College, Dublin. He won his first seat as Fianna Fáil TD for Dublin North East in 1957 (on his third attempt) and rapidly rose to prominence. As Minister for Justice 1961–64, he formally abolished the death penalty and passed the Succession Act, which gave women a right to share in family income. He was Minister for Agriculture 1964–66 and Minister for Finance 1966–70, during which time he introduced a tax-free scheme for writers and artists. In 1970 he was dismissed from Lynch's cabinet after allegations that he had attempted to import arms into the state to supply to the nationalist community in Northern Ireland.

Haughey was found not guilty at the arms trial and spent five years of political exile consolidating his base of support. In 1977 he was appointed Minister for Health in Jack Lynch's government, succeeding Lynch as Taoiseach in December 1979.

Haughey's years as Taoiseach were marked by adverse economic conditions and violent conflict in Northern Ireland. The 1980s saw many political scandals and changes in government. Haughey's leadership was strong within his own party but his style of leadership did not appeal to all. The Progressive Democrats, led by Desmond O'Malley, broke away from Fianna Fáil in 1985.

In June 1989 Haughey reluctantly took Fianna Fáil into its first ever coalition partnership with the Progressive Democrats. In 1990 he was President of the EEC Council of Ministers and in 1991 he signed the European Union Treaty at Maastricht. He resigned as Taoiseach in February 1992.

♣ **Garret Fitzgerald** (1926–) was born in Dublin and graduated from University College, Dublin. He worked for Aer Lingus, the national airline, from 1951 to 1958, where his skills as an economist and statistician became apparent. He turned to journalism and wrote for the *Irish Times*, *The Financial Times* (London) and the *Economist* (London) as well as contributing to many foreign journals. He was elected to the Senate in 1965 and was first elected as Fine Gael TD for Dublin South East in 1969. As Minister for Foreign Affairs 1973–77, he promoted Ireland's new position within the EEC through nationwide lectures

and newspaper articles. He took part in negotiations for the Sunningdale Agreement for power-sharing in Northern Ireland in 1973. This, however, was broken by the loyalist general strike in 1974.

In 1977 he took over the leadership of Fine Gael following the resignation of Liam Cosgrave and began a comprehensive restructuring of the party. He was Taoiseach in coalition with the Labour Party for two terms during the 1980s. In November 1985 he signed the Anglo-Irish Agreement with the initially hesitant Prime Minister of Great Britain, Margaret Thatcher. The agreement has endured despite continuous opposition from Northern Ireland unionists and widespread indifference from nationalists. Fitzgerald retired as Taoiseach in 1987 and published his autobiography, *All in a Life*, in 1991.

♣ **Albert Reynolds** was born in Co. Longford in 1932 and was involved in local politics from 1974, when he joined the County Council. He was elected Fianna Fáil TD for the Longford/Westmeath constituency in 1977 and took up his first ministerial job at the Department of Posts, Telegraphs and Transport in 1979. In 1987 he was Minister for Industry and Commerce and the following year was re-located to the Department of Finance. He was Vice-President of the Fianna Fáil Party 1983–91, during the Haughey years, and eventually replaced Haughey as Taoiseach in November 1992. Reynolds has become a millionaire through the successful management of his pet food and leisure (dance hall) businesses.

NORTHERN IRELAND

Northern Ireland was established under the Government of Ireland Act 1920. It consists of six of the nine counties of the province of Ulster: Armagh, Down, Antrim, Derry, Tyrone and Fermanagh, covering an area of 5238 sq miles (13,570 sq km), about one sixth of the land area of Ireland. The population (1,583,000 in 1991) has averaged a little under one third of the population of the whole island. The parliament of Northern Ireland was opened by George V on 22 June 1921. It consisted of the King, Senate and House of Commons. The parliament had sovereign powers except in areas of foreign policy and defence. The Ulster Unionist Party formed all the governments of Northern Ireland until 1972. On 24 March of that year the government of Stormont was replaced by direct rule from Westminster under the Northern Ireland (Temporary Suspension) Act.

Prime Ministers

✤ **Sir James Craig, Lord Craigavon** (June 1921–November 1940). James Craig (1871–1940) was a Belfast-born stockbroker and veteran of the Boer War. He organised the Ulster Volunteer Force and was quartermaster-general in France of the 36th (Ulster) Division 1914–16, which was made up largely of its members. He was a participant in the drafting of the Government of Ireland Act, which led to the establishment of the parliament of Northern Ireland, and he became its first Prime Minister in 1921. Craig presided over the Special Powers Act, which gave unlimited powers of arrest and detention (made permanent in 1933), and the abolition of proportional representation in 1929. Under his supervision local government elections were 'fixed' by allowing business firms to have a multiple vote and by granting the franchise on a rate-paying basis. The constituencies were gerrymandered to ensure that areas with a nationalist majority (i.e. Derry, Fermanagh and Armagh District Councils) returned Unionist majorities. In 1934 Craig told the House of Commons, 'We are a Protestant parliament and a Protestant state.'

✤ **John Miller Andrews** (November 1940–May 1943). Andrews (1871–1956) was born in Comber, Co. Down. He was director of the family linen-bleaching company and of the Belfast Ropeworks. He was Unionist MP for Co. Down and was unopposed in every election from 1921. He was Minister of Labour 1921–37 and Minister of Finance 1937–40. He was County Grand Master of the Orange Institution in Co. Down.

✤ **Sir Basil Brooke, Lord Brookeborough** (May 1943–March 1963). Brooke (1888–1973), of Colebroke, Co. Fermanagh, graduated from Winchester and Sandhurst and received the Military Cross and Croix de Guerre for distinguished service in World War I. He was elected to the Northern Ireland Senate in 1921 but resigned within a year to become commandant of the Ulster Special Constabulary in the fight against the IRA. He became Unionist MP for Lisnaskea, Co. Fermanagh in 1929 and Minister of Agriculture in 1933. He sacked all Catholic workers on his vast estates to set an example for other landowners. In 1941 he was Minister of Commerce and Production, becoming Prime Minister in 1943. He held

Sir Edward Carson campaigns against Irish Home Rule in 1911. An Anglo-Irish lawyer and hard-line Unionist, Carson was the man most responsible for the secession of the six counties of Northern Ireland from the Irish Free State.

Sir James Chichester-Clark and Brian Faulkner in September 1969. Faulkner succeeded Chichester-Clark as Prime Minister of Northern Ireland in March 1971 and was the last man to hold that office.

office for 20 years, during which time he had no official contacts with trade unionists or Roman Catholics. He promoted strong links between the government and the Orange Order, of which he was a senior member.

♣ **Captain Terence Marne O'Neill** (March 1963– April 1969). O'Neill (1914–90) was born in London to Arthur O'Neill, Unionist MP for Mid-Antrim, and educated at Eton. He served in the Irish Guards 1939– 45 in Normandy, Belgium and the Netherlands. In 1945 he moved to Northern Ireland and took up politics. He was elected unopposed for Bannside in 1946. He was Parliamentary Secretary from 1948 and Minister of Finance from 1956 to 1963. As Prime Minister, he sought better relations with the Catholic/ nationalist community in Northern Ireland and re- newed contact with the Republic. His policies were opposed by hardline Unionists and he was unable to attempt the reforms that the growing civil rights movement was demanding. He lost the support of

three cabinet members – Faulkner, Morgan and Craig – and in 1969 almost lost his seat to the Reverend Ian Paisley. He resigned his position to James Chichester- Clark.

♣ **Major James Dawson Chichester-Clark, Lord Moyola** (May 1969–March 1971). Chichester- Clark (1923–) was born in Castledawson, Co. Derry and educated at Eton. After a career in the British Army, he was elected to the seat in South Derry vacated by his grandmother, Dame Dehra Parker*, in 1960. He became Assistant Whip of the Ulster Union- ist Party in 1963, Chief Whip 1963–69, Leader of the House 1966–67 and Minister for Agriculture 1967–69. He resigned from the cabinet of O'Neill (his cousin) in protest against O'Neill's attempted reforms and took over as Prime Minister in May 1969. When violence erupted in Belfast in August he requested, and was granted, British troops. Unable to contain the rapidly deteriorating situation in Northern Ireland and un- willing to make the necessary reforms, he resigned within two years.

** **Dehra Parker** was **the only woman member of the Northern Ireland cabinet**. She was Unionist MP for Derry City and County 1921–29. In 1932 she was returned as MP for South Derry, one of the single-seat constituencies created after the abolition of proportional representation in 1929, and re- mained there until her retirement in 1960.*

❀ Arthur Brian Deane Faulkner, Lord Faulkner of Downpatrick (March 1971–March 1972). Faulkner (1921–1977) was born in Helen's Bay, Co. Down and educated at St Columba's College in Dublin. When he was elected for East Down in 1949 he was **the youngest ever member of the Northern Ireland parliament**. He became Chief Whip in 1956, Minister for Home Affairs in 1959 and Minister for Commerce in 1963. He opposed concessions to the Northern Ireland Civil Rights Association and in January 1969 resigned in protest at the Prime Minister O'Neill's attempts to introduce reforms at Westminster's request. He was Deputy Prime Minister to Chichester-Clark and took over in March 1971. As Prime Minister, he conceded that reform was necessary, and alienated many Unionist supporters. He announced in May 1971 that soldiers could shoot to kill on suspicion alone, and he introduced internment without trial in August 1971.

In March 1972 he refused to accept the need for power sharing or direct rule from Westminster, despite the efforts of the British Prime Minister, Edward Heath. He was, however, powerless to prevent the abolition of Stormont and direct rule took force.

Political Parties

❀ The Ulster Unionist Party provided all the governments of Northern Ireland between 1921 and 1972. It remained united until the 1960s, when the leadership of Terence O'Neill and the rise of the civil rights movement led to division and the resignation of party members. The gradual splitting of the UUP culminated in the foundation of the Democratic Unionist Party in 1971. The *raison d'être* for the UUP is the preservation of the Union with Great Britain. It remains the largest and most powerful party in Northern Ireland. It has often been aligned with the Conservative Party of Great Britain.

Party leaders: (As Prime Ministers above 1921–72), Arthur Brian Deane Faulkner (1971–74), Henry William West (1974–79), James H. Molyneaux (1979–).

❀ The Social Democratic and Labour Party was founded in August 1970 by members of the old Nationalist Party of Northern Ireland, the Northern Ireland Labour Party, the Republican Labour Party and civil rights activists. Its aims were to promote the cause of Irish unity, based on the consent of the majority of the people of Northern Ireland, and to cooperate with the Irish Congress of Trade Unions (ICTU) in joint action. The SDLP has since moved to

John Hume, leader of the Social Democratic and Labour Party (SDLP), arrives at 10 Downing Street for talks with British premier Margaret Thatcher in 1980. A moderate nationalist seeking to achieve Irish unity by constitutional means, Hume succeeded Gerry Fitt as leader of the SDLP in 1979.

the centre of the political spectrum and captures most of the Catholic/nationalist vote.

Party leaders: Gerry Fitt (1970–79), John Hume (1979–).

❀ The Democratic Unionist Party was founded in 1971 by the Reverend Ian Paisley and Desmond Boal. More militant than the Ulster Unionist Party, the DUP has continued to seek the maintenance of the Union with Great Britain and Unionist control of the parliamentary institutions. Ian Paisley has dominated the party since its foundation. The DUP is a radical right-wing party and poses a constant threat to the Ulster Unionist Party's traditional domination.

Party leaders: Ian Paisley (1971–).

❀ Provisional Sinn Féin is an all-Ireland party originally founded in 1905, whose goal is a united republican Ireland (see p. 63). Sinn Féin split in January 1970 into Official Sinn Féin and Provisional Sinn Féin. Official Sinn Féin, now known as the

Ian Paisley – the only 20th century European politician to found his own church and political party (the Democratic Unionist Party; DUP). Implacably opposed to Roman Catholicism, the Irish Republican Army and its goal of a united republican Ireland, Paisley has long been a spokesman of the more militant brand of Ulster Unionism.

Workers' Party, was the smaller of the two factions. Provisional Sinn Féin, led by Ruadhri O'Bradaigh, sought an all-Ireland 32-county republic and was preoccupied with the Northern Ireland situation. Sinn Féin, the Workers' Party, led by Tomás MacGiolla, was more Dublin-oriented, more socialist and unsympathetic to republican doctrine. Provisional Sinn Féin contests elections in the jurisdictions of Northern Ireland and the Republic. It is in Northern Ireland that the focus of its policy lies and it is here that it draws most of its support.

Presidents from 1962: Tomás MacGiolla (1962–70), Ruairí O'Brádaigh (1970–83), Gerry Adams (1983–).

🍀 **The Alliance Party** was formed in 1970 and is a moderate, centrist unionist party, which subscribes to power-sharing.

Party leaders: Phelim O'Neill (1970–72), Oliver Napier (1972–84), John Cushnahan (1984–87), John Alderdice (1987–).

IRISH NOBEL PEACE PRIZE WINNERS

🍀 **Seán MacBride** (1904–88) was born in Paris, the son of John MacBride (who fought in the 1916 Rising and for the South African Boers 1899–1902) and Maud Gonne (see p. 59), founder of the revolutionary women's society, Inghinidhe na hEireann.

Seán MacBride's first language was French (he received his early schooling in France), but he was sent to Mount St Benedict's in Gorey, Co. Wexford to complete his education. He became involved in the independence movement and saw active service in the War of Independence. He was an opponent of the Anglo-Irish Treaty of 1921 and remained a member of the Irish Republican Army, for which he spent time in jail and on the run. He moved between Paris and London, earning a living as a journalist, and then returned to Dublin in 1936 as chief-of-staff of the IRA.

With the passing of the 1937 constitution into law, MacBride resigned from the IRA, accepting that it was now possible to achieve national objectives by political means. He founded Clann na Poblachta in 1946 and joined in the first coalition government in February 1948 as Minister for External Affairs. During his term of office Ireland rejected membership of NATO and joined the Council of Europe. MacBride's influence also encouraged the repeal of the External Relations Act and the formal declaration of an Irish Republic on Easter Monday 1949.

Continuing his career at the bar, MacBride became increasingly prominent on the world stage as a defender of human rights. He took **the first case to be heard by the European Commission on Human Rights,** the Lawless internment case, and became a founder-member of Amnesty International and its international chairman 1961–74. He was Secretary-General of the International Commission of Jurists 1963–71, which was set up to monitor abuses in human rights around the world. In 1969 he became executive chairman of the International Peace Bureau in Geneva and in 1974 its president. As Assistant Secretary-General of the United Nations, he was appointed UN Commissioner for Namibia 1973-76.

MacBride was awarded the Nobel Peace Prize in 1974. In 1977 he was given the Lenin Peace Prize and in 1978 the American Medal for Justice. In his last campaign, he proposed the 'MacBride Principles', which sought to eliminate employers' discrimination against the Catholic/nationalist community in Northern Ireland. The principles have won widespread support in the USA and American multinationals in Northern Ireland frequently chose to adopt them.

(above) *Seán MacBride in 1967. MacBride's career took him from the outlawed Irish Republican Army (IRA) to the Secretary Generalship of the International Commission of Jurists and culminated in the award of a Nobel Peace Prize in 1974.*

❧ **Mairead Corrigan** and **Betty Williams** were founders of the Peace Movement in Northern Ireland in 1976. The movement was founded to mobilise public opinion against violence after three children in Belfast were killed by a car that had left the road when its occupant, a member of the IRA, had been shot by the British Army. Corrigan and Williams were joined by Ciarán McKeown and the 'Peace People' movement spread to the rest of Ireland and to the United Kingdom. The founders were awarded the 1976 Nobel Prize for Peace on 11 October 1977. At 32, Mairead Corrigan (b. January 1944) was **the youngest ever recipient of this prize**.

❧ **The last Secretary-General of the League of Nations** (1940–46), **Sean Lester** (1888–1959) of Carrickfergus, Co. Antrim was educated at the Methodist College, Belfast before taking up a journalistic career with the *North Down Herald* and later the *Freeman's Journal*. He became active in the independence movement and, following the Anglo-Irish Treaty of 1921, joined the new Free State government in the Department of External Affairs. In 1929 he was sent to the League of Nations in Geneva as Ireland's

(below) *Mairead Corrigan (far right) and Betty Williams (far left), founders of Northern Ireland's ill-fated Peace Movement and joint Nobel Peace Prize winners for 1976, pictured here with Joan Baez, Caran McKeown and Jane Ewart-Biggs at a rally in London's Trafalgar Square in 1976.*

representative and in 1934 was appointed High Commissioner for the League in Danzig (Gdansk), where he was an outspoken opponent of Nazi persecution of the Jews. In 1940 he was made Secretary-General of the League but had little chance of preventing the escalation of World War II. At the end of the war the United States had still not joined the League of Nations, while the Soviet Union had been expelled. When the Charter of the United Nations was drawn up in San Francisco that year, the League was not involved. This left Lester with the task of closing it down. Lester returned to Ireland, where he retired in 1947. He died in Recess, Co. Galway in 1959.

UNITED STATES

When the American Revolutionary war broke out in 1775, General Richard Henry Lee remarked: 'I do not believe that many of the native Virginians will offer themselves. The Irish, I am persuaded, will enlist in crowds.' His predictions were correct. The number of Irish recruits in the Revolutionary Army has been variously estimated at 35% to 50% of the total force. Ten generals in Washington's Army were Irish-born, and 20 were of Irish parentage. The Declaration of Independence was written in the hand of Irish-born Charles Thomson and was first read to the people by Irish-born John Nixon. The Declaration was first printed by John Dunlap (see p. 130) and signed by three natives of Ireland – James Smith from Dublin and George Taylor and Matthew Thornton from Derry. Five other signatories had Irish parents or grandparents: Thomas McKean, George Read, Robert Treat Paine, Edward Rutledge, Thomas Lynch Jr and Charles Carroll (see p. 78). The Constitutional Convention of 1787 had seven Irish members: Thomas Fitzsimmons, James McHenry, John Rutledge and Pierce Butler were all natives of Ireland, while George Read and Charles and Daniel Carroll were of Irish descent.

The Civil War saw a similar scale of Irish involvement, with some 144,000 Irishmen fighting in the Union Army. No fewer than 38 Union Army regiments had the word 'Irish' in their names. Some regiments, such as the 'Fighting 69th of New York' experienced terrible slaughter in constant front-line engagements. Perhaps the most famous of all regiments of all colours in the war, the '69th' fought in decisive battles in the Peninsular Campaign, at the Second Battle of Bull Run, Antietam, Fredericksburg and Chancellorsville. The Confederate Army also had a large Irish contingent. The Louisiana Irish Regiment, the Texas Rio Grande Regiment and the South Carolina Emerald Light Infantry comprised mostly Irish troops.

At Gettysburg National Military Park in Pennsylvania – the monument to those killed in the 1863 Civil War battle – there is a mourning Irish wolfhound at the foot of a Celtic cross. Most of the 7000 killed and 45,000 wounded were Irish. The Irish Brigade of Colonel Michael Corcoran of Co. Sligo was almost wiped out and the brigade ceased to exist thereafter.

✦ **The first Catholic governor in the American colonies, Sir Thomas Dongan** (1634–1715), was born in Celbridge, Co. Kildare. Having served in the Irish Regiment of the French Army, He went to London in 1678, was appointed Lieutenant-Governor of Tangier and in 1682 Governor of the bankrupt state of New York. Within six years of office, Dongan set the current boundaries of the state, set up a post office, negotiated with the Iroquois Indians, granted charters to the cities of New York and Albany and drafted a Charter of Liberties that guaranteed religious freedom and proposed the principle of no taxation without representation. His ideas were far ahead of his time and were influential in the revolution that was to follow a century later. He was replaced in 1688 and returned to England in 1691. He succeeded his brother as Earl of Limerick.

✦ **'The father of the American Navy', Commodore John Barry** (1745–1803), was born in Tacumshane, Co. Wexford and went to sea at 14. At the outbreak of the Revolutionary War he was a merchant captain in Philadelphia. He was the first naval commander appointed by the Continental Congress and in 1776, in the brig *Lexington*, he seized the British ship HMS *Edward*, **the first warship to be captured by the American Navy.** He made several successful engagements with British ships, but was seriously injured in 1782. He superintended the progress of the US Navy from 1782 until his death, and was called back into service in 1798 to organise a fleet of ships when war with France appeared imminent. Barry is commemorated by a statue on the quays of Wexford Town.

✦ **Jeremiah O'Brien** (1740–1818), born in Co. Cork, captured the British schooner *Margaretta* in what is considered **the first naval action of the American Revolution.** The *Margaretta* was a storeship and was seized in Machias Bay off the coast of Maine.

Major-General Charles O'Hara delivers the British surrender to George Washington at Yorktown, 1781. Large numbers of Irishmen fought in both the British and American armies during the American War of Independence.

Jeremiah O'Brien was the highest ranking of the five O'Brien brothers involved on that day.

✤ **The first admiral on the retired list of the United States Navy** was the maternal grandfather of Charles Stewart Parnell (see p. 54). **Admiral Stewart** of the US Navy commanded the USS *Constitution* during the Anglo-American War of 1812. His parents, Charles and Sarah Stewart, emigrated from Belfast. In the early years of his career, he served under Commodore John Barry (see p. 76).

✤ **Thomas MacDonough** (1738–1825), born at The Trap, now called Macdonough, Delaware, was described by Franklin D. Roosevelt as '...to the time of our Civil War ... the greatest figure in our naval history'. He was the grandson of John MacDonough, who had left Co. Kildare in 1730. Commodore MacDonough's greatest achievement was his victory over the British at Lake Champlain, Vermont on 11 September 1814. This was strategically vital as it sealed off naval access to the US through Canadian territory.

✤ **'General Washington's General', Henry Knox** (c. 1750–1806), was born in Derry and emigrated to America. He was **the first Commander-in-Chief of the American Army** before the Constitution invested that authority in the presidency. A close friend and adviser of Washington, his skill as a military strategist was unequalled. He travelled constantly with Washington and accompanied him at the battles of Trenton, Princeton, Monmouth, Valley Forge and Yorktown. He was chosen as Secretary of War by Congress in 1785 and served until 1797.

✤ **Governor of New Hampshire and commander of continental forces in the northern colonies, John Sullivan** (1740–95) was born in

Somersworth, New Hampshire, the son of immigrants from Ireland. He began his career as a lawyer and was a major in the New Hampshire militia when he was sent as a delegate to the Continental Congress in 1774*. He was promoted to brigadier-general in 1775, in charge of the forces in the northern colonies, and to major general in 1776. He was captured at the Battle of Long Island and later released in a prisoner exchange. He fought at the critical battles in Trenton and Princeton before retiring through poor health in 1779. He continued to serve as a delegate to the Continental Congress, representing New Hampshire, and was governor of that state for three years.

♣ **Charles Carroll** (1737–1832), born in Carrolltown, Maryland into **America's first Irish-Catholic dynasty,** was given an underground education at a time when Catholics were prohibited from voting, serving in government, receiving an education or worshipping in public. Despite the discriminatory laws, Carroll won the respect of the citizens of Maryland and became a leading figure of the American Revolution. He was a signatory of the Declaration of Independence and a senator in the first Congress in 1789. His business acumen helped him to finance much of the American war effort as well as the building of the new nation's first canals and railroads. He was widely favoured for selection by the Federalist Party to be the first president in the event of George Washington refusing the post. When he died, at 95 years of age, he was reputedly **the wealthiest man in America**.

♣ The British surrender at Yorktown in October 1781 was delivered to George Washington by **Major-General Charles O'Hara** (c. 1740–1802), second in command to General Cornwallis (see p. 77). He was the illegitimate son of Lord Tyrawley (Sligo/Mayo). Given the level of participation of Irish soldiers in both armies, it was appropriate that he should be the person formally to acknowledge the triumph of the American Revolution. O'Hara represented the third generation of generals in a family that originated in Sligo. Charles O'Hara himself was actually born in Lisbon, Portugal, where his father, James O'Hara (1690–1773), Baron of Tyrawley and member of the Privy Council, was serving as British envoy 1752–55.

* *The Continental Congress 1774–89 was the federal legislature of the 13 colonies and later of the United States under the Articles of Confederation. It created the Continental Army, named George Washington commander-in-chief, and adopted the Declaration of Independence on 4 July 1776.*

♣ **Patrick R. Cleburne** (1828–64) was a native of Cobh, Co. Cork and is considered the most famous of the Irish officers in the Confederate Army. With three years' experience in the British Army, he emigrated to the USA in 1850, studied law, and was running his own legal practice in Helena, Arkansas when the Civil War broke out. He enlisted as a private in 1861. He did not fight for slaveowners, for whom he had no sympathy, but for the defence of the community in Arkansas, where he had settled and made friends. Always a practical soldier, he made powerful enemies when he proposed that the southern slaves be armed to fight for the confederacy after Lincoln's Emancipation Proclamation had weakened the position of the south.

Cleburne rose to the rank of major-general. Known popularly as 'the 'Stonewall' Jackson of the West' after his exploits along the Mississippi, he was, as the name suggests, the most successful general in the western theatre of the war. Cleburne was killed at the battle of Franklin, Tennessee on 30 November 1864 and was buried nearby.

♣ Union Army general **James Shields** (1806–79), **the only person ever elected US senator by three states**, was born in Altmore, Co. Tyrone and emigrated to America in 1826, where he settled in Illinois. He studied law and became a Supreme Court judge 1843–45. He served with distinction as a brigadier-general in the Mexican War 1846–48. After a term as Governor of the Oregon Territory in 1848, he was elected US Senator for Illinois 1849–55 and for Minnesota 1858–59. He founded the town of Shieldville in Minnesota and encouraged Irish immigrants to move west. During the Civil War he led 7000 Union troops against 'Stonewall' Jackson in the famous 'Shenandoah Valley' campaign on 23 March 1862. After the war Shields moved to Missouri and was elected State Senator in 1879, the year of his death.

♣ **Commander-in-Chief of the US Army, Philip H. Sheridan** (1831–88) was taken to the United States as a child from his birthplace in Killinkere, Co. Cavan. He was educated at West Point Military Academy 1848–53 and later distinguished himself as a cavalry commander. He rose to the rank of major-general in command of a cavalry corps in the Northern Army of the Potomac in 1864 during the Civil War, defeated General Lee in a series of successful engagements and was appointed Union commander in the Shenandoah Valley. He won the last great battle of the Civil War at Five Forks on 1 April 1865. His continuing harassment of Lee's retreating army forced the surrender of the Confederates at Appomattox on 9 April. He was later appointed Military Governor of Texas and Louisiana and saw further active service in Indian campaigns, where he was ruthless and efficient in the relentless slaughter and dispossession of the Plains Indians. He became Commander-in-Chief of the US Army in 1883, succeeding William T. Sherman.

🍀 **Myles Walter Keogh** (1840–76) was born at Leighlinbridge, Co. Carlow and fought in Italy alongside 700 other Irish volunteers with the Papal Brigade in 1860 against Garibaldi's Redshirts. For this he was awarded the *Pro Petri Sede* Medal by Pope Pius IX. Keogh moved to America and joined the Union Army in the American Civil War. He was an able cavalry officer and, at the age of 25, became a lieutenant-colonel with 3000 men under his command.

After the Civil War, Keogh took a drop in rank in order to stay in the army. He joined the newly formed 7th Cavalry of General Custer as a captain and rode and died with him at the Battle of Little Big Horn against the Sioux. Indian survivors of the battle said in later years that Keogh was the last to be killed. His horse, Comanche, was the only creature left alive on the US Army side at the end of the battle. Keogh was not scalped, nor was his body mutilated in any way. This was perhaps because of the papal medal that he wore around his neck. The Sioux wore pendants to ward off spirits and it is likely that he was left intact for fear of angering his spirits. (Mutilation after death was performed by the Plains Indians in order that revenge would be more difficult for the victim to carry out in the next world.) Keogh's personal effects were found on an Indian arrested in Canada a year later. His medal was not found, but it is said that Sitting Bull (1834–90), Chief of the Dakota Sioux, wore it himself.

🍀 **Union Army General, and Governor of Montana, Thomas Francis Meagher** (1823–67) was born to a wealthy merchant family in Waterford. He abandoned his legal studies in the 1840s to become involved in O'Connell's Repeal Association. In a famous speech to the Association in 1846, he hailed the sword as a sacred weapon, championing physical force against the campaign for moral force favoured by the O'Connellites (see p. 54). William M. Thackeray dubbed him 'Meagher of the Sword', a name that remained with him. He was a founder-member of the Irish Confederation, but stood unsuccessfully as a parliamentary candidate for Waterford in 1848. In that same year he became the first person to propose the tricolour as the national flag after he had travelled to Paris to seek French support for an Irish revolution. For this he was subsequently arrested and sentenced to be hanged, drawn and quartered. His sentence was commuted to transportation and Meagher was sent to Tasmania. He escaped to America in 1852 and became a journalist and lecturer in New York. During the American Civil War Meagher organised the 69th Second Irish Regiment of the New York State Militia to fight for the Northern cause. The 'Fighting 69th' saw decisive action in several of the major battles of the American Civil War, suffering heavy casualties. Meagher was promoted to brigadier-general in the Union Army and was appointed Governor of Montana territory in 1865, after the war ended. Having survived execution, banishment and two years of Confederate gunfire, he fell overboard on a steamboat on the Missouri River in July 1867 and drowned. He is commemorated today by an equestrian statue in front of the Montana State Capitol.

🍀 **Stephen C. Rowan** (1808–90), born in Dublin, was a sailor on the *Vincennes* 1826–30, **the first American ship to circumnavigate the world.** He later fought in the Mexican War 1846–48, where his supportive action in aid of US ground troops was vital in the capture of San Diego, Los Angeles and eventually the state of California. He was an admiral in the Civil War, his most famous action being the defeat of the Confederate force, under his Irish-American rival Commodore W.F. Lynch, off the coast of North Carolina in 1862.

🍀 **Founder of the Office of Strategic Services, now the Central Intelligence Agency (CIA), Colonel William J. 'Wild Bill' Donovan** (1883–1959) led New York's 'Fighting 69th' regiment in France during World War I and won the Congressional Medal of Honor. His awards paved the way for a political career in the Republican Party and a position as head of the Office of Strategic Services, founded by him during World War II. Donovan's father was born in Co. Cork.

US Presidents

Perhaps the clearest evidence of Ireland's contribution to the history of the United States is that no fewer than 21 of the nation's presidents have been, to varying degrees, of Irish descent. They are listed in chronological order on the next three pages.

♣ **John Adams (1735–1826), 2nd President (1797–1801)**. His mother, Susanna Boylston Adams, was descended from an Ulster farming family.

♣ **James Monroe (1758–1831), 5th President (1816–20)**. Monroe was descended from an Ulster family who took their name from Mount Roe near Limavady, Co. Derry. His 17th-century ancestor, Andrew Monroe, was serving as a major under his kinsman Sir George Monroe, Governor of Coleraine, but was banished to Virginia as a loyalist. James Monroe was born in Westmoreland County, Virginia in 1758.

♣ **John Quincy Adams (1767–1848), 6th President (1825–29)**. John Quincy Adams was the son of John Adams and shares the same family roots.

♣ **Andrew Jackson (1767–1845), 7th President (1829–37)**. Jackson's father, also Andrew Jackson, was born in Carrickfergus, Co. Antrim c. 1730 and emigrated to South Carolina in 1765. His mother, Elizabeth Hutchinson, was also born in Ireland. Both the President's brothers, Hugh and Robert, were born in Antrim, but Andrew, the youngest son, was born two years after the family arrived in America. (Some historians maintain that he was, in fact, born at sea *en route* for America from Ireland.)

♣ **James Knox Polk (1795–1849), 11th President (1845–49)**. The descendant of Robert Pollock, a Scots planter who received grants of land in Coleraine, Co. Derry c. 1605–08. Polk's ancestral family home is at Cavanacor House, Ballindrait, Lifford, Co. Donegal.

♣ **David Riche Atchison (1807–86)**, the son of an Irishman, is rarely recorded as a US president. By holding that office for a single day, he has the distinction of holding the record for **the shortest ever US presidency**. The situation arose when President Polk left office and his successor, Zachary Taylor, refused to be inaugurated on a Sunday. Atchison was appointed President *pro tempore* at midnight on 3 March 1849 and left office 24 hours later.

♣ **James Buchanan (1791–1868), 15th President (1857–61)**. The son of James Buchanan Snr who was born in Ramelton, Co. Donegal c. 1761 and emigrated to Pennsylvania in 1783.

♣ **Andrew Johnson (1808–75), 17th President (1865–69)**. Both parents were of Irish descent.

His grandfather emigrated from Ballyeaston, near Larne, Co. Antrim c. 1750. His mother, Mary Polly McDonough, was also from an Ulster family.

♣ **Ulysses S. Grant (1822–85), 18th President (1865–77)**. Although the Grant name and line is essentially English, his maternal great-grandfather is recorded as having emigrated from Derigna, Ballygawley, Co. Tyrone in 1738, while his paternal grandfather married an Irish woman by the name of Rachel Kelly in 1792. (The 'S.' in his name stands for Simpson after his mother Harriet Simpson.)

♣ **Chester Alan Arthur (1830–86), 21st President (1881–85)**. Chester Alan was the son of the Reverend William Arthur, a baptist minister from The Draen, near Ballymena, Co. Antrim, who emigrated to America in 1815.

John Adams, 2nd President of the United States of America, was of Ulster descent through his mother. John's cousin, Samuel Adams, was a signatory to the Declaration of Independence, while his son, John Quincy Adams, became 6th President of the USA.

🍀 **Grover Cleveland (1837–1908), 22nd and 24th President (1885–89) and (1893–97).** Born in Caldwell, New Jersey, Cleveland's mother, Anne Neal, was of Ulster descent.

🍀 **William McKinley (1843–1901), 25th President (1897–1901).** His grandfather James McKinley was born in 1783 at Conacher's Farm, Dervock, Co. Antrim.

🍀 **William Howard Taft (1857–1930), 27th President (1909–13).** The Taft family is an English line, but William Howard's father, great-grandfather and great-great-grandfather all married into Irish families.

🍀 **Woodrow Wilson (1856–1924), 28th President (1913–21).** Wilson's grandfather, James Wilson, emigrated to Philadelphia in 1807 from Strabane, Co. Tyrone. His grandmother, Amy Adams, was from Sion Mills, also in Co. Tyrone. (John Dunlap – see p. 130 – and James Wilson both worked at Gray's Printing Press in Strabane, Co. Tyrone before emigrating to the US.)

🍀 **Warren Gamaliel Harding (1874–1923), 29th President (1921–23),** born in Blooming Grove, Ohio. The family name is English but is intermarried with Scots-Irish families.

🍀 **Herbert Clark Hoover (1874–1964), 31st President (1929–33).** Hoover's grandfather, Eli Hoover, married Hannah Leonard, born in Ireland 14 February 1832.

🍀 **Harry S Truman (1884–1972), 33rd President (1945–53).** Truman's maternal grandmother, Harriet Louisa Gregg, was Irish. Again, the Truman line is English, but inter-married with Scots-Irish.

🍀 **John Fitzgerald Kennedy (1917–63), 35th President (1961–63).** The Kennedy roots can be traced back to a tenant farmer named Kennedy in Dunganstown, Co. Wexford. His son Patrick emigrated to the US in 1848 and married an Irishwoman named Bridget Murphy. One of their children, Patrick Joseph Kennedy (1858–1929), became a Boston saloon-keeper. He married an Irishwoman, Mary Hickey, and their son, Joseph Patrick Kennedy (1888–1969), father of the US President, was a millionaire banker, business tycoon and US Ambassador to Britain.

John F. Kennedy was perhaps the best-known American of the 20th century. His administration was characterised by youth, glamour and stalled attempts at reform. He was sworn in during January 1961 at the age of 43 – **the youngest man ever elected President of the United States** and **the first Roman Catholic in that office**. His election was greeted with euphoria in Ireland as a symbol of the final acceptance of the lost millions of Irish in America. Even today his photograph occupies a prominent place on the walls of many Irish homes. He made a state visit to his ancestral home at Dunganstown, near New Ross, Co. Wexford in June 1963, where he was treated to dinner by his third cousin, Mary Ryan. A memorial, arboretum and visitor's centre stand there today.

As a senator, Kennedy had campaigned consistently for law reform, civil rights and the suppression of organised crime. As President he continued to pursue these aims with the help of his brother Robert Kennedy (1925–68), who was Attorney-General during his administration. In October 1962 he brought the world to the brink of nuclear war when he ordered the removal of Soviet missiles from Cuba and imposed a blockade of the island. The situation was only resolved when the Soviet leader Nikita Khrushchev complied with US demands.

On 22 November 1963 Kennedy was shot and mortally wounded while travelling in a motorcade through Dallas, Texas. Robert Kennedy was shot in 1968 during his Democratic Party presidential nomination campaign. A third brother, Edward Kennedy, was elected senator in 1962 and is a prominent spokesman of the liberal wing of the Democratic Party. The family still holds considerable political power in the US and has consistently maintained an active interest in Irish affairs. Jean Kennedy-Smith, sister of the late President, was made US Ambassador to Ireland in 1993.

Jacqueline Kennedy (1929–94), née Bouvier, wife of John F. Kennedy, was of French-Irish ancestry. Her great-grandparents were immigrants from Ireland who arrived in the United States with no money. The family fortune was made in real estate by James T. Lee, a first-generation Irish-American and the grandfather of Jacqueline.

🍀 **Richard Milhous Nixon (1913–94), 37th President (1969–74).** Nixon's mother, Hannah, was the daughter of Franklin Milhous, a Quaker whose ancestor, Thomas Milhous, emigrated from Kildare to Chester County in Pennsylvania in 1729. His first American ancestor, James Nixon, was born

in Ireland c. 1705 (probably at Timahoe*, Co. Laois) and emigrated to America, where he was first recorded in Delaware in 1731. He visited his probable ancestral home at Timahoe on 5 October 1970.

John Fitzgerald Kennedy, the most famous of the Massachusetts family of Irish descent active in US politics, on the occasion of his marriage to Jacqueline Lee Bouvier at Newport, Rhode Island on 15 September 1953.

🍀 **Ronald Reagan (1911–), 40th President (1980–88)**. Reagan's paternal great-grandparents, Michael and Catherine Reagan, have been traced to the village of Ballyporeen, Co. Tipperary, from where they emigrated to Fairhaven, Illinois. Reagan was **the oldest US President** (69 years 349 days old) when he took the oath of office. He was re-elected at the age of 73.

🍀 **William Clinton (1946–), 42nd President (1992–)**. Although the Clinton family name is English, the president's mother, Virginia Cassidy Kelley,

is the granddaughter of Irish immigrants, probably from Co. Fermanagh. Clinton was given an early education at a Catholic Grade School in Hot Springs, Arkansas run by Irish nuns and visited Ireland when a student at Oxford University, England. During his run for presidency, Clinton has taken a stronger position on Irish issues than any other president, including Kennedy, and has had frequent meetings with Irish-American groups.

* *President Nixon owned an Irish setter called Timahoe.*

Other Irish-American Political Figures

❧ **Vice-President of the United States** (1805–12), in the administrations of Thomas Jefferson and James Madison, **George Clinton** (1739–1812) was the son of an emigrant from Co. Longford, who left Ireland in 1729. Clinton was the first Governor of New York State (1775–95).

❧ The state of Pennsylvania is named after Admiral **William Penn** (1644–1718), who was born in Co. Cork, the son of William Penn Snr, who had been awarded confiscated lands in Ireland by Cromwell. William Penn Jr joined the Quakers in Cork and left for America in 1682, where he founded the state of Pennsylvania. The state, encompassing 45,333 square miles (117,413 square km) was, in fact, named Pennsylvania (Penn's Woods) by Charles II in honour of William Penn Snr rather than his son.

❧ **Joseph Raymond McCarthy**, born in Appelton, Wisconsin in 1908, was one of Timothy and Bridget McCarthy's seven children. Bridget (née Tierney) was born in Ireland, Timothy in America, with an Irish father and a German mother.

Appelton, Wisconsin was a predominantly Irish enclave in an area of the country populated mostly by Scandinavian and German settlers. This may have contributed to the paranoid mentality of Joseph McCarthy, who gave his name to 'McCarthyism', the practice of making unsubstantiated claims of Communist sympathies, and orchestrated the notorious anti-Communist witchhunts of the early 1950s. A more plausible explanation for McCarthy's infamous career would be his ruthless ambition, disregard for the truth and excellent oratorical skills.

He began his political career as a worker for the Democratic Party, but switched allegiance to the Republicans in 1936. He was Senator for Wisconsin 1947–57, during which time he rose to international prominence and then sank into oblivion. Capitalising on Cold War tensions and American involvement in Korea, he hit the headlines in February 1950 with the accusation that 205 known communists were operating in the State Department. A four-year campaign of

Ronald Reagan enjoys a pint of Ireland's most famous stout at O'Farrell's Bar, Ballyporeen, Co. Tipperary on 3 June 1984. Reagan's great-grandfather left the area in 1829. Kennedy and Nixon also made highly publicized visits to their Irish ancestral homes.

censorship and vilification took hold of America until the true demagoguery of McCarthy was exposed to the nation in May–June 1954 in televised hearings of his cross-examination of army and government personnel. In December 1954 he was 'condemned' by a Senate Committee and his influence steadily declined. He died in 1957.

CANADA

♣ **Canada is the only nation in the world to be subjected to invasion by an Irish army.** The Fenians were a republican organisation founded in New York on 17 March 1858 by James Stephens and named by John O'Mahoney in honour of the ancient Irish warriors known as the Fianna. They were dedicated to the forcible removal of British rule in Ireland and the establishment of an independent Irish republic. The Fenians were an American auxiliary of the Irish Republican Brotherhood – an organisation founded by Stephens in Ireland. The organisation as a whole became known as the Fenians in the public mind. In 1866 there were three dissenting factions within the movement: the Fenian Brotherhood (led by O'Mahoney), the Senate Wing (led by W.R. Roberts) and the United Irishmen (who supported the idea of attacking Britain through Canada). The ranks of the Fenians were largely made up of veterans of both sides in the American Civil War. Recruiting took place in Ireland and in the US among the Irish regiments of the Union army and the defeated Confederates.

The invasion of Canada was a fiasco that did not have the unified support of the factions of the movement. In the end it was John O'Mahoney who launched the raid on Campo Bello, off the coast of New Brunswick, in April 1866. In June a second force of 800, led by General John O'Neill, crossed the Canadian border, but were easily defeated. In March 1867 the Kerry rising in Ireland was equally unsuccessful and the movement was later reorganised. Clan na Gael was founded and was a parallel organisation to the Irish Republican Brotherhood. These organisations endured and were later vital to the success of the Irish independence movement.

Irish Prime Ministers of Canada

♣ **Sir Francis Hincks (1807–85), Prime Minister (1851–54)**, was born in Cork, the son of the Reverend Thomas Dix Hincks, founder of the Royal Cork Institution. He was eduated at the Belfast Aca-

Brian Mulroney at a meeting of Commonwealth leaders in London, 3 August 1986. Prime Minister of Canada from 1984 to 1992, Mulroney's ancestors come from Leighlinbridge, Co. Carlow.

demical Institute 1824–29 before emigrating to Toronto. Whilst pursuing a successful business career in banking and journalism, he was elected to the Legislative Assembly of Canada in 1841 as a representative of the Oxford constituency. In 1843 he retired from office as a cabinet member of the Baldwin-Lafontaine administration. Five years later he re-entered politics and resumed his position as Inspector-General in the second Baldwin-Lafontaine government. Following their joint retirement in 1851, Hincks became Prime Minister of Canada.

Hincks' government was characterised by the expansion of Canada's railway network and a reciprocity agreement with the United States in 1854. In that year the government was forced to resign and Hincks left Canada to take administrative positions as Governor of the colonies of Barbados, British Guiana and the Windward Islands. He later returned to serve as Minister of Finance in the MacDonald government 1869–73. He died in Montreal in 1885.

♣ **Arthur Meighen** (1874–1960), **Prime Minister (1920–21)**, was born in Ontario, the grandson of Arthur Meighen Snr, who was a yeoman of the City of Derry and emigrated to Canada in 1839. Meighen was a gifted parliamentary speaker and an accomplished lawyer. His selection as successor to the outgoing PM, Robert Laird-Borden, was an unpopular decision at the time. His term was marked by instability in the Conservative party and strong anti-trade union policies.

✿ **Brian Mulroney (1939–), Prime Minister 1984–92**, whose ancestors came from Leighlinbridge, Co. Carlow, was born in Quebec and was a graduate of the Université Laval. He was President of the Iron Ore Co. 1976–83, leaving to take the leadership of the Canadian Progressive Conservative Party. He was elected Prime Minister of Canada in September 1984 with 211 seats, **the largest number of seats ever won in a Canadian election**. His greatest achievement in office was probably the Free Trade Agreement with the USA in 1987. In 1985 he met Ronald Reagan (see p. 82) at the so-called 'Shamrock Summit', where an early-warning defence system between Canada and the US was agreed.

Irish Governors General of British North America/Canada

Canadian Governors General were the highest-ranking British officials in the colony of Canada after confederation in 1867. They were not continuously in office and various administrators took over the role, if not the office, of Governor General in the intervening years.

✿ **Sir Charles Stanley, Lord Monck** (1819–94), Governor General of British North America 1861–67, was a landowner from Templemore, Co. Tipperary. He was the son of Charles and Bridget Kelly, who sent him to Trinity College, Dublin to be educated for colonial service. In 1867, following the federation of British North America, he became **the first Governor General of the Dominion of Canada**.

✿ **Frederick Temple Blackwood, first Marquis of Dufferin and Ava** (1826–1902), was born in Florence, Italy. After his education at Eton and Oxford he spent ten years on his family estates in Clandeboye, Co. Down. He occupied a number of positions in the colonial service and was Governor General of Canada 1872–78. He was British ambassador to Russia, Turkey, Egypt, Italy and France and Governor General of India 1884–88.

✿ **Henry Charles Keith Petty Fitzmaurice, Lord Lansdowne** (1845–1927), Governor General of Canada 1883–88, was descended from the Dublin-born British Prime Minister William Petty, 2nd Earl of Shelburne. Lansdowne succeeded to his Irish peerage in 1866 and died at Clonmore in Ireland in 1927.

✿ **Vere Brabazon Ponsonby** (1880–1956), **Lord Bessborough**, was born in London into the Irish peerage. He was Governor General of Canada 1931–35.

✿ **Lord Athlone** (1874–1957), an Irish peer, was Governor General of Canada 1940–46.

✿ **Earl Alexander of Tunis and Errigal** (1891–1969; see also p. 98) was Governor General 1946–52. He was born in Caledon, Co. Tyrone and was a field marshal in the British Army during World War II, serving with great distinction in the North African campaign.

✿ **The 'father of the Canadian Confederacy', Thomas D'Arcy McGee** (1825–68), born in Carlingford, Co. Louth, was a leading member of the Young Ireland movement. He first emigrated to Boston in 1842 and joined the *Boston Pilot* newspaper. He returned home in 1845, however, and began writing for *The Nation*, the organ of the Young Ireland movement. He was implicated in the rebellion of 1848 and was compelled to escape back to America. In New York he founded the *New York Nation*, but had little success. He returned to Boston and published the *American Celt* 1852–57. On the invitation of Canadian friends, he moved to Montreal and founded the *New Era* newspaper in 1857. The following year he was elected to the Legislative Assembly of Canada for Montreal West.

During his political career he was the most eloquent and forceful advocate of a 'new nationality', his arguments successfully convincing Canadians of the need for a confederacy of states. In 1867, when the first cabinet of the Dominion of Canada was being formed, he stood aside in order that the Catholic Irish and Nova Scotia vote would not be split and would be represented at top level by his fellow Irish-Canadian, Edward Kenny. This magnanimous act, largely out of character, was recognised for what it was – a political move that crossed the boundaries of individual states and therefore a declaration symbolising a confederate Canada.

McGee was initially aligned with the reformers, but changed his allegiance to the Conservatives in 1863 and was appointed Minister of Agriculture in the 'Great Coalition' government of MacDonald and Tache. He grew less anti-British as the years passed and eventually became a loyal subject of Britain within the Dominion of Canada. He vehemently condemned the abortive Fenian invasion of Canada in 1866 and was assassinated in April 1868 by a Fenian named Whalen.

♣ **The founder and first Commissioner of the North West Mounted Police, the 'Mounties'** (called the Royal Canadian Mounted Police since 1920), was **Lieutenant-Colonel George French**, born in Roscommon in 1841. French was educated at Sandhurst and Woolwich military academies and was commissioned in the Royal Artillery in 1860. In 1873 he founded the North West Mounted Police in Canada and led their famous march to the foot of the Rockies in 1874 to extend the rule of law across the country. He resigned his position in 1876 and undertook colonial service in India and Australia. Today there are more than 19,000 members of the force in all of the Canadian provinces bar Ontario and Quebec.

SOUTH AMERICA

♣ **Governor of Chile and Viceroy of Peru, Ambrosio O'Higgins** (c. 1720–1801) claimed noble ancestry as a descendant of the Baron of Ballinary in Co. Sligo, but was probably born in more humble surroundings in Co. Meath. As a child he was employed as an errand boy by Lady Bective at Dangan Castle near Summerhill in Meath. As a young man he was sent to Cadiz in Spain to be educated for the church. Finding that he had no vocation, he tried various jobs before leaving for Peru in 1756. He ran a toy shop in Lima and studied engineering until he was commissioned as a draughtsman in Chile with the Council for the Indies in 1761, working as an assistant to another Irish ex-patriot, John Garland, Governor of Valdivia. He constructed and improved the Andean roads and founded a successful postal system that linked Chile with Buenos Aires and Mendoza. He also founded the towns of San Ambrosio de Ballenar and Osorno and built the highway from Santiago to Valparaiso. His grand plans for the large-scale colonisation of Chile and Peru by adventurous and displaced Irishmen and women never came to fruition. He moved through the ranks of the Chilean Army to brigadier-general and in 1787 was appointed Governor of Chile. He set about modernising colonial administration. In 1795 he became the Viceroy of Peru, the most important Spanish official in South

America. He defended the coast of Peru when war broke out with Italy in 1797. He died suddenly in Lima in 1801 at 80 years of age.

♣ **'The Liberator of Chile', first President of Chile and founder of the Chilean Navy, Bernardo O'Higgins** (1778–1842) was the son of Ambrosio. He was born in Talca in southern Chile and sent to England to be educated. There he met supporters of Latin American independence and was converted to the cause. He returned to Chile in 1802 to claim the estate left to him by his father and joined the independence movement. He was elected to the Patriot Congress in 1810 and campaigned for liberal reforms. He commanded patriot forces against the Spanish in 1813 and 1814 but was defeated at Rancagua in October 1814 and forced to flee to Argentina, where he joined up with the invasion force of José de San

Bernardo O'Higgins and José de San Martín on the battlefield of Maipó, 1817. O'Higgins played a major role in Chile's struggle for independence from Spain and became first leader ('supreme dictator') of the new Chilean state in 1817.

Martín. In February 1817 he commanded the forces that defeated the Spanish at the Battle of Chacabuco. He formally declared Chilean independence on 12 February 1812 and was proclaimed *Director Supremo*. He introduced many liberal reforms and founded a Chilean Navy, employing another Irishman, Captain George O'Brien*, to organise it.

From 1817 to 1823 O'Higgins was virtual dictator of Chile. By abolishing titles of nobility and expelling the royalist archbishop of Santiago, he made many enemies and in 1823 was forced to flee to Argentina, where he saw military service under Simón Bolívar. Plans to invade and liberate Peru came to nothing. He died in 1842 and is remembered today as the father of Chilean independence. He is buried beneath a monument in Santiago, where the city's main street – Avenida O'Higgins – is named in his honour.

O'Higgins' remains were repatriated from Callao, Peru to Santiago at the end of the Chilean–Spanish War of 1865–66 by Charles Condell (1844–87), who was a distant relation of the last principal of Dublin's Hibernian Marine School. Condell was a rear-admiral at the time of his death.

🍀 **Colonial Governor and revolutionary general to Bernardo O'Higgins, John/Juan MacKenna** (1771–1814) was born in Clogher, Co. Tyrone. His kinsman Alexander O'Reilly (see p. 91), a general in the Spanish army, enrolled him in the Royal Academy of Mathematics in Barcelona in 1784. In 1787 he joined the Irish corps of military engineers in the Spanish army. He sailed for Peru in 1796 and served under Ambrosio O'Higgins (see p. 86). In 1797 he was appointed Governor of Osorno, but by 1810 had joined the revolutionary army of Carrera as Commander-in-Chief of Artillery and Engineers. In 1813 he was promoted to brigadier-general and commander of Santiago. He allied himself with Bernardo O'Higgins (see above), when O'Higgins replaced Carrera as Commander-in-Chief of the revolutionary army, and served as his second-in-command. He was

---

* O'Brien died in an action that led to the capture of several Spanish ships. The Chilean Navy today still names ships in his honour. He was the first Chilean naval officer to die in action.

killed in a duel with Luis Carrera, brother of the revolutionary leader, in Buenos Aires in November 1814.

❧ Foremost hero of the Chilean Navy, Patricio Lynch was born in 1824, the son of a wealthy Irish merchant living in Chile. Lynch served for seven years in the British Navy and saw action in the Opium Wars against China. He commanded the final assault on Lima in 1880, during the war against Peru, and ruthlessly put down Peruvian resistance. His draconian methods were denounced by a leading Chilean-Irish liberal politician named Benjamín Vicuña MacKenna (1831–86). In 1884 Lynch was appointed Ambassador to Spain, the leading diplomatic post in Chile.

Since his death in 1886, the Chilean Navy has permanently had an *Almirante Lynch* in commission. The first of these made history in 1891 by being **the first warship to sink another with a launched torpedo** (during the Balmacedist war of 1891).

❧ Aide-de-camp to José de San Martín, the liberator of Argentina, **John Thomond O'Brien** (1796–1861) was born in Co. Wicklow and emigrated to Argentina in 1814. In that same year he fought for the liberationists at the siege of Montevideo and subsequently joined the army of the Andes in Mendoza. His promise was recognised by San Martín, who appointed him his personal aide-de-camp. O'Brien took part in all the major actions of the independence struggle in Chile and Peru and was present in a position of honour when Peruvian independence was formally declared in Lima in July 1826. He returned to Ireland in 1827 to persuade Irish emigrants to settle in Argentina, but met with little success. In 1828 he was back in Buenos Aires addressing a group of Irish residents on how best they could help the struggle for Catholic Emancipation in Ireland. He died in Lisbon in 1861 and his remains were repatriated to Argentina in 1935.

❧ Founder of the Ecuadoran Navy, Thomas Charles Wright (1799–1868) of Queensborough, Drogheda, Co. Louth, was a veteran of the British Navy who had fought in the Napoleonic Wars and in the Anglo-American War of 1812. He left for South America to join the independence struggle of Simón Bolívar and, after some military service, was asked to organise a naval force to patrol the Pacific coast. In a decisive battle at Callao, Spain's main naval base in the Pacific, he prevented the arrival of supplies and

reinforcements for the Spaniards. According to the naval historian John de Courcy Ireland, he 'was in no small way the architect of the final overthrow of Spanish power in South America'. Wright commanded the *Chimborazo*, which took Bolívar to Chile and also witnessed the Chilean independence struggle. He returned to Ecuador, settled in the port of Guayaquil and later fought with fellow-Irishman Daniel Florence O'Leary (see p. 89) in the war against Peru. When Ecuador achieved independence in 1830, he was asked to found the new state's navy. He spent 15 years in exile (1845–60), when the liberal regime he actively supported was overthrown, but later returned to his adopted country and died there in 1868. The naval academy in Guayaquil, Ecuador is named after him.

❧ Founder of the Argentine Navy, William Brown (1777–1857) of Foxford, Co. Mayo emigrated to Pennsylvania with his family in 1786, when he was nine years old. He began his life at sea as a cabin boy in US merchant ships before he was pressed into the British Navy in 1796. By 1809 he had succeeded in obtaining the command of a British merchant ship trading with Argentina. He became involved in the independence struggle in 1813, when he arrived in Buenos Aires port during the revolution only to find it blockaded by the Spanish, who commandeered his ship. Brown responded by organising an expedition to capture one of the blockading ships. He was subsequently offered the command of a small fleet by the Argentine authorities and in March 1814 he broke the Spanish blockade of Montevideo, allowing the patriot army to capture the city and effectively ending Spanish control of the newly independent state. In 1816 he was in the Peruvian port of Callao, blockading the city for three weeks and crippling the heart of Spanish rule in South America. He retired from active service in 1819 and settled in Buenos Aires, but was recalled in 1825 when war broke out with Brazil. Again he took command of the Argentine navy and gained a number of victories. During the Uruguayan Civil War 1842–46 Brown fought against the Italian patriot and future leader of the Risorgimento, Garibaldi. The two eventually became good friends. Brown died in Buenos Aires in 1857 and was given a public funeral and buried with full honours. The main square in central Buenos Aires, Plaza del Mayo, is named in honour of Brown's birthplace.

The following is quoted from a document in the Spanish National Library, section: *La Colección de Documentos de América*. Translated in the *Irish Sword*, Vol III, no. 6 by Dr Michelene Walsh. This has been reproduced by John de Courcy Ireland in *Ireland and the Irish in Maritime History* (1986):

> *The Irishman William Brown came to Buenos Aires in 1810 in command of a ship bringing a cargo to the English firm of Thomas Jones. He remained in Buenos Aires, where he made numerous journeys to the colony of Sacramento as a trader. At the beginning of 1813 the ships (Spanish) of Montevideo captured two of his boats bringing cargoes from Sacramento to Buenos Aires. Brown wrote a letter to General Vigodet (Spanish), governor of Montevideo, requesting him to release the crews, for they were innocent people who were doing nothing more than earning a living. General Vigodet answered him in unsavoury terms, telling him that should he fall into his hands he would receive the same treatment. This caused Brown to become so indignant that, having until then remained indifferent to events, (ie the revolt of Buenos Aires province against Spanish colonial rule), he declared himself openly for the patriots. After this he was asked to take the supreme command, which he accepted, of the ships which the government of Buenos Aires was enlisting for attack on the (Spanish) naval base of Buenos Aires. When Vigodet was made prisoner in Montevideo he was sent aboard Brown's ship, who, despite what happened between them, procured for him what clothes he needed and even lent him 100 crowns in gold for his journey, a sum which Vigodet returned to him as soon as he reached Spain. This conduct was greatly to Brown's credit.*

🍀 **Richard Wright**, brother of Thomas Charles Wright, fought at the Battle of Lake Maracaibo on 24 July 1823 in which 22 rebel Colombian ships and 770 men defeated 29 Spanish ships and 1000 men. This battle was considered the turning point in the anti-colonial war and was the first real victory of the Colombian Navy. (Lake Maracaibo is now in Venezuela.)

🍀 **Founder of the Uruguayan Navy, Peter Campbell** of Tipperary was part of the British invasion force that landed in Buenos Aires in 1806. (Francis Beaufort – see p. 20 – was also a member of the expedition.) He was imprisoned by the Argentines but later joined forces with José Artigas, the liberator of Uruguay, who commissioned him to found a naval force in 1814. Campbell obliged by arming the first Uruguayan flotilla. Artigas was defeated in 1819 and Campbell was exiled to Paraguay, where he made his

living in his old trade as a tanner. He died in Paraguay in 1832 and his remains were repatriated to Uruguay.

🍀 **Aide-de-camp to Simón Bolívar and national hero of Venezuela, Daniel Florence O'Leary** (1800–54) was born in Cork City and was the most eminent of a series of Irish aides-de-camp and officers in Bolívar's revolutionary army. O'Leary joined the 1st Division of the Red Hussars of Venezuela following a recruitment drive in Britain and Ireland. Arriving in Venezuela in 1817, his distaste for the indiscipline of the other troops impressed his commander, who made him an aide-de-camp. He was injured in battle during Bolívar's epic march across the Andes in 1819, but was present at Bolívar's triumphal procession through Bogotá and was decorated with the Order of the Liberator. In April 1820 he was appointed aide-de-camp to Bolívar, who entrusted him with negotiating peace with the Spanish commander General Pablo Morillo. Following several diplomatic and military representations, O'Leary was promoted to the rank of colonel in 1825. In 1826 he was requested to negotiate the formation of a unified federal South American state. Although unsuccessful, he remained Bolívar's closest adviser and was given command of Venezuelan troops during the war against Peru in 1829. He spent the years 1834–39 on diplomatic missions to Madrid, Paris and London, seeking the recognition of the Venezuelan state. He met the Irish liberator Daniel O'Connell (see p. 54) in London in 1834 and returned briefly to Ireland. He was home again in 1852 to visit his sons at school in England, and donated a collection of South American plants, animals and minerals to Queen's College, Cork (now University College, Cork). His three-volume *Narración* remains a main source of the history of the independence struggles of the northern countries of South America.

O'Leary died in Bogotá in 1854 and his remains are now housed in the National Pantheon in Caracas, near those of Bolívar. One of the principal city squares in Caracas, Plaza O'Leary, is named in his honour. The Venezuelan government have placed a plaque at his birthplace in Cork.

🍀 **The First Lady of Paraguay, Elisa Alicia Lynch** (1835–86) was born in Ireland in 1835 and married a French army doctor at 15. Leaving her husband after three years, she remained in Paris until 1853 when she met Francisco Solano López, the son of the dictator of Paraguay who was visiting Paris at the time. Lynch returned with him to Asunción and bore five children. In 1862 López inherited his father's presidency and Lynch as his mistress was *de facto* First Lady of Paraguay. She actively participated in the running of the country and was present when her lover was killed in 1870 during the War of the Triple Alliance 1865–70. She buried him, together with their first-born son, and was deported at the end of the war, leaving her great personal fortune behind. She returned to live in Paris and died in obscurity whilst on a visit to Jerusalem in 1886.

❦ **Spain's last viceroy in Mexico and a hero of Mexican Independence, Juan O'Donoju (O'Donohue)** was a Spanish general of Irish descent who defied the instructions of Madrid and negotiated a settlement with the rebels (the Plan of Iguala, 1825) which recognised Mexican independence. He is buried in Mexico City's cathedral.

❦ **The San Patricio Battalion** comprised a group of Irish soldiers, fighting in the American Army in the Mexican–American war (1846–48), who became convinced that they were fighting an unjust war and deserted to join the Mexican side. Led by John O'Reilly, they won special decorations at the Battle of Buena Vista, but were later defeated and taken prisoner after the last battle of the war at Churubusco on 20 August 1847. They were later court-martialled by Colonel Bennett Riley of the United States Army. Despite sharing his name with the San Patricio commander, O'Reilly, Colonel Riley was unsympathetic. Sanctioned by General Scott of the US Army, 16 of the 87 men taken prisoner were executed immediately, while the remainder were taken to Mexico City, where they watched the US flag being raised over the fortress of Chapultepec before they too were hanged. Those whose lives were spared were given 50 lashes and branded with the letter 'D' on their cheeks to mark them out as deserters.

Approximately 50% of the US Army troops recruited for the Mexican War 1846–48 were foreign-born. Irish recruits are estimated to have numbered about 24% of the entire force. Emigration from Ireland was reaching a peak at this time, as the Famine continued to ravage the country. Many emigrants were recruited straight off the ships. This suggests that a large number of the Irish executed that day were killed for deserting the US Army before they actually had a chance of living in America. Nobody knows for certain why they deserted to the Mexican side, but the suffering of impoverished Mexican farmers at the hands of a powerful US army probably reminded them of the repression they had suffered in their native Ireland.

The execution of the San Patricio Battalion caused outrage throughout Mexico and the executed men became national heroes. They are now part of Mexican folklore and their story is on the history curriculum in schools. The San Patricio Battalion is commemorated every September in San Jacinto Plaza, where a plaque stands in their honour.

(The Texan County of San Patricio, near the Mexican border, was founded on 17 March 1836 in commemoration of St Patrick. Evidently a particularly Irish settlement, it may have inspired the name of the Mexican battalion – or provided local recruits for the US Army. Today, San Patricio County has a population of about 60,000 and includes some of the suburbs of Corpus Christi.)

❦ **Ernesto 'Che' Guevara** (1928–67), the Cuban revolutionary hero and cult figure for radical students in the 1960s and 70s, was born in Rosario, Argentina of Spanish-Irish descent. He was the son of Ernesto Guevara Lynch, whose mother was a native of Galway, and Celia de la Serna. Guevara completed his medical studies in 1953 and became convinced of the need for violent revolution to overcome the poverty he had seen when travelling throughout Latin America. He joined Fidel Castro in 1956 in the campaign to overthrow the dictator Fulgencio Batista, and went on to become one of his lieutenants and an administrator and ambassador of the revolutionary government which came to power in 1959. He fought in the Congo with supporters of the Congolese prime minister Patrice Lumumba, and trained a team of guerrillas in the Santa Cruz region of Bolivia. In 1967 he was captured by troops of the Bolivian army and later executed.

Guevara wrote of his experiences and on the theories of revolution. His principal works include: *Guerrilla Warfare* (1961), *Reminiscences of the Cuban Revolutionary War* (1963) and *Bolivian Diary* (1969).

(Suggestions that the name 'Che' is a Latinisation of the Irish name 'Shay', short for 'Seamus', are unfounded! However, the ambiguity of the name 'Che' is unlikely to have gone unnoticed by the Guevara-Lynch family, who were very aware of the Argentine–Spanish–Irish triangle of their ancestry.)

SPAIN

❦ **Secretary of State of Spain, Richard/Ricardo Wall** (1694–1778) was born at Coolnamuck, Co. Waterford. He began his career in the army and served as a naval and military officer, rising to the rank of lieutenant-general. It was his diplomatic skills that were exemplary, however, and he was a chief negotiator for Spain at the peace settlement of Aix-la-Chapelle in 1748 at the end of the War of the Austrian Succession. He was the Spanish ambassador to England, Minister of External Affairs 1752–54, Secretary of State 1754–64 – Chief Minister of the King.

♣ Prime Minister of Spain, Leopoldo O'Donnell (1809–67) was a descendant of the 'Wild Geese' who fled Ireland after the Treaty of Limerick in 1691. He entered colonial service and amassed a fortune as governor-general of Cuba, before returning to Spain in 1846. In 1854 he was appointed War Minister by Espartero. Two years later he supplanted Espartero in a coup, but was himself replaced after only three months by Naváez. In 1858 he became Prime Minister once more and in 1859 led a successful campaign against the Moors in Morocco, for which he was made Duke of Tetuan. He was Prime Minister for brief periods again in 1863 and 1865–66.

♣ Field-Marshal of the Spanish army, Alexander O'Reilly (c. 1722–94), born in the Co. Meath/Co. Cavan area, took Louisiana from the French colonists in 1768. He reformed the Spanish army, remodelling it in the Prussian style.

♣ Sir Charles Wogan (c. 1698–1754), born in Rathcoffey, Co. Kildare, was Governor of La Mancha and a brigadier-general in the Spanish army. He was a Jacobite *émigré* and soldier of fortune who made his living in the service of France, Spain and the exiled Pretender, James Edward Stuart of England. His adventurous life is first documented with certainty from 1715, when he fought in the Stuart rising at the Battle of Preston and was captured. He escaped from Newgate prison to France, where he served with Dillon's Irish Regiment until 1718. James Edward Stuart, seeking further influence, asked Wogan to win him the hand of a Russian princess. However, Wogan failed to persuade the lady in question and Maria Clementia Sobieski, granddaughter of Polish King Jan Sobieski (the deliverer of Europe from the Turks), was chosen instead. On her way to Bologna, where she was to meet Wogan, Maria Clementia was arrested in Innsbruck by agents of the Austrian emperor, who sought the goodwill of the British government and did not wish to be seen to be involved in a Jacobite plot. However, Wogan managed to rescue Maria in April 1719 and took her to meet her husband-to-be.

James rewarded him with a baronetcy and the Pope conferred on him the title of Roman Senator.

Wogan then took up service as a colonel in the Spanish Army and soon distinguished himself at Santa Cruz. He was promoted to brigadier-general and made Governor of La Mancha. From La Mancha, he corresponded with the Dublin-based writer Jonathan Swift (see p. 134), whom he had earlier befriended. (Swift's extensive wine cellar in the deanery at St Patrick's in Dublin was augmented by Wogan, who sent him several casks of Spanish wine. Wogan also wrote extensively, but Swift's attempts to find him a publisher were unsuccessful.)

♣ The largest ship (and the only four-decker) **at the Battle of Trafalgar** on 21 October 1805 was the Spanish vessel *Santíssima Trinidad*, which was built in Spain by the Mullens, a father and son partnership who came from London, but whom the Spanish record as being Irish. The ship was the largest in the world at the time, at 1900 tons. It held a crew of 1200 within its 23½ in (60 cm) thick walls. The Mullens were master shipwrights who built many of Spain's finest ships in the 18th century.

Another Spanish ship at Trafalgar was the 100-gun *Rayo,* captained by **Enrique Macdonnell** of Irish ancestry. The *Rayo* survived the battle but in a later encounter Macdonnell, trying to recapture some prizes taken by the British on that day, was captured by two British ships (one of which was, incidentally, the previously French-owned *Hoche*, which had been captured in Lough Swilly, Co. Donegal in 1798 as part of Wolfe Tone's final and unsuccessful attempt to recruit French aid for the United Irishman rebellion).

Macdonnell also fought for the Swedish Navy 1788–90, and is reported to have held off an entire Russian squadron at Kynmeme, Finland. He retired as a commodore of the Spanish Navy c. 1818.

♣ Rear-Admiral of the Spanish Navy, Manuel McCrohon y Blake was born in Spain in 1816 of recent Irish ancestry. He received several awards in a distinguished career of imperial service, including a special medal from the king of Cambodia. He rose to the rank of rear-admiral in 1869 and was appointed Commander-in-Chief of the Philippines in 1871.

McCrohon supported the short-lived Spanish Republic when it was declared in 1873 and was consequently recalled from the Philippines after the regency was restored in 1874. He was, however, retained in service and was appointed Captain-General of Cadiz, where he died in 1877.

BRITAIN

Prime Ministers

♣ **Sir William Petty, 2nd Earl of Shelburne (1737–1805), Prime Minister of Britain (1782–83)**, was born in Dublin in 1737. His ancestor, Sir William Petty, was Surveyor-General in Ireland for Oliver Cromwell. The family acquired vast estates in Co. Kerry and had an annual rent-roll of £22,000 at the time of his inheritance.

William Petty was educated at Christ Church, Oxford and joined the Scots Guards. He inherited his father's seat in the House of Lords in 1761. In 1766 he was Secretary of State for the Southern Department (in charge of American colonial and Indian affairs). He resigned his post in 1768 in protest at the government's intention to use force in America. After some years of political inactivity, he was recalled as Home Secretary by Rockingham's government, becoming Prime Minister after Rockingham's death in July 1782. He made a peace settlement with the American revolutionaries that was rejected by Parliament. In economics he applied the free-market theories of Adam Smith, while he was more liberal in social policy than contemporaries such as William Pitt.

William Petty was a highly unpopular politician. He was more intellectual than many of his political peers and his home at Bowood House was frequented by David Hume, Dr Johnson and Jeremy Bentham. He hoped to establish a federal-style relationship between America and Britain, but was opposed to American independence. He was bitterly attacked in Parliament by Edmund Burke (see p. 135) and became disillusioned with politics altogether when King George III failed to support his American peace settlement. The King despised and distrusted him, calling him 'the Jesuit of Berkeley Square' (where he had his London home).

He was twice married, first to Lady Sophia Carteret in 1765 and, following her death, to an Irish woman called Lady Louise Fitzpatrick. When injured in the groin after a duel with a Lt-Colonel William Fullerton, Petty is quoted as saying 'I don't think Lady Shelburne will be any the worse for it'. With this sort of conceit, coupled with his Irish and Catholic background and an intellectual leaning in a political environment, it is a wonder he rose so high in his career.

♣ **George Canning (1770–1827), Prime Minister of Britain (1827)**, was born in Dublin in 1770. Of all British Prime Ministers, until those of recent decades, Canning's background was perhaps the least favourable. His father, George Canning Snr, born in Garvagh, Co. Derry, was a failed wine merchant and lawyer. He escaped to London after an illicit love affair and married an unsuccessful Irish actress, Mary Ann Costello. Following the marriage his allowance was stopped by his disapproving father. George Canning Jr lived a precarious existence with his parents for most of his childhood: his father abandoned the family to fend for themselves and later died in a garret in Holborn, London. Meanwhile, Mary Ann Costello had moved to London to continue her undistinguished acting career, taking her son with her. However, with the financial assistance of his uncle, Stratford Canning – who owned a banking house in the City of London, George Canning was able to complete his education at Eton and Christ Church, Oxford, where his intellect and wit were quickly recognised.

He was a member of the Irish Club in London but, despite his Whig background, joined the Tory Party. It is said that he became a Tory when he was told that the revolutionary Jacobins planned to make him their leader when the time came for action. Canning was

George Canning, the 19th Prime Minister of Great Britain, was born in Dublin – as was his mother, Mary Ann Costello. His father was a native of Garvagh, Co. Derry. Canning was the shortest-serving British PM ever, lasting only 100 days in 1827.

Dublin-born Arthur Wellesley, Duke of Wellington, in a painting by Goya. England's greatest general since Marlborough and one of the most decorated soldiers of all time, he proved an unpopular Tory Prime Minister.

not a radical; he was more interested in a prosperous future for himself.

Canning was chosen as MP for the rotten borough of Tralee, Co. Kerry in his native Ireland, and secured a fortune by marrying Joan Scott, daughter of General Scott. He was Foreign Secretary by the age of 37 and successfully scuppered Napoleon's plans for a Northern Alliance against Britain by a preemptive attack against Napoleonic forces in Copenhagen. Canning's promotion was hampered however by public knowledge of his affair in earlier years with Queen Caroline of Brunswick, the estranged wife of the Prince of Wales.

In 1812 he became MP for Liverpool and over the next ten years served, amongst other positions, as Ambassador to Portugal and President of the Board of Control. In 1822 Castlereagh (see p. 95) committed suicide and George IV was reluctantly obliged to offer the vacant post of Foreign Secretary to Canning, his wife's former lover.

As Foreign Secretary, Canning made various appointments designed to please the King and he was offered the position of Prime Minister in 1827, when Lord Liverpool suffered a crippling stroke. Canning had an innate Whig liberalism and his appointment alarmed the right wing of the Tory Party, who had pressed George IV to appoint the less liberal Dubliner, the Duke of Wellington (see below). Canning convinced the King with the teasing observation: 'Sir, your father broke the domination of the Whigs. I hope your Majesty will not endure that of the Tories.' Canning's period in office lasted only 120 days. He succeeded in making an alliance with the Russians and the French Bourbons and he gave assistance to the Greek independence movement. But Wellington, his long-time rival, resigned in protest at Canning's appointment and Robert Peel refused to serve in his government. The liberalism of his foreign policy and his pursuit of Catholic emancipation (although not matched in his dealings with social unrest in Britain) were unpopular with his own party. He died in office, his term of office being **the shortest ever served by a British Prime Minister** – 120 days from 10 April to 8 August 1827.

♣ **Arthur Wellesley, 1st Duke of Wellington (1769–1852) Prime Minister of Britain (1828–30).** Field-Marshal, Commander-in-Chief of the British Army and Prime Minister of Great Britain, Wellesley was born in Mornington House, 24 Upper Merrion Street, Dublin. He was sent to Eton at the age of 12 and entered the army as an ensign in 1787. He showed few signs of promise early in his career and his promotions at this time were partly due to the growing political clout of his eldest brother. From 1787 to 1793 he was aide-de-camp to the Lord Lieutenant in Ireland and from 1790 to 1795 he was an MP for Trim, Co. Meath in the Irish Parliament. He served in Flanders 1794–95 and was sent to India in 1797. He won a military reputation in India, where his brother, Lord Mornington, was appointed Governor General in 1798. He was knighted in 1804 and was elected MP for Rye in 1806. From 1807 to 1809 he served as Secretary for Ireland before being appointed Commander-in-Chief of the British Army in the Peninsular Wars. He drove Napoleon's army out of Spain and occupied Toulouse in 1814, for which he was made a field-marshal and Duke of Wellington. Parliament awarded him £400,000 and he received distinctions from all over Europe. He was appointed Ambassador to Paris and went on to negotiate for peace at the Congress of Vienna in 1814–15. When Napoleon escaped from Elba in March 1815, Wellington took command of British forces and defeated him at Waterloo on 18 June. He was acclaimed internationally and awarded a £263,000 estate in Hampshire by the British nation.

Wellington became a member of the cabinet in 1819 and Prime Minister in 1828. With Peel, he succumbed to the pressure of the national movement in Ireland to secure Catholic emancipation and passed the enabling law in 1829. A staunch Conservative who opposed parliamentary reform, he brought down his own government in 1830. He served in Cabinet twice again in 1834 and 1841–46.

Wellington is possibly **the most decorated soldier of all time**. In addition to his British honours, he was a prince of the Netherlands, a duke in France, Spain and Portugal, a marshal of seven European armies and a knight of 24 orders. Wellington died in Walmer, Kent in September 1852 and is buried in St Paul's Cathedral.

♣ **Sir Robert Peel (1788–1850), Prime Minister of Britain (1834–35 and 1841–46)** became MP for Cashel, Co. Tipperary in 1809, when the seat was purchased for him by his father. Peel was Chief Secretary in Ireland 1812–18. In 1814, as part of a coercion bill, he set up in Ireland **the world's first organised police force, the 'Peace Preservation Police'**, who were (un)popularly known as 'Peelers'. The Royal Ulster Constabulary still carry the nickname in Northern Ireland.*

The London Metropolitan Police Force was established in 1829, also by Peel, using his experience in Ireland. This time his first name was used as a nickname for the police force, whose members were called 'bobbies'. (It should be noted that while 'bobby' is almost a term of endearment, 'peeler' is quite the opposite.)

Robert Peel and Daniel O'Connell (see p. 54) were bitter rivals. O'Connell was aware of Peel's opposition to Catholic emancipation and labelled him 'Orange Peel'. In 1815 relations between the two men were so low that Peel challenged O'Connell to a duel. After a series of postponements a time and place were agreed. However, O'Connell was arrested *en route* and a confrontation was avoided.

♣ **Sir Henry John Temple, 3rd Viscount Palmerston (1784–1865), Prime Minister of Britain (1855–58 and 1859–65)**, although English born and bred, came from an Anglo-Irish landowning family which had held lands in Ireland from Elizabethan times. In 1722 his ancestor, Henry Temple (1673–1757), was created a peer of Ireland as Baron Temple of Mount Temple, Co. Sligo and Viscount Palmerston of Palmerston, now a suburb of Dublin City. Palmerston was **the oldest Prime Minister of Britain** when he assumed office at the age of 70 years 109 days on 6 February 1855.

♣ **Andrew Bonar Law (1858–1923), Prime Minister of Britain (1922–23)**, was born in Kingston, New Brunswick, Canada, to the Reverend James Law, a Presbyterian minister from Portrush, Co. Antrim. (His mother, Elizabeth Kidston was the Canadian-born daughter of a Glasgow iron-merchant.) Bonar Law's Ulster roots were evident in his hardline Unionist approach to the Irish question as Prime Minister.

♣ **Stanley Baldwin (1867–1947), Prime Minister of Britain (1923–24, 1924–29 and 1935–37)** and Rudyard Kipling (1865–1936), Nobel Prize-winner for literature, author of *The Jungle Book* (1894) and *Kim* (1901) amongst many other books, were first cousins who shared the same great-grandfather, the Reverend James MacDonald of Co. Fermanagh.

* *The first attempt to establish a police force in Ireland was by an Act of George III in 1787. The 'barnies', as they were known, were inadequate for the job. The Police Preservation Force was strengthened by the County Constabulary in 1822. Under an Act of 1836, a unified Irish Constabulary was formed, and given the 'Royal' prefix in 1867 as a reward for suppressing the Fenian uprising.*

♣ **James Callaghan, Prime Minister of Britain (1976–79)** (born in Portsmouth in 1912), is the great-grandson of a weaver who left Ireland during the Famine. He was created Baron Callaghan of Cardiff in 1987. Lord Callaghan has the unique distinction of having held four different cabinet positions in his political career: Foreign Secretary, Home Secretary, Chancellor of the Exchequer and Prime Minister. (He is also **the tallest ever British PM** at 6ft 1in (1.85m).)

Other figures

♣ **British Foreign Secretary at the Congress of Vienna, Robert Stewart, Viscount Castlereagh, second Marquess of Londonderry** (1769–1822), was born in Dublin and educated at the Royal School, Armagh and St John's College, Cambridge. In his early years he was a Liberal and supported the United Irishmen. However, horrified by the enormous upheaval that followed the French Revolution, he turned to Conservative politics. He was elected to the Irish Parliament in 1790 and appointed Chief Secretary in 1798. The Irish rising of that year convinced him of the necessity of unity between Britain and Ireland to preserve the Empire. The Act of Union between Britain and Ireland was passed in 1800, following a huge outlay for 'compensation for disturbance' to members of the house.

In 1805 Stewart was appointed Secretary for War and began his dominant role in British policymaking. As Foreign Secretary from 1812, he was the chief architect of the coalition against Napoleon. His skills as a negotiator secured the acceptance of the terms of the Congress of Vienna in 1815. His popularity diminished after the wars and he was closely associated with the repressive policies of the post-Napoleonic years in Britain. He took his own life in August 1822, unable to endure the continuing strain of his position.

♣ **General in the British Army and Commander-in-Chief in India, Eyre Coote** (1726–83) was born on the family estate in Ash Hill, Co. Limerick. He fought in Germany and against the Jacobite rebels in 1745. In 1754 he went to India with the 39th regiment, the first English regiment ever sent there (it retains the motto 'Primus in Indus'). As a captain of the 39th, he served in Bengal in 1756 taking part in action against the Surajah Dowlah in revenge for the 'Black Hole of Calcutta' atrocity. His advice to senior officers on what action should be taken was successfully followed and won him promotion. His victory

Charles Beresford, son of the 4th Marquess of Waterford, entered the Royal Navy at 13 and rose to the rank of admiral. An Irish speaker, he initiated Britain's imperial expansion into Egypt and the Sudan in 1882.

over fellow Irishman Lally (see p. 102), who was in the service of France, effectively ended France's involvement in the East Indies. In 1762 Coote returned to England, purchased the estate of West Park in Hampshire and was presented with a diamond-hilted sword worth £700 by a grateful East India Company. He was promoted to colonel in 1765 and in 1768 was elected MP for Leicester. The following year he was appointed head of the Madras Presidency, but disagreed with the Governor of Madras, Josias du Pré, and returned home by the overland route. He was one of the first to take this route and his successful journey encouraged subsequent exploration. He was MP for Poole 1774–80 and was appointed Commander-in-Chief in India as a lieutenant-general in April 1777. He assumed command in Calcutta in March 1779.

♣ **Viceroy of India, Richard Southwell Bourke, 6th Earl of Mayo** (1822–72), a native of Dublin, was educated at Trinity College and entered political life. In 1852, at the age of 30, he became Chief Secretary for Ireland. He held the position again in 1858 and 1866. He represented Kildare, Coleraine and Cockermouth (England) in Parliament between 1847 and 1868. In 1868 he was appointed Viceroy and Governor General of India. He cultivated friendly relations with the neighbouring states of Afghanistan, Nepal and Burma, thus drawing them into the trade and infrastructure of the British Empire. He encouraged the decentralisation of the Indian administration and reformed public finances. He was assassinated in February 1872 while inspecting a penal settlement at Port Blair in the Andaman Islands.

❦ **Admiral Lord Charles Beresford** (1846–1919), son of the 4th Marquess of Waterford, was born in Philipstown, King's County (known as Daingean, Co. Offaly since independence in 1922). Beresford's bombardment of the port of Alexandria in 1882 marked the first stage of Britain's imperial expansion into Egypt and Sudan. Beresford became a full admiral in 1907 and in 1909 he was placed in charge of the Channel Fleet. A Gaelic speaker who insisted that all his ship stewards came from Ireland, Beresford was a controversial figure who openly criticised his peers and had serious disagreements with Winston Churchill. He died in 1919, having trained many of the distinguished sea commanders of World War I.

❦ **British hero of the Boer War, the Rt Hon Sir Bryan Mahon** (1862–1930), was born in Belleville, Co. Galway. He was commissioned as a lieutenant in the King's Royal Irish Hussars in 1883 and received a DSO in the Dongola campaign of 1896. He was sent to South Africa as brigadier-general in 1900 to break the siege of Mafeking. Following his success, the extravagant celebrations in London added the new word 'mafficking' to the English language. After further service in India and Egypt, he was appointed to command the 10th (Irish) Division and took part in the ill-fated Gallipoli campaign of 1915. He was Commander-in-Chief in Ireland 1916–18 and, following his retirement in 1921, was nominated to the first Irish Free State Senate in 1922.

❦ The brigadier-general who gave the order for the notorious Amritsar massacre on 13 April 1919, **General Reginald Edward Harry Dyer** was born in Murree in the Punjab in 1864, the son of an Irish brewer. He was educated at Midleton College, Co. Cork and then at Sandhurst. 379 people were killed and 1200 wounded in the massacre as Dyer ordered his troops to open fire without warning on about 10,000 angry protesters demonstrating against the arrest of two Indian National Congress leaders. The Governor of the Punjab at the time was the Irish-born Sir Michael O'Dwyer, who was later shot by Undahn Singh, a survivor of the massacre who travelled to England. Singh was captured, tried and hanged at Pentonville Prison in 1939.

❦ **Field-Marshal and Commander-in-Chief of the British Army, Herbert Horatio Kitchener, 1st Earl Kitchener** (1850–1916), was born at Crotter House, Ballylongford, Co. Kerry on 24 June 1850. He was educated in Switzerland and at the Royal Military Academy, Woolwich. He joined the Royal Engineers in 1871 and served in the Near East. In 1898, as Commander-in-Chief of the Egyptian Army, he defeated the Khalifa Abdullah at Omdurman to secure British control of the Sudan, for which he was awarded a peerage. Chief-of-staff and then commander-in-chief during the Boer War 1900–02, he was subsequently made a viscount and received the Order of Merit. He was Commander-in-Chief in India from 1902 to 1909 and was promoted to field-marshal on his return. In 1911 he was appointed the government's Consul General in Egypt. At the outbreak of World War I in 1914 he was appointed Secretary of State for War and mobilised the British Army. He died when HMS *Hampshire* sank off the Orkneys in June 1916.

❦ **The first recipient of the Victoria Cross** was the Irishman **Charles David Lucas**, born in either Clontibret, Co. Monaghan, or Drumargole, Co. Armagh, according to differing accounts. (The VC is awarded for conspicuous bravery and takes precedence over all other decorations in the British Armed Forces.) Lucas joined the Navy in 1848. On 21 June 1854, in one of the first engagements of the Crimean War, he hurled an unexploded Russian shell from the deck of HMS *Hecla* during a bombardment in the Baltic Sea at the entrance to the Gulf of Bothnia. The fact that the shell actually exploded before hitting the water emphasises the bravery of the deed. Lucas received his Victoria Cross on 26 June 1857. He later married the daughter of the captain of HMS *Hecla*. By the time of his death in 1914, Lucas had risen to the position of rear-admiral.

❦ The woman soldier **Christian Davies, also known as 'Kit' Cavanagh or 'Mother Ross'** (1667–1739), was a Dublin-born innkeeper. The story of her life was recorded in her autobiography, published in 1740. At the age of 21 she married one of her barmen, Richard Welsh, who disappeared suddenly after the wedding. A year later she received a letter from him saying that he had been pressed into the army in Flanders. She set out to find him and enlisted in Marlborough's army under the assumed name of Christopher Welsh, later fighting at the Battles of Blenheim and Nijmegen. She was finally reunited with her husband 13 years after their wedding.

Richard Welsh continued in military service for three more years (1702–04) and was accompanied by Christian – as his wife – until he was killed at the Battle of Malplaquet in 1709. Christian then married Hugh Jones, who was mortally wounded in 1710 at the siege of St Venant. She then went to England, where she was presented to Queen Anne, who awarded her a pension of a shilling a day for life. Back in Dublin she married a soldier called Davies and spent 25 years of obscurity and illness on the streets of Dublin, where she died on 7 July 1739.

Although her story has undoubtedly been exaggerated, it is certain that Christian did fight for several years with the Royal Inniskilling Regiment. There are conflicting accounts of when her true sex was discovered. She was injured in several battles, but according to the *Dictionary of National Biography* it was when she received a fractured skull at the Battle of Ramillies in 1706 during the Marlborough campaigns that army surgeons discovered she was a woman. She was discharged automatically, but remained as a companion to her husband and cook to her regiment. When her husband Richard Welsh was fatally injured at Malplaquet in 1709, her uncontrollable grief moved Captain Ross to commiserate with her – whence she gained the soubriquet of 'Mother Ross' which remained with her for life. Other sources claim she was injured and her sex discovered at the Battle of Aughrim in Ireland in 1691.

🍀 Soldier, author and explorer **William Francis Butler** (1838–1910) of Suirville, Co. Tipperary, joined the British Army in 1858 and served in Canada 1867–73, where his experiences with fur trappers and Indians were recounted in *The Great Lone Land* (1872), which went into four editions. He later took part in the Zulu Wars and was a member of the relief expedition sent to rescue General Gordon from the besieging forces of the Mahdi in Khartoum in 1885. He was knighted in 1886 and in 1905 retired with the rank of lieutenant-general to Bansha Castle, Co. Tipperary.

🍀 **Field-Marshal in the British Army and Commander-in-Chief in India and Natal, Sir George Stuart White** (1835–1912) was born in Whitehall, Co. Antrim and educated at Sandhurst. After a slow start to his career, he distinguished himself in campaigns against the Afghans 1870–80, receiving the Victoria Cross. He was appointed Military Secretary to the Viceroy of India and in 1893 was made Commander-in-Chief of all forces. In September 1899 he was sent to Natal following the outbreak of the

Sir Henry Wilson, Chief of the Imperial General Staff from 1918, was elected MP for North Down in 1922. An ardent unionist and friend of British Prime Minister David Lloyd George, he was assassinated outside his London home by two IRA gunmen.

Second Boer War. Besieged by Boer forces at Ladysmith in November 1899, his forces held out for 118 days before relief arrived. White was awarded the Order of Merit in 1905 and served as Governor of Gibraltar and of the Chelsea Hospital, where he died in June 1912.

☘ **Field-Marshal in the British Army and military representative of Britain at the Paris Peace Conference** in 1919, **Sir Henry Wilson** (1864–1922), born at Currygrane, Edgeworthstown (Mostrim), Co. Longford, was educated at Marlborough College and joined the British Army in 1884. After service in South Africa and Burma, he was appointed Commandant of the Camberley Staff College as a brigadier-general. He was Director of Military Operations 1910–14 and, during World War I, formed a close relationship with Lloyd George, who appointed him Chief of the Imperial General Staff in 1918. In this capacity he represented Britain at the Treaty of Versailles, and was further promoted to field-marshal in July 1919. A staunch unionist, he consistently opposed Home Rule for Ireland and advocated repressive measures against the Sinn Féin movement. Wilson left the army in 1922, having been elected Conservative MP for North Down in 1921. Wilson became security adviser to the new state of Northern Ireland. He was shot dead outside his London home by two IRA assassins, Reginald Dunne and Joseph O'Sullivan. Both were ex-British Army war veterans, O'Sullivan having lost a leg at Ypres. Dunne and O'Sullivan were tried, found guilty and executed.

☘ **Field-Marshal in the British Army and Supreme Allied Commander in the Mediterranean (1944–45), Harold Rupert Leofric George Alexander, 1st Earl Alexander of Tunis and Errigal** (1891–1969). The Alexanders were a family of Scottish settlers who had been established in Ireland for several centuries, settling first in Donegal and then in Derry, where they became prominent in the business life of the city. A large family house was built at Boom Hall on the banks of the Foyle to the north of the city. In the 18th century an ancestor made a fortune in India and built Caledon Castle in Co. Tyrone, which became the family seat. James Alexander became the first Earl of Caledon in 1801.

Harold Alexander was born in London and taken home to Caledon a few days later. He was educated at Harrow and Sandhurst and served in the Irish Guards in France in World War I, where he was twice wounded and subsequently received the Military Cross, Legion of Honour and the Russian Order of St Anne. After the war he worked for the Imperial Defence College and also served in India. By the outbreak of World War II he had reached the rank of major-general. He was GOC Southern Command 1940–42, was then promoted to general and sent briefly to Burma. In 1942 he was appointed Commander-in-Chief Middle East and then Commander-in-Chief Eighteenth Army Group in North Africa, where he oversaw the defeat of Rommel. He was Commander of Allied Forces in Italy 1943–44 and then Supreme Allied Commander in the Mediterranean until the end of the war.

In 1946 Alexander was appointed Governor General of Canada (see p. 85). In 1948, at the Ottawa Conference, he offended the visiting Irish Taoiseach, John Costello*, who promptly announced Ireland's withdrawal from the Commonwealth. He returned to Britain in 1952 and served as Minister of Defence under Winston Churchill until 1954.

☘ **Chief-of-staff and Field-Marshal of the British Army, Sir John Dill** (1881–1944) was born in Lurgan, Co. Armagh. Educated at Cheltenham and Sandhurst, he saw service in South Africa and World War I. He rose to become commandant of the British Army Staff College and then Director of Military Operations at the War Office as a lieutenant-general. He was appointed chief-of-staff in April 1940 and as such was the chief military adviser to the British government in the early stages of World War II. He was often in conflict with Churchill and was sent to Washington in 1942 as chief representative of the British military there. Much admired in America, he became a close friend and adviser to President Roosevelt and General Marshall. He died in Washington in 1944 and is buried in Arlington Cemetery.

☘ **Bernard Law Montgomery, 1st Viscount Montgomery of Alamein** (1887–1970), was born in London to an Anglican vicar who shortly afterwards became Bishop of Tasmania. Montgomery came from a family that had settled in Ireland in the 17th century. The family fortune, made from the wine trade in Derry, bought a large estate on the Inishowen penin-

* *At a dinner reception in honour of Costello, Alexander chose a silver replica of 'Roaring Meg' (the cannon used against King James's forces at the Siege of Derry in 1689) as a centrepiece for the table. This powerful symbol of Ulster Unionism provoked Costello into a burst of temper and he formally announced the withdrawal of the 26 counties of southern Ireland from the Commonwealth. Although the repeal of the External Relations Act was planned before the Ottawa incident, it was not a foregone conclusion. The Republic of Ireland Act was passed on 21 December 1948.*

Field-Marshal Alexander (later Lord Alexander of Tunis) as Commander-in-Chief of Allied forces in Italy, 1943–44. The third son of the 4th Earl of Caledon, whose family seat was Caledon Castle, Co. Tyrone, Alexander was one of the most successful British generals of World War II.

sula, called New Park, near Moville, Co. Donegal. It was here that Montgomery's widowed mother spent the years of World War II.

Montgomery entered the Royal Military College, Sandhurst in 1907 as a cadet. In World War I he was wounded while a platoon leader of the Warwickshire Regiment. In 1920 he was posted to Co. Cork as brigade major to 17th Infantry Brigade which was involved in anti-guerrilla warfare against the IRA. At the outset of World War II he commanded the 3rd Infantry Division in the British Expeditionary Force, forming part of II Corps, commanded by another Irish general, Sir Alan Brooke (see p. 100). At the evacuation of Dunkirk he was highly commended for his skill and efficiency. In 1942 he was given command of the 8th Army in Egypt, with Alexander (see p. 98) as his commander-in-chief. On 31 August 1942 Alexander and Montgomery repulsed a combined Italian and German attack led by Rommel at Alam al Halfa. On 23 October Montgomery launched the Second Battle of El Alamein against Rommel's weakened forces

and, after a week of fighting, secured the first major victory of the war for the Allies. Joining with Eisenhower's forces, Montgomery had driven the Germans from North Africa by May 1943. In July 1943 Montgomery's 8th Army invaded Sicily with the US 7th Army under General Patton, and began the assault on the Italian mainland.

Montgomery was then recalled to prepare for the D-Day landings and was given control of all Allied ground forces for the invasion of 6 June 1944. Following the German retreat across France, Eisenhower took over as commander of all Allied ground forces while Montgomery commanded the 21st Army group fighting in Belgium and Holland. Operation Market Garden, involving a parachute assault on the Rhine Bridge at Arnhem, was one of his few military failures. Now a field-marshal, his strategy and influence created tensions between British and American high command. However, during the Battle of the Bulge in 1944, Montgomery saved an American force that had been cut off by a massive German surge. Meanwhile, the remainder of the US Army was able to cross the Rhine, forcing the German surrender in early May 1945.

After World War II Montgomery served as Chief of General Staff (1946–48) and was Deputy Commander of NATO forces 1951–58. As early as 1946 he had suggested the need for a European defensive strategy to counter the Soviet threat. He publicly announced that friendly relations with the Soviets should cease and prompted the British Prime Minister to begin the series of military and political conferences that led directly to the creation of the Western European Union (WEU) and then to NATO. Montgomery published his *Memoirs* in 1958 and *The Path to Leadership* in 1961.

❧ Parliamentary Private Secretary to Winston Churchill and Minister of Information in 1941, Brendan Rendall Bracken, Viscount Bracken (1901–58) was born in Templemore, Co. Offaly, the son of John K. Bracken (a founder-member of the Gaelic Athletic Association). He left school at 15 and went to Australia to work on a sheep station. In 1919 he returned to Ireland, collected his father's legacy and moved to England. He concealed his background by claiming that he was an outright Australian and that both his parents had died in a bush fire. He applied for entrance to Sedbergh public school at the age of 19 (passing himself off as being 16) and paid his own fees for two years.

He moved to London to work as a school teacher and there met J.L. Garvin, editor of the *Manchester Guardian*, who recommended him to Winston Churchill as an election worker. He joined the publishing company Eyre and Spottiswode in 1924 and later succeeded in gaining a directorship in the firm. He bought the *Financial News,* founded the *Banker* and acquired control of *Investors' Chronicle* and *The Practitioner*. From 1928 to 1945 he was managing director of the *Economist*.

Bracken was elected Conservative MP for North Paddington in 1929 and at the outbreak of World War II was appointed Parliamentary Private Secretary to Churchill, becoming one of his closest wartime associates and advisers. As Minister for Information 1941–45 he was popular with the press, who enjoyed his informal approach. After the war he left politics and became chairman of the amalgamated *Financial News* and *Financial Times*. He accepted his viscountcy in 1952.

❧ Field-Marshal and wartime adviser to Winston Churchill during World War II, Alan

William Joyce, American-born Nazi propagandist of Irish parentage. 'Lord Haw-Haw's' sneering upper-class voice became familiar to thousands of homes in Britain and Ireland during World War II.

Francis Brooke, 1st Viscount Alanbrooke was born at Bagnères-de-Bigorre in the French Pyrenees in July 1883. He was the ninth child of Sir Victor Brooke of Colebrook, Co. Fermanagh, and Alice Sophia Bellingham. He entered the Royal Academy at Woolwich at 18 and saw service in Ireland from 1902 and in India from 1906. He fought in the artillery in World War I and was awarded the DSO. He continued his army career after the war, working as an instructor, and advanced to become Director of Military Training at the War Office. Serving in France in 1940, he became critical of both French and British tactics and advised a withdrawal. In 1941, after the evacuation of Dunkirk, he became Chief of the Imperial General Staff. He cooperated closely with the Royal Navy and Royal Air Force and advised Churchill to promote Alexander (see.p. 98) and Montgomery (see p. 98). He worked closely with Churchill, accompanying him to the Allied Conferences at Casablanca, Quebec and Moscow in 1943. In 1944 he was made a field-marshal and the following year became Baron

Alanbrooke of Brookeborough. He retired from the army in 1946 and in 1949 became chancellor of Queen's University, Belfast. He died in Hampshire in 1963.

The Brooke family is one of the best known in Ulster and has a long military tradition. They were granted confiscated land in Donegal during the reign of Queen Elizabeth I. Henry Brooke held Donegal Castle against the rebels during the Great Rebellion of 1641 and was rewarded for his tenacity by 30,000 acres in Co. Fermanagh taken from the executed rebel Concobhar Rua Maguire. The Brookes have featured significantly in British military history since. It was a Brooke who burned down the presidential home in America in 1812. (The rebuilt version, designed by Irish architect James Hoban (see p. 114), had concealed the indelible scorch marks by whitewashing the walls – hence the name of the *White House*.) Over 50 members of the family fought for Britain in the two World Wars and many have been decorated.

❧ First Sea Lord and Commander-in-Chief of the Mediterranean Fleet in World War II was **Admiral Andrew Browne Cunningham** (1883–1963), born in Dublin. Cunningham was the son of a professor of anatomy at Trinity College, Dublin. At an early age he decided to go to sea and was educated at Edinburgh Academy and Stubbington House, Fareham for service in the Royal Navy. He joined up in 1897 and saw service in the Second Boer War and in World War I. He moved steadily through the ranks and, after 42 years of service, was appointed Commander-in-Chief of the Mediterranean Fleet in 1939.

In 1940 Cunningham successfully immobilised the French fleet at Alexandria – thus preventing the Axis from taking the port. He held the Italian Navy at bay with a skeleton fleet of ageing ships and secured the safe passage of Allied convoys. He provided sea cover for the Operation Torch landings in North Africa in November 1942, the invasion of Sicily in July 1943 and the Salerno landings in September 1943. He accepted the surrender of the Italian Admiral Lachino in Malta.

Cunningham was confirmed a full admiral of the fleet and, after the war, became President of the Institute of Naval Architects 1948–51. His leadership was characterised by his independent decision-making and he frequently chose to ignore orders from London. He had a strained relationship with Winston Churchill and considered many of the Prime Minister's judgements impetuous and unwise.

❧ Brendan 'Paddy' Finucane, born in Dublin in 1921, became a British Royal Air Force flying ace in World War II and downed 32 enemy planes, making

him the RAF's fourth most successful pilot ever. He was shot down and killed off the coast of northern France in 1942.

❧ The first in-flight refuelling tests were conducted by **Captain J.C. Kelly-Rogers** (1905–81), who was born in Dún Laoghaire, Co. Dublin. He joined the Royal Naval reserve in 1921 and in 1927 became a pilot in the Royal Air Force. He joined Imperial Airways (later BOAC and now British Airways) in 1935 and in 1938 made the first in-flight refuelling tests, a process which he then used in piloting **the first British transatlantic air-mail flight.** During World War II he commanded the aircraft used by Winston Churchill on his transatlantic flights. He was the chief North Atlantic pilot for BOAC from 1941 and in 1946 set up **the first land-plane service between London and New York**. He joined Aer Lingus, Ireland's national airline, in 1947 and was deputy manager by 1952. He was prominent in founding the Irish Aeronautical Museum, was a Freeman of the City of London and a fellow of the Royal Aeronautical Society. He died in Dublin.

❧ Nazi propagandist and recipient of the *Kriegsverdienstkreutz* **(war service cross) from Adolf Hitler, William Joyce, 'Lord Haw-Haw'** (c. 1906–46) was born in Brooklyn, New York of an Irish father and an English mother. His father, Michael Joyce, was a successful building contractor in New York who returned home to Galway in 1909. William Joyce followed him in 1914 and was educated at St Ignatius' Jesuit College before the family moved to England in 1922. William was profoundly influenced by his father, an ardent anglophile who acted as an informer for the Black and Tans during the War of Independence. Following independence the family were forced to flee to England for fear of reprisals. In London Joyce took first class honours in English and History at Birkbeck College and pursued his cherished ideal of becoming the perfect English gentleman. Having first joined the Conservative Party, he moved to Sir Oswald Mosley's British Union of Fascists (BUF) in 1933. Expelled in 1937, he founded his own National Socialist Party, which supported Hitler. He arrived in Germany in 1939 before the outbreak of the war and from September 1939 until April 1945 broadcasted Nazi propaganda from Radio Hamburg, with the call-sign 'Germany calling, Germany calling'. He earned his nickname from his upper-class British accent and was known in every household in Britain and Ireland. He was captured after the war trying to escape to Denmark and brought to trial in London at the Old Bailey. Captured in the possession of a British passport (probably false), he was convicted of treason and hanged at Wandsworth Prison on 3 January 1946. He is buried in Galway.

🍀 **Lawrence of Arabia, Thomas Edward Lawrence** (1888–1935) was born in Tremadoc, North Wales, where his Irish father, Thomas Robert Chapman, had settled and adopted an assumed name after eloping with the family governess from South Hill, Devlin, Co. Westmeath. A graduate of ancient history at Oxford University, Lawrence was working as an archaeologist in the Middle East at the outbreak of World War I. His knowledge of Arab culture, history and politics made him a natural choice for army intelligence work and he became liaison officer and adviser to King Feisal during the Arab revolt against the Turks. (Lawrence was short of the 5ft 5in height requirement for the regular army.) Britain's promise of Arab independence after the war was not honoured and Lawrence returned to England in disillusionment. He assumed the name of Shaw and joined the Royal Air Force in an attempt to avoid the publicity that followed him after his wartime exploits. Lawrence's own book, *Seven Pillars of Wisdom*, gives a detailed account of the Arab campaign. He wrote with a desire to establish a literary reputation and was honoured by his friend George Bernard Shaw (see p. 137), who invited him to join the Irish Academy of Letters on its foundation in 1932.

🍀 **Political economist John Elliot Cairnes** (1823–75) was born in Castlebellingham, Co. Louth, and graduated from Trinity College, Dublin in 1848. Appointed Whately Professor of Political Economy in 1856, his most celebrated work, published in 1862, *The Slave Power,* was a defence of the Northern states in the American Civil War and was the most influential treatise in moving the British government to support their cause. In 1866 he was appointed professor of political economy at University College London.

🍀 **Colonel Anthony William Durnford** (1830–79), who died with all his troops at the hands of the Zulus at the Battle of Isandhlwana in January 1879, was a native of Manorhamilton, Co. Leitrim. He was educated at the Royal Military Academy at Woolwich and saw service in Ceylon (now Sri Lanka) and Malta before being posted to South Africa. A liberal who opposed the poor treatment of natives by the colonial government, he was widely respected.

FRANCE

🍀 **Mistress to King Louis XV of France, Marie Louise O'Morphi** (1736–1815) was born in Rouen, the daughter of Irish parents. Her father was a shoemaker who died when she was very young, leaving her mother, Margaret Murphy, with five daughters to support. Margaret moved to Paris, changed her name to O'Morphi and encouraged her daughters to attract the attention of wealthy Parisians. None was more successful than Marie Louise. She drew the attentions of the infamous Casanova who, in turn, introduced her to the court painter, François Boucher. Boucher was mesmerised by her beauty and she posed for many of his voluptuous nudes that were highly fashionable at the time. She became mistress to the painter, who called her 'Louison', a name which remained with her. Eventually the king called to meet her and she became the 'Royal Mistress' at 17. As 'maîtresse en titre', she had a marked effect on the king who, uncharacteristically, began to show some of the vivacious and humorous characteristics that were so evident in Marie Louise. Madame de Pompadour, the former favourite of the king, while initially accepting Louison, arranged for her to marry a wealthy and elderly army officer once she felt that the Irish girl had become a threat to her own standing. The elderly officer died in 1757 and Louison married a court official. The king died in 1774 and Louison's second husband in 1790. During the Reign of Terror that followed the Revolution, Louison was imprisoned for two years. She later married a revolutionary called Dumont, 20 years her junior, who divorced her after two years. She had three children by King Louis XV and was separated from each of them at birth. She died in Paris in 1815, living long enough to see Louis XVIII, the grandson of her former lover, returned to the throne.

🍀 **Lieutenant-general in the French army and commander-in-chief of French establishments in the East Indies, Thomas Arthur Lally** (1702–66) was born in Romans in Dauphiné, the son of Sir Gerard Lally, an Irish *émigré* from Tullaghnadaly, Co. Galway. Lally, known as 'Tollendal' (a corruption of Tullaghnadaly) to the French, joined Dillon's Irish Regiment of the French Army at a very early age and rose through the ranks to become a brigadier on the field. In 1756 Louis XV sent him to India to further French interests in the face of continuing British expansion. He was made a lieutenant-general and appointed Commander-in-Chief of all French establishments there. After many delays, he finally arrived in 1758 and began reforming the corrupt operations of the French East India Company.

In his confrontation with the British in India, Lally was defeated by Eyre Coote (see p. 95) of Co. Limerick at the Battle of Wandiwash in January 1760. In 1761 French imperial designs on India came to an end at Pondicherry. Coote said of Lally, who was taken prisoner: 'There is certainly not a second man in all India who could have managed to keep on foot, for so long a period, an army without pay and without any kind of assistance.' Used as a scapegoat when he returned to France, Lally was arrested, thrown in jail without trial for 15 months and finally executed on 9 May 1766. His fate enraged Voltaire and Mme de Pompadour. The corruption demonstrated by the parliament at his trial was a contributory factor in the series of events that led to the French Revolution. The Irish Brigade itself, vitally important to the French Army, was near revolt over the scandal and joined with Voltaire and Lally's son in pleading his case. In 1778 an official pardon was decreed by Louis XVI in council, but it was not until 1929 that the French Army publicly exonerated Lally.

The affair effectively ended Irish recruitment into the French army. Frustrated by nepotism, corruption and the failure of the Stuarts to regain the English throne, many sought careers in the service of other European monarchies.

♣ **President of the Third French Republic, Patrick Maurice, Comte de MacMahon** (1808–93) was the grandson of John Baptist MacMahon who was born in Limerick in 1715 and, as a Catholic, was forced abroad to France to receive his education. John Baptist MacMahon, having heard that an Irishman of the same name had won fame as the principal doctor of the Paris military school, decided to follow that profession. He had two sons, the elder of whom, Charles Laurence, fought with Lafayette for American independence and became a field-marshal of the French Army and a peer of France. The second son, and father of the future President, became a colonel in the famous Hussars of the Guard Regiment in 1789. Although the family were royalist exiles, they befriended republicans and this allowed Patrick to become an acceptable compromise candidate for the presidency in future years.

Patrick MacMahon was one of nine surviving children and graduated from the military school of St Cyr in 1827. By 1830 he was a lieutenant in the 4th Hussars and won the Knight of the Legion award in Algiers in 1831. Rising quickly through the ranks, he became general of brigade with command of the province of Oran in 1848. He was appointed Military Governor of Constantinople in 1852 and three years later was awarded the Grand Cross of the Legion of Honour and appointed a senator of France following his success in the Battle of Sebastopol. In 1858 he was commander of all land and sea forces in Algeria. His dukedom was conferred in 1859 for his victory over the Austrians at the Battle of Magenta. He was finally defeated by the Prussian Army at Sedan in 1870, but was given command of the Army of Versailles in 1871 and defeated the Communards. He was appointed President of the Third Republic in 1873, holding office for six years.

His presidency is remembered, with justification, for its reactionary and monarchical leanings. The highlight of his career was his capture of Malakoff Fort at Sebastopol in the Crimean War. His reply when advised by central command to abandon the fort because the Russians had left it mined – 'J'y suis, j'y reste' ('Here I am and here I stay') – became legendary.

♣ **Confessor to King Louis XVI at his execution, Abbé Henry Essex Edgeworth** (1745–1807) was born in Edgeworthstown, Co. Longford, son of a Protestant rector who was converted to Catholicism while on a visit to Toulouse. Henry Edgeworth was educated at the Sorbonne, ordained a priest and joined the *Seminaire des Missions Etrangers*. He devoted himself to the poor of Paris for ten years before his health began to fail. He ministered to English and Irish residents in Paris and, in 1791, became spiritual director to Elizabeth, sister of Louis XVI. He was called to hear the king's confession before his execution and saw him guillotined in 1793.

Edgeworth fled France and spent some time hiding in England. The then British Prime Minister, William Pitt, offered him a pension and from Ireland came nomination for his presidency of Maynooth. He turned down both and went into the service of Louis XVIII as chaplain to the exiled court at Blankenberg, Brunswick. He was later sent to Tsar Pavel in St Petersburg. The Tsar was deeply impressed by him and awarded him a pension of 500 roubles. Edgeworth contracted fever while ministering to French prisoners of war and died at Mitau in 1807.

♣ **Henry James Clarke** (1765–1818), friend, confidant and **Minister of War to Napoleon Bonaparte**, was born in Landrecies, France to Irish parents from exiled families fighting in Dillon's Irish Brigade.

Clarke was educated at the École Militaire in Paris and commissioned to Berwick's Irish Regiment. When the French Revolution broke out in Paris in 1789, he was working as a diplomat in the French Embassy in London. After spending some time in Ireland visiting relations, he returned to Paris in 1791 to fight in the first of the Revolutionary Wars. In 1795, whilst working in the Ministry of War, he frequently met with the Irish revolutionary Wolfe Tone (see p. 53), who recorded their conversations in his *Diaries*. Clarke was sent to Austria on a secret diplomatic mission in 1797 to assist Napoleon in the drawing up of the Treaty of Campo Formio. In 1804 his services were recognised by the Emperor, who appointed him his Private Secretary for Military Affairs with the rank of general. From 1807 to 1814 he was the Minister of War of the revolutionary government. He was honoured with the titles of Comte d'Huneborg in 1808 and Duc de Feltre in 1809.

In 1815, after Napoleon's defeat and exile to Elba, he was recalled briefly as Minister for War to the restored Bourbon King Louis XVIII.

♣ **A general in Napoleon's revolutionary army, William Lawless** (1772–1824) of Dublin was a surgeon and anatomist who joined the United Irishmen (see p. 53). Outlawed, he fled to France, where was appointed a captain in the Irish Legion in 1803. He was personally decorated with the Legion of Honour after the siege of Flushing in 1806 and promoted to lieutenant-colonel. After the Battle of Lowenberg in August 1813, at which he lost a leg, he

THE STORMING OF THE BASTILLE – 14 JULY 1789

was promoted to general of brigade. On the restoration of the Bourbons in 1814 he was pensioned on half pay with the rank of brigadier-general.

🍀 **Admiral Armand de MacKau (McCoy)** of the French navy was one of only 13 French admirals since the Napoleonic wars. He was a pupil of Macdermott at the Collège Irlandais in St Germain-en-Laye and was a regular visitor to his cousins in Ireland.

As Minister for the Marine 1843–47 he modernised French state dockyards and the ships of the military and mercantile marine. More than anyone else, he was responsible for changing the French navy from sail to steam power. He improved the pay and working conditions of French sailors and introduced the first legislative steps towards the abolition of slavery in the French Empire. In 1847 de MacKau was made a full admiral and in 1849 his modernising drive was realised when he commissioned France's first steam-powered naval frigate, *Pomone*. In 1851 he was made a senator and a member of the Admiralty Council.

MacKau was a close friend of Jerome Bonaparte* (1784–1860), brother of Napoleon, the two having met as schoolmates at the Collège Irlandais.

* *In 1803 Jerome Bonaparte married Elizabeth Patterson, daughter of William Patterson of Fanad, Co. Donegal, who had emigrated to Phildelphia in 1760 and made his fortune by supplying ammunition and provisions to the American revolutionary army. The marriage was annulled by Napoleon, who later had Jerome married to a German princess.*

🍀 **The leader of the storming of the Bastille**, 14 July 1789, was **James Bartholomew Blackwell** (1763–1820), a native of Ennis, Co. Clare. Leaving Ireland at the age of 11, he was sent to the Irish College in Paris to seek the education denied him at home under the Penal Laws. He studied medicine at the University of Paris and later became a lieutenant in the regiment of Hussars. He made friends with the revolutionaries Danton and Desmoulins and was chosen as leader of the Faubourg St Antoine to lead the attack on the Bastille. He fought in the early revolutionary campaigns before sailing to Bantry Bay in Co. Cork in December 1796 with Wolfe Tone and General Hoche in an ill-fated attempt to liberate Ireland (see p. 53). He tried again with Napper Tandy in 1798, was caught by the British, and sent to Kilmainham Gaol in Dublin for two years, where he was denied prisoner-of-war status.

On his return to France Blackwell was appointed *Chef de Bataillon* of the Irish Legion and fought with Napoleon in the Prussian and Austrian campaigns. Blackwell received many wounds in battle and retired as colonel and commandant of the town of Bitche in Lorraine. He died in Paris in 1820 and is buried in the cemetery of Père Lachaise.

🍀 Another man of Irish descent involved in the taking of the Bastille was **Joseph Kavanagh**, a bootmaker from Lille who came from a Co. Clare family. His exploits are recorded in a pamphlet, *Exploits glorieux du célèbre Cavanagh. Cause première de la liberté française.* On 14 July 1789 he was prominent in the huge crowd that stormed Les Invalides in search of weapons and is recorded as having commandeered a carriage and drove through the streets of Paris with two companions shouting 'To the Bastille! Let's take the Bastille'.

Kavanagh was appointed a police inspector in Paris in 1791 and took an active role in the Reign of Terror. He was closely involved with the investigation into the death of Marat and it was he who searched the hotel room of the assassin Charlotte Corday. He disappeared after the fall of Robespierre and seems to have avoided capture.

🍀 When the crowd finally reached the Bastille on 14 July, there were only seven inmates. However, one of the prison chaplains was a Clonfert priest, **Thomas MacMahon**, from Eyrecourt, Co. Galway, then 70 years old. The most famous prisoner, the Marquis de Sade, had been removed to an asylum in Charenton just two weeks before, but during his stay he had been accompanied by **Comte Whyte de Malleville**. Whyte was, in fact, a 60-year old Dubliner and former officer in the Irish Regiment. He had been committed to Vincennes after being declared insane, and transferred to the Bastille in 1784 with the Marquis de Sade. He later followed the Marquis to Charenton.

Meanwhile, at La Force prison, the mob had succeeded in liberating **Clotworthy Skeffington, 2nd Earl of Massereene** (1742–1805), who was born in Co. Antrim. In 1765, whilst on a visit to France, Skeffington was caught cheating at cards (or, according to another version, tricked into signing bonds for large amounts) and thrown into a debtor's prison for 20 years.

❦ **General Cluseret** (1823–1900), French-born soldier of fortune, reversed the normal pattern of military service and was commissioned by the Irish revolutionary movement, the Fenians, to become commander-in-chief of the Fenian army. Cluseret was a veteran of the Crimean War who had been awarded the Legion of Honour in 1855. He fought with Garibaldi in Sicily and then joined the Confederates in the American Civil War. He accepted an invitation by James Stephens, founder of the Fenian movement, to take command of the Fenian army on the condition that it would number 10,000. He travelled in England using documents provided by the Fenians that allowed him to inspect Woolwich Arsenal and Aldershot. He returned to France, however, when the rising was launched prematurely in Kerry in March 1867.

❦ **Charles de Gaulle's** (1890–1970) maternal ancestors were the MacCartan family of Donegal who left Ireland c. 1690–91 after the Williamite victory over the armies of James II in Ireland. They settled in France where they were employed by the French Army. De Gaulle was President of France 1958–69.

RUSSIA

❦ **Governor of Livonia (Latvia) and field-marshal in the Russian army, Count Peter Lacy** (1678–1751) or 'Russian Peter' was born in Killedy, Co. Limerick and served as an ensign in the defence of Limerick against the forces of William III when he was only 13 years old. After the Treaty of Limerick in 1691, he left Ireland and joined the Irish Brigade in the French Army. His father, who had been a field-marshal and king's bodyguard in the service of Austria, and his two brothers had died before him, fighting in the Irish Brigade. Lacy fought in Italy with the brigade until its disbandment in 1696 following the Treaty of Ryswick. He travelled to Russia and entered the service of Peter the Great, who placed him in command of the Grand Musketeers, a hundred Russian nobles armed and horsed at their own expense. In 1708 he was appointed colonel and served with distinction in the Northern War against Sweden. He continued in service throughout wars with the Danes, Swedes and Turks between 1709 and 1721. In 1728 he was made a general and became governor of Livonia. He led an expedition of 30,000 men to establish Augustus of Saxony on the Polish throne, entering Warsaw in triumph in 1735.

He was a favourite of the Russian Tsarina Catherine (and almost certainly one of her many secret lovers) and later of the Tsarina Anna. He received many awards and marks of favour and was promoted to field-marshal in 1736. He retired to his estates in Latvia in 1743 and died there in May 1751. He is considered one of Russia's most successful generals.

❦ **John Delap** of Kerry joined the Russian Navy in 1714 and was a lieutenant on board the flagship of Peter the Great, *Ekaterina*. In 1719 he served as a captain in the war against Sweden.

❦ **Governor of Livonia (Latvia) and Russian field-marshal, Count George de Browne** (1698–1792) was born in Camas, Co. Limerick and educated at the Limerick diocesan school. A Catholic and a Jacobite, he had to leave Ireland to pursue his career and served under the Elector Palatine before joining the Russian army in 1730. He won fame and promotion for his service in the wars against Poland, France and the Turks and rose through the ranks to become a general. At one point he was captured and imprisoned by the Turks and sold as a slave. His freedom was eventually secured by the intervention of the French ambassador to Constantinople, but as a slave he had discovered important state secrets which he was able to bring back to St Petersburg. The Tsarina Anna rewarded his service by making him a major-general under his compatriot Count Lacy (see above). After further service in the Seven Years War (1756–63), he was named field-marshal by Peter III. He was put in charge of the Russian forces during the Danish war, but argued that it was an ill-advised campaign, thereby angering the Tsar, who stripped him of his rank and ordered him into exile. The Tsar later backed down and appointed him Governor of Livonia, where he ruled with ability until his death in February 1792.

❦ **Commander-in-chief of Russia's Baltic fleet**, Irishman **Commodore Cronin** (c. 1752–1841; called 'Crown') was appointed in 1812 when Napoleon invaded Russia. He was entrusted with this position following his achievements during the Russo-Swedish War of 1788–90, when he came very close to capturing the Swedish king, Gustavus III.

His son, Admiral Cronin Jnr, corresponded with the Fenian leader John Devoy in the US during the Balkan Crisis 1877–78. They discussed the possibility of landing a Russian force in western Ireland should Anglo-Russian hostility have erupted into full warfare. (Devoy was simultaneously negotiating a possible alliance with the Emperor of Ethiopia.) At this time the Fenians were also financing the development of John Philip Holland's submarine (see p. 9).

♣ It has been claimed that an Irishman, **David Butler**, was the founder of the Russian Navy. This is not entirely true, but it is worth noting that when the shipmaster Brandt built the *Orel* – the first Russian warship of any significance – for Tsar Alexis (who reigned from 1645 to 1676), David Butler was given its command. Butler is recorded as being an Irishman with a history of service in the British Navy. His place of birth is unknown.

♣ **Ivan Beshoff**, a survivor of the 1905 mutiny on the battleship *Potemkin*, settled in Dublin and opened a fish and chip shop. Beshoff's is still in business today. Ivan Beshoff died in 1987 at the age of 104.

SWEDEN

♣ The *Svenska Adelns Attartaflor* – ('Genealogies of the Swedish Nobility'), describe **Hugo Hamilton** (d. 1679), commander in the Swedish army, as the second son of Malcolm Hamilton, Archbishop of Cashel and Emly, a second-generation settler whose family originated in Lanarkshire, Scotland. Hugo Hamilton was sent to Sweden in 1624 and rose through the ranks of the army. He was ennobled as Baron Hamilton de Deserf. In 1662 he returned to Ireland after the restoration of Charles II. The king made him Baron Hamilton of Glenawley, Co. Fermanagh and he took up his father's estate nearby in Ballygawley, Co. Tyrone.

♣ **Malcolm Hamilton** (1635–99), born in Ballygawley, Co. Tyrone, joined his uncle Hugo in Sweden in 1654 and served in the lifeguards of Queen Christina. He was naturalised in 1664 and in 1693 was ennobled with his younger brother, Hugh, as Barons Hamilton de Hageby. Malcolm Hamilton also rose through the ranks of the Swedish Army to become a major-general and Governor of Wester-Norland in 1698. He died in Stockholm and is buried in Gothenburg.

♣ **Hugh Hamilton** (d. 1724) was the younger brother of Malcolm and joined him in Sweden in 1680. Hugh Hamilton's career in the Swedish Army was the most distinguished of his family. He was decorated for service in the wars of Charles XII against the Danes in 1710 at Helsingburg and against the Russians in 1719 at Gefle. He became a general and Master of the Ordnance. Hugh Hamilton died in the province of Jonkoping and is buried there. He had married Lady Ardvisson of Gothenburg and they had numerous children. Their sixth son, Gustavus David, created Count Hamilton in 1751, attained distinction in the Seven Years War and became a field-marshal. The present-day Swedish Counts Hamilton are direct descendants of their Co. Tyrone forebears.

GERMANY AND THE AUSTRO-HUNGARIAN EMPIRE

The extent of Irish involvement in the Austrian Army in the 18th century in particular can be seen in the Austrian annual register of 17 March 1766. Count O'Mahony, ambassador from Spain to the Austrian court, gave a banquet in honour of St Patrick. Among the guests invited that evening were Count Lacy – President of the Council of War – generals O'Donnell, McGuire, O'Kelly, Browne, Plunkett and McEligot, and a host of the counsellors, governors and officers from Ireland who were in the service of the Austrian Empire.

♣ **Austrian field-marshal, Count Lavall Nugent** (1777–1862) of Ballincor, Co. Wicklow, joined the Austrian engineer corps as a cadet in 1793 and had become a captain by 1799. He distinguished himself in the Napoleonic Wars at the Battle of Monte Croce (1800) and the Battle of Caldiero (1805). After several years out of commission, he was re-engaged into the Austrian army in 1813, shortly before war was declared on France. Nugent defeated the French in a series of battles in Italy and commanded the Austrian troops in Naples in 1816. Pope Pius VII made him a prince of the Holy Roman Empire and in 1826 he became a magnate of Hungary with a hereditary seat in the upper house of the Hungarian diet. He was appointed field-marshal in 1849 and continued to volunteer his service. In 1859, at the age of 82, he was present at the Battle of Solferino. He died at Bosiljero, near Karlstadt (Karlovac), in August 1862.

♣ **Austrian field-marshal and military and civil governor of Dalmatia and Albania, Baron Thomas von Brady** (c. 1752–1827), born in Cavan (probably at Cootehill), joined the Austrian Army in 1769. He moved steadily through the ranks, distinguishing himself in battle as a lieutenant, and in 1788 received the Maria Theresa Cross for personal bravery during the Turkish War. (He was reputed to be a lover of the Empress Maria Theresa.) In 1796 he was promoted to major-general and commanded the Austrian Army in Italy at the Battle of Cattaro in 1799. He was appointed Governor of Dalmatia in 1804 and in

1807 made a privy councillor in recognition of his services as a general of division in Bohemia. In 1809 a large part of the Austrian Army was under his command at the Battle of Aspern-Essling. He retired as a general on full pay in that same year.

♣ **Austrian field-marshal, town commandant of Prague and commanding general in Bohemia, Marshal Maximilian Ulysses Von Browne**, commander of the O'Neillan Regiment (previously O'Nolan – an Irish family that intermarried with the Brownes while both were in the service of Austria), was the Austrian-born son of an Irish Jacobite who owned Clongowes Wood in Co. Kildare. A general in 1751 and a field-marshal in 1754, he was a recipient of the Order of the White Eagle in Poland and a member of the Order of the Golden Fleece.

♣ **The founder of the imperial navy of the Austro-Hungarian Empire** in the Adriatic was **George Forbes**, from Granard, Co. Longford, whose services were lent by King George I to the Emperor Charles VI in 1719. With an expertise that was obviously apparent to Britain's admiralty, Forbes assembled and armed a flotilla at Trieste that was designed to combat piracy and to protect Austrian trade. Forbes was **the first Commander-in-Chief of the Austrian Navy** and rose to the rank of vice-admiral in 1736. The naval force he established lasted 198 years, until the end of World War I, when Austrian access to the sea was lost at the Treaty of Versailles. During that time many Irishmen served in all ranks of the Austrian Navy. John Forbes, the son of George, was a commander in the British Navy in 1781. His daughter married the brother of the Duke of Wellington.

♣ **Nicholas Taaffe** (1677–1769), born at O'Crean's Castle, Co. Sligo, the sixth Viscount Taaffe, was educated in Lorraine and joined the Austrian Army, in which he rose to the rank of lieutenant-general by 1752. His Irish estates were sold under an act of British parliament to a Protestant claimant and he received only one third of their value. Making his estate in Austria his home, **he introduced the potato to Silesia**. He served the Austrian Army with distinction at the Battle of Kolin in 1757.

♣ **Alfred Ritter von Barry**, born in 1830 to an Irish family, was commissioned by the Austrian emperor and fought in **the last naval battle between squadrons of wooden battleships** at Heligoland in 1864, in the German–Danish war, where he distinguished

himself by saving the emperor's flagship. Two years later, he was at the Second Battle of Vis as captain of the *Prinz Eugen*. This was **the first naval battle between two fleets of ironclads**. Alfred Barry became an admiral of the Austrian Navy.

Alfred's brother, **Captain Richard Barry**, was born in Ireland. Napoleon III charged him with the task of escorting Archduke Ferdinand Maximilian and his wife to Vera Cruz, Mexico, to become emperor and empress of that country.

Alfred Barry's son, **Richard Barry Jr**, born in Austria, was one of the leaders of the Austrian Arctic expedition that discovered and named the previously unknown island north of Siberia, which they named Franz Josef Land after the then Austrian emperor.

♣ **The most decorated Austrian of World War I and the last recipient of the exclusive Order of Maria Theresa**, **Gottfried von Banfield**, born in 1890 in Hercegnovi, Crna Gora (previously Yugoslavia), was of a famous Irish-Austrian military family. Gottfried was the grandson of an *émigré* soldier from Castle Lyons, Co. Cork on one side of the family and a fifth-generation descendant of a Clonmel, Co. Tipperary family on the other.

Von Banfield was a pioneer of the Austrian Air Force. In 1912, while serving in the navy, he became aware of the importance that aircraft would have in future naval conflicts. He took flying lessons and later undertook numerous scouting and offensive missions during World War I. His skill as a pilot was such that the Austrian emperor bestowed upon him every medal there was and then invented a new one to give him: the Gold Cross. Von Banfield lived in Trieste in what is now Italy. He was particularly proud of his Irish background and made a visit to Dublin in 1984 as an honorary guest.

♣ **'Lola Montez, the Spanish Dancer'** belongs in many categories and to many countries. She was born **Marie Dolores Eliza Rosanna Gilbert** in Limerick in 1818 and was educated in Montrose, Scotland and Paris. At 19 she eloped to Ireland with a Captain Thomas James in order to avoid an arranged marriage with a gout-ridden judge, but was divorced within five years. She trained in dancing for a short time, making her debut in London in 1843 as 'Lola Montez, the Spanish Dancer'. Despite her lack of dancing skills, she was employed to perform in Dresden, Berlin, St Petersburg and Paris. While in Paris, she had an affair with a newspaper editor, Dujarrier, who was killed in a duel shortly afterwards. In 1847 she danced in Munich, where the mad king of Bavaria,

Ludwig I, and the Hungarian composer Franz Liszt fell in love with her. Ludwig made her Comtesse de Lansfield and gave her a pension of 20,000 florins. He then built her a magnificent castle.

King Ludwig being insane, Lola Montez became the effective ruler of Bavaria. Her reign did not last long, however. Her liberal reforms alarmed the rich and powerful and an insurrection to get rid of her and Ludwig was successfully organised in 1848. She was forced to move on again (before her Bavarian castle was fully complete). She went to Australia, where she publicly horsewhipped the editor of the *Ballarat Times* for libellous accusations against her character. In 1849 she married an Australian, Lieutenant Heald who died within two years. She moved once more in 1851, this time to the USA, where she married her third husband, P.P. Hull, in San Francisco in 1853. This marriage ended in divorce and in 1859 she settled in New York to devote herself to the care of the inmates of the Magdalen Asylum. She had supported herself in Australia and the United States by giving lecture tours on such diverse topics as 'heroines of history' and 'the secrets of beauty'.

She died in Asteria, New York in January 1861 and is buried in Brooklyn's fashionable Greenwood Cemetery. She was hailed as the 'toast of three continents' and was the most popular entertainer of her day. Ireland's claim is the strongest, but she could have belonged to many countries: born in Ireland, her father was an English soldier; she was educated in Scotland and then France; she was a Comtesse and effective ruler of Bavaria; she married an Australian and then an American, becoming a naturalised citizen of the USA. Although she was known as 'the Spanish Dancer', Spain was, in fact, one of the few countries she did not have any known connection with.

GREECE

✤ **'The Liberator of Greece', Sir Richard Church** (1784–1873), was born in Co. Cork, the son of a Quaker merchant. He ran away from home to join the British Army and saw active service in Egypt and Italy. Whilst on an expedition to the Ionian Islands, he met Greek leaders in exile and grew sympathetic to their cause. Following the end of the Napoleonic Wars, he pleaded the case for Greek independence in London and at the Congress of Vienna in 1815, but to no avail. He entered the service of the Neapolitan government in 1816, but in 1820, as Commander-in-Chief in Sicily, he was expelled by revolutionaries. He was invited to join the leaders of the Greek Revolution

in 1821 and was appointed Commander-in-Chief of the campaign against Turkish rule in western Greece during the Greek War of Independence (1821–32). He became a Greek citizen, a member of the Council of State and Inspector-General of the army. He died in Athens in March 1873.

AUSTRALIA

Irish-Australian PMs

✤ **James Henry Scullin** (1876?–1953), Labor Prime Minister of Australia 1929–31, was born near Ballarat, Victoria, the son of an Irish railway worker. He left school at an early age and was educated at evening classes, where he won prizes as a debater. He joined the Labor Party in 1903 and was elected to the House of Representatives as a member for Corangamite in 1910. He became leader of the Labor Party in 1928 and Prime Minister in 1929 at the height of the Depression. His leadership was brief and he was put out of government in 1931. He remained leader of the Labor Party until 1935, when illness forced him to resign. He was a close adviser to his successor, John Curtin (see below), during World War II.

✤ **Joseph A. Lyons** (1879–1939) succeeded James Scullin and lasted in office until 1939. Born near Stanley, Tasmania of an Irish farming family, he worked as a teacher and entered politics as the Labor member for Wilmot in the Tasmanian House of Assembly. He was leader of the party from 1916 and between 1923 and 1928 was premier of Tasmania. He joined the Australian House of Representatives in 1929, but resigned from cabinet over financial policy in 1931 and founded his own political party, the United Australia Party. He became Prime Minister in the same year following the Labor Party's electoral defeat and remained in office until 1939.

His wife, Dame Enid Lyons, was **the first woman member of the Australian House of Representatives** and of the federal cabinet.

✤ **John Joseph Ambrose Curtin** (1885–1945) was Prime Minister for most of World War II. Born in Creswick, Victoria, the son of an immigrant from Cork who worked as a police sergeant, Curtin left school at 13 and worked in a Melbourne printing office. He became active in trade union organisation and campaigned against conscription in World War I, in common with most of his Irish-Australian compatriots. He first entered the federal parliament in

1928 as the member for Fremantle. He lost his seat in 1931, but was re-elected in 1934. In 1935 he became leader of the Australian Labor Party and led it for six years in opposition. As Prime Minister in 1941, he mobilised Australian resources to resist Japanese invasion. He invited General Douglas MacArthur to use Australia as a base for fighting Japan. Curtin laid the groundwork for Australia's post-war economy and introduced social welfare benefits such as those for unemployment and sickness and widows' allowances. He died in office in 1945.

🍀 **Joseph Benedict Chifley** (1885–1951) was born in Bathurst, New South Wales. A close colleague of John Curtin (see above), he was a member of the House of Representatives and treasurer and minister for post-war reconstruction in the war cabinet during World War II. He took over from Curtin following Curtin's death in 1945 and served as Prime Minister until 1949. As Prime Minister, he continued the Labor Party's nationalisation and welfare programmes. He

is also remembered for initiating the post-war immigration policy and the Snowy Mountains hydroelectric scheme. He died in opposition in 1951 and is commemorated by a plaque in Thurles, Co. Tipperary, from where his paternal grandfather emigrated in 1845. (Chifley's mother, Mary-Anne Corrigan, was Irish born and emigrated to Australia as a child.)

🍀 **Paul Keating, Prime Minister of Australia** (1991–), visited his ancestral home in Tynagh, Co. Galway on his state visit to Ireland in September 1993. Parish registers clearly record the movements of his Galway forebears, John and Mary Keating (née Larkin), who left their small farm for Australia and arrived in Sydney Cove on 29 July 1855 after a voyage of six months on board the *Mangerton*, a ship carrying 305 emigrants from Ireland to Sydney on that voyage. The Keatings brought their eight children with them, amongst whom was the future prime minister's great-grandfather, Matthew, then 16 years old.

Wartime Australian PM John Curtin (right) with General Douglas MacArthur, 5 June 1942. The son of an immigrant from Co. Cork, Curtin was a robust supporter of the Allied struggle against Fascism who mobilised Australian resources to resist Japanese invasion in World War II.

Paul Keating grew up in Bankstown, west Sydney, an Irish and Labor Party stronghold. His vision of an Australian republic by the turn of the century – a direct inheritance of his Irish-Australian background – seems likely to be achieved, as Australians re-orientate themselves toward new regions of diplomatic, cultural and commercial influence in Asia.

NEW ZEALAND

Irish-New Zealand PMs

🍀 **John Ballance** (1839–93), born in Glenavy, Co. Antrim and apprenticed to an ironmonger in Belfast at 14, emigrated to New Zealand and set up a shop in Wanganui before turning to journalism and founding the *Wanganui Herald*. He entered the House of Representatives in 1875 and joined the Liberal Party. He was Minister of Lands and Native Affairs 1884–87 and leader of the opposition in 1889. He became Prime Minister in 1891 but died in office in 1893. Ballance made major tax and land ownership reforms and was instrumental in introducing women's suffrage in New Zealand in 1893, making it **the first country in the world to have universal suffrage**.

🍀 **William Ferguson Massey** (1856–1925) was born in Limavady, Co. Derry, the son of a local farming couple who emigrated to New Zealand in 1862. Massey followed his parents in 1870 and took up farming near Auckland. In 1894 he won a seat in the conservative interest in the House of Representatives, as a member for Waitemata. He was chief opposition whip 1895–1903 and then leader of the opposition, which in 1904 renamed itself the Reform Party. In July 1912 he became Prime Minister and held office for 13 years. He formed a national government in 1915 and led the country through World War I. He became **the only premier in the world to retain office before, during and after World War I**. He was a firm supporter of the British Empire and pledged New Zealand's loyalty during the war. He was a plenipotentiary to the Paris Peace Conference in 1919 and a signatory of the Treaty of Versailles.

🍀 **Michael Joseph Savage** (1872–1940), **the first Labour Prime Minister of New Zealand** (1935–40), was born in Victoria, Australia of Irish parents. He moved to New Zealand in 1907 and became active in the trade union movement in Auckland. Joining the Labour Party on its formation in 1916, he was elected National Secretary in 1919. He was elected as repre-

Brendan Bolger, Prime Minister of New Zealand from 1980. His parents emigrated from Co. Wexford in 1930. In October 1990 Bolger led the conservative National Party to the biggest electoral victory in New Zealand's history.

sentative of Auckland West in 1919 and in 1923 became deputy leader of the parliamentary party. In 1933 he took over party leadership following the death of Henry Holland. In 1935 Labour won the general election with ease and Savage was Prime Minister until his death in 1940. His term was marked by far-reaching social security legislation and humanitarian politics, which he called 'applied Christianity'.

🍀 **The current President of New Zealand, James Brendan Bolger** (1935–), is the son of Dan and Cecilia Bolger (née Doyle) who left their homes near Gorey, Co. Wexford on the day they were married in 1930 and settled in Taranaki on New Zealand's North Island to farm.

Prime Minister since October 1990 as head of the conservative National Party, Bolger typifies the new breed of conservatives who have abandoned the protectionist and colonial outlook and have embraced the free market. His 1990 election victory saw a 10% swing against the Labour Party, the biggest political change in New Zealand in 55 years. His policies are anti-union and pro-privatisation. Considered by New Zealanders to be an 'ordinary bloke', he is in many ways an antipodean equivalent of British premier John Major.

Bolger is a contributor to the International Fund for Ireland and a regular visitor to his cousins in Wexford and Dublin. He paid his first visit to Ireland as Prime Minister in February 1993.

♣ **The 'Pakeha Maori', Frederick Edward Maning** (1812–83), born in Johnville, Co. Dublin, was brought to Van Diemen's Land (Tasmania) when his parents decided to emigrate in 1824. In 1833 he set off in a trading schooner for New Zealand, not then a British colony, in search of adventure. He was made welcome by the Maoris and in turn embraced their culture and way of life. He was installed as *Pakeha Maori* ('naturalised stranger'), settled in Onaki and married a Maori. In 1865 he became a judge in the courts established under British rule to settle land titles. He published two books: *Old New Zealand,* a record of Maori life, and *The History of the War in the North with Heke* in 1845.

♣ **Captain William Hobson** (1793–1872), born in Waterford, was **Britain's first Consul and Governor of New Zealand.** In 1840 he secured the Treaty of Waitangi, by which the Maoris ceded their lands to Queen Victoria in return for British protection.

Hobson began his career in the British Navy in 1803 and was captain of the *Rattlesnake* in 1834. The following year he was sent to India and in 1836 visited Australia and New Zealand. In 1839 his leadership qualities and knowledge of the area were considered sufficient to appoint him governor of New Zealand. Despite his incorporating their homeland into the British Empire under the terms of the Treaty of Waitangi, Hobson was revered by the Maoris, who recognised that his rule in the new colony was applied with justice.

♣ **Wellington**, the capital of New Zealand and the site of the first permanent European settlement in 1840, is named after the Dublin-born soldier and Prime Minister of Great Britain (see p. 93).

CHINA

♣ **Head of the Chinese imperial maritime customs, Sir Robert Hart** (1835–1911) was born in Portadown, Co. Armagh. He was educated at the Wesleyan School in Taunton, Somerset, England, the Wesleyan Connexional School in Dublin and then at Queen's University, Belfast, from where he was appointed to the British diplomatic service in 1854 and sent to China.

He quickly rose to head the imperial maritime customs service and in this capacity proposed the founding of the Anglo-Chinese imperial navy. The new fleet included eight steamships but was highly ineffective from the start. However, Chinese officials working in the new force were quick to realise the potential of a modern navy and began to set up an infrastructure suitable for 20th-century shipbuilding.

In 1866 Hart returned briefly to Ireland, and was accompanied as far as Paris by **the first Chinese diplomats in Europe**. In 1896, after a career of service in customs, he founded the Imperial Chinese Post Office. Hart had a greater respect for the Confucian ethics of the Chinese than most of his fellow-imperialists and was awarded the highest decoration ever bestowed on a foreigner, the Ancestral Rank of the First Class of the First Order for three generations. He was commemorated by a public statue in Shanghai that did not survive the Cultural Revolution. He was given the freedom of the cities of London and Belfast. He died in September 1911 and is buried under a Celtic cross in Bisham, Buckinghamshire.

♣ During the Sino-Japanese War of 1894–95, a native of Waterford by the name of **Mellows** was in command of one of the Taku ports controlling the entrance to the harbour in Tianiin (Tientsin) – the port of Peking. Mellows served in the Chinese Navy until his death in 1927 or 1928.

THAILAND

♣ **Michael Deasy**, born in West Cork in the mid-19th century, the son of the coastguard at Old Kinsale Head, left the British Navy complaining that his religion and background denied him the opportunity of promotion, despite his skills. He went to the Far East and eventually became a lieutenant in the Siamese navy. At the end of his career he was the harbour master of Bombay in India.

ISRAEL

🍀 **President of Israel** (1983–93), **Chaim Herzog** was born near the Cliftonville Road in Belfast in 1918. The family moved to Dublin when Dr Helevi Herzog was appointed Irish Chief Rabbi and they settled in Dublin's Jewish district of Portobello, when Chaim was nine months old. Chaim was educated at Wesley College, Dublin before moving to Palestine in 1935, where he studied for two years at a 'yeshiva' in Jerusalem. He then moved to England, where he studied at Cambridge and London universities, and was called to the bar. In 1939 he joined the British Army, graduated from the Royal Military Academy, Sandhurst and served with distinction in northwest Europe in World War II. He was among the first Allied troops to cross the Rhine and among the captors of Himmler, head of the Nazi SS. He was a personal representative of field-marshal Montgomery (see p. 98) to the first displaced persons conference at Bergen Belsen at the end of the war.

Discharged from the army in 1947, he returned to Palestine to rejoin the Jewish underground militia, *Hagana*. He was appointed Head of Intelligence Department of General Staff of the Israeli Defence Force when it was formed in 1948. He later served as Defence Attaché to Washington for the IDF 1948–50 and 1959-62. He was the first Military Governor of the West Bank. He retired from the army as a major-general. In 1975 Herzog was sent to Washington as Ambassador for Israel, but resigned three years later to rejoin his law practice and join the leadership of the Labour Party. He entered the *Knesset* (parliament) in 1981 and was elected President of Israel in March 1983. He returned to Ireland on a controversial state visit in June 1985. Speaking with a marked Dublin accent, he was the source of much pride and amusement to the local populace.

Chaim Herzog, President of Israel (1983–93), born in Belfast and raised in Dublin. He was Head of Intelligence in the Israeli Defence Forces, Military Attaché to Washington and first Military Governor of the West Bank.

INDIA

🍀 **'The Rajah from Tipperary', George Thomas** (1756–1802) was born on a small farm near Roscrea, Co. Tipperary. He joined the British Navy, but deserted in 1781 from a man-of-war at Madras and became a mercenary in the service of the Nizam of Hyderabad. In 1787 he went to Delhi and entered the service of the Begum Sumru of Sirdhana, who appointed him as commander of her army. He lost favour with the Begum in 1792 and transferred to the service of Appa Rao, the Maratha governor of Meerut. When the Appa Rao died in 1797, Thomas seized power and made himself rajah of a vast territory. He founded a mint and a gun factory and extended his territory with frequent raids.

He proposed to the British government that he conquer the Punjab for them. Recognising his military might, the Sikhs who had been dispossessed by him sought French aid and finally deposed him in 1802. He was escorted to the British frontier, intending to return to Ireland, but died of fever at Baharampur in August 1802 and was buried there at the military cemetery.

🍀 **William Tone** (1764–1802), brother of **Theobald Wolfe Tone** (see p. 53), joined the British East India Company and travelled to India. There he joined the army of the Nizam of Hyderabad, George Thomas (see above), although it is not known if the two ever met. Tone died in 1802, fighting as a mercenary in the army of Holkar.

the arts

ARCHITECTURE

Architects

✿ **Developer of the skyscraper and 'the father of American modernism', Louis Sullivan** (1856–1924) was born in Boston, the son of an immigrant from Co. Cork and a Swiss mother. He revolutionised American architecture and transformed the face of US cities with designs that adapted to modern materials and confined space. Classical tradition was abandoned for buildings 'whose form followed their function'. Sullivan's work was an inspiration to Frank Lloyd Wright, who trained under him up to 1893. The buildings that made his name were the Chicago Auditorium and Gage Buildings in 1889. Other major works include the Transportation Building for the World's Columbian Exposition (1892–3) and the Schlessinger Department Store, Chicago (1904).

✿ **Architect of the TWA Terminal at John F. Kennedy Airport**, New York, **Kevin Roche** (1922–) was born in Dublin, where he worked with Michael Scott before emigrating to the USA in 1948. He has worked on over 50 major commissions, including the CBS Headquarters, the United Nations Plaza and the Ford Foundation Building in Manhattan. The American Wing of the Metropolitan Museum and the Oakland Museum in California are also his creations. He is one of the USA's leading architects and was awarded the Pritziker Prize in 1982 and the Gold Medal from the American Institute of Architects in 1993.

✿ **Peter Rice** (1935–92) was an architectural engineer from Belfast. He graduated from Queen's University and Imperial College, London and was employed by Ave Orup. He was sent to Australia, where he drew plans to raise the roof of the Sydney Opera House. He worked on many prominent contracts including the Pompidou Centre in Paris, Kansai International Airport in Japan, the new pavilion at Stansted Airport, Essex, England, the Lloyd's Build-

ing in the City of London and the Expo Pavilion for Seville in 1992. Rice was director of Arup's in London and ran a private practice in Paris. He was awarded the Royal Gold Medal for Architecture.

✿ Winner of the Royal Gold Medal of the Royal Institute of British Architects (1975), **Michael Scott** (1905–) is the leading figure of Irish modernism. The Gold Medal is considered the highest architectural award in the world and Scott shares his distinction with Walter Gropius, Frank Lloyd Wright, Le Corbusier and Mies van der Rohe. Born in Drogheda, Co. Louth, he was educated at the Dublin School of Art and the Abbey School of Acting. He worked in a private practice 1928–77 and established the Scott, Tallon, Walker partnership. His designs include the Offices and Central Bus Terminal, Store Street, Dublin (1953, with R. Tallon) and Dublin's Abbey Theatre (1965).

✿ **The leading Mexican architect of his day, Juan O'Gorman** (1905–82), a graduate of the University of Mexico and third-generation Irish on his father's side, was also an accomplished muralist. From 1932 to 1935 he was head of the Department of Construction in the Ministry of Public Instruction and designed 30 new schools. He was professor of architecture at the National Polytechnic Institute. His work is complex and imaginative and makes use of distinctly Mexican decorative motifs. His anti-fascist and anti-clerical murals at Mexico City airport were destroyed in 1939 during a political swing to the right. The enormous work in Gertrudis Bocanegra Library at Patzcuaro, portraying in narrative 1000 years of the history of the state of Michoacan, is one of the most elaborate murals ever painted.

✿ **Architect of the White House, Washington DC, James Hoban** (c. 1762–1831) was born near Callan, Co. Kilkenny and studied drawing under Thomas Ivory at the school of the Dublin Society. He was employed as a joiner in the construction of the Royal Exchange (now City Hall) and the Custom House. He emigrated to America in 1785, finding employment in Philadelphia. He moved to South Carolina, where he designed the State Capitol at Columbia in 1791. In 1792 he won a competition for a design for the president's residence in Washington (later called the White House). The completed work resembled the Duke of Leinster's residence in Dublin (now Leinster House, An Dáil, the seat of the Irish government) and its cornerstone was laid by George Washington on 13 September 1793. Hoban also built

The National Gallery of Dublin was largely built with funds provided by railway pioneer William Dargan (whose statue can be seen in the foreground) and was opened in 1866. It was designed by Francis Fowke who also designed the Royal Albert Hall in London. It is home to 2400 paintings and 300 pieces of sculpture.

the Great Hotel in Washington between 1793 and 1795 and the Little Hotel in 1795. Hoban became a captain in the Washington Artillery 1799 and, when the city was incorporated in 1802, was elected a member of council, retaining his seat until his death. After the British Army destroyed the White House in 1814, he was employed to reconstruct it. The present building was completed in 1829. Hoban also built the State Department and the War Office. He died in 1831, leaving a large estate valued at £60,000.

🍀 **Architect of the Royal Albert Hall,** London, **Francis Fowke** (1823–65) was born in Ballysillane near Belfast. He was educated at Dungannon College in Co. Tyrone and at the Royal Military Academy, Woolwich. A captain in the Royal Engineers, he served in Bermuda and Paris. He was appointed architect and engineer to the Art and Science Department in London. His designs include the National Gallery of Ireland (1864) and the Museum of Science and Art in Edinburgh (1862). His plans for the South Kensington Museum (now the Victoria & Albert

Museum) won first prize in a 1864 competition, but their adoption was prevented by his death. The Royal Albert Hall was designed in 1865 and the plans accepted before Fowke's premature death in December of that year.

Buildings and structures

🍀 **The National Gallery of Ireland**, when opened in January 1864, was **the first public gallery in the world to be illuminated by gas**. Over 2000 gas jets were used.

🍀 **The Pigeon House chimneys** in Dublin are **the tallest structures in Ireland**. They were built by Vierrum & Partners Ltd of Belgium. The first chimney stack was commissioned in 1969 and stands 680ft 1in (207.48m). The second stack was commissioned in 1977 and stands 681ft 2in tall (207.08m). Their respective base circumferences are 45ft (13.71m) and 51ft (15.6m) and at the top they measure 16ft (4.88m) and 19ft 6in (6m). They have a gas velocity of 76ft (23.16m) per second. They are part of the Electricity Supply Board's (ESB) coal-fired power station on Dublin's South Wall. The South Wall stretches over four miles from Butt Bridge at the Customs House to the Poolbeg Lighthouse and was constructed between 1708 and 1762 to improve the navigation of the Liffey.

A 720ft (220m) radio mast, known as a Loran C. long-range radio transmitter, is planned for Loop Head, Co. Clare by the Commissioners of Irish Lights. The project's go-ahead is pending the results of an environmental impact study.

❧ **The Wellington Monument** in Phoenix Park, Dublin, begun in 1817, is **the tallest obelisk in Europe** at 205ft (62.5m). It is the second highest obelisk in the world after the Washington Monument in Washington, DC, USA, which stands at 555ft 5in (169.3m). The Wellington Monument was built to the competition-winning design of Sir Robert Smirke. The rebuilt British Museum in London was also designed by Smirke.

❧ **The Blennerville Windmill** at Tralee, Co. Kerry is **the largest windmill in Ireland and Great Britain**. Constructed in 1796, it stands 196 ft (59.7 m) high, with sails 74ft (24.2 m) in diameter.

❧ **The City Hall in Belfast** was commissioned in 1888, when Belfast became a city, and completed in 1906. It was built by the architect Brumwell Thomas and is Belfast's most impressive public building, with a 300ft- (91m-) long Portland stone façade and a central dome that rises to 173 ft (53m). Durban City Hall in South Africa is an exact replica.

❧ **The largest house in Ireland** is **Castletown House** in Celbridge, Co. Kildare. Built for the MP for Donegal and Speaker of the Dublin parliament 1715–29, William Conolly, between 1719 and 1722, it was inhabited by Conolly's descendants until 1966. It is now preserved and run by the Castletown Foundation, set up by the Hon. Desmond Guinness. The house is 400ft (121m) in length. It was built to the design of the Florentine architect Alessandro Galilei, with sections by Edward Lovett Pearce. It is now the headquarters of the Irish Georgian Foundation.

❧ **The oldest building in Ireland** cannot be dated with any certainty. However, the remains of what is probably **Ireland's oldest settlement**, excavated at the **Carrowmore** site in Co. Sligo, date from the

Mesolithic period c. 7500 BC. (Ireland became separated from Britain c. 9050 BC.)

The Mesolithic site at **Mountsandel** near Coleraine in Co. Derry has been dated to 7000 BC. The remains of the hearths of the wooden houses that stood there 9000 years ago can still be seen today. The Mountsandel site is a 200ft (61m) mound with a hollowed centre that the Normans used as a fortification in the 12th century. It served that function until the 1600s.

❧ **The Ceide Fields**, a Neolithic site recently discovered in Co. Mayo, is **the site of the largest Stone Age community to have been unearthed in Europe**. Covering over four square miles (10.36 square km) of hillside, the farming community which lived there until c. 3000 BC probably numbered as many as 5000.

❧ **Newgrange, Knowth and Dowth** in the Boyne Valley are **the oldest Neolithic structures in Europe**, dating from c. 3100 BC. Newgrange is Ireland's best-known prehistoric monument and arguably the finest architectural achievement on the island. Dating from over 5000 years ago, it could also be said to be **Ireland's first astronomic observatory and the oldest known astronomically aligned megalith in the world.** The passage graves at Newgrange are 500 years older than the oldest Egyptian pyramids, but their purpose remains unclear. The Newgrange mound is 36ft (11m) high and 300ft (91m) in diameter. Surrounding the base of the mound are 12 standing boulders, out of an original estimated 38, measuring up to 8ft (2.4m) high. The base of the mound is lined with large stones bearing geometric decorations, the most famous and intricate of which is the stone marking the entrance.

The structure contains a 62 ft (19 m) passageway to a central chamber. Above the entrance there is a lintel stone that is aligned so that the first rays of the sun on the winter solstice will enter the passageway and fill the chamber deep inside with light. Every winter solstice this phenomenon is watched eagerly from within by those interested and patient enough to tolerate the five- or six-year waiting list.

Equally fascinating and less remarked upon is the engineering feat that the actual construction entailed. Leaving aside the mathematics needed to align the structure, the stones used in its construction include massive capstones weighing several tons that, under examination, are revealed to have come from both the Wicklow Mountains, approximately 40 miles (64km) to the south, and the Mourne Mountains, about the same distance to the north. In 3100 BC the land between Newgrange and the two mountain ranges was covered by dense forest. The builders had no wheels to move nor metal tools to cut the stone. Archaeologists assume that the right stones were chosen and simply dragged by men and oxen to the site.

A further fascinating feature is the location chosen for the passage grave. The Boyne Valley in Co. Meath is one of the most fertile pasturelands in Europe and today continues to yield a very high ratio of crops and dairy produce to the acre. The settlers in the Boyne Valley were Ireland's earliest farmers and the fertility of the earth is very likely to be linked to the function of the structures.

In December 1993 UNESCO designated Newgrange and the Boyne Valley archaeological complex as a world heritage site. The Giant's Causeway in Co. Antrim is the only other world heritage site in Ireland.

Other names on UNESCO's prestigious list include the pyramids of Egypt, Machu Picchu in Peru, Hadrian's Wall and Mont St Michel.

♣ **The oldest castle in Ireland** is **Ferrycarrig Castle**, near Wexford, dating from c. 1180. Carrickfergus Castle in Co. Antrim is Northern Ireland's oldest castle, dating from c. 1210. Trim Castle in Co. Meath, built c. 1205, has the largest fortifications – 1455ft (443m) long.

♣ **The oldest pub site in Ireland**: a public house has stood on the site currently occupied by the **Brazen Head in Dublin** since the late 12th century, but the present structure dates from 1668 and is a mixture of 17th-century and modern architecture. **Grace Neill's Bar** in Donaghadee, Co. Down, built in 1611, is **the oldest pub building in Ireland** dating from the 12th century.

St Patrick's Cathedral, Dublin, at 300 ft (91.44 m) in length, is Ireland's largest church. It was home to Dean Jonathan Swift who is buried there. The site was founded as a church in 1190. The present structure is a mixture of different restorations and reconstructions from 1225 to modern times.

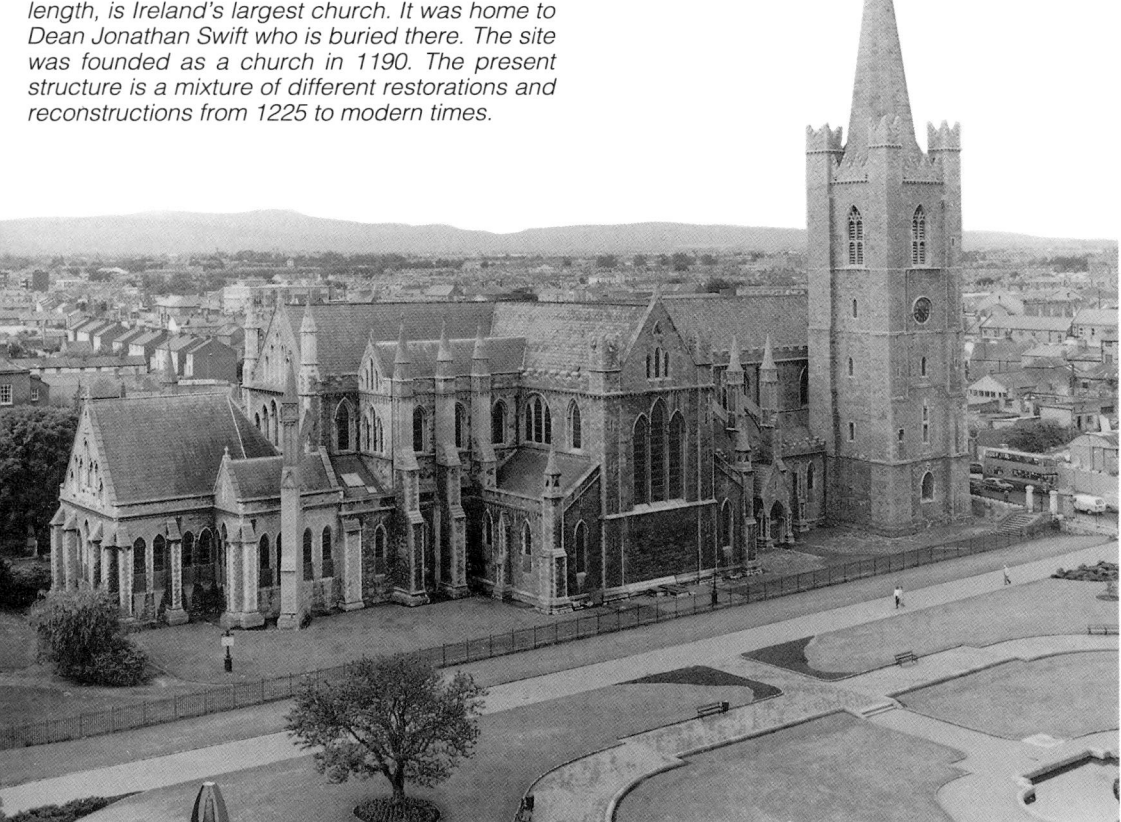

🍀 **The longest bar in Ireland** is the **Grandstand Bar** at the Galway Racecourse, measuring 210ft (64m) in length. It was built in 1955.

🍀 **The oldest lighthouse in Ireland** is **Hook Lighthouse** at Hook Head in Co. Wexford. Dating from the 13th century, it is said to be one of the four oldest lighthouses in the world.

🍀 **St Patrick's Cathedral** in Dublin is **the largest church in Ireland**. It was built on the site of an earlier church from 1191. Most of the building dates from the 13th to the 14th centuries. It was extensively restored 1864–69. The cathedral is 300ft (91.44m) long. The 147ft (44.8m) high Minot Tower was built c. 1362 and was topped with a 100-ft (30.48m) granite spire 1749–50. Among the principal monuments in the cathedral are the graves of Jonathan Swift, Dean of St Patrick's (see p. 134) and his partner Stella Johnson.

🍀 **The smallest church in Ireland** is **St Gobban's church** in Purl Braddan, Co. Antrim. It measures 12ft 1½in by 6ft 6in (3.7m × 2m). It is also **the smallest church in the UK**.

🍀 **The Gallarus Oratory is the oldest church in Ireland**. Built c. AD 750, it is situated at Kilmalkedar on the Dingle Peninsula in Co. Kerry.

VISUAL ARTS

🍀 **Georgia O'Keefe** (1887–1986) was born near Sun Prairie, Wisconsin, USA, the daughter of Francis Calixtus O'Keefe, a native of Ireland. O'Keefe was one of the great pioneers of modernism in America. Educated at Chatham Episcopal Institute, Virginia 1901, The Art Institute, Chicago 1904–05 and the Arts Student's League, New York 1907–08, she worked as an art teacher before exhibiting in the famous 291 Gallery of Alfred Stieglitz in New York in 1916 (and again in 1917 and 1926). Her works have been widely exhibited, including a definitive retrospective at the National Gallery in Washington, DC in 1988, two years after her death.

🍀 **John Singleton Copley** (1738–1815) was born in Boston, Massachusetts to Richard and Mary Singleton Copley, from Limerick and Clare respectively, who had recently arrived in the New World. John Singleton had become a portrait and historical painter by the age of 16. At 17 he painted George Washington

(who was then not quite as famous as he was later to become). In 1774 Copley moved to England and was well received by Sir Joshua Reynolds and London art circles. He became a member of the Royal Academy in 1783.

Copley was one of the finest artists to emerge from colonial America. His skills were stifled in London, however, where he seemed ill at ease with the classical 'grand manner'. Despite this, he made several commissions including *The Children of King George III* (1785, The Queen's Collection). The Tate Gallery, London holds some fine examples of his work, but his best-known painting, *Watson and the Shark* 1778, hangs in the Museum of Fine Arts in Boston.

🍀 **The highest price ever paid for a miniature** was £352,000 by the Alexander Gallery of New York, USA at Christie's in London on 7 November 1988, for a 2.13in-high (54mm) portrait of George Washington by the Dublin-born miniaturist **John Ramage** (c. 1748–1802), made in 1789.

Ramage entered the Dublin Society School in 1763. He emigrated to the USA in 1775 and established himself as a goldsmith and artist in Boston. He was a member of the city's Royal Irish Volunteers and fought in the War of Independence. The miniature of Washington was the result of a sitting at Ramage's studio in William Street, New York.

🍀 **William Blake** (1757–1827), English painter, engraver, mystic and poet, ignored by many until long after his death, was the son of an Irish hosier. Blake's life and work were highly individual and unconventional. *Poetical Sketches* (1783) was his only book to be commercially published. The rest he wrote, illustrated and published himself with the help of his wife, Catherine Boutcher.

In *Songs of Innocence* (1789) he produced a new method of printing his own poems by combining the text and illustration into a single decorative unit. His major works include *The Marriage of Heaven and Hell* (1790), *Songs of Experience* (1794), *Milton* (1804–08) and *Jerusalem* (1804–20). In these works and in his illustrations of Biblical stories for private patrons, Blake created a unique style that placed studies of human and other natural forms within a mystical and fanciful setting rich with symbolism.

🍀 **Pioneer photographer Matthew Brady** (1823–96) was born in Warren County, New York to an impoverished Irish immigrant. In 1839 Brady first heard of Louis Daguerre's image-printing discovery, and began experimenting himself. (The daguerreotype was a photograph produced on a silver-coated copper plate treated with iodine. The first one was made in 1837.) By 1843 he was running his own studio on Broadway in New York and attracting hundreds of customers.

In 1850 Brady produced *The Gallery of Illustrious Americans* and the following year he attended the World Fair in London. In 1855 his association with the Englishman Alex Gardner led to success in a new wet-plate process of photography. The new images were far clearer than before and Brady's studio enjoyed enormous success.

Brady persuaded Abraham Lincoln to allow him to document the Civil War in photographs and his company collected over 3500 images during the war years. Brady's photographs provide the most comprehensive visual documentation of 19th-century American history.

♣ **Augustus Saint Gaudens** (1848–1907), **America's leading public sculptor of the 19th century**, was born at Charlemount Street in Dublin. His father, from Aspet in France, lived for seven years in Dublin, where he married Mary McGuinness. The family emigrated to New York City, where Augustus trained as a cameo cutter and studied at the National Academy of Design. He spent several years training in Paris at l'Ecole des Beaux Arts and in Rome.

He received his first major commission in America in 1878 for the Admiral Farragut Monument in New York City, which was well received. His Lincoln Memorial (1887) in Chicago established a style of American sculpture that endured long after his death. His masterpieces are considered to be the Adams Monument at Rock Creek Cemetery, Washington, DC, The Shaw Memorial (1897) in Boston, and the Sherman equestrian statue (1903) in New York City. The Sherman statue is often hailed as America's finest equestrian monument. Saint Gaudens' style was simple and technically well crafted. His taste epitomised the America of his time. He was responsible for the Parnell Monument on O'Connell Street in Dublin which was erected in 1911. His studio in the Cornish Hills of New Hampshire now houses the memorial collection of his work.

♣ **Sir Francis Bacon** (1909–92) was born in Dublin of English parents. He moved to London in 1925 and began painting the following year. He had no formal training throughout his life and never adhered to one particular school of art. Always seeking to agitate the spectator, he portrayed the human figure stripped of all its beauty. Major retrospectives of his work were held in 1971–72 at the Grand Palais, Paris and the Kunsthalle, Düsseldorf, during which he was internationally acclaimed and judged by some critics to be the finest painter alive.

The painting 'Triptych May–June' was sold at Sotheby's in New York for $6.27m on 2 May 1989. This was **the highest price ever paid for a painting during the lifetime of an artist born in the UK.** (Dublin was part of the UK in 1909.)

♣ **Eileen Grey** (1879–1976), born in Enniscorthy, Co. Wexford, studied in London at the Slade School while apprenticed to the Japanese lacquer craftsman Sugawara. In 1907 she moved to Paris and designed the furniture and carpets which were sold from her gallery at 217 Faubourg St Honoré. Her design became famous and her major works were two houses completed in 1925 at Roquebrune and Castellar on the Côte d'Azur, one of which was decorated by Le Corbusier, the other becoming the home of the artist Graham Sutherland. Grey became a Fellow of the Royal Irish Architects Institute in 1975.

Flying was always a favourite pastime of Grey's and in the early 1920s she flew America's first airmail service from New Mexico to Acapulco. She died in Paris in October 1976 and is buried in Père Lachaise cemetery.

♣ **Sir Robert Sidney Nolan** (1917–92) was born in Melbourne, Australia, the son of Irish immigrants. His father was a Melbourne tram driver. Nolan took up painting in 1938 after attending evening classes at Prahan Technical College and at the National Gallery School. In 1940 he had his first one-man show, shocking the Australian public with his avant-garde style. Nolan served in the Australian army 1941–45 and, while stationed in the Wimmera district of Victoria, painted a series of landscapes that established his originality. In 1946 he travelled through northeastern Victoria, visiting the places associated with the Irish-Australian bushranger Ned Kelly (see p. 40). The series of paintings that followed are perhaps Nolan's most celebrated. Kelly is portrayed as a folk hero in a deliberately naive style. The *Fraser Series* depicts images of an escaped convict in an Australian desert landscape, which became a recurrent theme in his work. In 1949 Nolan completed a series of paintings on glass, the *Eureka Stockade*, depicting a gold-miner's uprising led by Peter Lalor*, which holds

* *Peter Lalor (1823–89) was a Co. Laois-born Australian politician and leader of the miners at the Eureka stockade in 1854, when he won the battle for electoral representation for the miners.*

special significance for Australian labour history. He also evoked the lives of explorers such as Burke and Wills (see p. 33) in the dry, harsh light of the outback.

Nolan exhibited at UNESCO in Paris in 1949 and moved to London in 1950, where he was to live for most of the rest of his life. In 1953 he and John Heyer made the film, *Back of Beyond,* which won the Grand Prix at the Venice Film Festival the following year. He also exhibited at the Venice Biennale in 1954. In 1955 he made a second series of *Kelly* paintings and between 1957 and 1958 produced the *Gallipoli* paintings. The paintings he produced while based in London transposed the style of his earlier works to new environments and different countries. Nolan was a regular visitor to Ireland and donated a set of paintings to the Hugh Lane Municipal Gallery of Art in Dublin.

✿ **Sean Kenny** (1933–73), a designer and architect from Portroe, Co. Tipperary, studied in Dublin and then with Frank Lloyd Wright in the USA for two years. He worked in stage design in London and in 1963 redesigned the Old Vic Theatre for its occupation by the National Theatre Company. At Canada's Exposition in 1967 he designed the 'Gyroton' rollercoaster which brought him success outside the theatre. He also designed a glass underwater restaurant in Nassau and a multi-layered stage for a Las Vegas night-club. He was internationally famous when he died in 1973 at the age of 40.

✿ **Court painter to George I and George II of England**, **Charles Jervas** (c. 1675–1739) was born in Shinrone, Co. Offaly and studied under Sir Godfrey Kneller in London before furthering his training in Italy. His other famous sitters included Pope, Swift (see p. 134) and Addison. He succeeded Kneller as court painter in 1723.

✿ **Jack Butler Yeats** (1871–1957), born in London, was the youngest of the five children of John Butler Yeats and Susan Pollexfen and the brother of William Butler Yeats, the winner of the Nobel Prize for Literature in 1923 (see p. 139). At eight years of age he went to live in Co. Sligo with his mother's parents. At 17 he returned to London, where he trained at the Westminster, South Kensington and Chiswick schools of art. He worked as an illustrator in London, but visited Ireland frequently, where he befriended Lady Gregory and John Millington Synge (see p. 147). In 1910 he went to Ireland to live permanently, first in Greystones, Co. Wicklow and then in Dublin. He started to use oils from this time and produced some of his best works

in subsequent years, inspired by the 1916 Easter Rising in Dublin and the independence movement.

✿ **Louis le Brocquy** (1916–) is probably Ireland's leading international artist. He is a self-taught painter who left his family business in the 1930s. He has had an impressive list of retrospective exhibitions including: the Venice Biennale 1956, the Municipal Gallery, Dublin 1966 and 1978, Ulster Museum 1967 and 1987, Musée d'Art Moderne, Paris 1976, New York State Museum 1980 and City Museum of Contemporary Art, Hiroshima 1991.

MUSIC

Composers and performers

✿ The actor, composer and singer who sang in the first performance of Mozart's *Le Nozze di Figaro,* **Michael Kelly** (1762–1826), was born in Dublin. He appeared on stage as a child and went to Italy for training in 1779. He moved to Vienna, where he was made the principal tenor to Emperor Joseph I 1783–87 and took the stage-name Occhelli. In this capacity he met Wolfgang Amadeus Mozart and the two became close friends and colleagues. Kelly created the roles of Don Curzio and Don Basilio in Mozart's *Le Nozze di Figaro.*

Vienna marked the climax of Kelly's career as one of the most celebrated tenors of his day. In 1787 he moved to England, where he toured successfully and became musical director at Drury Lane, remaining there for 20 years. He made his last public appearance in Dublin in September 1811 and afterwards concentrated on running his business affairs at Drury Lane, and at the King's Theatre in Haymarket, London.

✿ **Catherine Hayes** (1825–61) of Patrick Street, Limerick was **the most celebrated prima donna of her day.** Born into poverty, her voice was discovered by a Bishop Knox who overheard her singing an Irish love song as a child. She was sent to Dublin, where she studied under an Italian singing teacher, Antonio Sapio. She gave her first public concert in the Rotunda, Dublin in May 1839. In 1842 she went to Paris and then to Milan to train as an opera singer. She made her continental debut in Bellini's *I Puritani* at Marseilles in May 1845, causing a sensation. She was promptly employed as prima donna at La Scala, Milan.

Hayes established her supremacy as an interpreter of Italian opera and performed the works of Donizetti,

Ricci, Mercadante, Rossini and Verdi in Venice, Vienna and London. At Covent Garden in 1849 huge crowds turned out to greet her and she was invited to Buckingham Palace. She returned to Ireland and sang publicly in Limerick and Cork to a rapturous reception. She toured Canada, America and Australia and received unprecedented acclaim there too. Tickets for her recitals were bought for up to $1150 in San Francisco and her fees there averaged £650 per month. She settled in London in 1856 and married her agent, William Avery Bushnell. His premature death in 1858 and her bad health following a riding accident contributed to her own death in 1861. She is buried in Kensal Green Cemetery in Kensington, London.

✿ The prima donna from Castlebar, Co. Mayo, **Margaret Burke Sheridan** (1889–1958) was the orphaned daughter of the town's postmaster. Whilst in the care of the Dominican School in Eccles Street, Dublin, her singing talent was discovered. She was taught by Vincent O'Brien, whose other pupils included John McCormack (see below) and James Joyce (see p. 141). In 1908 she won a gold medal at the Feis Ceoil (the annual national music competition) and a move to London was financed by benefactors. She studied at the Royal Academy of Music for two years and was taken up by Lord and Lady de Walden, who introduced her to London society as the new musical prodigy. The Irish-Italian inventor Marconi (see p. 11) was enchanted by her and said, 'Yours is the voice I have been waiting for all my life.' He then sponsored her studies in Italy.

She made her operatic debut in 1918 as a replacement – at four days' notice – for Lucrezia Bori as Mimi in Puccini's *La Bohème*. Her reception was enthusiastic. *La Corriere della Sera* reported that 'Miss Sheridan is Irish but either by luck or by instinct she sings as an Italian . . . '

Sheridan was a favourite of Puccini, who coached her personally for the role of Manon Lescaut. She was invited to sing at La Scala in 1922 and was their representative at the international opera seasons at Covent Garden in 1919 and 1925–30. She never sang opera in Ireland but gave two concerts at the Theatre Royal. An ardent Irish nationalist, she refused to perform at the San Carlo Opera House in Naples following the death on hunger strike of the Lord Mayor of Cork City* in Brixton Prison, London in 1920.

* *Terence MacSwiney (1879–1920) was arrested in August 1920 following the capture of Cork City by the British Army during the Anglo-Irish War. He went on hunger strike and died on the 74th day, as a result of force-feeding.*

John Field, 'inventor' of the nocturne and teacher of the Russian composer Glinka. Possibly Ireland's greatest composer, he is buried in Moscow where he died in 1837.

She retired suddenly from Covent Garden and never sang in concert again. She worked as a member of the American National Arts Foundation and divided her remaining days between Ireland and the United States. She is buried in Dublin at Glasnevin Cemetery.

✿ **John McCormack**, acclaimed as **the greatest lyric tenor of his day**, was born in Athlone, Co. Westmeath in 1884. In 1902 he won the Feis Ceoil (annual national music competition) in Dublin and caused the audience to burst into spontaneous applause (thus contravening competition rules). He travelled to the USA in 1904 and represented Ireland at the St Louis Fair, making some of the earliest musical recordings for the Edison Bell Company in the same year. He studied in Italy and made his operatic debut in 1907 at Covent Garden in Mascagni's *Cavalleria Rusticana*. In 1909 he performed in Verdi's *La Traviata* at the Manhattan Opera House and afterwards sang with the Chicago and Boston opera companies and the Metropolitan Opera Company. He toured Australia with Dame Nelly Melba in 1911. He was always awkward in the acting roles, however, and in 1913 he turned to the concert stage where he achieved extraordinary popularity. He became America's foremost tenor after the death of the great Caruso in 1921 and made over 500 recordings. In 1928 he was made a hereditary papal count for his services to charity. McCormack became an American citizen in 1919. He performed to an audience of over one million people gathered in Phoenix Park, Dublin for the Eucharistic Congress of 1932. He died in Booterstown, Co. Dublin in 1945.

♣ **The first ever performance of George Frideric Handel's oratorio *Messiah*** was given on 13 April 1742 at Fishamble Street Music Hall in Dublin, during the composer's visit to the city 1741–42. *Messiah* delighted its audience of 700 and raised £400 for local charities. The rendition of the contralto aria 'He was despised', by the actress Susannah Cibber, prompted the Rev. Dr Delany to rise to his feet and cry out, 'Woman, for this be all thy sins forgiven thee.'

♣ Ludwig van Beethoven (1770–1827) was fond of traditional Irish tunes and prepared arrangements for several, including *Kitty of Coleraine*. His First Piano Concerto contains snatches of the Orange ballad *The Sash my Father Wore*, while the composition *Three Variations on an Irish Air*, Opus 105 No. 4 was based on the melody of *The Last Rose of Summer*.

♣ **Dominick Lynch, the man who introduced opera to America,** was the son of an Irish immigrant who fought in the American Revolution. Lynch was educated in Ireland and France and returned to the United States to set up a wine-importing business. He was responsible for popularising fine French wines in America and established himself as a leading figure of fashionable New York society. He travelled to Europe to recruit his own opera company which he personally helped to direct for the American première of Rossini's *The Barber of Seville* in the Park Theatre in November 1825. He died on a visit to Paris in 1837.

♣ **John Dowland** (1562–1626), possibly from Dalkey, Co. Dublin, was hailed as **the greatest lutenist and composer of his age**. He was court lutenist to the king of Denmark for many years, and to James I in London. A Catholic, he was known throughout Europe and is mentioned by many of the poets and dramatists of the European courts of the time. His melodies were often based on well-known folk songs and were widely published. His three *Books of Songs or Ayres* (1597–1603) established him as **the greatest song composer of his time**. He was paid huge salaries by his royal patrons, but spent freely and is said to have died impoverished in London.

♣ **Ireland's leading composer and the inventor of the 'nocturne', John Field** (1782–1837), was born at Golden Lane, Dublin and educated in music by his father and grandfather, who were orchestral musicians. He proved to be a child prodigy and at 10 played an entire concerto by Giordani at the Rotunda concert rooms in Dublin. In 1793 the family moved to Bath in England, where John Field was employed by the piano-maker Clementi to demonstrate the quality of his instruments. The two travelled across Europe and Field was soon recognised internationally as a musician and composer. In 1803 he settled in St Petersburg, where he was employed as the teacher of Mikhail Ivanovich Glinka (1804–57), who was to write the first Russian opera *A Life for the Tsar* (1836) and, more famously, *Ruslan and Ludmilla* (1842).

Field was the composer of seven concertos and four sonatas but, perhaps most importantly, he invented the 'nocturne' – a short piano piece in which a melody is accompanied by broken chords. His nocturnes (the first three being published in 1814) inspired many later composers, most notably Chopin.

Field gave concerts throughout Europe during his 30-year stay in Russia and was in great demand as a teacher. In 1832 he moved to London and scored a great success with his E flat piano concerto at a Philharmonic Society concert. He returned to Moscow but died there in January 1837, his health having been damaged by excessive drinking. He was given a grand public funeral and was buried in Moscow's Wedensky Cemetery, where a tombstone was erected in his honour. Dublin's National Concert Hall has also dedicated a room to his memory.

Descendants of John Field continued to live on Golden Lane until as recently as 1922. An elderly woman by the name of Field is known to have taught music to local children from her home, but after the Civil War (1922–23) records of her disappeared.

♣ **Harriet Smithson** (1800–54), also known as **Madame Berlioz**, was born in Ennis, Co. Clare and worked as an actress in Dublin, Belfast, Cork, Limerick and then at Drury Lane in London. Still relatively unknown, she travelled to Paris in 1828 and was widely acclaimed for her performances. Berlioz, the French composer, fell in love with her and his *Symphonie Fantastique* (1830) was composed for her. In 1833 the couple were married at the British Embassy in Paris. The marriage and financial fortunes failed, however, and they were separated in 1840.

include *Siege of Rochelle* (1835), *Falstaff* (1838) and, most famously, *The Bohemian Girl* (1843), which was translated into several languages. Balfe continued touring until he retired in 1864 and his operas were played in Vienna, St Petersburg and throughout Italy.

🍀 Another leading composer of English opera, **William Vincent Wallace** (1812–65), was born in Waterford and spent some years as a church organist and concert violinist before emigrating to Australia with his wife, a Miss Kelly. His marriage and attempts at sheep farming were both unsuccessful and he returned to music, earning his living as a musician on his travels through Tasmania, New Zealand, India, Nepal, Kashmir, South America and Mexico. He invested money in American tobacco and lost heavily. In New York in 1844 Wallace remarried, to Miss Stoepel, a pianist. In London the following year he achieved fame and fortune with the opera *Maritana*. In February 1860 *Lurline* was produced at Covent Garden and proved to be equally popular with the audiences. He wrote several more operas and piano pieces, but became seriously ill in 1864. He died in 1865 whilst resting in Château de Bagen in the French Pyrenees.

🍀 **Victor Herbert** (1859–1924) was born at 9 D'Olier Street, Dublin (where the offices of the *Irish Times* newspaper are currently located). His widowed mother remarried, to a German surgeon, and the family moved to Stuttgart in 1866, where Victor studied music. From 1874 to 1876 he studied cello with Cissmann and gave concerts in many cities, eventually becoming first cellist of Edward Strauss's orchestra in Vienna and **the foremost cellist of his time**. In 1866 he married Therese Forster, a Viennese prima donna, and emigrated to the USA to work with the Metropolitan Opera. In 1889 he founded the American Society of Composers, Authors and Publishers. He was highly popular in America and is best remembered for the 40 operettas he wrote there, including *Babes in Toyland*, *The Red Mill*, *Eileen* and *Sweethearts*. He made many early recordings for the phonograph and arranged Peadar Kearney's *The Soldier's Song* before it was adopted as the Irish National Anthem. He died in New York, where a bronze bust to his memory was unveiled in Central Park in 1927.

🍀 **Sir Arthur Sullivan** (1842–1900), composer of the Savoy comic operas (with words by W.S. Gilbert) such as *The Pirates of Penzance* (1879), *The Mikado*

Harriet Smithson, born in Ennis, Co. Clare, was a successful stage actress before she met Berlioz in Paris in 1828. She was the inspiration of his Symphonie Fantastique *(1830) and married him in 1833.*

🍀 **The most successful 19th-century composer of English opera** was **Michael Balfe** (1808–70), born at Pitt Street, later Balfe Street, Dublin. He quickly became a proficient violinist and gave his first public performance at nine years of age. He moved to London in 1823 and was apprenticed to Edward Horn, the noted singer. He played in the orchestra at Drury Lane before travelling to Italy under the patronage of Count Mazzara. Balfe was commissioned by La Scala to write the music for a ballet, *La Perouse*, which won instant success in 1826. He moved to Paris in 1827, where the composer Rossini arranged a lucrative deal for him at the Théâtre des Italiens. He returned to Italy in 1830 and met and married the Hungarian singer Lena Rosa. In 1833 he was back in London, where he wrote several operas for performance at Drury Lane. His works

(1885), *HMS Pinafore* (1878) and *The Gondoliers* (1889), was the son of an Irish musician and bandmaster at the Sandhurst Royal Military College. His mother, Mary Coghlan, was of Irish-Italian descent. Sullivan also wrote serious music, such as the oratorio *Kenilworth* (1864) and the opera *Ivanhoe* (1886).

🍀 **Dermot Troy** (1927–62), born in Wicklow, studied at the Royal Irish Academy of Music and was invited to join the Glyndebourne chorus following his victory in the *Irish Independent* Caruso competition in 1952. He was an excellent actor with a gift for languages, as well as being an outstanding natural tenor. He spent three years at Covent Garden and was invited to sing in Mannheim. After a successful tour of West Germany, he was offered a three-year contract in Hamburg. He suffered a heart attack in 1961, but returned the following year to sing as Lensky in Tchaikovsky's *Eugene Onegin*. It was to be his last performance and he died at the age of 35.

🍀 **James Galway** (1939–) was born in Belfast. His father was a riveter at the Harland & Wolff shipyard (see p. 48) and his mother a winder at a spinning mill. Both parents were musical and Galway inherited their skill and enthusiasm. At the age of nine he became a member of the Onward Flute Band and later joined the Belfast Military Band. He was taught by John Francis at the Royal College of Music in London. In 1959 he moved to the Guildhall School of Music and Drama in London before receiving a grant in 1960 to attend the Paris Conservatoire. He joined the Sadler's Wells Opera in 1961 and the Covent Garden Opera in 1965. He played with the London Symphony Orchestra from 1966 to 1967 as first flute, later joining the BBC Symphony Orchestra and the Royal Philharmonic Orchestra. In 1969 he joined the Berlin Symphony Orchestra as principal flautist under its conductor, Herbert von Karajan, with whom he travelled worldwide. In 1975 Galway left the Berlin orchestra to pursue a solo career. He continues to record and tour today, is a top-selling recording artist and is recognised internationally as **the world's most celebrated flautist**.

🍀 **Barry Douglas** (1960–) was born in Belfast and learnt to play the clarinet and cello as a child. He took up the piano at the somewhat advanced age of 17 and went on to study the instrument at the Royal College of Music. In 1986 he became **the first Irishman to win the Gold Medal at the Tchaikovsky International Piano Competition** in Moscow. He made his debut with the Berlin Philharmonic Orchestra in

1987 and has made regular concert appearances in major European, American and Far Eastern cities. He has made highly praised recordings of Tchaikovsky's Piano Concerto No. 1, Mussorgsky's Pictures at an Exhibition, Brahms's Piano Concerto No. 1 and Lizst's Piano Concertos Nos. 1 and 2.

Tunes and songs

🍀 **The American national anthem**, *The Star-Spangled Banner*, was written as a poem by Francis Scott Key while witnessing the bombardment by the British of Fort McHenry at Baltimore, Maryland in September 1814. It is claimed that the music for the song was the marching air of the Royal Inniskilling Fusiliers (of Enniskillen, Co. Fermanagh), but this is disputed. A possible alternative composer of the tune is the English composer John Stafford Smith, who is said to have set Scott Key's poem to the music of a drinking song, *To Anacreon in Heaven*. Though Francis Scott Key has often been claimed as an Irishman, this is not the case. The Key family was of pure English stock. Confusion may have arisen from his place of birth, namely the predominantly Irish Carroll County in Maryland. *The Star-Spangled Banner* was adopted as the United States' national anthem in 1931.

🍀 **The New Zealand national anthem,** *God Save New Zealand* was written in 1878 by Irish-born poet and citizen of New Zealand **Thomas Bracken**.

🍀 The music for *Waltzing Matilda,* Australia's unofficial anthem, was composed by **Robert Barton** of Co. Fermanagh to the lyrics of the Australian poet Andrew 'Banjo' Paterson.

🍀 *The Red Flag,* the socialist anthem, was written by **Jim Connell** (c. 1850–1929) of Co. Meath, to the Irish tune *The White Cockade*. In later years the British Labour Party changed the tune to that of *Tannenbaum*, but kept Connell's original lyrics.

🍀 The celebrated American band tune, *When Johnny Comes Marching Home,* was written by **Patrick Sarsfield Gilmore**, who was born in Co. Dublin in 1829 and later emigrated to the United States. The song is famously associated with the American Civil War and the Spanish-American War.

🍀 *The Teddy Bears' Picnic,* written in 1932 by **Jimmy Kennedy** (1902–84) of Omagh, Co. Tyrone, became internationally famous and sold over 4 million records. Kennedy wrote many popular tunes including *Red Sails in the Sunset,* inspired by the evening view of Portstewart Bay in Co. Antrim. Collaborating with Michael Carr, he was responsible for the British wartime favourites *Siegfried Line, The Hokey Cokey* and *Chestnut Tree.* He lived in turn in Switzerland, Dublin and London. He was a chairman of the British Songwriters Guild and is buried in London. His funeral oration was given by Denis Thatcher, husband of the then British Prime Minister.

Top-selling contemporary Irish and Irish-related popular music artists

♣ The band **U2** originated at the Mount Temple Comprehensive School in Dublin in 1977. Drummer Larry Mullen founded the band and was joined by Bono (Paul Hewson) vocals, The Edge (Dave Evans) on guitar and Adam Clayton on bass. They first reached number one in the UK charts in February 1983 with the single 'New Year's Day'. *War* reached number 10 in the UK album charts in 1983 and the following year the live album *Under a Blood Red Sky* reached number 28 in the US and number 2 in the UK.

In 1984 U2 set up their own record label, Mother Records, with the intention of promoting new talent in Ireland. *The Unforgettable Fire*, produced by Daniel Lanois and Brian Eno, reached number one in the UK and included the hit single 'Pride'. By 1987 the group's position as one of the most popular in the world was confirmed with *The Joshua Tree* – **the fastest-selling album in British musical history**.

U2 have collaborated with Clannad (see p. 127), Roy Orbison and BB King and have continued to top the charts internationally with their latest albums *Achtung Baby* and *Zooropa*. They have sold in excess of 90 million albums worldwide and are worth over IR£100 million.

The Zooropa World Tour finished in Ireland in August 1993 and was simultaneously broadcast by RTE Radio 2 in **the largest live radio broadcast to an international audience** of over 400 million.

♣ **George Ivan 'Van' Morrison** (1945–) was born in Belfast and raised as a Jehovah's Witness. His mother was a jazz singer and he grew up listening to records of American jazz, country and blues from his father's extensive collection. He could play guitar, harmonica and saxophone at 13 and at 14 left school to join a local showband. In 1963 Morrison joined with guitarist Bill Harrison and the band Them was born. Them attracted a regular audience at Belfast's Mari-

time Hotel and was signed up by Decca Records. In 1964 the single 'Baby Please Don't Go' reached number six in the UK charts and in 1965 'Here Comes The Night' reached number two. Morrison's name was already well known when Them broke up in 1966. He signed with Warner Brothers and soon established his solo career with two classic albums, *Astral Weeks* (1968) and *Moondance* (1969). He spent much of the 1970s in the USA and founded his own record company, Caledonia Productions. He currently lives in Ireland and continues to record popular and critically acclaimed music after more than 30 years.

His other albums include: *Hardnose the Highway* (1973), *Wavelength* (1978), *Inarticulate Speech of the Heart* (1983), *No Guru, No Method, No Teacher* (1986), *Irish Heartbeat* (1988) with the Chieftains (see p. 127) and *Enlightenment* (1993).

♣ **Bob Geldof** (1951–) was born in Blackrock, Co. Dublin. He joined with ex-school friends in 1975 to

Bob Geldof on stage with the Boomtown Rats at Wembley Stadium during the Live Aid concert, 13 July 1985. Band Aid and Live Aid raised in excess of £110 billion for famine relief in Ethiopia.

The Chieftains modernised traditional Irish music and introduced it to an international audience. They were particularly popular in Germany, where they inspired a new Volkmusik *movement in the 1970s.*

form the Nightlife Thugs, who soon changed their name to the **Boomtown Rats**. The band were approached by several record companies in 1977, following a successful tour of the UK and Ireland. Signing with Ensign Records, their first album, *Boomtown Rats* (1977), included the single 'Looking after number one', which reached number 11 in the UK charts. The second album, *Tonic For The Troops* (1978), was awarded a golden disc and their first number one single, 'Rat Trap', came in November 1978. In August 1979 another single, 'I don't like Mondays', reached number one and brought them international success.

In October 1984, having watched BBC reporter Michael Buerk covering the famine in Ethiopia, Geldof was moved to raise money by assembling leading performers in the pop industry to make a record. Within three weeks of the report Geldof and singer/songwriter Midge Ure had written 'Do they know it's

Christmas?' The single, sung by Band Aid, went straight to number one in the UK charts and became **the UK's second-highest-selling single**, with 3.6 million copies sold by May 1987, and a further 8.1 million worldwide. All profits were donated to the Ethiopian Famine Relief Fund and its accounts were closed in 1992 at £110 million.

Developing this idea, Geldof organised with Bill Graham the Live Aid concert of 13 July 1985. The world's leading popular performers sang in simultaneous concerts in London and Philadelphia and were **watched by an unprecedented 1.6 billion people (one third of the world's population) over ten hours. A record twelve satellites transmitted television pictures to every country on earth.** Within a week £30 million had been collected (with Ireland alone contributing over £7 million). By January 1986 £70 million had been raised. The money bought 200 trucks, nine ships and 17,000 tons of grain and built schools, houses and clinics. Geldof was nominated for the Nobel Peace Prize in 1986 and was given an honorary knighthood by the British queen in the same year. His autobiography, *Is That It?* (1986), was an international bestseller.

♣ **Sinead O'Connor** (1966–), born in Dublin, signed her first record deal with Ensign Records in 1987. Her debut album, *The Lion and the Cobra* (1988), sold one million copies and was nominated for a Grammy award. In 1989 she released the single 'Nothing compares 2 U', which reached number one in the Irish and UK charts. Her second album, *I do not want what I have not got*, sold six million copies worldwide and topped the US and UK Billboard charts. She received a Grammy award in 1991 and her work won her credit as Artist of the Year, Best Album, Best Single and Best Female Singer by readers and critics of *Rolling Stone* magazine. Her third album, *Am I not your girl?*, was released in 1993.

♣ **Chris de Burgh** was born Christopher Davidson in Argentina in 1948, the son of a British diplomat. He began writing pop songs whilst a student at Trinity College, Dublin and was signed by A & M Records. He was supporting act for Supertramp in 1975 and that year released his debut album, *These Castle Walls*. His early career met with success in South America, South Africa and Canada, but this was not matched in Ireland, the UK or the USA. However, his 25th single release in the UK, 'Lady in Red', reached number one in the charts and was an enormous success worldwide, creating a soaring interest in his earlier records. De Burgh now lives in Dublin.

De Burgh's albums include: *Far beyond these Walls* (1975), *Eastern Wind* (1980), *Into the Light* (1986) and *Power of Ten* (1992).

♣ **Clannad***, from Gaoth Dobhair (Gweedore) in the Co. Donegal Gaeltacht (Irish-speaking area), are the most successful of the Irish folk-rock bands. The line-up consists of Máire Ni Bhraonáin, Pól O'Bhraonáin, Ciarán O'Bhraonáin, Padraig Duggan and Noel Duggan. The band was formed in Leo's Tavern, Gweedore in 1970 and consisted at the time of three of the O'Bhraonáin (Brennan) children and two of their uncles. Their first commercial success came in Germany in 1975 after a successful tour, but it was the theme tune to the television film *Harry's Game* in 1982 that brought them to the attention of a wider audience. The single reached number five in the UK

* Clannad is the Irish word for family.

charts and received an Ivor Novello award in 1984. Clannad also recorded the soundtrack for the BBC television series *Robin of Sherwood* in 1984, which won a British Academy award for best soundtrack the following year. In 1986 they combined with Bono of U2 (see p. 125) for the duet 'In a Lifetime', which was a UK Top 20 hit.

Albums include: *Clannad* (1973), *Crann úll* (1980), *Legend* (1984), *Atlantic Realm* (1989) and *Banba* (1993).

♣ **Enya (Eithne Ní Bhraonáin)** from Gweedore, Co. Donegal, was a member of Clannad (see above) before she began her solo career. She is a classically trained pianist and played keyboards for Clannad from 1979 to 1982. Her distinctive mystical style failed to make much impact until her UK number one single, 'Orinoco Flow', in 1988. She records in collaboration with lyric writer Roma Ryan and producer Nicky Ryan. Enya achieved further single success with 'Caribbean Blue' in 1990 and her album sales have steadily increased worldwide.

Albums include: *Enya* (1987), *Watermark* (1988) and *The Celts* (1992).

♣ **The Chieftains** have brought traditional Irish music to an international audience and continue to sell thousands of records after 30 years. The original group members – Paddy Moloney, Seán Potts, Michael Tubridy and Martin Fay – met up as members of Ceoltóirí Chualann, a traditional music organisation set up in 1961 by Seán O'Riada (1931–71).

The Chieftains performed and recorded on a semi-professional basis on the Claddagh Records label and quickly established themselves as the leading exponents of Irish traditional music. Following the death of O'Riada, Seán Keane, Peader Mercier and Derek Bell joined the band and gained popularity on the British folk scene with *Chieftains 4* in 1974. It was *Chieftains 5*, recorded with Island Records in 1975, that earned the group a truly international reputation. They were lauded by Eric Clapton and Mick Jagger and collaborated with Mike Oldfield on his *Ommadawn* album. In 1975 the band played on the soundtrack of *Barry Lyndon* by Stanley Kubrick.

Peadar Mercier was replaced by Kevin Conneff in 1976 and Matt Malloy joined their ranks in 1979. They continue to record and have collaborated in recent years with James Galway (see p. 124) and Van Morrison (see p. 125).

Albums include: *Celtic Wedding* (1987), *The Chieftains in Ireland* (1987) with James Galway, *Irish Heartbeat* (1988) with Van Morrison and *The Celtic Harp* (1993).

♣ **Feargal Sharkey** was born in Derry in 1958. In 1974 he joined **The Undertones** with Damian O'Neill, John O'Neill, Mickey Bradley and Billy Doherty. They were favourites of the English DJ John Peel, who helped their particular brand of pop-punk to receive plenty of airtime. The Undertones released several top-selling singles, including 'My Perfect Cousin' (1980) and 'It's Going to Happen' (1981). Their first three albums were all top 20 hits in the UK album charts.

Sharkey's solo career began in earnest in 1984, when his single 'Listen to your Father' reached number 12 in the UK charts. This was followed by the number one hit 'A Good Heart' in 1985. His debut solo album, *Feargal Sharkey*, produced by Dave Stewart of Eurythmics, reached number 12 in the UK charts in 1985.

♣ **Thin Lizzy** was formed in Dublin by Phil Lynott, Eric Bell and Brian Downey. A series of changes in the line-up brought a variety of musicians in and out of the band, including Gary Moore, Andy Gee, Scott Gorham and Midge Ure. Between 1973 and 1983, Thin Lizzy had nine hits in the UK singles chart and eight in the top 20 album charts.

Albums include: *Jailbreak* (1976), *Chinatown* (1980), *Thunder and Lightning* (1983).

♣ In December 1993 the Limerick band **The Cranberries** made Irish popular music history when sales of their debut album, *Everybody else is doing it, so why can't we?*, passed the one million sales mark in the USA. This makes the album, recorded in Dublin, **the most successful Irish debut album ever released**. The band were presented with their first platinum disc on 9 December 1993.

The London-Irish

♣ **John Lydon** or **Johnny Rotten** (1956–) of **The Sex Pistols**, one of the instigators of the punk revolution, was born and raised in London, where his Irish parents had moved in the 1950s in search of work. His father was from Tuam, Co. Galway and his mother from Cork.

In the volatile atmosphere of London in the early 1970s, Rotten's punk revolution was waiting to happen. In 1975 the Sex Pistols were formed with the sponsorship of entrepreneur Malcolm McLaren, who was able to market the violent disaffection of the group and their followers. The Sex Pistols were signed up by EMI Records and released their first single, 'Anarchy in the UK'. The group suffered bans on their records, distribution problems and violent attacks by objectors to their 'God Save the Queen' single in 1977 (with Virgin Records), but their first album, *Never Mind the Bollocks Here's the Sex Pistols*, went straight to number one in the UK album charts.

In 1978 Lydon formed Public Image Limited, whose 11th album, *That what is not*, was released in 1992. He published an autobiography, *No Irish, No Blacks, No Dogs*, in 1994.

♣ **Boy George** was born George O'Dowd in London in 1961 to Irish immigrants from Co. Tipperary. His group **Culture Club** signed with Virgin Records and became one of the most successful of the 1980s, producing a string of hit records. 'Karma Chameleon' reached number one in the charts in 1983. His ambiguous sexuality made Boy George a favourite target for the tabloid press, but ultimately it was drug abuse that led to the downfall of the band.

Shane McGowan of The Pogues, who unleashed a unique blend of traditional Irish music and punk rock on the unsuspecting London-Irish in the 1980s.

After successfully overcoming his drug problem, Boy George began a solo career. In 1987 he reached number one with a cover version of 'Everything I Own' by Ken Boothe of Bread. In 1989 he formed his own record label, More Protein, and fronted a new band, Jesus Loves You. In 1992 he sang a cover version of 'The Crying Game' by Dave Berry for the soundtrack of the film of the same name by Neil Jordan (see p. 158).

❧ **Elvis Costello**, or Declan Patrick Aloysius McManus (1955–), was born in Paddington, London to Irish immigrant parents. His father, Ross McManus, was a singer and bandleader. Elvis Costello signed with Stiff Records* but, although acclaimed by critics from the start, his popular appeal was slower to develop. He joined with The Attractions to produce the album *Armed Forces*, which was a top 10 hit in the UK and USA and included the hit single 'Oliver's Army'. In 1981 he experimented with country music and recorded *Almost Blue in Nashville* with Billy Sherrill, the single 'Good Year for the Roses' becoming the major hit of the album. While continuing to record his own music, Costello produced albums with Squeeze, The Specials, The Bluebells and The Pogues (see below), meeting his first wife, Cáit O'Riordan, while working with the latter.

He collaborated with Paul McCartney and co-wrote a number of songs on the album *Flowers in the Dirt*. *Spike* (1989) was highly acclaimed and commercially successful. Costello also co-wrote the soundtrack for the television series *GBH* by Alan Bleasdale. Since the late 1980s his song-writing has been greatly influenced by traditional Irish music.

❧ **The Pogues** were born in 1983 when Shane MacGowan, Jem Finer and Spider Stacey began busking and singing rebel songs in the Irish pubs of North London. Finer was a London Jew who enjoyed traditional Irish music. The rest of the band, including accordionist James Fearnley and drummer Andrew Ranken, were London-Irish.

Shane MacGowan was reared in Tipperary by his mother, a folk singer. He was sent to Westminster School in London, but was expelled for bad behaviour and spent years in labouring jobs and experimenting

* *Stiff Records was co-founded by Irishman David Robinson, who bought a recording console from Eamonn Andrews and took it to London, where he began recording from the basement of a pub. There he recorded leading new wave bands such as Graham Parker and The Rumour, Ian Drury and the Blockheads and later The Pogues.*

with punk rock. The Pogues made a deliberate attempt to inject some ethnic vitality into the London-Irish of Kilburn. Cáit O'Riordan joined the band on bass and they were eventually signed by Stiff Records in 1983. Their first album, *Red Roses for Me* (1984), was the first ever blend of punk and Irish traditional music. Conservative taste in Ireland did not warm to it and the British press was fiercely critical. Elvis Costello (see above), however, liked the sound and the band toured with him, making festival appearances across Britain and Ireland. They were joined by Terry Woods on banjo and Philip Chevron on guitar.

In 1985 their second album *Rum, Sodomy and the Lash* won critical acclaim and MacGowan was accepted as a gifted songwriter. They were voted Britain's best live act in 1986 and set off on a tour of the USA. In 1987 The Pogues recorded *The Irish Rover* with The Dubliners – an indication of their final acceptance among Irish traditionalists.

FASHION AND COUTURE

❧ **John Rocha** became **the first Irish-based designer to win the British Fashion Awards Designer of the Year** in October 1993. Born in Hong Kong, the son of a Chinese Buddhist and a Portuguese Catholic, Rocha has been an Irish resident since 1979. His inspiration comes from the Irish environment. Consequently his clothes tend to be made with traditional, natural Irish fabrics – wool, linen and tweed – in muted colours, with a strong Celtic influence in the design. He is currently manufacturing from a factory in Clanbrassil Street, Dublin.

❧ **Paul Costello** (1945–) was educated at Blackrock College, Dublin and the Chambre Syndicale de la Haute Couture in Paris. He worked in design in Paris, Milan and New York before setting up his own design and manufacturing company in Dungannon, Northern Ireland, with offices in London and a retail outlet in Brown Thomas department store in Dublin. His designs are internationally acclaimed and he has a selection of high-profile clients, including the Princess of Wales and the Duchess of York. He has been nominated twice for the Designer of the Year award in the UK, has won the Fil d'Or award in France on three occasions and was Designer of the Year in Ireland in 1991.

❧ **Philip Treacy** (1967–), born in Galway, established himself as a milliner of international standing when he won his third consecutive British Fashion Design award in 1993. His creations are ordered for the couture shows of Christian Lacroix, Karl Lagerfeld and Valentino.

❧ **Ib Jorgensen** was born in Denmark in 1932. He came to live in Ireland as a child and was educated in Dublin at Castleknock College and the Grafton Academy of Dress and Design. He opened his own salon in Dublin in 1956 and established an international clientele through outlets in Dublin and London.

❧ **Sybil Connolly** (1921–) was born in Waterford and educated in dress design at Bradleys of London. She returned to Dublin in 1940 and set up her own couture business there in 1953. She has been an international dress designer for three decades and is currently a designer for Tiffany's of New York.

❧ **The greatest distance covered by female models on a catwalk** is 71.1 miles (114.4km), by Roberta Brown and Lorraine McCourt at Parke's Hotel, Dublin from 19 to 21 September 1983. Male model Eddie Warke covered a further 11.9 miles (19.1km) on the catwalk.

JOURNALISM, PUBLISHING AND LITERATURE

Journalism

❧ **The first daily newspaper in the United States**, the *Philadelphia Packet,* was founded by the printer and journalist from Strabane, Co. Tyrone, **John Dunlap** (1747–1812). Dunlap emigrated in 1771 and, in common with so many of his contemporary Irish-Americans, became involved in the revolutionary movement. He printed the *Declaration of Independence* and, during the Revolution, subscribed £4000 to supply Washington's army. He was also a member of the general's personal bodyguard.

Dunlap had his earliest experience of the printing trade at Gray's Printers in Strabane, where James Wilson, grandfather of the future American President, Woodrow Wilson (see p. 81), served his apprenticeship before he emigrated in 1807. Gray's Printing Press was in business throughout the 18th and 19th centuries. Strabane was a centre of the printing trade in these years and at one point had ten printers and two newspapers running simultaneously. Gray's is now preserved as a heritage museum.

❧ *The Southern Cross* weekly newspaper, founded in 1875 by Dean Patrick Dillon and published in Buenos Aires, is **the oldest Irish newspaper published outside Ireland.**

❧ **The first daily English-language newspaper in South America** was *The Standard,* founded in 1861 by **Michael George Mulhall**, born at St Stephen's Green, Dublin. *The Standard* grew to become the leading Argentine paper for over a century, although it was never very popular with the Irish community for whom it was launched. Mulhall was a gifted statistician whose works were widely published. His *Dictionary of Statistics* (1883) became a standard reference book, while *Handbook of the River Plate* (1869) was **the first English-language book to be published in South America.**

❧ **The highest price ever paid for a broadsheet** was $1,595,000 for one of the 24 known copies of the *Declaration of Independence,* printed by John Dunlap in Philadelphia, Pennsylvania, USA in 1776. It was sold by Samuel T. Freeman & Co. to Ralph Newman of Chicago, Illinois on behalf of an undisclosed client at Sotheby's, New York on 3 March 1990.

❧ **Maurice Anthony Coneys Gorham** (1902–75), born in London, son of Dr J.J. Gorham of Clifden, Co. Galway, joined the *Radio Times* in 1926 and was appointed art editor in 1928. He was general editor 1933–41 and then joined the BBC as director of North American services 1941–44. He was director of Allied Expeditionary Forces programmes 1944–45 and was then appointed head of the BBC television service. He resigned in 1947 and returned to journalism until 1953, when he took up the post of director of Radio Eireann. He resigned in 1959, shortly before the Irish Government's disclosure of the organisation of the new national television service. He wrote the officially sponsored *Forty Years of Irish Broadcasting* (1967).

❧ **The pioneer of reform journalism, or 'muckraking', Samuel S. McClure** (1857–1949) emigrated from Co. Antrim with his parents and began his career in journalism while still a student in Illinois. He launched **America's first syndicate** in 1884, which was soon supplying American newspapers with columns written by leading American and European writers. In 1893 *McClure's Magazine* was published and continued for three decades, featuring exposés by leading social crusaders such as Ida Tarbell and Lincoln Steffens.

❧ Founder of the *Daily Mail* and *Daily Mirror* newspapers, **Alfred Harmsworth, Viscount Northcliffe** (1865–1922), was born in Chapelizod, Co. Dublin. He conceived the idea of a popular newspaper to capitalise on the growing literacy of the public following the 1870 Education Act. The result was *Answers to Correspondents* founded in 1888 – soon shortened to *Answers*. His ability to read public taste brought huge success. Further cheap periodicals led to the establishment of Amalgamated Press, then **the world's largest news publishing empire**. He bought and rescued the ailing *London Evening News* in 1894 and in 1896 founded the *Daily Mail*, pioneering a completely new form of popular journalism. The *Daily Mail* became **the first British newspaper to achieve daily sales of one million copies** in March 1900. Working with the motto 'Explain, simplify, clarify' he had equal success in founding the *Daily Mirror* and the *Sunday Dispatch* in 1903. His career reached its peak in 1908 with the takeover of *The Times*. However, his political influence remained relatively slight and, despite his best efforts, he was unable to mould public opinion through his newspapers.

❧ War correspondent **Edmund O'Donovan** (1844–83), born in Dublin, began his career with the *Irish Times* in 1866. He joined the French Foreign Legion at the outbreak of the Franco-Prussian War in 1870 and was wounded and captured. He sent reports to London and Dublin from his internment camp. He was reporter for *The Times* during the Carlist uprising in Spain 1873 and worked in Turkey for the *Daily News* in 1876. In 1879 he was detained by the Ottoman authorities in Merv in Central Asia on suspicion of being a Russian agent. His adventures are recorded in his book *The Merv Oasis* (1882). In 1883 he went to the Sudan for the *Daily News* and joined the army of Hicks Pasha which marched on Al-Obeid. In November of that year the army was ambushed and O'Donovan was never heard of again.

❧ O'Donovan was accompanied in the Sudan in 1883 by **Frank Power** (1858–84), born in Co. Laois. Power did not join O'Donovan and the army of Hicks Pasha after he contracted a fever that left him bedridden. Consequently he survived to be appointed acting British Consul and he welcomed General Gordon to Khartoum. During the siege of the city Power sent dispatches to *The Times* by telegram. General Gordon sent him down the Nile by steamboat with Colonel Stewart, but they struck a rock near Berber and were killed when they came ashore. *Letters from Khartoum, Written during the Siege* was published in 1885.

❧ War correspondent **Windham Thomas Wyndham Quin, fourth Earl of Dunraven and Mount Earl** (1841–1926), born in Adare, Co. Limerick, was privately educated and was a skilled yachtsman and steeplechaser. He was war correspondent for the *Daily Telegraph* in Abyssinia in 1867 and covered the Franco-Prussian War from 1870. He succeeded to the earldom in 1871 and in that year hunted buffalo in the USA with Texas Jack and Buffalo Bill (see p. 39).

Quin lived on his estate in Adare, established a successful stud there, and took an active interest in Irish politics. He was colonial under-secretary 1885–87. He competed in the America's Cup in 1893 and 1895, but failed to win. He was expelled from the New York Yacht Club for protesting at the conduct of the 1895 race. During World War I he commanded his own hospital ship, *Grianaig*, in the Mediterranean. He is best remembered in Irish history as the leader of the landlords who agreed to accept land purchase and so facilitated the passing of the Wyndham Land Act of 1903, which enabled Irish tenant farmers to become the owners of their land. He was an advocate of devolution and federalism as solutions to the Irish political crisis. Quin was nominated to the Free State Senate in 1922. His memoirs *Past Times and Pastimes* were published in 1922.

❧ War correspondent **James O'Kelly** (1845–1916), born in Dublin and educated at Trinity College, Dublin and the Sorbonne, joined the French Foreign Legion in 1863 and was sent to Mexico in 1866 to support the Emperor Maximilian. He was imprisoned by the Mexican General Canales but escaped and returned to France. He served as a captain in the French Army until the fall of Paris to the Prussians in 1870.

O'Kelly joined the *New York Herald* and was sent to Cuba to report on the Cuban revolt. He penetrated Cuban lines and succeeded in interviewing General Cespedes, President of the Republic. He was arrested by the Spanish and sentenced to death as a spy but was reprieved following the intervention of the Irish Home Rule MP, Isaac Butt, amongst others. *The Mambiland, or Adventures of a Herald Correspondent in Cuba* was published in Philadelphia in 1874. He later served with the US Army in the war against the Sioux chief, Sitting Bull.

O'Kelly was elected Home Rule MP for Roscommon in 1880 and served time in Kilmainham Gaol with Charles Stewart Parnell. He covered the Mahdi revolt in the Sudan for the *London Daily News* and was reporter from the House of Commons for the *Irish Independent* 1892–95.

♣ **Sir William Howard Russell** (1820–1907), born in Tallaght, Co. Dublin, left his legal studies to take up journalism with *The Times*. He reported from Ireland on O'Connell's Repeal Movement and on the general election of 1841. He went to Gallipoli in 1854 to report on the Crimean War, where his description of the infantry at Balaklava as the 'thin red line' entered the English language. His reports, highlighting the mismanagement of food and medical supplies and the sufferings of the troops, made him popular with the public but a bitter enemy of army command. This was particularly so after his critical account of the infamous Charge of the Light Brigade.

In 1860 Russell founded the *Army and Navy Gazette*, which he edited himself. In 1861 he witnessed the First Battle of Bull Run in the American Civil War. He wrote in opposition to slavery and faithfully recorded the disorderly retreat of the Federal troops at Bull Run. Having thus made enemies on both sides, he moved to London. In 1870 he accompanied the Prussians in the Franco-Prussian War and in 1879 sent his last dispatch from South Africa during the Zulu War. He was knighted in 1895 and received awards throughout Europe. He has been called **'the first modern war correspondent'**. He died in London and is buried at Brompton Cemetery.

♣ War correspondent and author of *The Longest Day*, **Cornelius Ryan** (1920–74) was born and educated in Dublin before moving to London, where he joined the Reuters News Agency in 1941. In 1943 he was appointed war correspondent of the *Daily Telegraph* and covered the D-Day invasion of Normandy on 6 June 1944 and the subsequent progress of General Patton's Third Army. In 1945 he opened a *Daily Telegraph* office in Tokyo and reported on US atomic testing in the Pacific. In 1947 he moved to New York and worked for *Time* Magazine and later for *Newsweek* and *Collier's Magazine* until, in 1956, he moved to the *Reader's Digest*. He was now devoting most of his time to writing books and decided to write a history of the D-Day Landings. After ten years of research, during which he interviewed more than 1000 participants, he published *The Longest Day* in 1959. The $20,000 spent in researching the book was quickly paid off as it became an instant best-seller and made him a millionaire. The film rights were sold and the movie also became a box-office hit. Ryan spent an-

William Howard Russell, born in Tallaght, Co. Dublin, has been called 'the first modern war correspondent'. In his report from the battle of Balaklava in the Crimea he first used the term 'the thin red line', which has since entered the phraseology of the English language.

other five years researching a book on the fall of Berlin, *The Last Battle* (1960), which was another best-seller. More than 10 million hardcover copies of these two books were sold and they were translated into 20 different languages. Malcolm Muggeridge described Ryan as 'the most brilliant journalist in the world'. *A Bridge Too Far* (1974), which was also made into a successful film, describes the mismanaged Allied 'Operation Market Garden' and Battle of Arnhem in 1944 and took seven years of research. Ryan died in New York.

♣ **Founder of the original *Tatler*, *Spectator* and *Guardian* journals, Richard Steele** (pseudonym Isaac Bickerstaff; 1672–1729) was born in Dublin and educated at Oxford. He conceived the idea of a periodical addressed to those who frequented London's coffee-houses and in April 1709 the first issue of the *Tatler* appeared, with Joseph Addison as a contributor. The magazine advocated gentlemanly conduct and respect for ladies. It was succeeded in 1711 by the *Spectator*, which was followed in 1713 by the *Guardian*. Steele entered Parliament as a Whig in 1713 and was knighted in 1715. The partnership with Addison in the *Spectator* was to have a lasting influence on the style of periodical writing in English. Steele provided originality and enthusiasm, while Addison was a master of the essay.

❦ **The first penny-daily newspaper in the United Kingdom**, the *Liverpool Daily Post* was founded in 1855 by **Michael James Whitty** (1795–1873), of Enniscorthy, Co. Wexford. The idea of a popular newspaper for a mass audience was later developed on a national scale by Alfred Harmsworth (see p. 131). Whitty combined his journalistic skills with his position as Chief Constable of Liverpool 1836–48. During his term of office he modernised the force and formed the city's first efficient fire brigade.

❦ **The founder of the Press Club** in 1896 and its president 1896–97, **Charles Williams** (1838–1904), of Coleraine, Co. Derry, joined the *Evening Standard* in 1859. He reported on the Franco-Prussian War of 1870 and in 1877 worked from the HQ of Turkish command during the Armenian War. He accompanied the Nile expedition to relieve General Gordon besieged in Khartoum in 1884. He left the *Standard* for the *Daily Chronicle* and reported from the Balkans 1885–87. His last war dispatches were from Kitchener's 1898 Sudanese campaign.

❦ **Nellie Bly** (1867–1922), the daughter of an Irish immigrant, was **America's first leading woman journalist.** Born Elizabeth Cochrane in Cochrane Mills, Pennsylvania, a town founded by her father, she inherited the adventurous blood of her relations, including that of a grand uncle, Thomas Kennedy, who travelled around the world in three years. Nellie Bly took up the challenge and embarked upon a round-the-world trip on 14 November 1889, returning in triumph on 25 January 1890, just 72 days, 6 hours and 11 minutes later. *The World*, for which she wrote, headlined her achievement with 'Father Time outdone!' Bly had outdone Jules Verne's fictional hero Phileas Fogg, who took 80 days to complete the journey. Such was her confidence, Bly actually stopped *en route* at the home of Jules Verne in France for an interview. She later published an account of her travels in *Around The World in 72 Days* (1890).

Bly was an active crusader against injustice. She began her journalistic career by touring the factories and workshops of Pittsburgh, reporting on the deprivation suffered by the workers. She made much money for herself and raised even more for the causes she championed. In particular, she raised money for the Salvation Army, dressing up as a volunteer to witness the organisation's work and then describing to the general public what she had seen. She interviewed murderers, described the misery of slum-dwellers, went down in a diving-bell and up in a balloon, and posed as a beggar, a lunatic and a factory worker. She was the most successful writer *The World* ever had and it prospered as a reforming journal while she was a contributor. Bly died of pneumonia in January 1922.

Publishing and printing

❦ **The first subscription publishing enterprise** was founded by **Peter Fenlon Collier** (1846–1909) of Myshall, Co. Carlow. Collier emigrated to Cincinnati, Ohio in 1866 and, after a brief period as a novice priest, moved to New York, where he began to print books from his basement workshop in 1875. In 1888 he launched a popular magazine, *Once a Week,* which became *Collier's, The National Weekly* in 1895 and grew to a circulation of over three million copies. With his son, he published *Dr Eliot's 'Five Foot Shelf of Books',* or *The Harvard Classics.* By 1950 over 400,000 of the 50-volume set had been sold.

❦ **'The father of the printing profession'**, **Michael Henry Gill** (1794–1879), the Dublin-born son of a woollen draper and leading United Irishman, was widely considered to be the most accomplished printer of the 19th century. By 1842 Gill had become the sole lessee of Dublin University Press, which produced the seven volumes of the *Annals of the Four Masters.* He was among the most outstanding academic printers in Europe, expanding into publishing with the purchase of the stock, copyrights and premises of publisher James McGlashan in 1856. M.H. Gill & Son was formed in 1876. The company merged with Macmillan of London in 1968.

Literature

In no other field of achievement has the success of Irish men and women been recognised as it has in literature. To produce a list of the most excellent writers from Ireland, or those whose work and background is Irish, would require a book in itself. The writers listed below have been selected, for the most

Jonathan Swift, Dean of St Patrick's Cathedral, Dublin and author of Gulliver's Travels, Drapier's Letters *and* Tale of a Tub. Gulliver's Travel's *was intended as a savage satire on English misrule in Ireland. Ironically it has become one of the most popular children's stories of all time.*

part, for achieving world-wide fame. This, by necessity, excludes many excellent writers in the Irish language who are not well known outside Ireland.

❦ **Dublin has produced three winners of the Nobel Prize for Literature:** William Butler Yeats (1923), George Bernard Shaw (1925) and Samuel Beckett (1959). The only city to have produced more Nobel laureates in literature is Paris with six.

❦ **Jonathan Swift** (1667–1745), dean of St Patrick's Cathedral, Dublin, was born in Hoey's Court, Dublin and educated at Kilkenny School and Trinity College, Dublin, where he graduated without distinction. In 1689 he was appointed as secretary to the Whig statesman Sir William Temple at Moor Park, Surrey. He took holy orders and was sent to Kilroot, Co. Antrim in 1694, despite his wish to obtain a major

church appointment in England. He returned to Moor Park in 1696 and remained there until the death of Sir William in 1699. It was at this time that he was employed as the tutor of Hester 'Stella' Johnson, who became the enduring love of his life. *A Tale of a Tub* and *The Battle of the Books*, both published in 1704, were written at Moor Park.

In 1700 Swift returned to Ireland, where he was given the living of the vicarage at Laracor near Trim, Co. Meath. In 1701 he took his doctorate at Trinity College, Dublin and, for the following nine years, he divided his time between London and Dublin. In London he made his reputation as a wit, conversationalist and satirist. He met with Joseph Addison and William Congreve in the London coffee houses and became involved in politics. He espoused the Tory cause and was a close friend of the Lord Treasurer, Harley. He made stinging attacks on the Whig Party's war policy and contributed to the downfall of the Duke of Marlborough. The letters that make up Swift's *Journal to Stella*, written to Hester Johnson who had moved to Dublin with him, describe his political activities at this time. He hoped for a bishopric in return for his services but Queen Anne, offended by his attacks on religious cant in *A Tale of a Tub*, instead gave him the deanery of St Patrick's, Dublin in April 1713.

Being sent to Dublin was, in the beginning, akin to banishment for Swift and, when the Whigs returned to power within a year, his prospects seemed gone forever. However, while in St Patrick's, he became increasingly shocked and incensed by the scenes of poverty and misery in the neighbouring streets. Out of this sense of outrage came one of the most brilliant and biting pieces of satire written in English – *Gulliver's Travels*. Published in 1726, *Gulliver's Travels* very quickly became famous. Swift had become a champion of Irish economic independence, having witnessed the terrible effects of English policy on the country's citizens. *The Drapier's Letters* (1724) and *A Modest Proposal* (1729) exposed and bitterly ridiculed government corruption and the mismanagement of Ireland.

Swift's lifelong companion, Stella (Hester Johnson), died in 1728 and thereafter his sanity and health began to suffer. He continued to keep up voluminous correspondence with Pope, Gay, Arbuthnot and others of his English circle, but was increasingly suffering from loss of hearing, giddiness and mental decline. (His illness has since been diagnosed as Ménière's disease.) After suffering a stroke in 1742 which left him unable to speak, he was committed into care. He died in 1745 and is buried in St Patrick's Cathedral, where his own epitaph can be read: 'Fierce indignation can no longer tear his heart.'

🍀 **George Berkeley** (1685–1753), Ireland's most celebrated philosopher, continues to have a critical influence on European thought. Born in Dysart Castle, near Thomastown, Co. Kilkenny, he was sent to Trinity College, Dublin, where he was student, fellow and tutor until 1713. In 1709 he published *An Essay towards a New Theory of Vision*, followed in 1710 by *A Treatise concerning the Principles of Human Knowledge* and *Dialogues between Hylas and Philonous* (1713). In these works he first put forward and developed a psychological analysis of human perception. He used the 'Molyneaux problem'* to prove that the objects of vision and touch are not the same. Hume and Kant were influenced by his ideas, although neither perhaps grasped their full meaning. Berkeley showed the world from a new point of view by arguing that it is the mind that creates and that if the existence of something cannot be perceived by the mind, it cannot be said to exist at all. His doctrine is summed up in the phrase *esse est precipi* ('to be is to be perceived') – that nothing has any existence except in the mind of God.

Berkeley left Ireland to travel widely through France and Italy between 1714 and 1721. Upon his return to Ireland, he was appointed to the deanery of Derry in 1724. He was keen to found a college in America where colonists and native Americans could be educated side by side and was voted a government grant of £20,000. He sailed to America in 1728 and spent three years in Rhode Island, but his grant was withdrawn and he came home before a college was founded. His visit, however, did provide an impetus to found an American university and he is eponymously honoured by one of the nation's leading universities, in Berkeley, California.

In 1734 Berkeley returned to Ireland to take up his appointment as Bishop of Cloyne. He continued his

* *The 'Molyneaux problem' is named after the Dublin philosopher and patriot **William Molyneaux** (1656–1708). It highlighted the differences between the empiricists and the rationalists. It asked whether a man who is born blind and who can distinguish a globe from a cube by touch could tell which was which without touching them if he were suddenly to regain his sight. Molyneaux posed the question to his friend and colleague John Locke (1632–1704). As empiricists, they believed that the man would not be able to make the distinction, whereas rationalists, who maintained that some elements of knowledge are innate, believed that he could. Molyneaux also wrote a political and economic treatise,* The Case of Ireland's being Bound by Acts of Parliament in England Stated *(1698).*

Edmund Burke, born at Arran Quay, Dublin, was the leading political orator of his time. He expressed his opposition to the French Revolution in Reflections on the Revolution in France *(1790). Burke's political philosophy formed the basis of modern British Conservative thought.*

philosophical writings and made a critical examination of Newton's mathematics in the interest of the Christian mysteries in *The Analyst* (1734). In 1735 he published the first of three volumes of *The Querist*, which contained some five hundred questions on the social and economic problems of Ireland. The last of his philosophical works, *Siris* (1744), advocates the drinking of tar water for its medicinal properties and then moves on to consideration of religious questions. He resigned his bishopric in 1752 and moved to Oxford. He died there in 1753 and was buried in Christ Church Cathedral.

🍀 **Edmund Burke** (1729–97) was born at 12 Arran Quay, Dublin, to a Catholic mother and Protestant father. He was educated at the Quaker school in Ballitore, Co. Kildare kept by Abraham Shackleton. Burke entered Trinity College, Dublin in 1744 (where he was a founder of the college historical society). He moved to London in 1750, studying law at the Middle Temple, but was not called to the bar. In 1757 *A Philosophical Inquiry into the Origin of our Ideas of the Sublime and Beautiful* was published and favourably received. In 1759 he became founding editor of the *Annual Register*, a yearly survey of world affairs, and remained involved with it for 30 years. In 1761 he moved back to Dublin to become secretary to W. G. Hamilton, Chief Secretary of Ireland, but resigned his post two years later and moved back to London, where he became an associate of Johnson, Garrick and Reynolds and where, in 1764, they formed their famous Garrick Club.

By 1765 he was MP for Wendover and secretary to Prime Minister Lord Rockingham. At Westminster his brilliant skills as an orator and wit were developed. In two great parliamentary speeches, 'American Taxation' (1774) and 'Conciliation with the Colonies' (1775), and 'A Letter to the Sheriffs of Bristol' (1777) Burke criticised British policy towards the American colonies. Burke also advocated legislative independence for Ireland and drew charges of 'Catholicism' which lost him the seat as MP for Bristol which he had held from 1774 to 1780. He became MP for Malton, a pocket-borough of Lord Rockingham's, in 1781. When Rockingham was returned as Prime Minister in 1782, Burke was made Privy Councillor and Paymaster of the forces. He immediately reduced his own salary from £20,000 to £4000 and introduced similar reforms to other public offices. In 1788 Warren Hastings, Governor-General of India, was impeached largely at the instigation of Burke, who opened the proceedings with a speech that lasted four days. The trial lasted eight years and ended in the acquittal of Hastings on all charges.

Reflections on the Revolution in France (1790), Burke's most famous work, went into 11 editions and became the bible of those – throughout Europe – who were opposed to the Revolution. His work provoked many responses, not least Thomas Paine's *Rights of Man*. Burke's writings advocated a liberal and reasoned approach to political conflict that was opposed by the landed aristocracy in Britain. He was, however, fundamentally a conservative, favouring tradition, inherited values and the ordered system of the society of his day. His writing inspired conservative political theory in the 19th century.

♣ **Oliver Goldsmith** (1728–74) was a contemporary of Burke and also a member of Samuel Johnson's Literary Club, but he never enjoyed the same fame or worldly success. Goldsmith was born in Pallas, Co.

Longford, and educated at Trinity College, Dublin, and at the universities of Edinburgh and Leiden. He earned a precarious living as a hack in London's 'Grub Street' and wrote numerous reviews, introductions, histories and addresses for magazines and periodicals. These pieces are of varying quality, as his main concern in writing them was to earn a living. *The Citizen of the World* (1762) was a series of satirical essays that contributed to his growing fame in literary circles. His novel *The Vicar of Wakefield* (1766) enhanced his fame and remains a classic today. Goldsmith next turned to the stage and enjoyed moderate success with *The Good-Natur'd Man* in 1768 before his ultimate triumph with *She Stoops to Conquer* in 1773. His finest work in poetry was *The Deserted Village*, published in 1770. His eloquence, wit and humour on paper was evidently not matched by his speech. David Garrick composed a mock epitaph:

> *Here lies Nolly Goldsmith,*
> *for shortness called Noll,*
> *Who wrote like an angel*
> *but talked like poor Poll.*

Samuel Johnson made a similar observation: 'No man was more foolish when he had not a pen in his hand, or more wise when he had.'

♣ **Maria Edgeworth** (1767–1849), born at Black Bourton, Oxfordshire, the daughter of Richard Lovell Edgeworth (see p. 52). She was educated in England before moving to Ireland with her father who was returning to manage his estates at Edgeworthstown (Mostrim), Co. Longford. Edgeworth was **the first modern Irish fiction writer**. Her novel *Castle Rackrent* (1800) could be described as **the first European regional novel**. It was her first novel and was an instant success. Written in the year of the Act of Union, the novel is not only a masterly work of fiction, but a cautionary tale to Irish landlords and an historical record of Ireland at that time. Edgeworth's most notable follower, Sir Walter Scott, wrote in the original edition of *Waverley* that his aim was 'in some distant degree to emulate the admirable Irish portraits drawn by Miss Edgeworth'. Her subsequent works were no less successful: *Belinda* (1801), *Essays on Irish Bulls* (1802), *The Absentee* (1809), *Tales of Fashionable Life* (6 vols.; 1809–12) and *Ormond* (1817). She made several visits to London, where she was courted by society and more particularly by many individuals who sought her hand in marriage. Her friendship with Scott was a lasting one and her influence on his writing and that of the 19th-century Realists was enormous.

❀ **Joseph Sheridan Le Fanu** (1814–73) was born in Dublin of a family of Huguenot origins. His paternal grandmother was the sister of Richard Brinsley Sheridan (see p. 149). After graduating from Trinity College he was called to the bar, but quickly turned to writing. His early short stories were published in the *Dublin University Magazine*. From 1840 he was increasingly involved in Irish journalism. In the 1860s he published a series of novels, including *Uncle Silas* (1864), that established him as a best-selling writer of tales of the sinister and the supernatural. Largely forgotten in the early part of the 20th century, Le Fanu is now recognised as being in the front rank of ghost story and mystery writers. His tale of female vampirism, 'Carmilla', from his short-story collection *In a Glass Darkly* (1872), was an influence on Bram Stoker's *Dracula* (see below).

❀ **Abraham (Bram) Stoker** (1847–1912), author of *Dracula*, was born in Dublin at Marino Crescent and was a graduate of Trinity College, Dublin. He entered the civil service and wrote unpaid theatre reviews for the *Evening Mail*. In 1878 he was invited to work as secretary to the actor and stage-manager Sir Henry Irving. He accepted and held the post until the death of Irving in 1905. Stoker wrote a dozen novels in all; most are now forgotten. *Dracula*, written in 1897, was influenced by *Carmilla*, a tale of vampirism by fellow-Dubliner Sheridan Le Fanu (see above). Many parallels have been drawn between the character of Count Dracula and that of Henry Irving, whose *Personal Reminiscences* were published by Stoker in 1906, but it is of course as a horror story that *Dracula* caught the public imagination, and innumerable reprints, adaptations, translations and film productions of Stoker's novel have been made, the story of the Transylvanian vampire becoming familiar to audiences worldwide.

❀ **Oscar Fingal O'Flahertie Wills Wilde** (1854–1900) was born at Westland Row, Dublin, the son of the eminent surgeon Sir William Wilde (see p. 15) and Jane Francesca Elgee, 'Speranza' of the *Nation*. Wilde was educated at Portora Royal School, Enniskillen, Trinity College, Dublin and Magdalen College, Oxford. He won the Newdigate Prize for poetry in 1878 and graduated with first class honours in classics and the humanities.

Wilde moved to London after graduation and acquired a reputation as an outstanding wit, being burlesqued as Bunthorne in Gilbert and Sullivan's *Patience* (1881). He was founder of the aesthetic cult of 'art for art's sake' that glorified beauty for itself alone.

After a successful tour of North America in 1882, he worked in London as a book reviewer and was editor of *Woman's World* 1887–89. In 1888 he published *The Happy Prince and Other Tales,* a collection of fairy tales that launched his literary career. *The Picture of Dorian Gray,* his only novel, was not well received on publication in 1891. *Lady Windermere's Fan* (1892) was Wilde's third play and his first success and he followed it with *A Woman of No Importance* (1893), *An Ideal Husband* (1895) and *The Importance of Being Earnest* (1895). In 1894 he also wrote *Salomé*, a French work translated by his friend and lover Lord Alfred Douglas. The play was banned in England for portraying biblical characters. It was, however, staged in Paris, where the lead role was played by Sarah Bernhardt, and was later made the libretto of an opera by Strauss.

The Marquess of Queensberry, father of Lord Alfred, objected to Wilde's liaison with his son. When Wilde took him to court in 1895 on criminal libel charges, he was himself arrested following a scathing cross-examination by Edward Carson, later champion of the Irish Unionist cause (see p. 71). On 25 May 1895 Wilde was sentenced to two years' hard labour in Reading Gaol for committing homosexual acts. In November of the same year he was declared bankrupt and, on his release in 1897, he left England and lived out his last years in Italy and France, surviving on a small annuity paid for by friends. In 1898 he published *The Ballad of Reading Gaol,* an account of his sufferings in prison. He died of cerebral meningitis in Paris at the Hôtel d'Alsace on 30 November 1900 and is buried in Père Lachaise cemetery.

❀ **George Bernard Shaw** (1856–1950), winner of the Nobel Prize for Literature in 1925, was born at Synge Street, Dublin into a poor family. He spent many summers in Dalkey, Co. Dublin in the home of his mother's close friend and music teacher, George Vandeleur Lee. Shaw attributed his education more to his music-filled environment and the long hours spent in Dublin's National Gallery than to the teaching system at Wesley College. In 1876 he left Dublin to follow his mother and sisters to London. For the next nine years he strove to establish himself as a writer and completed five unsuccessful novels. In 1884 he joined the Fabian Society, whose socialist ideals remained central to Shaw's work and way of life. He overcame his chronic shyness and grew to become a brilliant public speaker. He served as a local government councillor in the London borough of St Pancras 1897–1903.

In 1885 Shaw found employment as a book re-

George Bernard Shaw, Nobel Prize winner for Literature in 1925, photographed with members of the cast during rehearsals of his play Buoyant Billions, *Ayot St. Lawrence, Hertfordshire, July 1949.*

viewer for the *Pall Mall Gazette* and as an art critic for *The World*. In 1888 he adopted the pen-name Corno di Bassetto and wrote musical criticism in a fresh and direct style for the *Star*. He was less successful with his plays. *The Philanderer, Mrs Warren's Profession, Arms and the Man, Candida* – all internationally acclaimed today – were not to the critics' taste in the 1890s. In 1895 he took up a post as dramatic critic for the *Saturday Review*, under the editorship of Frank Harris*, and championed the work of Henrik Ibsen.

The Devil's Disciple was acclaimed in New York and brought Shaw his first royalties in 1897. The

** **James Thomas (Frank) Harris** (1856–1931) was born in Galway. As a teenager, he ran away to the USA and, at the age of 27, re-emerged to begin a literary career in London. He edited the* Evening News, *the* Fortnightly Review *and the* Saturday Review. *He was imprisoned for contempt of court in a libel suit in 1914 and returned to the USA after his release. He published biographies of George Bernard Shaw and Oscar Wilde and a shamelessly boastful autobiography in five volumes.*

following year he gained financial security through his marriage to Charlotte Payne-Townshend, a wealthy Anglo-Irish associate of Shaw's Fabian friends. Shaw now began to write plays at a prolific rate. It was not until 1904 that his genius was recognised in Britain, when Harley Granville-Barker took over as producer at the Royal Court Theatre in London, where *John Bull's Other Island, Man and Superman* and *The Doctor's Dilemma* established Shaw's reputation.

Shaw's pacifism during World War I earned him notoriety and he was expelled from the Dramatists' Club. His popularity in Britain took another knock when he protested against the executions of the leaders of the Easter Rising in Dublin in 1916.

Although Shaw considered *Heartbreak House*, produced in New York in 1920, to be his best play, many would have chosen *St Joan*, produced in London in 1924. *St Joan* established Shaw as the world's greatest living playwright and was probably the decisive work in his claim to the 1925 Nobel Prize for Literature.

William Butler Yeats (right) with his friend John Masefield (1878–1967), the English poet laureate 1930–67. In 1923 Yeats became the first Irish writer to receive the Nobel Prize for Literature. Yeats was at the forefront of the Irish literary renaissance.

Shaw returned to political writing in 1928 with *An Intelligent Woman's Guide to Socialism and Capitalism*. He declined British honours, turning down an Order of Merit and a peerage. A lifelong socialist, pursuer of women's rights and advocate of a new phonetic alphabet, he lived to the age of 94. His will benefited the National Gallery of Ireland and its value was later vastly increased by the royalties earned from *My Fair Lady,* a film version of *Pygmalion* that earned him an Oscar for Best Screenplay. At his death in November 1950 the lights on New York's Broadway were extinguished in his honour.

✿ **William Butler Yeats** (1865–1939), winner of the Nobel Prize for Literature in 1923, was born in Sandymount, Dublin, the eldest child of the painter John Butler Yeats. He spent his first 15 years in London, where he went to the Godolphin School in Hammersmith, but spent his summer holidays in Sligo. When the family returned to Ireland in 1880, he went to the High School, then on Harcourt Street. He studied at the Metropolitan School of Art 1884–85 and then at the Royal Hibernian Academy 1886. Having made friends with George Russell* and a group of mystics, he decided to abandon his artistic studies and develop his experiments in poetry.

He met with John O'Leary and Standish O'Grady who awakened in him a sense of Ireland's epic past. This inspiration lay behind the *Wanderings of Oisin*. In 1887 he was back in London and maintained his interest in the occult by joining Madame Blavatsky's Theosophists and the Order of the Golden Dawn. He founded the Irish Literary Society of London in 1891 and the National Literary Society the following year.

* *George Russell, pen-name A.E. Russell (1867–1935), poet and painter, was born in Lurgan, Co. Down and brought up in Rathmines in Dublin. His home was a meeting-place for those interested in the artistic and economic fate of Ireland. He was editor of the* Irish Homestead, *the organ of the Irish Agricultural Organisation Society, and a friend of W.B. Yeats. He was a theosophist and wrote on economics and politics while continuing to paint and write poetry.*

The Countess Cathleen, his first poetic play, was published in 1892 and his first volume of folk stories, *The Celtic Twilight*, appeared the following year. In 1895 he published *A Book of Irish Verse and Poems*. His life-long obsession with Maud Gonne (see p. 59) began after their first meeting in 1889 and his first marriage proposal to her was refused in 1891.

With Lady Gregory (see p. 145) he formed the Irish Literary Theatre, which began in 1899 with a performance of *The Countess Cathleen*. He worked with George Moore on *Diarmuid and Grainne* in 1901 and wrote *Cathleen Ni Houlihan* in 1902 for Maud Gonne. The Irish National Theatre became the Abbey Players in 1904 after Annie Horniman, a wealthy patroness from Manchester, bought the Mechanics Institute on Abbey Street for a venue. Yeats remained a director of the new theatre until his death. The Abbey established Dublin as an important theatrical centre in the early years of the century.

Yeats toured the US successfully in 1903, but returned to discover that Maud Gonne had married Major John MacBride. Yeats abandoned active politics and devoted his time to writing. In 1908 he met the American author Ezra Pound, who was strongly influenced by him and later worked as his secretary in 1913 and 1915. He turned down a knighthood in 1915 and proposed to Maud Gonne for the second time in 1916 following the execution of her husband for his participation in the 1916 Easter Rising – only to be refused again. In 1917 he married Georgie Hyde-Lees and settled once again to writing poetry in homage to the leaders of the Easter Rising. From 1922 he lived in Thoor Ballylee, a small Norman castle near Lady Gregory's Coole Park in Co. Galway. His poetry collections *The Tower* and *The Winding Stair* evoke this place. He received honorary degrees from Queen's University, Belfast and from Trinity College, Dublin in 1922, and was appointed to the Senate of the newly formed Irish Free State.

Yeats' major volumes of poetry appeared in the 1920s and 30s: *The Wild Swans at Coole* (1919), *Michael Robartes and the Dancer* (1921), *The Tower* (1928) and *The Winding Stair* (1933). His poetry deals with Ireland's political strife, his own personal troubles and recollections and an examination of his consequent emotions. *Collected Poems* appeared in 1933 and *Collected Plays* in 1934. His autobiography is contained in three volumes written over his lifetime: *Reveries over Childhood and Youth* (1915), *The Trembling of the Veil* (1922) and *Dramatis Personae* (1936).

From 1927 he spent winters in Italy and southern France to preserve his health. He died in Roquebrune near Monaco on 28 January 1939 and was buried there. In September 1948 his remains were returned to Drumcliff, Co. Sligo, 'under bare Ben Bulben's head'. Yeats wrote his own epitaph, now inscribed on his gravestone:

> *No marble, no conventional phrase;*
> *On Limestone quarried near the spot*
> *By his command these words are cut:*
> *Cast a cold eye*
> *On life, on death.*
> *Horseman, pass by!*

Yeats is judged by many to be **one of the greatest poets in the English language of the 20th century** and his work continues to be a source of inspiration and the subject of research and analysis all over the world.

James Joyce, master of the Modernist novel, photographed in 1941. Joyce opened Ireland's first cinema house in 1909. He was also an excellent singer and came third in the tenor competition of the 1904 Feis Ceoil (national music competition).

♣ **James Augustine Joyce** (1882–1941) was born at Brighton Square, Rathgar, Dublin and was educated at Clongowes Wood, Belvedere College and University College, Dublin, where he studied languages and learned to speak Latin, French, Italian, German and Norwegian. His first published work appeared in the *Fortnightly Review* in April 1900 and was an essay on the Norwegian playwright Ibsen, who remained a lasting influence on Joyce's own writing career.

In 1904 he met Nora Barnacle (who became his wife in 1931) and they moved to the continent, where they lived in Zurich and later in Pola and Trieste. Joyce made a brief return to Dublin in 1909 and **opened Ireland's first cinema**, the Volta on Mary Street. He made another visit in 1912 to arrange the publication of his collection of short stories, *Dubliners*, but argued with his publisher and never returned to Dublin again. By 1904 he had begun *Stephen Hero*, which he later rewrote as *Portrait of the Artist as a Young Man*. This was his first full-length work and was published in the United States in 1916. A highly autobiographical work, it describes the difficulties facing the artist in the stifling and conservative environment of Dublin. This is also evident in *Dubliners* (1914). Encouraged by the success of these works, Joyce undertook the writing of *Ulysses*. He moved to Paris in 1920 at the invitation of Ezra Pound and it was there, in 1922, that his masterpiece was published by Sylvia Beach, the owner of the bookshop Shakespeare and Company. Although it was banned in the USA and Britain, the book was widely available and brought him international fame. In *Ulysses*, Joyce employed the narrative technique known as 'stream of consciousness', juxtaposing past and present through references and parallels to other works such as the *Odyssey, Hamlet* and the Bible. The richness of Joyce's use of language is unrivalled in Western literature and the novel has become an undisputable classic of the 20th century. *Finnegans Wake*, published in 1939, reaches the limits of linguistic sophistication (see p. 22). Joyce intended his readers to take a lifetime to interpret the book and many have taken up the challenge.

Joyce's writings have immortalised the streets of Dublin. Admirers of his work, who come from all over the world to visit Dublin, constitute a minor tourist industry. Their numbers increase towards 'Bloomsday' (16 June), the day on which Leopold Bloom experienced his series of (mis)adventures as described in *Ulysses*.

James Joyce had an excellent singing voice and was third in the tenor competition at the 1904 Feis Ceoil (the annual national musical competition). The Feis Ceoil also unearthed the talents of John McCormack (see p. 121) in 1902 and Margaret Burke Sheridan (see p. 121) in 1908.

♣ **Samuel Barclay Beckett** (1906–89), writer, playwright and winner of the Nobel Prize for Literature in 1969, was born in Foxrock, a wealthy suburb of Dublin. He was educated at Earlsfort House school

---

Samuel Beckett, author of the hugely influential Waiting for Godot, *became the third Dublin-born recipient of the Nobel Prize for Literature in 1969. He spent most of his life in France and fought for the resistance in World War II.*

in Dublin, Portora Royal School in Enniskillen, Co. Fermanagh, and at Trinity College, Dublin. He graduated from Trinity in 1927 with distinction in English, French and Italian. He taught in Belfast briefly before leaving for Paris in 1928. There he met and befriended James Joyce (see p. 141), who was a major influence on his later work. Beckett returned to Dublin in 1930 to lecture in French at Trinity College. He left his job to tour Germany, France, England and Ireland. He published poetry and, in 1934, his first book of stories, *More Pricks than Kicks*, but these were not well received. He settled in Paris and married Suzanne Dumesnil. In 1938 his first novel, *Murphy*, was published in English.

When World War II broke out, Beckett joined the French Resistance movement and was involved in providing information on the movements of the German Army. He was awarded the Croix de Guerre in 1945 for his services. His second novel, *Watt*, was completed in 1945, although it was 1953 before it was published.

After the war, Beckett wrote only in French and finally achieved recognition with *Molloy* (1951), the first of a trilogy of novels (*Malone Dies* (1951) and *The Unnamable* (1953) being the other two). However, it was with *Waiting for Godot* in 1952 that he achieved international recognition. This tragi-comedy, first produced for the stage in Paris in 1953, caused a furore with its bleak nihilism. *Endgame* was premiered in London in April 1957, followed by *Krapp's Last Tape* in 1958. He wrote a series of works for BBC Radio, including *All That Fall* (1957) and *Embers* (1959). Later works include *Happy Days* (1961), *Breath* (1969) and *Not I* (1972). Beckett always shunned publicity and he refused to attend the prize-giving ceremony at which he was awarded the Nobel Prize for Literature. The philosophy of Beckett's writing is harsh and uncompromising in its fatalism – where mankind's only dignity is in his endurance of the futility and suffering of his existence.

♣ **Brian Friel** (1929–), widely regarded as **the leading contemporary playwright in the English language,** is a native of Killyclogher, near Omagh in Co. Tyrone. He was educated at St Columb's College in Derry and then in 1945 he went to St Patrick's, Maynooth. He took a postgraduate course at St Joseph's Training College, Belfast, qualifying as a teacher in 1950.

As a teacher in various Derry schools, Friel began to develop his writing career and wrote short stories for the *New Yorker* magazine. He married Anne Morrison in 1954 and they have five children. His first

Brian Friel, from Killyclogher, Co. Tyrone, has become one of the leading contemporary playwrights in the English language. Dancing at Lughnasa (1990), his most successful play to date, won three Tony Awards in 1992.

stage play, *A Doubtful Paradise*, was performed in Belfast in 1959. He retired from teaching in 1960 to concentrate on his writing. In 1962 his short stories were collected in *The Saucer of Larks*. The following year the Abbey Theatre in Dublin staged *The Enemy Within* and subsequently premiered most of his plays. *Philadelphia Here I Come* (1964) was his first international success. It concerns a reluctant emigrant to the USA whose divided mind is represented by two actors.

Subsequent works include *The Gold in the Sea* (1966) short stories, *The Loves of Cass Maguire* (1967), *Freedom of the City* (1973) based on the events of 'Bloody Sunday' in Derry in January 1972, *The Faith Healers* (1980), *Aristocrats* (1981) and *Translations* (1981). *Translations* is one of Friel's most admired works, exploring the trauma of the loss of identity

«here with a loaf of bread beneath the bough a flask of wine-a book of verse-and Thou....

Brendan Behan, the Dublin-born IRA volunteer who was arrested on a bombing mission in Britain in 1940. His autobiographical Borstal Boy recounts his experience in a juvenile prison. Behan was rearrested in Dublin in 1942 and sentenced to 14 years for a shooting offence.

following the anglicisation of Irish place-names by the Ordnance Survey of Ireland begun in 1830 by the British Army's Royal Engineers. It was the first theatrical production of the Field Day Theatre Company and publishing house, founded by Friel and actor Stephen Rea (see p. 162).

With the Field Day Theatre Company, Friel adapted *Three Sisters* (1981) and wrote *The Communication Cord* (1983) and *Making History* (1988). *Dancing at Lughnasa* (1990) was a huge success in Britain, Ireland and the USA. It was staged at the Abbey Theatre and the National Theatre in London and received an Olivier Award. On Broadway in 1992 it received three Tony Awards. Friel has been an honorary Doctor of Literature of the University of Ireland since 1982 and in 1987 became the first writer since W.B. Yeats to be appointed to the Seanad (Irish Senate).

☘ While Brian Friel may be considered the best living playwright in the English language, his friend, fellow-graduate of St Columb's College, Derry, and co-director of the Field Day Theatre Company, **Seamus Heaney** (1939–) has been hailed by many as **the best living poet in the English language**. Heaney was born on a farm in Bellaghy, Co. Derry and won scholarships to St Columb's and then Queen's University, Belfast, where he gained a first-class degree in English. At Queen's University, under the tutorship of the English critic Philip Hobsbaum, Heaney worked with some of contemporary Ireland's leading writers and critics, including Seamus Deane, Michael and Edna Longley and Stewart Parker.

Heaney's ability was quickly recognised and his first collection of poems, *Death of a Naturalist* (1966), was well received. He lectured in English at Queen's University and contributed to the *Listener*. *Door in the Dark,* his second volume of verse, appeared in 1969. He was invited to the University of California at Berkeley as a visiting lecturer in 1970, where he absorbed the wider range of writing techniques and cultures that became evident in his third volume, *Wintering Out* (1972).

With the worsening of the troubles in Northern Ireland, Heaney resigned from Queen's University, Belfast and moved with his family to Ashford, Co. Wicklow. Subsequent collections include: *North* (1975), *Field Work* (1979), *Station Island* (1984), *The Haw Lantern* (1987). He also edited a collection of verse – *The Rattle Bag* (1982) – with the English poet (now Poet Laureate) Ted Hughes. His plays include: *No Cure at Troy* (1990), an adaptation of *Philoctetes* by Sophocles (1991) and *Seeing Things* (1991). Heaney was appointed resident poet at Harvard University, Boston in 1982 and was elected to the Boylston Chair of Rhetoric and Oratory there in 1984. In 1989 he was elected to the prestigious Chair of Poetry at Oxford University.

Other leading Irish writers

♣ **John Banville** (1945–), born in Wexford, worked as a sub-editor on the *Irish Press* until 1984. In 1988 he was appointed literary editor of the *Irish Times*. His work has won many awards. In 1989 *The Book of Evidence* was nominated for the Booker Prize and won the Guinness Peat Aviation Literary Award. Other major works include: *Long Lankin* (1970), *Birchwood* (1973), *Doctor Copernicus* (1976), *Kepler* (1981), *The Newton Letter* (1982), *Mefisto* (1986) and *Ghosts* (1993).

♣ **Brendan Behan** (1923–64), born in Dublin, became involved with the Republican movement and was captured in Liverpool on a bombing mission in 1939. He subsequently spent two years in a juvenile detention centre. In 1941 he was deported to Ireland, where he was re-arrested after several months for shooting at a policeman. He was released in a general amnesty in 1946, having served five years of his 14-year sentence. His experiences in these years are recounted in his works. *Borstal Boy* (1958), considered to be his finest work, is an autobiographical account of prison life. He wrote poetry, prose and plays in English and Irish and won international fame with *The Quare Fellow*, first performed at the Pike Theatre, Dublin in 1954 and then at a Theatre Workshop Production in London in 1956. *An Giall* was first produced at the Damer Irish Language Theatre in 1958 and an English adaptation, *The Hostage*, was performed that same year, bringing the author even greater acclaim. He was a popular media personality, particularly in Dublin where he became something of a folk hero. His premature death was caused by alcoholism and diabetes. His funeral in Dublin was attended by thousands.

♣ **Elizabeth Bowen** (1900–73), the Dublin-born novelist, essayist and local historian, was educated at Trinity College, Dublin and at Oxford. She also wrote the short story collections *Encounters* (1923), *Look at all those Roses* (1941), *The Collected Stories of Elizabeth Bowen* (1980), and novels such as *The Hotel* (1927), *The Last September* (1929), *The Heat of the Day* (1949) and *Eva Trout* (1969). Her historical writing includes *Bowen's Court* (1942), a history of the family home in Co. Cork, and *The Shelbourne Hotel* (1951), a history of the famous Dublin institute and landmark.

♣ **John Burke,** born in 1787 in Tipperary, compiled with his son, **John Bernard Burke**, *A Genealogical and Heraldic Dictionary of the Peerage and Baronetage of the United Kingdom*, the first edition of which

Roddy Doyle, the second Irish-born recipient of the Booker Prize (after Iris Murdoch), for his novel Paddy Clarke Ha Ha Ha *in 1993. Doyle's novels have been successfully screened on television and in the cinema.*

appeared in 1826. This was followed in 1838 by *A Genealogical and Heraldic History of the Commoners of Great Britain and Ireland*. Still published today as *Burke's Peerage* or *Burke's Landed Gentry*, it is a standard reference book of inestimable importance. It has been called the 'stud book of humanity' by its more anglophile admirers. John Bernard Burke became Governor of the National Gallery of Ireland in 1874.

✿ **Padraic Colum** (1888–1972), born in Longford, was one of the first playwrights at the Abbey Theatre. *Broken Soil* (1903), *The Land* (1905) and *Thomas Muskerry* (1910) presented harsh and realistic contrasts to the contemporary Celtic mysticism of W.B. Yeats.

Colum went to the USA in 1914. In 1924 he was invited to visit Hawaii to investigate native Polynesian folklore and to convert elements of it into stories for local children. He published *Collected Poems* in 1932 and *The Legend of St Columba* in 1937. The third edition of *Irish Elegies* was published in 1963. In 1959 his major historical work, *Sinn Féin: The Story of Arthur Griffith and the Origin of the Irish Free State*, was published in New York.

✿ **Cecil Day-Lewis** (1904–72), born in Ballintubber, Co. Mayo, became Britain's Poet Laureate in 1968 (the second Irish person to do so*). Day-Lewis was educated at Oxford and was a contemporary and friend of Auden and Spender. His first volume of poetry, *Beechen Vigil*, was published in 1925. He joined the British Communist Party but left in 1938 to work for the British Ministry of Information during World War II. He was professor of poetry at Oxford 1951–56 and at Harvard 1964–65. He was also a member of the Irish Academy of Letters. Day-Lewis wrote many murder mysteries under the pen-name of Nicholas Blake, and published his autobiography, *Buried Day*, in 1960. He was the father of the Oscar-winning actor Daniel Day-Lewis (see p. 155).

✿ Dubliner **Roddy Doyle** (1958–) became, in October 1993, the second Irish-born author (after Iris

* ***Nahum Tate***, *born in Dublin in 1652, was England's first Irish Poet Laureate, succeeding Shadwell in 1692. Although a poor poet in general, his* Supplement to the New Version of the Psalms *(1703) was of better quality than his usual work. The hymn contained therein, 'While Shepherds Watched Their Flocks by Night', remains one of the most famous carols in English. He also rewrote Shakespeare's* King Lear, *adding a happy ending in which Cordelia marries Edgar. This was the preferred version on the English stage until the 1850s.*

Murdoch in 1978) to be awarded the Booker Prize, for his novel *Paddy Clarke Ha, Ha, Ha*. Doyle has achieved international fame with the successful filming of two parts of his *Barrytown Trilogy*: *The Commitments* and *The Snapper*. The third book in the series, *The Van*, has yet to reach the screen. *The Commitments* (1991), directed by Alan Parker, was a box-office hit across Europe and America. *The Snapper* (1993) directed by Stephen Frears, although so far less successful commercially, received equal critical acclaim.

✿ **Lady Gregory, Isabella Augusta Persse** (1852–1932), was born in Roxborough, Co. Galway. She married Sir William Gregory of Coole Park, a former Governor of Ceylon, in 1880. Although raised in the Protestant landed gentry tradition, she became a convinced and active nationalist. She studied the Irish language and Irish folklore and organised the Gaelic League in her locality. In 1896 she met W.B. Yeats (see p. 139) and a life-long friendship developed. Together they formed the Irish Literary Theatre, which put on its first production, Yeats' *The Countess Cathleen*, in 1899. Her house at Coole Park became a meeting place for Yeats, Synge and other writers of the Literary Revival. She was the crucial policy-maker at the Abbey Theatre, which opened on 27 December 1904 with a production of her one-act play *Spreading the News*, along with Yeats' *On Baile Strand*. She was one of very few writers with whom Yeats could collaborate and the ideas and dialogue of many of his plays are attributable to her. When the Abbey was in need of more plays, she turned to writing herself, with great success. She wrote 27 in all, mostly short, sympathetic observations of Irish rural life highlighting the negative results of Britain's misgovernment of Ireland. Her best-known works are *Spreading the News* (1904), *Kincora* (1905), *The Rising of the Moon* (1907) and *The Workhouse Ward* (1908). Her contribution to modern Irish culture was recognised in Yeats' elegy, 'Coole Park and Ballylee', 1931.

✿ **Patrick Kavanagh** (1904–67), born in Iniskeen, Co. Monaghan, published his first book of poetry, *Ploughman and Other Poems*, in 1936. Other major works include: *The Green Fool* (1938), *The Great Hunger* (1942), *A Soul for Sale* (1947) and a novel entitled *Tarry Flynn* (1948). *Collected Poems* (1964) consolidated his reputation and attracted a large readership outside Ireland.

✿ **Clive Staples Lewis** (1898–1963), born in Belfast, was a graduate of Oxford and a veteran of World

War I. C.S. Lewis tutored at Magdalen College, Oxford from 1925 to 1954, when he was appointed professor of medieval and renaissance literature. A critical work, *The Allegory of Love* (1936), won him the Hawthornden Prize. He wrote allegorical fantasy fiction and several religious works. *The Chronicles of Narnia* (1950–56), an allegorical series of six books for children, has become a best-seller worldwide. Other works include: *The Problem of Pain* (1940) and *The Screwtape Letters* (1942), letters from a senior to a junior devil on the art of temptation. Lewis was a convert to Christianity and described his experience in his autobiography, *Surprised by Joy* (1955).

♣ **Louis MacNeice** (1907–63), born in Belfast, was a member of the group of left-wing poets in England, along with Spender, Auden and Cecil Day-Lewis (see p. 145). He joined the BBC in 1941 and wrote many radio plays over his 20 years working there, including *Christopher Columbus* (1944) and *The Dark Tower* (1947). It was his poetry, however, that was most praised by the critics: *Autumn Journal* (1938–89), *Holes in the Sky* (1947), *Collected Poems* (1925–48) and *Autumn Sequel* (1954). His autobiography, *The Strings Are False*, was published posthumously in 1965.

♣ **Brian Moore** (1921–), born in Belfast, served in North Africa, Italy and France with the British Ministry of War Transport during World War II. He emigrated to Canada in 1948 and took Canadian citizenship. After several years struggling as a journalist and fiction writer in Montreal, his first novel, *The Lonely Passion of Judith Hearne,* was published in 1955 to great critical acclaim. He moved to New York in 1959 and later settled in Malibu, California. He received the Governor-General of Canada's Award for Fiction in 1960. His novels sell worldwide and many have been adapted for the cinema. He also writes film scripts and worked for Alfred Hitchcock (see p. 158).

Moore's other major novels include: *The Luck of Ginger Coffey* (1960), *The Emperor of Ice-cream* (1965), *Catholics* (1972), *The Mangan Inheritance* (1979), *Black Robe* (1985), *The Colour of Blood* (1987), *Lies of Silence* (1990) and *No Other Life* (1993).

♣ **Thomas Moore** (1779–1852), born at 12 Aungier Street, Dublin, in 1794, became one of the first Catholics admitted to Trinity College, Dublin. There he made friends with the doomed patriot Robert Emmet. In 1799 he moved to London to study law. In London his singing and poetical skills made him a huge social success. *Odes of Anacreon,* published in 1800, was highly praised. He gained an admiralty post in Bermuda in 1803 but, after spending only a few months there, delegated his duties to a deputy and undertook a tour of the United States and Canada. *Irish Melodies,* written in ten parts between 1808 and 1834, ensure his enduring fame and he was acclaimed as Ireland's national lyric poet. His fame, even in England, rivalled that of his friend Byron.

In 1812 Moore was offered £3000 by Longman, the publishing firm, to write an oriental romance. *Lalla Rookh* was published in 1817 and was very popular, despite its considerable length. He was forced to leave London in 1818 to avoid the debtor's prison after discovering that his deputy in Bermuda had absconded, leaving Moore responsible for a debt of £6000. In Italy he renewed his friendship with Byron, who left him his memoirs. He returned to Dublin in 1835 on a civil list pension of £300 per year.

♣ **Edna O'Brien** (1932–) was born in Tuamgraney, Co. Clare and educated at the Convent of Mercy, Loughrea, Co. Galway and at the Pharmaceutical College in Dublin. She moved to England in 1958 and has lived there ever since, visiting Ireland regularly as a popular media personality. Her novels include: *The Country Girls* (1960), *The Lonely Girl* (1962), *Casualties of Peace* (1966), *A Pagan Place* (1970), *Johnny I Hardly Knew You* (1977) and *The High Road* (1988). O'Brien has also written the short stories collected in *The Love Object* (1968), *A Scandalous Woman and Other Stories* (1974), *Mrs Reinhardt and Other Stories* (1978), *A Fanatic Heart, Selected Stories* (1984) and *Lantern Slides* (1990).

♣ **Sean O'Casey** (1880–1964) was born at 85 Upper Dorset Street in Dublin. He was closely involved with the Irish Labour movement before 1916 and was Secretary of the Irish Citizen Army under James Connolly. He was part of the Marxist element of the Irish independence movement which was ultimately superseded by the nationalist faction. This defeat and an abiding hatred of the poverty and injustice suffered by Dublin's working class were the source of his three critically acclaimed plays for the Abbey Theatre. Encouraged by Lady Gregory (see p. 145), he submitted plays to the theatre and was eventually successful with *The Shadow of a Gunman* (1923), which instantly established him as a leading new literary voice. (O'Casey was already 43 years old.) *Juno and the Paycock* (1924) and *The Plough and the Stars* (1926) followed and were enormous financial boosts to an ailing Abbey Theatre. *The Plough and the Stars* caused much controversy over the parading of the revolutionary flag and the characterisation of a prostitute in a leading and heroic role.

The three Abbey productions are considered O'Casey's best. *The Silver Tassie* (1928) was turned down by Abbey directors, Lady Gregory, W.B. Yeats and Lennox Robinson, who all agreed that it was an unsuitable production to appear at the Abbey, dealing as it did with the theme of war rather than the realistic portrayal of human characters. O'Casey, then living in London, was bitterly disappointed and decided to stay abroad. He wrote many plays for the London stage but none were as successful as his first three. However, more recently some critics have come to regard *The Silver Tassie* and *Red Roses for Me* (1946) as forerunners of the new experimental English theatre from which writers like Harold Pinter, who was trained in Irish repertory, received a grounding in free artistic expression.

✤ **Brian O'Nolan** (1911–66) wrote under the pen-names **Flann O'Brien** and **Myles na gCopaleen**. He was born in Strabane, Co. Tyrone and graduated from University College, Dublin in 1932 with a degree in Celtic languages. His first novel, *At Swim-Two-Birds*, a Joycean concoction of folklore, humour and poetry published in 1939, is now regarded as a masterpiece of wit and scholarship. As Myles na gCopaleen, he wrote the column 'Cruishkeen Lawn' in the *Irish Times*, in which he championed the Irish language and poured scorn on the self-important and the generally stupid. His writings include *The Hard Life* (1961), *The Dalkey Archive* (1965) and *The Third Policeman* (posthumously published in 1967). He also wrote the play *Faustus Kelly*, produced at the Abbey Theatre in 1943. *An Béal Bocht* (The Poor Mouth), his only book in Irish, was written in 1941 and published in 1973.

✤ **Somerville and Ross: Edith Somerville** (1858–1949) was born in Corfu, where her father was stationed as a British Army officer. The following year he returned with his family to their home in Drishane, Skibbereen, Co. Cork. Edith was educated at Alexandra College in Dublin and studied painting in London, Paris and Düsseldorf. On 17 January 1886 she met her cousin **Violet Martin** (1862–1915), born in Ross, Co. Galway, and they undertook a literary partnership under the names Somerville and Ross. Their first book, *An Irish Cousin*, appeared in 1889 and was followed by a more serious work, *The Real Charlotte* (1894), *Some Experiences of an Irish RM* (Resident Magistrate; 1899), *Further Experiences of an Irish RM* (1908) and *Mr Knox's Country* (1915). In their novels the way of life on the decaying estates of the landed gentry in the west of Ireland is described with humour and accuracy. Some criticise the stereotyping of the Irish peasant characters, but that is to ignore the mockery that is made in equal measure of the landowners and the fact that the authors would have had little or no knowledge of the harsher facts of life faced by tenant farmers and labourers. The literary merit of their work is undisputed. It is generally believed that Violet Martin (Ross) was the source of much of the wilder humour and that Somerville added more factual detail and knowledge of Ireland and the Irish language.

Martin died in 1915 but Somerville continued to write under both names, believing that her partner remained with her after death as a source of inspiration. Later books included *The Big House at Inver* (1925), *The States Through Irish Eyes* (1931) and *An Incorruptible Irishman* (1932).

✤ **John Millington Synge** (1871–1909) was born in Rathfarnham, now a suburb of Dublin. He was educated at Trinity College, Dublin and the Royal Academy of Music. He travelled to Germany in 1893 to study and work as a musician but two years later moved to Paris, having decided to pursue a literary career. He was the best playwright the Abbey Theatre produced, although his initial reception from his Irish audience was violently hostile. Synge was the first playwright to write about Ireland for an Irish audience and was a scholar of Irish language and culture. On the advice of W.B. Yeats, whom he met in Paris, he spent consecutive summers on the Aran Islands from 1899 to 1902, where the traditional Gaelic culture and way of life remained practically untouched. He travelled through the remotest parts of County Wicklow, visiting the homes of the local people and absorbing their stories and language. The 'poetic prose' of Hiberno-English speech, and the vivid and energetic imagination of those who speak it, was reproduced on stage in stylised form. *The Shadow of the Glen,* his first play, performed in the Abbey in 1903, dealt with a loveless marriage and was extremely controversial, but it was *The Playboy of the Western World* (1907) that caused riots at the Abbey. Five hundred policemen were required to control an audience of under 500 people. The portrayal of Irish women competing for the affections of a man who had reputedly killed his own father – and was revered for it in the community – proved too much for Dublin audiences, who were outraged by a work that appeared to belittle the ideal of Irish womanhood. The comic irony of Synge's work was interpreted as mocking laughter and exacerbated the hostile reception of critics and public alike. The play also caused riotous scenes in America (where the whole cast of the touring Abbey Theatre Company were briefly held in jail). *The Playboy of the Western World* is now recognised as a classic of the Irish theatre and receives countless annual productions.

Synge's other major works are *Riders to the Sea* (published in 1903 and first performed the following year), *The Tinker's Wedding* (1907), *The Aran Islands* (1907; a novel) and *Deirdre of the Sorrows* (published posthumously in 1910). *Collected Works Volume I: Poems* was published in 1962 and *Collected Works Volume II: Prose* in 1966.

♣ The novelist and short-story writer **William Trevor** (1928–) was born William Trevor Cox in Mitchelstown, Co. Cork. He graduated from Trinity College, Dublin and was a sculptor before he took up writing. He has won many awards, including the Hawthornden Prize in 1965 for *The Old Boys* (1964), the Whitbread Prize for Fiction and the Allied Irish Banks Prize. He is **the only writer to have won the Whitbread Prize twice** – for *The Children of Dynmouth* (1976) and *Fools of Fortune* (1983). *Angels at the Ritz* (1975) won the Royal Society of Literature Prize.

Irish authors abroad and Irish-related writers

♣ The poet, critic and short-story writer **Edgar Allan Poe** (1809–49), born in Boston, was one of America's most brilliant writers. He is considered to be one of the creators of modern horror fiction and was a master of mystery and the macabre. Poe had a strong Ulster background. His father's family emigrated from Ireland c. 1748 and his grandfather, David Poe, married Elizabeth Cairnes of an established Boston-Irish family. His mother, Elizabeth Arnold, was of English ancestry. Poe was orphaned in 1811 and in 1820 was sent to school in Richmond, Virginia to be taught by Joseph H. Clarke of Trinity College, Dublin, who had been employed to educate the 'best' families of Richmond. It was with Joseph Clarke that Poe developed an interest in poetry, publishing three volumes before he was 25.

His *Tales of the Grotesque and Arabesque* established the tone of writing with which his name became synonymous – that of terror and mystery. The collection includes some of Poe's best-known stories: 'The Masque of the Red Death', 'The Fall of the House of Usher' and 'The Murders in the Rue Morgue'.

♣ **Eugene Gladstone O'Neill** (1888–1953), 1936 Nobel Prize Winner for Literature, was born in America to **James O'Neill** (1849–1920) of Co. Kilkenny. His mother was from a middle-class Catholic Irish-American family long established in the US. James O'Neill was a stage actor who, in 1882, first appeared as Edmond Dantes in a stage version of *The Count of Monte Cristo* and was so successful that he never played in another role. He ended up playing the part more than 4000 times. The play was finally made into a film in 1913 for which O'Neill, who was by then almost synonymous with the character of Edmond Dantes, received 20% of the profits. This was **Hollywood's first ever percentage deal contract**.

Eugene Gladstone O'Neill (whose father had given him his middle name after the British Prime Minister because he considered him to have been the only

Eugene O'Neill, the only American to have won the Nobel Prize for Literature, was the son of a Kilkenny-born stage actor. His daughter, Oonagh, married Charlie Chaplin.

British politician to have ever tried to do anything for Ireland) attended Princeton University briefly from 1906 to 1907 and then drifted for six years in the merchant navy and gold prospecting. His travels were symptomatic of a restless nature, the inheritance of a childhood spent on the move following his father's theatrical engagements. He made three suicide attempts in these years and was prone to bouts of heavy drinking. He later saw that this part of his life was the source and inspiration for much of his writing. By 1914 he had decided to become a playwright. In his travels he had encountered a touring company from the Abbey Theatre and in the early stages of his writing career he was given encouragement by Joyce (see p. 141) and O'Casey (see p. 146), who both considered that he wrote like an Irishman. His work was also greatly influenced by Synge (see p. 147) and Yeats (see p. 139). His first play, *Bound East for Cardiff*, was produced in Provincetown, Massachusetts in 1916 and was restaged in New York later the same year. In 1920 his first full-length play, *Beyond the Horizon*, was shown on Broadway and was attended by James O'Neill who told his son: '... people come to the theatre to be entertained, not to be depressed. Do you want them to go home and commit suicide?'

O'Neill wrote 20 full-length plays and several shorter pieces between 1920 and 1943. He won four Pulitzer Prizes for drama and is **the only American playwright to have won the Nobel Prize**. He died in a Boston hotel, withdrawn and waiting for death like one of his own characters. He was a deeply disturbed man who had rejected the austere and doctrinaire Catholicism of his parents and who strived to find spiritual solace elsewhere. He wrote that 'the theatre must give us what the Church no longer gives us – a meaning'. He was profoundly caught up in his Irish heritage and once mused in a letter to his brother that 'the critics have missed the important thing about me and my work, the fact that I am Irish'.

❧ **Francis Scott Key Fitzgerald** (1896–1940), 'spokesman of the roaring twenties', born in St Paul, Minnesota, ranks as one of the best writers America has produced. Raised in the Hibernian surrounds of St Paul, he was the grandson of Philip Francis McQuillan, who emigrated from Co. Fermanagh in 1843. McQuillan moved to Minnesota and set up a wholesale grocery business in St Paul. When he died in 1877 he left a fortune of $250,000. F. Scott's mother, Mollie McQuillan, married her longtime suitor Edward Fitzgerald. He was also of Irish ancestry and was related to several influential Maryland families.

Francis Scott Key (see p. 124), after whom he named his son, was among his ancestors.

F. Scott Fitzgerald was sent to New Jersey for his secondary education and entered Princeton University in 1913, but left to join the army. His writing chronicles the carefree decadence of the jazz-age generation. The tension in his works is partly produced by his desire to belong to America's high society and an innate instinct to despise it. It was a dilemma facing many Irish-Americans at the beginning of this century as they began to reach a point where the dominance of the Anglo-Saxon Protestant culture could be challenged. Among the best-known works of F. Scott Fitzgerald are *This Side of Paradise* (1920), *The Beautiful and the Damned* (1922), *The Great Gatsby* (1922), *Tender is the Night* (1934) and *The Last Tycoon* (1941; unfinished).

❧ **Richard Brinsley Sheridan** (1751–1816) was the son of the Irish actor-manager Thomas Sheridan and the novelist and dramatist Frances Sheridan. He eloped to France with one Eliza Linley, a singer, with whom he entered into an invalid marriage contract. In 1773 the pair were lawfully married. Sheridan, short of cash, turned his hand to play-writing and produced *The Rivals* in a few weeks. The play was a triumphant success at Covent Garden in 1775. In 1776 he became manager of Drury Lane Theatre and in 1777 became a member of Dr Johnson's Club. *The School for Scandal* (1777) had 73 performances between 1777 and 1789 and made a profit of £15,000. Sheridan now turned to politics, becoming MP for Stafford in 1780, Under-Secretary for Foreign Affairs in 1782 and Secretary to the Treasury the following year. He established a reputation as a brilliant orator in the Commons and became a friend of the Prince Regent. However, by the early 1790s his financial situation was deteriorating, largely owing to expenditure on his theatre business. His political career reached its nadir when he did not receive an appointment to Grenville's 'ministry of all the talents' in 1806. When Drury Lane was destroyed by fire in 1809 Sheridan lurched deeper into debt. In 1812 he lost his parliamentary seat and in 1813 was arrested for debt.

❧ **The Brontë sisters**, Charlotte (1816–55), Emily (1818–48) and Anne (1820–49), were the daughters of **Patrick Brontë** (1777–1861) of Ballynaskeagh, Co. Down. Born with the name of Prunty, he changed his name to Brontë when he left Ireland for St John's College, Cambridge in 1802. He graduated in 1806 and took holy orders. He held curacies in various places in England until 1820, when he secured a permanent position as curate of Haworth, a wild moorland district of Yorkshire. He is chiefly remembered for his three novelist daughters and his eccentric and spartan upbringing of them.

☘ **Ethel Lilian Voynich** (1867–1947), author of what is probably **the best-selling novel of all time by an Irish author**, was born in Cork to George Boole (see p. 20), the professor of mathematics at Queen's College, Cork. She was involved in revolutionary politics from an early age and met Oscar Wilde (see p. 137) and George Bernard Shaw (see p. 137) in London at gatherings for the Friends of Russian Freedom. In 1890 she met a revolutionary Polish count, Wilfred Michail Voynich, an escapee from a Siberian labour camp who remembered seeing her three years previously standing outside the Warsaw Citadel where he was a prisoner. They married, but the romance only blossomed briefly. Ethel began a passionate affair with Sydney Reilly, a Polish-Russian Jew and a master spy for the British Secret Service, whose real name was Sigmund Rosenblum.

It is widely believed that Reilly's life story inspired the creation of Ian Fleming's James Bond. He was certainly the inspiration for the hero of Ethel's first novel, *The Gadfly* (published in New York in 1897), a radical and anti-clerical story set in Italy, with a revolutionary patriot, Arthur Burton, as the hero. The novel was an enormous success worldwide. It was translated into Russian in 1898 and later became the virtual bible of the Revolution, selling over five million copies in 100 editions. It is estimated that over 250 million Russians have read *The Gadfly* and the book's hero became a favourite role model of Soviet youth. Further translations sold another one million copies in Eastern Europe and China, while in the West over two and a half million English-language copies were sold. Soviet critics regarded her as one of America's finest novelists – she spent the later part of her life in the United States. Not all critics in Western Europe were so enthusiastic. Joseph Conrad reviewed the book and said, 'I don't remember ever reading a book I disliked so much.'

☘ **Margaret Mitchell** (1900–49), author of *Gone With the Wind,* based the character of Gerald O'Hara on her grandfather Thomas Fitzgerald. Both sides of her family had Irish roots, her mother's being the more recent emigrants. The O'Hara family of her epic novel emanate from Co. Meath and call their Georgia plantation Tara after the seat of the High Kings of Ireland. *Gone With The Wind* (1936) received a Pulitzer Prize, has been translated into 30 languages, has sold in excess of 28 million copies and continues to sell 250,000 paperbacks per year in the United States alone.

☘ **Sir Arthur Conan Doyle** (1859–1930) was born in Edinburgh, Scotland to Charles Altamount Doyle and Mary Foley. His background and environment were Irish and Catholic and his family made a distinguished contribution to art and literature in Victorian Britain. His grandfather was **John Doyle** (1797–1868), the celebrated caricaturist who was born in Dublin and who trained at the Royal Dublin Society before moving to London in 1821. He was the leading caricaturist of his time and is praised in the writings of Thackeray, Wordsworth and Haydon. John Doyle's distinctive 'HB' signature was contrived by the combination of two Js and two Ds.

Arthur Conan Doyle's uncle, **Richard Doyle** (1824–83), joined *Punch* magazine in 1843, two years after its launch, and became a regular contributor of sketches and caricatures until 1850. He is best remembered for creating the enduring cover-design for *Punch*.

Conan Doyle was educated at Stonyhurst and Edinburgh University, graduating in medicine in 1885. He practised at Southsea until 1890, before devoting his time to writing. Sherlock Holmes was introduced in 1887 in his novel *A Study in Scarlet*. His novels were relatively unsuccessful at first and it was his short stories, *The Adventures of Sherlock Holmes*, published in *The Strand* magazine from July 1891, that brought him fame. The character of Holmes is said to be derived from Dr Joseph Bell who taught Conan Doyle in Edinburgh. Bell had always advocated the diagnosis of patients by the careful and minute observation of all facts so that an informed deduction could be made. The Sherlock Holmes stories ran in *The Strand* until December 1893, when the character of Holmes plunged over the Reichenbach Falls with his arch-enemy Professor Moriarty. In October 1903, through popular demand, *The Adventures of Sherlock Holmes* was revived. *The Hound of the Baskervilles* ran in *The Strand* from August 1901 to April 1902 and later appeared as a separate volume. None of Conan Doyle's other works captured the public imagination as much as Sherlock Holmes. Holmes has proved particularly adaptable to the cinema screen and the character has been played by 75 actors in 211 films produced between 1900 and 1993, making him **the most portrayed character in cinematic history**. (Count Dracula, the creation of 'Bram' Stoker (see p. 137), is the second-most portrayed character in cinema, appearing in 159 films.)

Conan Doyle was active in publicly seeking a reprieve for Roger Casement*, who was hanged in Pentonville prison in August 1916 as a British traitor.

🍀 **Raymond Chandler** (1888–1959) was born in Chicago, the creator of Philip Marlowe and classics such as *Farewell My Lovely* (1940) and *The Big Sleep* (1939). Chandler's mother, née Thornton, was from Co. Waterford and the author was a frequent visitor to his uncle, Ernest Thornton, in Co. Waterford, during his childhood.

🍀 Jean **Iris Murdoch** (1919–), the novelist and philosopher, was born in Dublin. She was educated at Somerville College, Oxford and entered the British Treasury Department in 1942. She worked for the United Nations in 1944 and later taught at St Anne's College, Oxford. She is the author of many distinguished and popular novels, of which *The Sea, The Sea* (1978) won the Booker Prize. Murdoch was **the first Irish-born author to win this award**. *The Red and the Green* (1965) was a fiction based on the period of revolution and civil war in Ireland between 1916 and 1923 and describes the dilemmas and conflicting loyalties facing Anglo-Irish families such as her own.

Murdoch's other – highly individual and symbolic – novels include *Under the Net* (1954), *A Severed Head* (1961; adapted as a play with J.B. Priestley in 1964), *The Italian Girl* (1964), *Bruno's Dream* (1969), *The Black Prince* (1973), *Nuns and Soldiers* (1980), *The Philosopher's Pupil* (1983), *The Good Apprentice* (1985), and the philosophical works *The Sovereignty of the Good* (1970) and *The Fire and the Sun* (1977).

🍀 **George Kelly** (1887–1960), uncle of Princess Grace of Monaco (see p. 160) and son of an Irish immigrant bricklayer, was an accomplished playwright. His most famous work, *Craig's Wife*, was awarded the Pulitzer Prize in 1925.

🍀 **William Somerset Maugham** (1874–1965) was born in Paris to an Anglo-Irish father who was legal adviser to the British Embassy there. Maugham was for many years considered one of Britain's leading writers of the 20th century. In 1907 his first play, *Lady Frederick*, made him the most popular playwright in Britain and the following year he had four plays running simultaneously in London. Before World War I he was working on his major novel *Of Human Bondage* (1915), which contained much autobiographical experience.

During the war Maugham worked as a British spy in Geneva and St Petersburg, where his mission was to try to prevent the outbreak of the Russian Revolution. *Ashenden* (1928) is based on these experiences. He continued to write best-selling novels, including *The Moon and Sixpence* (1919), *The Painted Veil* (1925) and *Cakes and Ale* (1930). He settled in France in 1928 and worked briefly as a spy again before the German occupation of France. He then escaped to the United States, where he wrote most of his short stories, many of which were made into films. His short story collections included: *Quartet* (1949), *Trio* (1950) and *Encore* (1951). His last major novel, *The Razor's Edge*, was published in 1945. In 1962 he published the notoriously bitter memoir, *Looking Back,* which recounted his marriage to Syrie Wellcome between 1916 and 1927. (Syrie Wellcome was the first wife of the pharmaceutical manufacturer Sir Henry Wellcome and the daughter of the Dublin philanthropist Dr Barnardo; see p. 27.)

THE CINEMA

Irish interest and participation in the film industry has been consistent from the time the Cinématographe of the Lumière brothers was shown for the first time in Paris in December 1895. Within four months, the Cinématographe had reached Dublin and was being shown at Dan Lowrey's Star Theatre of Varieties – now the Olympia Theatre.

🍀 **Ireland is the European country with the most frequent cinemagoers**. Cinema admissions for the year 1993 reached over 9.3 million or 2.6 cinema tickets per capita per annum.

🍀 **Ireland's first regular cinema house** was the Volta Picture Palace, which was opened in Dublin on 20 December 1909 by James Joyce (see p. 141). Joyce, who was living in Trieste at the time, persuaded some Italian entrepreneur acquaintances to set up a Volta Picture Palace in Dublin as a 'sister' to the one they were then running in Bucharest. The Volta was taken over within a year by British Provincial Cinematograph Theatres. By 1910 numerous cinemas had sprung up around the country.

🍀 **The first commercial films to be made in Ireland** were made by Sidney Olcott for the Kalem Film Company of America. In 1910 Olcott and his

---

* *An Anglo-Irish patriot and British knight, his controversial diaries were released by the office of Public Records in 1994.*

crew arrived in Ireland and began shooting *The Lad from Old Ireland* in Cork and Kerry. Each year until 1914 the Kalem company set up base in O'Sullivan's Hotel in Killarney. Over 30 silent films were produced, mostly based on the dramas of Dion Boucicault, such as *The Colleen Bawn, The Shaughraun* and *Arrah na Pogue*. The anti-British sentiment of these films was regarded as subversive by the British authorities in Ireland, who were particularly anxious at the rise of nationalism at the time.

Irish-born Oscar winners

🍀 **Designer of the first Academy Award (Oscar) statuette** in 1927 was Dublin-born art director **Cedric Gibbons** (1893–1960). One of the most influential production designers in the history of Hollywood, Gibbons began his career in cinema with the Edison company in 1917. He moved to MGM Studios in 1918 and from 1924 to 1956 was the leading art director there. Gibbons was nominated many times for the Academy Awards and actually won 11 of them for the following films: *The Bridge of San Luis Rey* (1929), *The Merry Widow* (1934), *Pride and Prejudice* (1940), *Blossoms in the Dust* (1941), *Gaslight* (1944), *The Yearling* (1946), *Little Women* (1949), *An American in Paris* (1951), *The Bad and the Beautiful* (1952), *Julius Caesar* (1953), *Somebody up there Likes Me* (1956). An honorary Oscar for 'consistent excellence' was also awarded to him in 1950.

Gibbons was involved in practically all of MGM's major productions for 32 years. His sets were invariably exotic and luxurious, even when this seemed unnecessary. He was the greatest exponent of the escapist fantasy style of Hollywood set design. His belief was that people would not pay to see the harsh realism of everyday life played back to them on the cinema screen. It is perhaps appropriate that the person who designed the Academy Award should be the one to receive it more often than anyone else other than Walt Disney, who won 32.

🍀 **Benjamin Glazer, the first Irish person to win an Oscar,** was born in Belfast in 1887, the son of Hungarian Jewish refugees. He studied law at the University of Pennsylvania and took to writing plays and adaptations. His first film as a writer was *A Trip To Paradise*. He became head of production at Pathé Studios in the late 1920s and then moved to Paramount. He received an Oscar for best screenplay in his adaptation of *Seventh Heaven* 1927-28 (the year of the first Academy Awards). His other productions included *A Farewell To Arms* (1933) and *Arise My Love* (1940). Glazer died in Hollywood in 1956.

🍀 **Barry Fitzgerald** (1888–1961), who went by the stage-name William Joseph Shields, was born in Dublin and joined the civil service in 1911. He acted with an amateur group before joining the Abbey Theatre 1916-29. As a full-time actor, he toured the United States in 1934 and was acclaimed as the best actor of the year by New York critics for his performance as Fluther Good in *The Plough and the Stars*. He settled in the USA in 1936 and went to Hollywood, where he appeared in many films over the next 20 years. He won a best supporting actor Oscar for his performance as Father Fitzgibbon in *Going My Way*. He starred with John Wayne and Maureen O'Hara in John Ford's *The Quiet Man* (1952). He returned to Ireland in 1959 and died in Dublin.

🍀 **George Bernard Shaw** (see also p. 137) won an Oscar for *My Fair Lady* (1938), the film version of *Pygmalion*. He is **the only person ever to have won both an Oscar and a Nobel Prize for Literature.** The former he did not accept, however, remarking 'I've been offered titles, but they get one into disreputable company.'

🍀 **Greer Garson** born in 1908 in Co. Down, won the best actress Oscar in 1942 for her performance in the title role in *Mrs Miniver*. (**Her acceptance speech was the longest ever made at an Oscar ceremony,** lasting five and a half minutes.) A leading Hollywood lady in the 1940s and 50s, she was nominated for an Oscar in six other films from 1939 to 1960. Garson was educated at University College London and went on to a career on the stage. In 1938 she was spotted by Hollywood director Louis B. Meyer, who considered her the personification of British refinement and beauty. She was taken to Hollywood and cast accordingly. Her Oscar nominations were for *Goodbye Mr Chips* (1939), *Blossoms in the Dust* (1941), *Mrs Miniver* (1942), *Madame Curie* (1943), *The Valley of Decision* (1945) and *Sunrise at Campobello* (1960).

🍀 **Shane Connaughton** from Duleek, Co. Cavan, won an Oscar in the short film category in 1981 for *Bottom Dollar*.

🍀 **Josie McAvin** (1923–), born in Dublin, was twice nominated for best art/set direction before finally winning her award in 1985 for Sidney Pollack's *Out of Africa*. She was first nominated in 1963 for her work in the Tony Richardson film *Tom Jones* and in 1965

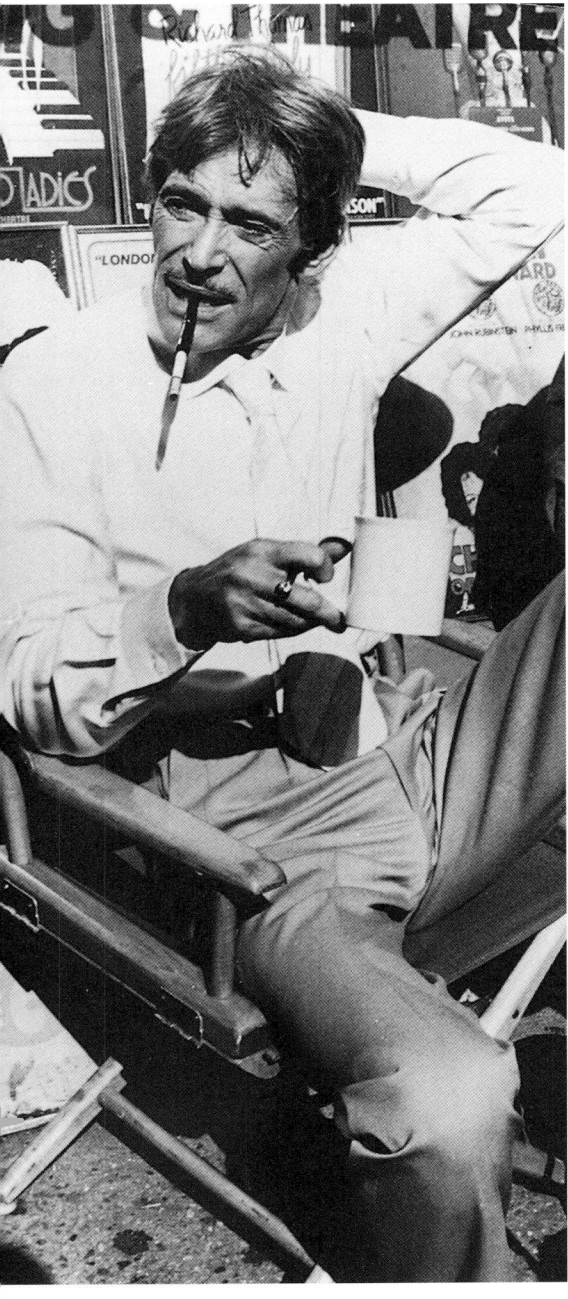

The Connemara-born actor Peter O'Toole, star of Lawrence of Arabia, The Lion in Winter and numerous other successful films, has been nominated for an Oscar on seven occasions without ever winning one.

for *The Spy Who Came In From The Cold*, directed by Martin Ritt and filmed on location in Dublin.

❀ **Michele Burke** of Co. Kildare is a winner of two Academy Awards, for best make-up in Jean-Jacques Annaud's *Quest for Fire (1981)* and *Bram Stoker's Dracula* (1993). She was also nominated for the best make-up award for *Batman* (1989) and *Cyrano de Bergerac* (1990).

❀ **Brenda Fricker** (1945–), Dublin-born winner of the best supporting actress award for her role as Mrs Brown in *My Left Foot* (1989), became well-known for her role in the BBC television series *Casualty*. She also starred in *The Field* (1990) and *The Woman who Married Clark Gable* (1985).

❀ **Neil Jordan** (see p. 158) won an Oscar for best screen play in *The Crying Game* (1992).

❀ **The most nominated actor never to receive an Academy Award** is **Peter O'Toole**, who has received no less than seven best actor nominations since 1962, when he played his first starring role as T.E. Lawrence (see p. 102) in David Lean's epic, *Lawrence of Arabia*. His subsequent nominations were for: King Henry II opposite Richard Burton in *Becket* (1964); King Henry II opposite Katherine Hepburn in *The Lion in Winter* (1968); the title role in *Goodbye Mr Chips* (1969); Jack, son of the Earl of Gurney, in *The Ruling Class* (1972); the lead in *The Stunt Man* (1980); Allan Swann in *My Favourite Year* (1982).

Peter Seamus O'Toole was born in Connemara, Co. Galway in 1933 and studied at the Royal Academy of Dramatic Art in London, the Bristol Old Vic and the Shakespeare Memorial Theatre Company.

Alphabetical hall of fame: actors, filmmakers and personalities

❀ **Kenneth Branagh** was born in Belfast on 10 December 1960. His family moved to Reading, England in 1970. He began his acting career with the local Progress Theatre Group as a teenager and in 1979 won a scholarship to the Royal Academy of Dramatic Art and earned fame for his West End debut in *Another Country* (1982). He joined the Royal Shakespeare Company and became the group's youngest ever Henry V in 1983. He set up his own theatre company, Renaissance, in 1986 and launched its first play, *The Public Enemy*, in 1987. He made his debut as a film director in 1989 with *Henry V* and was nomi-

Gabriel Byrne in a scene from Cool World *(1992). Byrne has emerged as one of Hollywood's leading actors, appearing in such films as* Defence of the Realm, Gothic, Miller's Crossing *and* Into the West.

nated Oscars as best director and best actor. He directed and starred in *Dead Again* in 1990, which was a box office success, making the top 20 list in the US. *Peter's Friends* enjoyed similar success. Branagh is married to the Oscar-winning actress Emma Thompson and lives in England.

🍀 **Alexander Herbert Reginald St John Brenon** (1880–1958), born in Dún Laoghaire, Co. Dublin, directed over 300 films. Educated in London, he emigrated to the USA in 1896, directing his first film for the Universal Company in 1910. From 1910 to 1914 he directed many films in Europe. Among his more famous works are *Ivanhoe*, *Neptune's Daughter* (1914), *A Daughter of the Gods* (1915), *Peter Pan, A Kiss for Cinderella* and the first version of *Beau Geste* (1926). He acted in and wrote the screenplay for many of his own films.

🍀 **George Brent** (1904–79), born in Shannonbridge, Co. Offaly, was acting with the Abbey Players

in Dublin in 1922 when he went on the run as a wanted IRA volunteer. By 1927 he had made it on the Broadway stage and starred with Clark Gable in *Love, Honor and Betray*. In Hollywood he was cast opposite Barbara Stanwyck, Greta Garbo and Bette Davis. His films include *Charlie Chan Carries On* (1931), *Dark Victory* (1939), *The Fighting 69th* (1940) in which he plays Wild Bill Donovan (see p. 79), *The Spiral Staircase* (1946) and *Temptation* (1946). After 25 years of retirement from the screen he returned, appositely, to appear in *Born Again* in 1978.

🍀 **Pierce Brosnan**, the Co. Meath-born Hollywood actor, has starred in *Taffin, Lawnmower Man* and *Mrs Doubtfire*. In 1994 he was chosen to be the next James Bond.

🍀 **Ellen Burstyn** (1932–) is the stage name of Edna Gilhooley, who was born in Detroit, Michigan to Irish parents. She won an Academy Award for best actress in *Alice Doesn't Live Here Anymore* (1974). Her other films include *The Last Picture Show* (1972), the biggest box-office hit of 1973, *The Exorcist, Resurrection* (1980) and *The Ambassador* (1984).

♣ **Gabriel Byrne** (1950–) was born in Walkinstown, Dublin and won a scholarship to University College, Dublin. His professional acting career began in 1977 in the Project Theatre, Dublin. In 1978 he starred in the television series *The Riordans* on Radio Telefis Eireann, the national TV station. He also starred in the sequel, *Bracken*, and was asked to take a cameo role in John Boorman's *Excalibur*, filmed in Ireland in 1980. Always willing to take on non-commercial projects, Byrne has appeared in films of varying success. His major films include: *Defence of the Realm* (1985), *The Courier* (1987), *Siesta* (1986), *Miller's Crossing* (1990), *Into the West* (1991) and *Cool World* (1992).

♣ **James Cagney** (1904–86) was born in New York, the son of James Cagney Snr, an Irish immigrant bartender from Co. Cork, and Carolyn Nelson, who was of Irish-Norwegian parentage. He made his name with *Public Enemy* (1931) and became the star of many 1930s gangster movies. In *Angels with Dirty Faces* (1938) and *The Roaring Twenties* (1939) Cagney epitomised the street-wise, tough screen image of the American-Irish – a cliché inherited by the Italians and Hispanics in later decades. He changed his role in 1942 in *Yankee Doodle Dandy*, in a wartime show of patriotism, where he showed great talent as a song-and-dance man and won an Oscar for best actor. He was awarded the American Film Institute's Lifetime Achievement Award in 1974.

♣ **The MGM lion, Caibre**, was born on 27 March 1927 and bred in Dublin Zoo. He was named after the son of Niall of the Nine Hostages of Irish legend.

♣ **Sir Charles 'Charlie Chaplin' Spencer** (1889–1977), the legendary clown and film-maker, was born in London in 1889 to Hannah Hill, who was a native of Cork and daughter of a cobbler. His fourth wife, Oonagh O'Neill (1926–91), was the daughter of the playwright Eugene O'Neill (see p. 148).

Chaplin was spotted by Mack Sennett, who signed him to the Keystone Studio in 1913. *Making a Living* was his film debut in 1914 and in it he introduced his character of the gentleman tramp. Chaplin's international fame was quickly established and in 1919 he co-founded United Artists with D.W. Griffith, Douglas Fairbanks and Mary Pickford. His leading films include: *The Kid* (1920), *The Gold Rush* (1925), *City Lights* (1931), *Modern Times* (1936), *The Great Dictator* (1940) and *Limelight* (1952).

Chaplin came under investigation by the Un-American Activities Committee (see Joseph Eugene McCarthy, p. 83) and was banned from the USA as a Communist sympathizer in 1952. He settled in Switzerland with Oonagh O'Neill. In 1973 he returned to the USA to collect a special Academy Award – his second Oscar, the first having been awarded 45 years earlier in 1928.

♣ **George M. Cohan** (1878–1942), considered the father of American musical comedy, was an actor, songwriter, playwright, director and producer. His composition *Over There*, a patriotic tune for World War I, won him a Congressional Medal of Honor. Other tunes, such as *You're a Grand Old Flag* and *Give My Regards to Broadway*, were equally popular. His life was celebrated by Cagney (see above) in the 1942 musical *Yankee Doodle Dandy*. Cohan was born in Providence, Rhode Island into a traditional Irish family. His grandparents were Michael Keohane and Jane Scott, who emigrated from Co. Cork in 1848, fleeing the Famine. His father, Jerry Cohan, was widely known as the best Irish dancer in New England and his speciality was working American variations on standard jigs and reels.

♣ **Cyril Cusack** (1910–93) was born in Kentani, Kenya, where his father was a sergeant in the mounted police. He spent 75 years in acting, making his first appearance in 1917 in Sidney Olcott's film version of *Knocknagow*. He was educated at Newbridge College and University College, Dublin and joined the Abbey Theatre in 1932. He acted in numerous plays with the Abbey, the Royal Shakespeare Company and the National Theatre, and appeared in many National Theatre productions worldwide. He won the International Critics Award as actor of the season in Paris in 1961, for his roles in *Krapp's Last Tape* and *Arms and the Man*. His four daughters, Sinéad, Sorcha, Niamh and Nora, are all well-known actresses. Sinéad is married to the successful British film and stage actor, Jeremy Irons. In Ireland Cusack is popularly remembered as Uncle Peter in the television soap series *Glenroe*. His leading films were: *Odd Man Out* (1946), *Shake Hands with the Devil* (1959), *The Spy who came in from the Cold* (1965), *Fahrenheit 451* (1966), *The Day of the Jackal* (1972), *Nineteen Eighty-Four* (1984) and *Little Dorrit* (1987).

♣ **Daniel Day-Lewis** was winner of the award for best actor in 1990 as Christy Brown in *My Left Foot*

(1989). He was born in London in 1958, the son of the Sligo-born British Poet Laureate Cecil Day-Lewis (see p. 145) and of Jill Balcon, the daughter of the British film producer Sir Michael Balcon. Daniel Day-Lewis began his cinema career in *Gandhi* (1982). Other films include: *The Bounty* (1984), *My Beautiful Laundrette* (1985), *A Room With A View* (1985), *The Last of the Mohicans* (1992), *The Age of Innocence* (1993) and *In the Name of the Father* (1993), the latter an account of the trial and wrongful imprisonment of the 'Guildford Four' on terrorist charges in the early 1970s.

♣ **Brian Dennehy**, star of *Gorky Park* (1983), *FX Murder By Illusion I & II* (1985 and 1991), *Best Seller* (1987), *The Belly of an Architect* (1987) and *Presumed Innocent* (1990), is also an accomplished stage actor. His most recent role as Hickey in Eugene O'Neill's *The Iceman Cometh* (1992), a Tony Award winner,

---

Daniel Day-Lewis and Brenda Fricker receive their Oscars for best actor and best supporting actress for their performances in My Left Foot *(1989). The film depicted the life of Dublin writer Christy Brown, who suffered from cerebral palsy.*

has received critical acclaim. In an interview with the *Cork Examiner* whilst on tour in Ireland in 1993, he spoke about his grandfather who had left Cork City as an uneducated and unskilled 13-year-old to live and fend for himself alone in the USA. Dennehy now runs his own theatre company, which he calls *Saoirse* (Irish for 'freedom') in honour of his grandfather. He currently lives in Santa Fe, New Mexico.

♣ **Walter Elias 'Walt' Disney** was born in 1901 in Chicago, Illinois to the Irish-born Mary Richardson. Disney's earliest American ancestors were Huguenots who settled in Co. Cork before emigrating in the late 17th century. In its original form the name was D'Isney. Walt Disney's career began as a commercial artist after graduating from Kansas City Art Institute. During World War I he worked in France as an ambulance driver for the Red Cross. After the war he began to draw cartoons or *Laugh-O-Grams*, which he unsuccessfully tried to sell to theatre halls. He moved to Hollywood in 1923 and spent four years trying to sell his live-action animation ideas. The breakthrough came in 1927 with *Oswald the Lucky Rabbit. Mortimer the Mouse*, later to become *Mickey Mouse*, followed within a year. Disney's fame was established after the success of *The Three Little Pigs* (1933) and its hit song 'Who's Afraid of the Big Bad Wolf?'. His full-length cartoons are recognised as masterpieces: *Snow White and the Seven Dwarfs* (1938), *Fantasia* (1940), *Pinnochio* (1940), *Bambi* (1942), *Lady and the Tramp* (1955) *and The Jungle Book* (1967). Disney also made several action movies of less merit, also geared to young audiences.

Walt Disney received more Academy Awards than any other person in the film industry, with 26 regular and 6 special trophies. He died in 1966 but productions have continued in his name. Disneyland Amusement Park was opened in Anaheim, California in 1955. Disneyworld 'theme parks' followed in Orlando, Florida in 1971, Tokyo 1983 and Paris 1992.

♣ **Mia Farrow**, born in Los Angeles in 1946, is the daughter of Maureen O'Sullivan (see p. 160) and the film director John Farrow. She is as famous for her marriages as she is for her film roles. She was married to Frank Sinatra 1966–68 and André Previn 1970–79 and also had a much-publicised relationship with Woody Allen. Her films include: *Rosemary's Baby* (1968), *The Great Gatsby* (1974), *Death on the Nile* (1978), along with those made with Woody Allen: *A Midsummer's Night Sex Comedy* (1982), *Zelig* (1983), *The Purple Rose of Cairo* (1985), *Hannah and Her*

Sisters (1986), *Radio Days* (1987), *New York Stories* (1989), *Crimes and Misdemeanours* (1989) and *Husbands and Wives* (1992).

❧ **Robert J. Flaherty** (1884–1951) has been called the 'father of the documentary film'. Born in Iron Mountain, Michigan to an Irish father and a German mother, he began as an explorer before deciding to record his experiences on film. His early explorations in the Canadian wilderness were undertaken with his immigrant father, who worked as a miner. His film on the life of Eskimos made over the 16 months he lived with them, *Nanook of the North* (1922), was his first film, and now his best-known, establishing him as a master of the documentary. His Polynesian documentary *Moana* was made in 1926 and *Industrial Britain* followed in 1931. *Man of Aran* was made off the Galway coast in 1934.

Flaherty worked on exterior shots for movie-makers and joined with Frank Capra in producing propaganda films for the US Film Unit. His wife, Frances Hubbard, whom he married in 1914, made essential contributions to many of his works.

❧ **Errol Flynn** (1909–59) was born in Hobart, Tasmania, the son of Professor Theodore Thomson Flynn MBE, an Irish emigrant who was a distinguished marine biologist and zoologist at the University of Tasmania and later professor of biology at Queen's University, Belfast (1931–48).

Errol Flynn was the archetypal swashbuckling, all-American hero, put forward as a model of American male sexuality despite the fact that he was not American and was refused entry to the US Army in World War II because of a heart condition and recurrent malaria and tuberculosis. Many of his films were centred around Irish characters or situations that figure elsewhere in this book. Some of the more successful Flynn films include: *Captain Blood* (1935); *The Adventures of Robin Hood* (1938); *The Charge of the Light Brigade* (1936); *They Died With Their Boots On* (1941); *Gentleman Jim* (1942) – possibly Errol Flynn's best film, in which he plays Jim Corbett; *The Adventures of Don Juan* (1948) and *Too Much Too Soon* (1958), which deals with the history of the Irish-American acting family, the Barrymores. Flynn emphasised his Hibernian background in the naming of his children Sean, Deirdre and Rory (all by his third wife Patrice Wymore).

❧ **John Ford*** (1895–1973), **winner of the most best director Academy Awards,** was born Sean Aloysius O'Feeney in Cape Elizabeth, Maine in 1895, the youngest of 13 children. His father was born in Galway and his mother was a native Irish-speaker from the Aran Islands. Ford made over 130 films and won best director Academy Awards for *The Informer* (1935), *The Grapes of Wrath* (1940), *How Green Was My Valley* (1941) and *The Quiet Man* (1952).

During World War II Ford was in charge of the Field Photographic Branch of the OSS (Office of Strategic Services – now the CIA). In this capacity he made several documentaries and received Oscars for *The Battle of Midway* (1942) and *December Seventh* (1943). *The Quiet Man* (1952), filmed in Co. Mayo, was one of a series of films made with John Wayne, including: *Stagecoach* (1939), *Fort Apache* (1948), *She Wore a Yellow Ribbon* (1949), *Rio Grande* (1950) and *The Horse Soldiers* (1959). Famous for his beautiful cinematography, Ford's work continues to influence and inspire directors today. Ford was awarded the Life Achievement Award from the American Film Institute and the Presidential Medal of Freedom.

❧ **John Frankenheimer**, director of *The Manchurian Candidate* (1962), *The Birdman of Alcatraz* (1961), *All Fall Down* (1962), *The Iceman Cometh* (1973) and *French Connection II* (1975), was born in Malba, New York in 1930 to an Irish mother.

❧ The stage and film actor **Richard Harris** was born in Limerick in 1932 and educated there at the Crescent College. His films include: *The Guns of Navarone* (1961), *This Sporting Life* (1962), *A Man Called Horse* (1969), *The Molly Maguires* (1970), *The Return of a Man Called Horse* (1970), *The Wild Geese* (1978) and *The Field* (1990).

❧ **Audrey Hepburn** (1929–93) was born in Brussels, Belgium of Dutch-Irish parentage. Her father was from an Anglo-Irish banking family. She won her Academy Award for best actress for her debut in *Roman Holiday* (1954) with Gregory Peck (see p. 162). Other films included: *Sabrina* (1954), *The Nun's Story* (1956), *Breakfast at Tiffany's* (1961), *My Fair Lady* (1964) and *Wait Until Dark* (1967).

---

* John Ford made his debut in the film industry as a Ku Klux Klan extra in D.W. Griffith's notorious cinematic masterpiece, The Birth of a Nation *(1914).*

🍀 **Sir Alfred Hitchcock**, 'the master of suspense', was born in London on 13 August 1899, the son of Emma Whelan from Cork. He was educated in London by the Jesuits and worked as a commercial artist before entering the film industry. His first film as a director was *The Pleasure Garden* (1925) and his first venture into sound came with *Blackmail* (1929). His wife, Alma Reville, whom he married in 1926, co-wrote many of his film scripts. It was some years before Hitchcock's films were recognised, but true success came in 1934 with *The Man Who Knew Too Much*. This was followed by *The Thirty-Nine Steps* (1935) and *The Lady Vanishes* (1938). Hitchcock's first American film, *Rebecca* (1940), won a best picture Oscar and he was nominated as best director. He subsequently settled in Hollywood and made numerous films of merit: *Spellbound* (1945), *Notorious* (1946), *Strangers on a Train* (1951), *Rear Window* (1954), *Vertigo* (1958), *North by Northwest* (1959), *Psycho* (1960), *The Birds* (1963) and *Frenzy* (1972). In each of his films, Hitchcock made a personal appearance, whether in a very small part, or as an extra in a crowd. In 1979 Hitchcock was presented with the American Film Institute's Life Achievement Award. He died in 1980.

🍀 **Reginald Ingram Montgomery Hitchcock** (1893–1950), a.k.a. **Rex Ingram**, was born in Grosvenor Square, Rathmines, Dublin, the son of a Trinity College lecturer and later rector of Kinnity, Co. Offaly. Ingram emigrated to the USA at 18 and studied sculpture in the Yale School of Fine Arts. In 1913 he met Charles Edison, son of the inventor Thomas Edison, and he was invited to join the Edison Company. He made his first film, *The Great Problem*, when 23 years old. With several films behind him, he joined the Metro Company in 1920 to direct *The Four Horsemen of the Apocalypse*. In this, his masterpiece, he introduced Rudolph Valentino and Alice Terry (later to become Ingram's wife) to the screen. The film was a huge commercial success and made the Metro Company's fortune. Other leading films by Ingram include: *The Conquering Power* (1922), *The Prisoner of Zenda* (1922), *Trifling Women* (1923) and *Scaramouche* (1923). Tiring of Hollywood, Ingram moved to Europe and North Africa. He founded the Victorine Studios in Nice and made several movies there. He made one sound-film, *Baround* (1931), and played the leading role himself. Because he left America before the sound era, he has been largely forgotten.

🍀 **Paul Hogan**, the Australian comedian and film star, best known for his role in the box-office smash hit, *Crocodile Dundee*, was born in 1939 in Lightning Ridge, New South Wales to an Irish-born father.

🍀 **Anjelica Huston**, daughter of John Huston, grew up on the family estate in Galway. Films include *Prizzi's Honor* (1985), for which she received an Oscar for best supporting actress, *The Dead* (1987), *The Grifters* (1990) and *The Addams Family* (the top-grossing movie in the USA in 1991).

🍀 **Neil Jordan** (1951–) was born in Sligo and educated in Dublin at St Paul's, Raheny and University College. He became involved in Dublin fringe theatre at an early age. He was co-founder of the Irish Writers' Co-operative and has published a collection of short stories, *Nights in Tunisia* (1978), and two novels: *The Past* (1980) and *Dream of a Beast* (1983). He has also been involved in television writing and a documentary on the making of John Boorman's *Excalibur*, which was filmed in Co. Wicklow in 1981. He directed his first film, *Angel*, in 1982. *Company of Wolves* (1984) won best director award from the British Critics Circle. *Mona Lisa* (1985) was an artistically acclaimed and commercial success and established his name. *High Spirits* (1988) and *We're No Angels* (1989) were less successful despite their all-star casts. *The Miracle* (1991) saw a return to low-budget art cinema and *The Crying Game*, made the following year, was a runaway success, gaining an Oscar for best screenplay in 1992.

🍀 **Muiris 'Kruger' Kavanagh** (1894–1971), of Dún Chaoin in the Kerry Gaeltacht, earned his life-long nickname at school during the Boer War. He emigrated to the USA in 1913 and went to night school for three years. He became publicity manager for MGM Studios and selected girls to dance for the Ziegfeld Follies. When Eamon de Valera (see p. 66) visited the USA in 1919 to win support for the Irish independence movement, he acted as de Valera's personal bodyguard. Kavanagh returned to Ireland to open a pub and guesthouse in Dún Chaoin. 'Kruger's' became the haunt of politicians, writers, actors and scholars from far and wide. Brendan Behan (see p. 144) wrote a song to celebrate the granting of his publican's licence.

🍀 **Joseph Francis 'Buster' Keaton** (1899–1966) began his career on stage at the age of three, performing in his Irish parents' acrobatic comedy routine, 'The Three Keatons'. He was given the nickname 'Buster' by the escapologist Harry Houdini after he fell down a flight of stairs as an infant and remained unscathed. Roscoe 'Fatty' Arbuckle introduced him to the silent screen and he made his debut movie, *The Butcher Boy*, in 1917.

By 1920 his own studio was producing popular slapstick comedies. *Saphead* (1920) established him as a star and many notable films followed, among them *The Playhouse* (1921), *The Boat* (1921) and *Cops* (1922). His full-length feature films included *Our Hospitality* (1923), *The Navigator* (1924) and *The General* (1927).

Keaton's skill as a mime artist did not lend itself to the sound era. He appeared in other films, including Charlie Chaplin's *Limelight* in 1935, and he was given a special Academy Award for screen comedy in 1959. In 1965 he made a silent short, *Film*, which was received with standing ovations at the Venice Film Festival.

🍀 **Gene Kelly** (1912–), born in Pittsburgh, Pennsylvania, was Irish on both sides of his family. His maternal grandfather was Billy Curran, who left Derry in 1845 and settled in New York, while his father, James Patrick Kelly, was the grandson of an immigrant who established himself in Peterborough, Ontario in Canada among the rival colonies of Irish, French and English loggers. The story goes that this ancestor left Ireland during the Famine along with his landlord, Lord Peterborough, who subsequently named the new Canadian settlement after himself.

Gene Kelly was the archetypal Hollywood song-and-dance man and starred in some of the most popular movies of the musical era. He made his debut in 1942 in *For Me and My Girl*. Other hits included: *Anchors Aweigh* (1945), *On the Town* (1949), *An American in Paris* (1951) and *Singing in the Rain* (1952). More than anyone, Kelly seemed to epitomise the confidence and prosperity of America after World War II. Kelly's success may have reflected the newly found acceptance of Irishness in American culture at this period. (Before the war, many Irish-Americans in Hollywood found it necessary to change their names to disguise their origins.) Gene Kelly also made non-musical films with some success, including *Morningstar* (1958) and *Inherit the World* (1960). In 1969 he directed his own film *Hello Dolly*. He was an Academy Award Winner in 1951.

Paul Hogan, Irish-Australian comedian and comedy actor from Lightning Ridge, New South Wales. The phenomenal success of Crocodile Dundee *shot him to international stardom.*

🍀 **Grace Kelly** (1929–82) was the granddaughter of an Irish immigrant who established a bricklaying firm in Philadelphia. Her father Jack built on the family fortune and was an Olympic medallist for the United States in rowing. Grace Kelly made her stage debut in 1949 and her talent was quickly recognised. Films include: *High Noon* (1952), *Dial M for Murder* (1954), *Rear Window* (1954), *To Catch a Thief* (1955), and *Country Girl* (1954), for which she won an Oscar for best actress. She married Prince Ranier and became Princess Grace of Monaco. She was a lifelong supporter of Irish charities and cultural projects. She died in a car crash in Monaco in 1982.

🍀 **Angela Lansbury,** the television and cinema actress, is best known as Jessica Fletcher in the TV series *Murder She Wrote*. She was born in London in 1925, the daughter of Belfast stage actress Moya McGill, but was evacuated to the USA in 1940. Lansbury has received three Oscar nominations, as best supporting actress in *Gaslight* (1944), *The Picture of Dorian Gray* (1945) and *The Manchurian Candidate* (1962). She lived in Ireland in the late 1960s and remains a regular visitor.

🍀 **Ray McAnally** (1925–89), of Buncrana, Co. Donegal, joined the Abbey Theatre in Dublin in 1947 and appeared in over 150 Abbey productions during his career. In 1987 he won the British Academy award for best supporting actor for his portrayal of a left-wing British Prime Minister in the TV drama *A Very British Coup*. His other films include: *Shake Hands with the Devil* (1959), *Billy Budd* (1962), *The Mission* (1987), *My Left Foot* (1989) and *We're no Angels* (1989).

🍀 **Siobhán McKenna** (1923–86), born in Belfast, took up acting at the Abbey Theatre after graduating from University College, Galway in 1944. She made her London debut in 1947 and was soon established as a leading actress. She received particular acclaim for her roles as Pegeen Mike in *Playboy of the Western World* (1962) and as the lead in *St Joan*. She appeared in eight films and her one-woman show, *Here are the Ladies*, staged in London in 1970, was hugely popular. Her film work includes: *King of Kings* (1961), *Of Human Bondage* and *Doctor Zhivago* (1965).

🍀 **Liam Neeson,** born in Ballymena, Co. Antrim, is a graduate of Queen's University, Belfast. He began acting with the Lyric Players in Belfast before moving to the Abbey Theatre in Dublin. He has appeared in many films, including the lead role in Steven Spielberg's highly acclaimed *Schindler's List* (1993), for which he was nominated for an Oscar as best actor. Other films include: *Lamb* (1985), *A Prayer for the Dying* (1987), *The Big Man* (1990) and *Husbands and Wives* (1992).

🍀 **Sam Neill,** born in Omagh, Co. Tyrone in 1946, left Northern Ireland in 1954 for New Zealand, his mother's home country. His Northern Irish father was a British Army officer with the Royal Irish Fusiliers at Gough Barracks in Armagh. Neil spent his early childhood in Ballykinlar by the Mourne Mountains. Recently he has been in the spotlight playing Dr Alan Grant in Steven Spielberg's 1993 box-office hit *Jurassic Park*. Other films include: *My Brilliant Career* (1979), *A Cry in the Dark* (1986), *Dead Calm* (1988), *Death in Brunswick* (1990) and *The Piano* (1993).

🍀 **Merle Oberon,** or Merle O'Brien Thompson (1911–79), was born into a Tasmanian-Irish family. She was educated in Calcutta and went to London in 1928, where she met Alexander Korda. In 1933 she starred in *The Private Life of Henry VIII* and, following its success, moved to Hollywood. Her Hollywood successes include: *The Dark Angel, Wuthering Heights* (1939, with Laurence Olivier), *The Lion Has Wings* (1939, made in Britain), *24 Hours of a Woman's Life* (1952), *Oscar* (1965) and *Hotel* (1966).

🍀 **Maureen O'Hara** (1921–) was born into a theatrical family in Milltown, Dublin. She emigrated to the USA in 1939, having trained as an actress in Ireland and England. She was chosen for many Hollywood productions and, with her striking red hair and strong features, was often typecast as the quintessential Irish woman. She was typically rebellious and anti-patriarchal in her roles but was inevitably subdued by John Wayne-type characters by the end of the feature. O'Hara was one of a few who could work easily with John Ford and she starred in *The Quiet Man* (1951), *How Green Was My Valley* (1941), *Miracle on 34th Street, Rio Grande* (1951) and *The Long Grey Line* (1955). She also starred in Alfred Hitchcock's *Jamaica Inn* (1939). She now lives in retirement on the Caribbean Island of St Croix and maintains a residence at Glengariff, Co. Cork.

🍀 **Maureen O'Sullivan** (1911–) was born in Boyle, Co. Roscommon. In her Hollywood career she is best remembered for the role of Jane Parker, starring opposite Johnny Weissmuller in the series of im-

(above) *Liam Neeson of Ballymena, Co. Antrim was nominated for best actor in 1994 for his portrayal of the character of Oskar Schindler in the film* Schindler's List, *based on the Booker Prize-winning book by the Irish-Australian author Thomas Keneally.*

(right) *Ray McAnally of Buncrana, Co. Donegal receives a BAFTA award for his performance as a left-wing British Prime Minister in* A Very British Coup *in 1989. He died later that year.*

mensely popular *Tarzan* movies in the 1930s and 40s. O'Sullivan attended secondary school at Roehampton Convent in London, where she was a classmate of Vivien Leigh and Gwen McCormack, daughter of the tenor John McCormack (see p. 121). O'Sullivan and John McCormack later starred together in *Song o' My Heart* (1930).

It would be unfair to relegate Maureen O'Sullivan to the permanent status of Tarzan's mate, however, as she showed true acting talent in films such as *David Copperfield* (1935), *The Barretts of Wimpole Street* (1934), *Pride and Prejudice* (1940) and *The Big Clock* (1948). She is the mother of the actress Mia Farrow (see p. 156).

♣ **Gregory Peck** (1916–): Peck's mother was Catherine Ashe*, born near Dingle, Co. Kerry. She emigrated to the USA and settled in Rochester, New York, where Peck was born. Gregory Peck was winner of the Oscar for best actor in 1962 in *To Kill a Mockingbird.* He was also nominated for his performances in *Keys of the Kingdom, The Yearling, Gentleman's Agreement* and *Twelve O'Clock High.* Peck is a regular visitor to Ireland and lived in Galway in 1970. He starred as Captain Ahab in John Huston's *Moby Dick,* filmed in Youghal, Co. Cork in 1956.

♣ **Mary Pickford** (1893–1979), born in Toronto, Canada, was idolised by millions. 'The world's sweetheart' of the silent screen, her real name was Gladys Mary Smith. Her maternal grandparents, John Pickford Hennessy and Catherine Feeley, both emigrated from Co. Kerry. The grandparents met for the first time in Canada and their daughter, Charlotte Hennessy, was Pickford's mother. Pickford made her first stage appearance at the age of five. In 1919, having already starred in several films, she co-founded the United Artists studio with Charlie Chaplin (see p. 155) and D.W. Griffith. *Pollyanna* (1920) and *Little Lord Fauntleroy* (1921) were her own successes. Her first sound movie, *Coquette* (1929), won her an Academy Award as best actress (an award she had also won in 1928), but the transition to talkies was ultimately unsuccessful. She made her last film, *Secrets,* in 1933 and retired from filmmaking.

♣ **Tyrone Power** (1914–58) was the great-grandson of the actor William Grattan Tyrone Power (1797–1841), of Kilmacthomas, Co. Wexford, who was a stage hit in London during his lifetime and earned up to £100 per week, a huge sum at that time. He bought property in Texas in 1840 and settled with his family in the USA. Tyrone Power starred in over 40 movies, including *The Black Rose* and *Blood and Sand.* He introduced John Ford's film *The Rising of the Moon,* which was filmed in Ireland.

* *Catherine Ashe was a relation of Thomas Ashe (1885–1917), an insurgent of Easter 1916 who led the volunteers in an assault on the police barracks in Ashbourne, Co. Meath. Thomas Ashe went on hunger strike in Mountjoy jail in 1917 to win prisoner-of-war status. He died as a result of forcible feeding. His funeral was attended by 30,000 people.*

♣ **Anthony Rudolph Oaxaca Quinn** (1915–), perhaps best known for playing the title role of *Zorba the Greek* in the 1964 film and again on Broadway in 1983, was born in Mexico to a Mexican mother and Frank Quinn, an Irish immigrant. He has appeared in over 175 films and won Oscars for best supporting actor in *Viva Zapata* (1952) and *Lust for Life* (1956). Other notable films include *The Guns of Navarone* (1961), *Requiem for a Heavyweight* and *The Shoes of the Fisherman* (1968).

♣ **Stephen Rea**, born in Belfast, trained at the Abbey Theatre School in Dublin. He formed the Field Day Theatre Company with playwright Brian Friel (see p. 142) in 1980 and has acted in all of its productions except *Three Sisters,* which he directed. He has appeared in several films, most successfully in the Neil Jordan (see p. 158) productions *Angel* (1982), *Company of Wolves* (1984) and *The Crying Game* (1992), for which he received an Academy Award best actor nomination. He also appeared in the recent Robert Altman production *Pret à Porter*.

♣ **Honoured Artist of the Soviet Republics, Alexander Arthurovitch Row** (1906–73), born in Russia, a specialist in films for children, was the son of a Wexford-born milling expert and a Greek mother. *The Little Humpbacked Horse* (1941) was distributed worldwide and in 1965 *King Frost* won the Golden Lion Award in Venice.

♣ **Mack Sennett** (1880 or 1884–1960) was born Michael Sinnott in Richmond, Quebec, Canada to Irish parents. He directed and produced approximately 1000 films. Having been apprenticed to D.W. Griffith at Biograph, and working as an actor opposite leading ladies such as Mary Pickford and Mabel Normand (to whom he formally proposed 11 times), he established his own studios in 1912. Keystone Studios made its reputation with Sennett's creation, *The Keystone Cops,* and other slapstick comedies. He discovered and then directed Charlie Chaplin, 'Buster' Keaton, 'Fatty' Arbuckle, W.C. Fields and Frank Capra.

Mack Sennett Comedies succeeded Keystone and Harry Langdon and Mabel Normand made many films there before the end of the silent era. Sennett could not make the transition to sound films easily and he lost his entire fortune through a series of unpopular productions. In 1939 he joined Twentieth Century Fox as a producer and in 1941 received a Special Academy Award.

🍀 **Martin Sheen** (born Ramón Estevez; 1940–) was born in Dayton, Ohio to Francisco Estevez of Spain and Mary Ann Phelan of Borrisokane, Co. Tipperary. He is the father of actors **Charlie Sheen** and **Emilio Estevez**. Martin Sheen has been an established screen actor for 25 years, his films including *Catch-22* (1970), *Badlands* (1974), *The Eagle's Wing* (1978), *Apocalypse Now* (1979), *The Final Countdown* (1980), *That Championship Season* (1982), *Gandhi* (1982), *The Dead Zone* (1983), *Wall Street* (1987) and *Da* (1988).

Television and radio stars

🍀 **Patrick Duffy**, born on 17 March 1949 to Irish parents Tony and Marie Duffy, became best known for his television series roles as *The Man from Atlantis* and Bobby Ewing in *Dallas*. (The *Dallas* series was an enormous success in the 1980s and was sold to television stations in over 90 countries worldwide. An average episode of the series was budgeted at $700,000

Successful screen actor Martin Sheen is the son of Mary-Ann Phelan of Borrisokane, Co. Tipperary and Francisco Estevez of Spain. His sons Charlie Sheen and Emilio Estevez have followed him into screen acting.

– nearly seven times the cost of most contemporary soap opera productions.) Both of Duffy's parents were murdered in an armed raid on their shop in 1987.

🍀 **Michael Terence 'Terry' Wogan** was born in Limerick in 1938 and joined RTE in Dublin in 1963. In 1965 he began working for BBC radio and has remained a top-rating presenter for the BBC for 30 years. *Late Night Extra*, from 1967 to 1969, made his name across Britain and was followed by his own programme, *The Terry Wogan Show*, from 1969 to 1972. He worked on the BBC Radio 2 *Breakfast Show* from 1972 to 1984 and took up television presentation with *Blankety Blank* in 1977. The TV chat-show *Wogan* first went on air in 1982 and was an instant success, running three times a week from 1985. Wogan hosts the annual BBC *Children in Need* show.

🍀 **Eamonn Andrews** (1922–87), born at Synge Street in Dublin, began his broadcasting career in 1946 with Radio Eireann. He became famous through the popular BBC TV show, *What's My Line*. In July 1955 the BBC began broadcasting their own version of an American TV show, *This Is Your Life*, with Andrews as host presenter. The show was extremely popular and Andrews was voted top television personality in 1956 and 1957. In 1964 he presented **Britain's first TV chat show**, *The Eamonn Andrews Show*. Andrews worked on several other television programmes and enterprises in Ireland and Britain. His boxing commentaries were especially praiseworthy on 'World Title' nights, when his inside knowledge of the sport – he was Irish Junior Middleweight Champion in 1944 – added insight to his presentations.

🍀 **Terence Alan 'Spike' Milligan** (1918–) was born in Ahmadnagar, India. His father, Leo Alphonso Milligan, was born in Co. Sligo to William Patrick Milligan and Elizabeth Higgins. He made his radio debut on *Opportunity Knocks* in 1949. With Peter Sellers, Harry Secombe and Michael Bentine he co-wrote and performed *The Goon Show* (1951–59), which made an indelible mark on British humour. Milligan has made several film cameos and has written a variety of books for children, as well as autobiographical stories and a selection of humorous poetry. His publications include: *Puckoon* (1963), *Adolf Hitler, My Part in his Downfall* (1971) and *The Looney: an Irish Fantasy* (1987). *Puckoon*, his first novel, was set in rural Ireland and based entirely on the recollections of his father – Milligan himself had yet to visit the country at the time.

sport

1908, which were confined to the Home Country teams, and the cycling team of 1912, athletes did compete for Ireland.

Partition has ensured that the representation of Ireland has continued to be a contentious issue, while some sporting bodies choose to ignore the border and others prefer to recognise it. Athletes caught in the middle care very little for the politics of it all but it has made the selection of national teams particularly difficult.

Olympic medallists

1896 – Athens

♣ **John Mary Pius Boland** (1870–1958), born in Dublin, was **the first Irish Olympic medallist**, winning two gold medals. He beat Dionisios Kasdaglis of Egypt to win the singles tennis title and went on to win a second gold in the doubles with Fritz Traun of Austria, whose original partner withdrew because of injury. Boland was in Athens on an Easter holiday with a Greek friend who was a member of the organising committee and was invited to participate. He won with no practice and with borrowed equipment.

1900 – Paris

♣ **John Flanagan** (1873–1938), born in Co. Limerick, won his first gold medal in the hammer throw for the United States. He won again in 1906 and 1908. He set 18 world records, from 44.46m at Clonmel, Ireland on 9 September 1895 to 56.19m at New Haven, USA on 24 July 1909.

♣ **Denis St George Daly** (1862–1942), born in Co. Galway, and **John George Beresford** (1847–1925), born in Ireland, won gold with the Great Britain polo team.

♣ **Harold Sigerson Mahony** (1867–1905) won two silver medals – in the tennis singles and mixed doubles events. In the latter, his partner, the Englishwoman Charlotte Cooper, was the first woman to win an Olympic gold medal. Mahony, who also took a bronze in the men's doubles, was born in Dromore Castle, Co. Kerry. He was also a Wimbledon champion (see p. 196).

♣ **Pat Leahy** (1877–1926) of Charleville, Co. Cork was second in the high jump and third in the long jump. His brother, Con (1876–1921), was to be Olympic champion at Athens in 1906. The competition was

ALL-ROUND SPORTSMEN AND WOMEN

♣ Possibly **Ireland's greatest all-round sportsman** was **Trevor George McVeagh** (1906–68), born in Athboy, Co. Meath. He represented Ireland more than 70 times in four different sports. In one year, 1938, he won international caps for tennis, hockey, squash and cricket. As captain of what was probably Ireland's best ever hockey team, he led them to three successive Triple Crown victories 1937–39. In tennis, he represented Ireland in 17 Davis Cup matches. (He twice beat the great American Bill Tilden, Wimbledon, US and French Champion and World No.1 for six successive years 1920–25.) In cricket, McVeagh's batting average of 40.88 runs per innings is the second best ever of those playing four or more first-class matches for Ireland. He scored 695 runs in ten matches 1926–34, and scored a century and took five catches in the historic Irish victory over the West Indies in 1928. He was Irish national squash champion three times, 1935–37.

♣ All-round sportswoman, **Dorothy 'Tommy' Dermody** represented Ireland at international level in four different sports. She was Irish fencing champion seven times between 1940 and 1950 and competed for Ireland in the 1948 Olympics. She was also Irish ladies diving champion six times between 1936 and 1944 and was also an international at squash and lacrosse.

OLYMPIC GAMES

For all Olympic competitions prior to the Paris Games in 1924, Ireland was part of Great Britain and so Irish athletes represented Great Britain and Ireland. However, in cases such as the hockey and polo teams of

won by the American Irving Baxter who cleared 1.90m.

1904 – St Louis

🍀 **Thomas Francis Kiely** (1869–1951) won gold in the all-around ten-event title, winning four events and finishing 129 points ahead of the American Adam Gunn. Kiely declined sponsorship from the English authorities because it would have entailed his representing Great Britain, and he travelled to the USA at his own expense.

A native of Ballyneal, Co. Tipperary, he won a total of 53 Irish titles, including 18 at the hammer. On one day, 10 September 1892, he won a record seven Gaelic AA titles. He won the US all-around title in 1904 and again in 1906.

🍀 **Pat Flanagan** won a gold medal as a member of the victorious US tug-of-war team. It is believed that he was a native of Co. Limerick and was related to John Flanagan, the great Irish-American hammer thrower, although no firm evidence of this exists.

🍀 **Martin Sheridan** (1881–1918), born in Bohola, Co. Mayo, won gold in the discus throw for the first time while representing the USA. Sheridan had left his home town in 1900 at the age of 19 to join the New York police force. In a remarkable career, he won nine Olympic medals, five gold, three silver and one bronze. He set 13 world records for the discus and won eight US titles, four at discus, one at shot and three at the all-around event. King George of Greece had a statue of a discus thrower erected in his honour in the Athens Stadium. He died prematurely of pneumonia in 1918 and a memorial to him was erected in Bohola in 1966.

🍀 **James Mitchel** (1864–1921), born in Emly, Co. Tipperary, won a bronze medal in the 56lb weight throw while representing the USA. Mitchel won 76 national championship titles in the hammer throw in Ireland, England, Canada and the USA. He broke the world record for the hammer 11 times between 1886 and 1892. At St Louis in 1904 he also competed in the discus, hammer and the tug-of-war.

Mitchel was favourite for the throwing events in the 1906 Intercalated Games but he injured his shoulder when a freak wave hit the ship carrying the US team to Athens and had to withdraw.

🍀 **John J. Daly** (b.1880) of Ballyglunin, Co. Galway won silver in the 2,590m steeplechase in 7:49:60. He was later US 5-mile and Canadian 3-mile champion.

1906 – Athens (Intercalated Games)

🍀 **Cornelius 'Con' Leahy** (1876–1921) of Cregane, Charleville, Co. Cork, won the gold medal in the high jump and silver in the triple jump. (See also 1908.)

🍀 **John Flanagan** won the gold medal in the hammer throw for the United States, for the second time. (See also 1900.)

🍀 **Peter O'Connor** (1874–1957) of Ashtown, Co. Wicklow won gold in the triple jump and silver in the long jump. O'Connor was an outstanding jumper who set his first world record of 7.51m in 1900. The following year he broke his own record on four occasions. On 5 August 1901 he jumped 24ft 11¹ in (7.61m) in Ballsbridge, Dublin and this remained the world record for 20 years and was an Irish record until 1968.

O'Connor's Olympic medals were awarded in controversial circumstances. He was world record holder in the long jump, although past his best by 1906. After winning second place at 7.02m, however, he won the triple jump with 46ft 2in (14.07m). At the award ceremony, he caused a stir when he climbed the flagpole to replace the Union Jack with the Irish flag. He was AAA champion at the long jump each year 1901–06 and the high jump 1903 and 1904. In 1932 he was a judge at the Los Angeles Games.

🍀 **Martin Sheridan,** Mayo-born New York policeman, won gold in the discus and shot and three silver medals in the standing long jump, the standing high jump and the stone cast*. (See 1904.)

🍀 **John McGough** (1887–1967), of Co. Monaghan, took the silver in the 1500m representing Great Britain. (McGough emigrated to Scotland and settled in Glasgow as a young man.)

1908 – London

🍀 **Timothy Ahearne** (1885–1968) of Athea, Co. Limerick won gold and set a new world record of 14.92m in the triple jump. His record was later beaten by his own brother Dan Ahearn (he dropped the final 'e'), who in May 1911 jumped 15.52m.

🍀 **Joseph Edmund Deakin** (1879–1972) was Irish champion at one and four miles in 1901. He won

---

* *The stone cast was an Olympic contest, now discontinued, to see who could throw a 14lb stone the furthest.*

Olympic gold in the three-man team race over 3 miles.

❧ There was a clean sweep by Irish-born competitors in the hammer. John Flanagan won his third successive Olympic gold for the United States, with Matt McGrath (see 1912) second and Con Walsh (1881–1942), representing Canada, third. Walsh was born in Carriganimma, Co. Cork. He became Irish champion in the hammer throw in 1906 and emigrated to Toronto the same year.

❧ **John Hayes**, whose parents came from Nenagh, Co. Tipperary, won gold in the marathon representing the USA. He was awarded first place after the Italian, Dorando Pietri, was disqualified for being helped over the finishing line. His winning time was 2:55:18.4, half a minute behind Dorando.

❧ **Bobby Kerr** of Enniskillen, Co. Fermanagh won gold in the 200 metres in a time of 22.6 seconds while representing Canada. Born in 1882, Kerr went to Ontario, Canada as a child with his parents. Having won AAA titles at 100yds and 220yds, he was favourite to win both sprints in London 1908, but was a disappointing 3rd to take the bronze at 100m. He later represented Ireland at an international track meeting in Dublin in 1909. He retired from competition that year and later worked as manager of the Canadian track and field team.

❧ **Cornelius 'Con' Leahy** won silver in the high jump. Leahy was one of seven brothers who were all excellent athletes. Pat Leahy had won two Olympic medals in 1900, Tim achieved the best high jump in the world in 1910 (6ft 3 in), and Joe was one of very few men of those days who could beat 7m in the long jump. Con won four and Pat two AAA high jump titles.

❧ **George Cornelius O'Kelly** (1886–1947) of Gloun, Co. Cork won Olympic gold in heavyweight freestyle wrestling. O'Kelly, a fireman in Hull, England, was holder of the British heavyweight title.

❧ **Edward Barrett,** born in Ballyduff, Co. Kerry in 1880, achieved a unique double for an Irishman with medals at tug-of-war and wrestling. He won a gold medal as a member of the victorious City of London Police tug-of-war team, but wrestling was his forte, and he also won Olympic bronze in the heavyweight freestyle event, at which he was British champion in 1908 and 1911. He was beaten by fellow-Irishman Con O'Kelly. Barrett also won an All-Ireland Senior Hurling Championship medal as a member of the 1901 London-Irish team that beat Cork in the All-Ireland final.

❧ **James Clark** (1874–1929), a Liverpool policeman, was a member of the runners-up team in the 1908 tug-of-war and received a silver medal. Clark was from the tiny village of Bohola, Co. Mayo and was a cousin of Martin Sheridan. The cousins competed against each other in the heats of the tug-of-war, one representing Britain and the other the USA.

❧ **Martin Sheridan** of Co. Mayo won two gold medals, for the discus and the Greek-style discus, and bronze in the standing long jump. (See 1904.)

❧ **Joshua Kearney Millner** (c.1849–1931), born in Ireland, won gold in the free rifle – 1000yds event. Although his exact date of birth is unknown, he was not less than 58 years and 237 days old. This makes him **the oldest Irish Olympic medal winner.**

❧ The Ireland hockey team lost the final to England in 1908 to take the silver. Team: E.P.C. Holmes, Henry Brown, Walter Peterson, William Graham, Walter Campbell, Henry Murphy, C.F. Power, G.S. Gregg, Eric Allman-Smith, Frank Robinson, Robert Kennedy (W.G. McCormack).

❧ **Denis Horgan,** born near Banteer, Co. Cork in 1871, took silver for Great Britain in the shot put. Horgan still holds the British record for **the most national (Amateur Athletic Association) titles in a single event**, by winning the shot put 13 times between 1893 and 1912. Horgan had set seven world records to 14.88m in 1904, but entered the Olympic competition for the first time in 1908 when he was past his peak. In 1907, as a policeman in New York, he had been savagely beaten to the point of death. He returned to Ireland and recovered dramatically. By the summer of 1908 he had recuperated sufficiently to regain his AAA title and secure a place on the British Olympic team.

❧ **James Cecil Parke** (1881–1946) of Clones, Co. Monaghan took silver in the men's doubles tennis tournament. Parke also won 20 caps as a rugby international for Ireland and won two Wimbledon mixed doubles titles (see Tennis).

❧ **Hardness Lloyd, John McCann, Percy O'Reilly** and **Anthony Rotherham** won bronze for Ireland at polo. Only three teams competed in the event!

1912 – Stockholm

❀ **Kennedy McArthur** (1880–1960) of Dervock, near Ballymoney, Co. Antrim won the marathon (40.2km that year) in 2:36:54.8. McArthur had emigrated to South Africa in 1905 and represented that country in Stockholm.

❀ **Matthew McGrath** (1878–1941), a Tipperary-born policeman, won the hammer throw for the USA. McGrath's winning throw of 179ft 11in (54.84m) was an Olympic record that stood for the next 24 years. All of his 6 throws on the day were 15ft (4.5m) or more longer than any other competitor's. He also won Olympic silver medals in 1908 and 1924 and his best-ever throw was a then world-record 187ft 4in (57.10m) in 1911.

❀ **Pat J. McDonald** (1878–1954), a 6ft 8in (2.03m) giant from Co. Clare won the shot for the United States with a throw of 50ft 4in (15.34m). He was born McDonnell, but changed the spelling of his name because his sister, who emigrated before him, was given the name McDonald at Ellis Island and subsequent McDonnells including Pat accepted the name. He joined the police force in New York.

❀ **Mathias 'Matt' Hynes** (1883–1926) won a silver medal as a member of the Great Britain tug-of-war team. Hynes was born at Killanin, Co. Galway, also home to the future President of the International Olympic Committee, Lord Killanin (see p. 171). He was a member of the London police force and replaced fellow-Irishman and gold medal winner (1908) Edward Barrett in the GB tug-of-war team.

1920 – Antwerp

❀ **Frederick Whitfield Barrett** (1875–1949), born in Co. Cork, won gold representing Britain at polo. He later won a bronze in 1924 at the Paris Games.

❀ **Pat McDonald** (see above) won his second Olympic gold for the USA. His 56lb weight win at the age of 42 years 23 days makes him **the oldest ever Olympic gold medallist at athletics**.

❀ **Noel Mary Purcell** (1891–1962), born in Dublin, was a member of the winning British water-polo team. Purcell was Irish half-mile swimming champion and played on the Irish national side for 18 years. He captained the Irish team that competed for the first time in the Olympics as an independent nation in 1924 and was capped for Ireland at rugby four times in the 1920/1 season. By winning medals for two different countries, Purcell forced a change in the Olympic rule on nationality.

❀ **Paddy Ryan** (1883–1964) of Pallasgreen, Co. Limerick, won the hammer title for the United States with a throw of 173ft 5 in (52.87m), the fifth consecutive Olympic gold for an Irishman at this event. Ryan had set a world record of 189ft 6 in (57.77m) in Celtic Park, New York in 1913 which was not beaten until 1937 and remained an American record until 1953. Ryan won the hammer-throwing championship of the USA every year from 1913 to 1921, except 1918 when he was serving with the US Army in France. He was a close friend of John Kelly, father of Princess Grace of Monaco (see p. 160) and of Gene Tunney the world heavyweight boxing champion. Ryan returned to live in Ireland in 1919 and took up farming in Pallasgreen.

❀ **Frank Heggarty**, born in Ireland, won a team silver for Great Britain in the 8000m cross country event.

1924 – Paris

❀ **Terence Robert Beaumont Sanders** (1901–85), born in Ireland, was gold medal winner for Britain in the coxless fours rowing event.

❀ **Matt McGrath**, previous champion for the United States in the hammer throw, won a silver medal at the age of 45 years and 205 days, making him **the oldest medallist in the throwing events in Olympic history**.

❀ **F.W. Barrett** won bronze with the Great Britain polo team (as above, 1920).

1928 – Amsterdam

❀ **Patrick O'Callaghan** (1905–91) of Derrygallon, Kanturk, North Cork, won gold in the hammer with a throw of 168ft 7in (51.40m). This was **the first Olympic gold medal for Ireland as an independent nation.**

1932 – Los Angeles

❀ **Patrick O'Callaghan became the first and only sports person representing Ireland to retain an Olympic title.** His hammer victory also meant that seven of the first eight Olympic titles in the hammer throw were won by Irishmen*. His winning throw was 53.92m (176ft 11in). On 22 August 1937 he exceeded the world record with a throw of 195ft 5in (59.56m) in Fermoy, Co. Cork. However, this was not recognised, as the Irish federation – the National Athletic and Cycling Association of Ireland (NACAI) – was not a member of the International Amateur Athletic Federation (IAAF). This was because they were in dispute with that organisation.

❦ **Bob Tisdall**, born in Ceylon in 1907, and raised in Nenagh, Co. Tipperary, won gold in the 400m hurdles in a world record time of 51.7 seconds. Tisdall had only run in six previous races over the distance. However, in conformity with the rules at that time, Tisdall's record was not officially recognised because he had hit a hurdle. The American, Glen Hardin, in second place, was given the new record of 51.9 secs.

❦ **Sam Ferris** (1900–80) of Dromore, Co. Down took silver for Britain in the marathon in this, his third Olympics. He finished 19 seconds behind the winner, Juan Carlos Zabala of Argentina, who won in 2:31:36.

1936 – Berlin

❦ **Ireland did not participate at the Berlin Games.** This was as a result of disagreements between the national sporting bodies – mostly relating to partition and the nationality of Northern Irish athletes. In 1935 the NACAI refused to accept that athletes from Northern Ireland could not represent Ireland. In protest, an Irish team did not travel to Berlin.

❦ **Bryan J. Fowler**, born in Co. Meath in 1898, was a captain in the British Army who won silver with the British polo team. Britain were beaten 11–0 by Argentina in the final. The British team also included an English-born member of the Guinness family, Humphrey Patrick Guinness (1902–80). The Argentine team had two players, Laurence Duggan and Robert Cavanagh, who had Irish grandparents. This was the last polo match in Olympic competition.

** The hammer throw is the only event in the Olympics taken from the Celtic **Tailteann Games, the oldest of all sporting festivals known in Europe,** dating from c. 1800 BC. The first documentary evidence of the Olympics dates from 772 BC. Cuchulainn, legendary hero of the Red Branch Knights, could throw a huge stone tied to the wooden beam of a chariot wheel enormous distances.*

Patrick O'Callaghan of Kanturk, Co. Cork, winner of the first gold medal for Ireland at the 1928 Olympics in Amsterdam. He retained his title four years later at Los Angeles and remains the only Irish athlete to have achieved this feat.

1948 – London

🍀 Again the issue of partition and who might or might not represent Ireland was the cause of a war of words between British and Irish officials. A much reduced Irish team attended and no medals were won.

🍀 Irish-born **Christopher Barton** (1927–) won silver for Great Britain in the eights class in rowing.

1952 – Helsinki

Team selection continued to be hampered by the politics of partition.

🍀 **The first boxing medal to be won by an Irishman competing for the Irish Republic** was awarded to **John McNally** (1932–) from Belfast who won a silver medal in the bantamweight division. McNally had become Irish senior bantamweight champion earlier in 1952 and was an automatic selection for the Olympic team.

1956 – Melbourne

🍀 **Ronnie Delany** (1935–) won the 1500m. Delany, from Arklow, Co. Wicklow set a new Olympic record of 3:41.2. He was a master at indoor running, being undefeated throughout his career in 40 races in the USA 1956–9, including 34 at the 1 mile. These included three world indoor mile records: 4:03.4 in 1958 and 4:02.5 and 4:01.4 in 1959. His outdoor mile best was an Irish record 3:57.5 in 1958.

🍀 **Thelma Hopkins** (1936–), born in Hull, England and raised in Belfast, won silver in the high jump for Great Britain. She set a world record at 1.74m in 1956 and was also a hockey and squash international for Ireland.

🍀 **Fred Tiedt** (1935–) of Dublin won silver in the welterweight boxing division, while **Freddie Gilroy** (1936–) of Belfast, **Anthony Byrne** (1930–) of Drogheda and **John Caldwell** (1938–) of Belfast won bronze medals at bantamweight, lightweight and flyweight respectively. Caldwell, at 18 years 209 days, was **Ireland's youngest Olympic medallist**.

🍀 **The first woman to compete for Ireland in the Olympics** was **Maeve Kyle** (1928–) from Kilkenny who ran in the 100m and 200m, but failed to reach the finals. She competed again in Rome 1960 and Tokyo 1964, although not getting further than the semi-finals. She won a record 41 titles at Irish and Northern Irish championships between 1955 and 1975, and undoubtedly would have won more had there been more organised athletics in her younger days. She won a European Indoor bronze medal at 400m in 1966 and set numerous world age bests in her 40s and 50s after she had retired from hockey, at which she won 58 caps for Ireland.

🍀 Irish-born **Kevin Gosper** won silver with the Australian 4x400m relay team.

1960 – Rome

🍀 No medals were won by Irish competitors.

1964 – Tokyo

🍀 **Jim McCourt** (1944–) of Belfast won bronze in the lightweight boxing division, competing for Ireland.

1968 – Mexico City

🍀 No medals were won by Irish competitors.

1972 – Munich

🍀 **Mary Peters** (1939–), who won a gold medal for Britain in the Pentathlon, was born in Halewood, Lancashire, but she was raised in Northern Ireland and continues to live there. Her winning score of 4801 points was a new world record, but she was a mere 10 points ahead of her German rival Heide Rosendahl. Peters took part in her first pentathlon in Ballymena in 1955 and in her career won eight Women's Amateur Athletic Association (WAAA) pentathlon titles and gold medals in the Commonwealth Games of 1970 and 1974. At the shot she was twice WAAA champion and, in 1970, was the Commonwealth champion.

1976 – Montreal

🍀 No medals won by Irish competitors.

1980 – Moscow

🍀 **Hugh Russell** (1959–) of Belfast won bronze in the flyweight boxing division, competing for Ireland.

Yachtsmen **David Wilkins** (1950–) of Malahide, Co. Dublin and **Jamie Wilkinson** (1951–) of Howth, Co. Dublin won silver in the Flying Dutchman class. David Wilkins was the first Irish competitor to have appeared in four Olympic competitions, 1972/76/80/88.

1984 – Los Angeles

John Treacy (1958–) took the silver medal in the marathon behind Carlos Lopes of Portugal in a time of 2:09:56. Treacy, from Villierstown, Co. Waterford, was twice winner of the World Cross Country Championships – in Glasgow 1978 and Limerick 1979. With Olympic appearances also in 1980, 1988 and 1992, he emulated yachtsman David Wilkins as a four-time Olympian.

William McConnell (1956–) of Newry, Co. Down won bronze with the Great Britain hockey team. McConnell has won 117 caps for Ireland and 51 for Great Britain.

Stephen Martin (1959–) of Bangor, Co. Down was also a member of the Great Britain hockey team that won the bronze medal. Martin has made 92 international appearances for Ireland and over 65 for Great Britain.

1988 – Seoul

James Kirkwood (1962–) of Lisburn, Co. Down and **Stephen Martin** (see 1984) were members of the gold medal-winning Great Britain hockey team in Seoul. Kirkwood has won 48 caps for Ireland and 31 for Great Britain.

1992 – Barcelona

Michael Carruth (1967–) of Greenhills, Dublin won gold in the welterweight boxing by beating the Cuban world champion Juan Hernández, thus becoming the first gold-medal winner for Ireland since Ronnie Delany in 1956.

Mary Peters, born in Halewood, Lancashire and raised in Northern Ireland, won gold in the pentathlon at the Munich Olympics in 1972. Her winning score of 4801 was a world record at the time.

🍀 **Wayne McCullough** (1970–) from the Shankill Road in Belfast won silver in the light bantamweight boxing division, competing for Ireland.

🍀 **Jackie Burns-McWilliams** (1964–) of Ballymoney, Co. Antrim won bronze with the Great Britain women's hockey team. She has won over 65 caps for Ireland and 34 for Great Britain to date.

Winter Olympics

🍀 **The only Irish winner of a medal at the Winter Olympics was Thomas R.V. Dixon** (1935–), the heir of Lord Glentoran, who won gold for Britain on the two-man bobsleigh with partner Tony Nash at the 1964 Games at Innsbruck, Austria. Dixon is London-born, but has a family seat at Doagh, Co. Antrim.

Other Irish Olympians

🍀 **Sir Michael Morris, Lord Killanin, the sixth President of the International Olympic Committee 1972–80,** was born in Melbourne, Australia in July 1914. His father, Lieutenant-Colonel George Henry Morris, a member of the Irish Guards, died in action in France only one month later. The Morris family had been residents of Galway since the 14th century and Richard Morris, a direct ancestor of the future IOC President, was one of the first bailiffs of Galway in 1486, one year after the town had been granted its charter. The family intermarried with the O'Flaherty and Fitzpatrick clans and inherited land near Spiddal, Co. Galway in the 17th century. Lord Killanin's grandfather was Lord Chief Justice of Ireland in 1885.

Michael Morris, Lord Killanin, was educated in England at Eton, at the Sorbonne in Paris, and then at Magdalene College, Cambridge. He took to journalism and became diplomatic and political correspondent for the *Daily Mail* and its Sunday edition, the *Sunday Dispatch*. He reported on Neville Chamberlain's 'Peace in Our Time' speech after the Munich Agreement with Adolf Hitler in 1938. In World War II he served as a brigade-major of the 30th Armoured Brigade in the British Army.

After the war he took up his family seat in Spiddal, Co. Galway. He married Sheila Dunlop in 1945. (She had been awarded an MBE for her services on 'Ultra' which had helped to break the German coding system during World War II. Her father, Henry Wallace Doveton Dunlop, founded the Irish Champion Athletic Club and the **Lansdowne Road Rugby ground, now the oldest in the world.**)

In 1950 Lord Killanin was elected President of the Irish Olympic Council. Two years later he became a member of the International Olympic Committee. He was Vice-President by 1968 and on 10 September 1970 he assumed the presidency following the retirement of Avery Brundage.

His presidency was memorable for his innovation and the modernisation of the Olympic Games, particularly through the difficult years of boycotts at Montreal and Moscow. He has received many honorary degrees and awards in Ireland and abroad. At the 83rd session of the International Olympic Committee in Moscow in 1980 he was awarded the gold medal of the Olympic Order, the highest accolade of the Olympic movement. Lord Killanin has residences in both Dublin and Galway.

Lord Killanin has written several works, including *My Olympic Years* and *My Ireland*, and has edited the *Shell Guide to Ireland* with Michael Duignan. He also worked with the filmmaker John Ford (see p. 157) in his Irish productions, including *The Quiet Man, The Rising of the Moon* and *The Playboy of the Western World*.

🍀 **Desmond O'Sullivan** of Dublin was elected Treasurer to the Olympic Council of Ireland in 1957, General Secretary in 1972, Vice-President in 1975 and President of the OCI 1976-89. **In 1981 he was awarded the silver medal of the Olympic Order** in recognition of his contribution to the Olympic movement.

🍀 **Ken Ryan** has been General Secretary of the Olympic Council of Ireland since 1976. In 1979 he became a member of the European National Olympic Marketing Committee. He was **awarded the bronze medal of the Olympic Order in 1981** for his services to the Olympic movement.

Olympic arts medals

🍀 **Jack B. Yeats** (1867–1957; see p. 120), writer, artist and brother of Nobel Prize-winning author William B. Yeats, won an Olympic silver medal in Paris 1924 in the experimental painting division of the Olympic Art Contests for his entry, 'Swimming'.

🍀 **Oliver St John Gogarty** (1878–1957), doctor, wit, poet and Senator of Ireland, was invited by the Olympic Council of Ireland to submit an entry to the literature division of the Olympic Art Contests and won a bronze medal for 'Ode to the Tailteann Games'; he was joint third with the French entrant C.A. Gonnet.

🍀 **Letitia Hamilton** (1878–1964), born in Dublin, was a founder-member of the Dublin Painters' Group and was elected to the Royal Hibernian Academy in 1944. In 1948 she was invited, among others, to submit an entry for the painting division of the Olympic Arts Contest. Her entry, 'Meath Hunt Point-to-Point Races' was selected and won an Olympic bronze medal.

Athletics – track events

🍀 **Eamonn Coghlan** (1952–) has been the outstanding Irish athlete of recent years. Born in Drimnagh in Dublin, he showed early promise and was offered a scholarship to Villanova University in Pennsylvania. There the celebrated coach was Jumbo Elliot, who trained many Irish students, including Ronnie Delany. Between 1975 and 1983 Coghlan set Irish records at 1500m, the mile, 2000m, 3000m and 5000m. He also set European records at the mile, with 3:53.3 in 1975, with a best outdoor time of 3:51.59 in 1983. He was also a member of the 4×1 mile world-record-setting Irish team in 1985. Coghlan led off with a 4:00.2 leg, followed by **Marcus O'Sullivan** 3:55.3, **Frank O'Mara** 3:56.6 and **Ray Flynn** 3:57.0 for a time of 15:49.08. The previous record was 16:02.8.

In 1976 Coghlan was a strong favourite to win the 1500m at the Montreal Olympics, but he came a disappointing fourth. He was fourth again at the Olympics in Moscow in 1980, this time at 5000m, after falling ill. He damaged his achilles tendon in 1982, but despite his bad luck, he came back to become the **first man to break the 3min 50 sec barrier in the indoor mile** on 27 February 1983 at East Rutherford, New Jersey, USA in 3:49.78. This was his fourth indoor world record for the mile, following 3:55.0 and 3:52.6 in 1979 and 3:50.6 in 1981. Later that year he at last took a major championship gold medal, winning the world title at 5000m in Helsinki.

Popular in the United States, Coghlan's brilliance on the indoor circuit earned him the nickname 'Chairman of the Boards'. He won the celebrated Wanamaker Mile at the annual Millrose Games in Madison Square Garden a record seven times between 1977 and 1987 and in the 14 years 1974–87 won 52 of his 70 races at 1500m or 1 mile indoors. He set a world indoor record for the 2000m in Inglewood, California in 1987, with 4:54.07.

On 20 February 1994 in Cambridge, Massachusetts, Coghlan, at 41 years of age, became **the first runner over the age of 40 to run a sub-four-minute mile**, smashing that barrier with a marvellous time of 3:58.15.

🍀 **Frank O'Mara** (1960–), of Croom, Co. Limerick, was twice winner of the World Indoor Championships at 3000m – in Indianapolis in 1987 (beating fellow Irishman Paul Donovan into second place) and again in Seville in 1991. He has been Irish record holder at 5000m since 1987, with a time of 13:13.02.

🍀 **Marcus O'Sullivan** (1961–), born in Cork, inherited Eamonn Coghlan's role as the world's finest indoor miler. He won the Wanamaker Mile five times between 1986 and 1991. In Meadowlands in 1989 he set a world indoor record in the 1500m at 3:35.6. He is three-times World Indoor Champion at 1500m: Indianapolis 1987, Budapest 1989 and Toronto 1993.

🍀 **John Treacy** (1958–) of Villierstown, Co. Waterford, currently based in Rhode Island, USA, is Ireland's leading long-distance runner. He was twice world cross country champion 1978 and 1979. He won silver in the marathon in the Los Angeles Olympics 1984 and won the Los Angeles Marathon in 1992 and Dublin City Marathon in 1993. He finished third in the Boston City Marathon in 1988 and again in 1989. He was also third in the New York City Marathon in 1988 and second in the Tokyo Marathon in 1990. He is **the first sportsman to be given the Freedom of the City of Waterford**.

🍀 **Catherina McKiernan,** born in Cornafean, Co. Cavan in 1969, was national senior cross-country champion each year 1990–94 and was second in the World Cross-Country Championships in Boston in 1992 and again in 1993 and 1994. In 1991–92 she won three successive grand prix events in Belgium, France and Mallusk and went on to win the World Cross Country Challenge series. She won this series again in 1993 and 1994. She reached the final of the 10,000m in the 1993 World Championships in Stuttgart, but failed to finish.

🍀 **Sonia O'Sullivan** (1969–) of Cobh, Co. Cork became the **first Irish woman athlete to break a world track record** in the 5000m indoors in 1991 in a time of 15:17.28. She finished fourth in the 3000m in the 1992 Barcelona Olympics and was the second Irish woman to appear in an Olympic track final. In 1992 she broke five Irish records from 1500 to 5000m in eleven days. She emerged as an international athlete in 1992 and was favourite to win the 3000m in the World Championships in Stuttgart in 1993. Finishing fourth behind three Chinese athletes, she went on to take the silver in the 1500m – thus becoming the **first woman representing Ireland to win a medal at any major championship.** She won four IAAF grand prix events in 1993, finishing second overall in the series, and collected $100,000. She set a new world record in the women's 2000m at Meadowbank, Edinburgh, 8 July 1994.

Eamon Coghlan – 'Chairman of the Boards' – was an outstanding mile runner in the late 1970s and 1980s, excelling on the indoor circuit. He set a world record in Boston in February 1994 in the Masters' (over 40s) race with a time of 3:58:15.

❦ **Founder of the New York City Marathon, Fred Lebow** fled anti-Jewish persecution in his native Romania in 1947 and, after much travelling, ended up in Ireland where he lived for three years, gained an education and became an Irish citizen. In 1950 he moved to the United States, where he organised the first New York marathon race in 1970. His race came into its own when the course was changed from five laps of Central Park to a route through all five boroughs to celebrate the US Bicentennial in 1976. In 1977 there was a world record marathon field of 4823 runners, and this record has since been broken many times, reaching 27,797 in 1992.

The annual participation of approximately 25,000 runners come from over 100 different countries. In 1992, Lebow, who had run in 68 other marathons, competed in the New York race for the first time, despite suffering from cancer of the brain.

Athletics – field events

❦ **William Barry**, born in Cork in 1863, was a hammer pioneer who set eight world records from 33.00m at Tralee in 1885 to 39.41m in New York in 1888.

❦ **The Davin Brothers** of Carrick-on-Suir, Co. Tipperary set the standards of organised athletics in 19th-century Britain and held an unprecedented number of records in one family. **Tom** (1852–94) set a new world record in the high jump of 5ft 10in (1.785m) in 1873. This record was beaten by his brother **Pat** (1857–1949) who jumped 6ft 4in (1.93m) in 1880. Pat set a world record for the long jump at Monasterevin in 1883 when he jumped 23ft 2in (7.06m), equalling that jump at Portarlington a month later. He had previously won the British AAA titles at both long jump and high jump in 1881.

At the British AAA championships of 1881 the third Davin brother, **Maurice** (1842–1927), won the shot put and the hammer events at 39 years of age. Maurice Davin was the Irish all-round Champion in 1888. He was adept at many sports including rowing, swimming, running and jumping and was **the first President of the Gaelic Athletic Association**.

BADMINTON

❦ **Frank Devlin** (1900–88), born in Clane, Co. Kildare, was the best badminton player of his time. He won five successive All-England titles 1925–29 and a sixth in 1931. He was also a winner of seven doubles titles, the first with Englishman George Sautter in 1922 and the rest with his compatriot 'Curly' Mack. He won five mixed doubles titles, two of them with top tennis player Kitty McKane. He took up coaching in 1931 in Canada and eventually settled in the USA. His daughters, **Judith and Susan,** were both outstanding players.

♣ **Judy Hashman, née Devlin** (1935–), born in Winnipeg, Canada, is **the most successful badminton player in the history of the women's All-England Championships.** She won ten singles titles, 1954, 1957–58, 1960–64, 1966–67, and seven doubles Championships, six with her sister **Susan Devlin** (later Peard).

The two sisters won a record 10 doubles titles in the US Championships. Judy won 12 US Singles Titles, 1954, 1956–63, 1965–67 and eight mixed doubles titles. She played for the USA and helped them to three wins in five Uber Cup series. She moved to England in 1960 and qualified to play for the national team in 1970–72. In 1978 she was appointed manager and coach of the England team. An all-round sportswoman, she represented the USA at junior level in tennis and was also a member of the USA lacrosse team for five years.

♣ **Susan Devlin** was a member of the US Uber Cup team 1957–62 before moving to Ireland, where she played for the national team 1963–69 and directed a coaching school for children 1960–84.

BOXING

Ireland has always produced a disproportionate number of champions in boxing. As with many other Irish sportsmen and women, Irish boxers have made their careers abroad. In the United States the Irish ghettos of the major cities produced numerous boxing heroes who fought savagely for material reward and social recognition. The end of the 'golden age' of Irish-American boxing coincided with a new social acceptance for the Irish community that culminated in the election of John F. Kennedy as president (see p. 81). Since then, the black and Hispanic communities of America have taken over that role.

Irish World Champions

Flyweight

♣ **Rinty Monaghan** (1920–84), born in Belfast, was world flyweight champion 1948–50, competing for

Ireland, having beaten Jackie Patterson to take the title. When he won the European title in 1949, he became **the first boxer in history to hold five titles at the same weight simultaneously** – he was World, European, Commonwealth, British and Irish champion.

♣ **Dave 'Boy' McAuley** (1961–) of Larne, Co. Antrim, representing the UK, beat Duke McKenzie in Wembley Arena in June 1989 to win the International Boxing Federation (IBF) world flyweight title. He defended his title successfully five times before losing to Rodolfo Blanco (Colombia) in 1992.

Bantamweight

♣ **Johnny Caldwell**, born in Belfast in 1938, won his world title representing Ireland in 1961 when he beat Alphonse Halimi of France. He lost it to Eder Jofre (Brazil) in 1962. As a professional, Caldwell was British, European and World Champion at bantamweight.

Featherweight

♣ **Ike O'Neill Weir, 'the Belfast Spider',** born in Lurgan in 1867, became the **world's first featherweight champion** – according to some sources – in 1890.

♣ **Dave Sullivan** (1877–1929), born in Cork, won the world featherweight title in September 1898 at Coney Island New York. He lost the title 46 days later and remains today the **shortest lived world champion at that weight**.

♣ **Barry McGuigan, 'the Clones Cyclone',** born in 1961 in Clones, Co. Monaghan, took his World Boxing Association (WBA) title on 8 June 1985 by defeating the Panamanian Eusebio Pedroza. McGuigan lost his title a year later to the little-fancied Steve Cruz in Las Vegas. McGuigan won the Irish bantamweight title and the Commonwealth Games gold medal as an amateur in 1978, Having turned pro, he won the British featherweight title in 1983.

Lightweight

♣ **Jack McAuliffe** (1866–1937) of Meelin, Co. Cork won the world lightweight title in 1885 and held on to it for eleven years before retiring undefeated. He is one of the few world title-holding champions never to have lost a fight.

Jack Dempsey and Gene Tunney battle it out in a world heavyweight title fight in Philadelphia, 23 September 1926. Dempsey was of Irish, Jewish and Cherokee Indian descent, while Tunney's parents emigrated to the US from Kiltimagh, Co. Mayo.

Welterweight

🍀 **Jimmy Gardner** of Lisdoonvarna, Co. Clare won the world welterweight title in 1908, although this is not universally recognised. His brother George was world light heavyweight champion in 1903.

🍀 **Tom McCormick** of Dundalk, Co. Louth won a version of the world welterweight title in 1914.

🍀 **Jimmy McLarnin**, born at Inchicore in 1906, first won the title in May 1933 by defeating Young Corbett III. He fought three title fights against Barney Ross, losing the title in May 1934, only to win it back again in September 1934 and lose it in May 1935, all on points.

Middleweight

🍀 **Jack 'Nonpareil' Dempsey** (1862–95), born in Kildare, became **the world's first official middle-** **weight champion** in 1884 and held on to his title for seven years. (He was not related to the great heavyweight champion.)

Light Heavyweight

🍀 **George Gardner** (1877–1954), born in Lisdoonvarna, Co. Clare, won his world title in July 1903 and lost it in November that year. He was the older brother of Jimmy Gardner, world welterweight champion 1908.

🍀 **Mike McTigue** (1892–1966), born in Ennis, Co. Clare, became world champion on 17 March 1923 when he beat Battling Siki of Senegal in Dublin. He held the title for two years.

Irish-American boxers

From the very start of boxing as a spectator event in America, the Irish were beating all comers. In the

1840s Mike McCool and Joe Coburn reigned as heavyweight champions and were succeeded by James 'Yankee Sullivan' Ambrose from Co. Cork. Ambrose lost his title to Tipperary-born John Morrissey in 1853. In 1860, when Irish-American John Heanan lost a world heavyweight title bout in London on an alleged foul to Englishman Tom Sayers, a diplomatic crisis was caused when English dignitaries were met by hostile Irish demonstrators in Boston and New York.

The bare-knuckle boxing era came to an end on 7 February 1882 when world heavyweight champion **Paddy Ryan** of Thurles, Co. Tipperary lost his title to **John L. Sullivan** (1858–1918). Sullivan, born in Boston, was the son of recent immigrants, his father hailing from Tralee, Co. Kerry and his mother from Athlone, Co. Westmeath.

Thereafter, for the most part, the new rules of the Marquess of Queensberry took effect. **Sullivan was the first heavyweight champion under the Queensberry rules** and their greatest advocate. The first title fight under the new rules took place in Chester Park, Cincinnati, Ohio on 29 August 1885, between Sullivan and Dominick F. McCafferey, with both boxers wearing gloves over six three-minute rounds. The referee Billy Tait left the ring without giving a verdict, but stated two days later that Sullivan had won. Sullivan travelled to Ireland, England and Australia to maintain his world-champion status and became a national hero in the United States. He held his title for ten years before losing to **James Corbett** (1866–1933) on 7 September 1892.

♣ **James 'Gentleman Jim' Corbett**, as he was known, was born into San Francisco's large Irish community. His father was from Tuam in Galway while his mother was a Dubliner. Corbett is reputed to have soaked the bandages wrapped around his fists in plaster of Paris before each fight – not the sort of behaviour that one would expect, given his nickname.

The early years of the 20th century saw Irish-Americans such as O'Brien, Dillon, Ryan and O'Dowd continue to dominate in the ring.

♣ **William Muldoon** (1852–1933), **inventor of the medicine ball**, was born in Allegany, New York to Patrick and Maria Muldoon (née Donohue) from Ireland. Muldoon joined the New York Police Department (NYPD) in 1876 and trained as a wrestler and physical education instructor. He coached John L. Sullivan in 1889 for the fight against Jake Kilrain. His expertise as an athletic coach paid more than the NYPD, and by

1900 he was able to afford a mansion in wealthy Westchester County in upstate New York. His new home became a health and training centre and it was here that he developed the first medicine ball. He was a crusader against corruption in sport, particularly in boxing. With Gene Tunney he provided the Tunney–Muldoon Trophy in 1928 – as an emblem of the world heavyweight boxing championship.

♣ **William Harrison 'Jack' Dempsey** (1895–1983) of Manassa, Colorado – nicknamed Jack after the middleweight champion of 1882 (see p. 175) from Co. Kildare – took the world heavyweight title in 1919. **Gene Tunney,** in turn, defeated Dempsey in 1926 and again in 1927. The contest on 23 September 1926 at the Sesquicentennial Stadium, Philadelphia, attracted a crowd of 120,757. This is the **greatest ever paid attendance at any boxing bout.** (Tunney was first-generation American, the son of parents from Kiltimagh in Co. Mayo.) Tunney retired in 1927 while Jack Dempsey kept going until 1933.

♣ In 1935 **Jim Braddock** won the world heavyweight title. He was born in the USA to Irish parents who had first emigrated to Mottram, Lancashire, England before moving on to the USA. The 1930s was the end of an era of Irish domination of boxing that was so emphatic that, for its duration, fighters from other immigrant groups adopted Irish names in order to further their careers.

♣ **Muhammad Ali,** three-times world heavyweight boxing champion, 1964–67, 1974–77 and 1979, had a maternal grandfather by the name of O'Grady who came from Co. Clare.

CRICKET

♣ **Sir Tim O'Brien** (1861–1948), born in Dublin, scored 306 runs at an average of 43.73, the **highest average for Ireland in first-class cricket** of those who played four or more matches. A dashing batsman, he played in five Test matches for England, captaining them against South Africa once on the 1895/6 tour. He played for Oxford University 1884–85 and Middlesex 1881–98 before his Irish games in 1902–07.

♣ **Ivan Anderson** (1944–), born in Armagh, holds the record for the highest score for Ireland, 198 not out v Canada in 1973 and is the only Irish cricketer to score two centuries in an international match, against Scotland in 1976.

🍀 **Frank Fee** (1934–) has achieved the best bowling for Ireland, 9 wickets for 26 runs against Scotland in 1957.

CROQUET

🍀 **The most successful croquet player of his era, Cyril Corbally** (1880–1946), born in Ireland, won a record five Open Championships, 1902–03, 1906, 1908, 1913. His record stood until Englishman Humphrey Hicks won his sixth title in 1950. Corbally also won the mixed doubles in 1903 and 1911 and the men's doubles in 1913 with his brother Herbert. He was the best of the school of Irish players who adopted the centre-stance and his success led to the virtual abandonment of the old-style, side-stance favoured in Britain.

Stephen Roche of Dundrum, Dublin, won the grand Slam – the Tour de France, Tour d'Italia and the World Championship – in 1987. He is the only cyclist ever to have won all three competitions in one season.

CYCLING

🍀 Winner of the Grand Slam (Tour de France, Tour d'Italia and the World Championship) in 1987, **Stephen Roche** (1959–) of Dundrum, Dublin was the first to achieve the treble since Eddy Merckx in 1974. No other cyclist has ever won all three competitions in the one season.

Roche began his career with his local cycling club in Dublin, the Orwell Wheelers. His rise to the top was rapid. He was offered a contract with Peugeot on the professional circuit in 1981, having won the Paris–Roubaix and Paris–Reims classics as an amateur in 1980. He won the Paris–Nice race that year and in 1983 took the white jersey (best newcomer) in the Tour de France. In 1985, Roche finished 3rd in the Tour de France and he was widely fancied to win the following year. However, injury forced him out of contention for a season and he had to wait until 1987 to win the Tour de France. In a magnificent Grand Slam season he cycled over 27,000 miles (43,450km).

🍀 **Sean Kelly** (1956–) of Carrick-on-Suir, Co. Tipperary began racing with the local club Carrick Wheelers and joined the professional circuit in 1977. He rapidly established his reputation as one of the greatest ever riders in the one-day classics. In 1978 he won his first stage in the Tour de France, and although his biggest disappointment was that he never won the race outright, he was points winner a record four times 1982–83, 1985 and 1989. His highest race position was 4th in 1985 when he received the green jersey for the third time. Among his many successes in 1982 was victory in two stages of the Tour de France, overall victory in the Paris–Nice race and third place in the World Championship. **From 1984–89 Kelly was ranked as the number one cyclist in the world** and did more than anyone to break Franco-Belgian domination of the sport. He is unmatched in winning seven consecutive Paris–Nice races 1982–88.

🍀 **The first Irishman to win the World Championship title in cycling was Harry Reynolds, 'The Balbriggan Flyer',** of Balbriggan, Co. Dublin. In 1895 he had won the Irish 5-mile and 50-mile championships as well as the gold medal in the Surrey 100 Guinea Cup. He was overlooked for the Irish Olympic team in 1896, but travelled to Copenhagen to compete in the World Championship in August of the same year. He won the title by beating the first Olympic champion Paul Masson. (**Stephen Roche**, Austria 1987, was the next Irish world champion.)

Crowds of up to 250,000 greeted him on his return home. He turned professional and won many races in Australia, Ireland, England, New Zealand and Sweden. It is said that he trained by racing the Balbriggan–Skerries train in Co. Dublin and by cycling up Barnageera hill backwards. He died in his home town in 1940 and is commemorated there by a monument.

GAELIC SPORTS

The Gaelic Athletic Association (GAA) is an amateur sporting association that owes its origins to Michael Cusack and Maurice Davin who issued a circular on 27 October 1884: '...a meeting (which) will be held at

ALL-IRELAND SENIOR FOOTBALL FINALS – ROLL OF HONOUR	
Kerry (30 wins)	1903, 1904, 1909, 1913, 1914, 1924, 1926, 1929, 1930, 1931, 1932, 1937, 1939, 1940, 1941, 1946, 1953, 1955, 1959, 1962, 1969, 1970, 1975, 1978, 1979, 1980, 1981, 1984, 1985, 1986
Dublin (21 wins)	1891, 1892, 1894, 1897, 1898, 1899, 1901, 1902, 1906, 1907, 1908, 1921, 1922, 1923, 1942, 1958, 1963, 1974, 1976, 1977, 1983
Galway (7 wins)	1925, 1934, 1938, 1956, 1964, 1965, 1966
Cork (6 wins)	1890, 1911, 1945, 1973, 1989, 1990
Meath (5 wins)	1949, 1954, 1967, 1987, 1988
Wexford (5 wins)	1893, 1915, 1916, 1917, 1918
Cavan (5 wins)	1933, 1935, 1947, 1948, 1952
Tipperary (4 wins)	1889, 1895, 1900, 1920
Kildare (4 wins)	1905, 1919, 1927, 1928
Down (4 wins)	1960, 1961, 1968, 1991
Louth (3 wins)	1910, 1912, 1957
Mayo (3 wins)	1936, 1950, 1951
Offaly (3 wins)	1971, 1972, 1982
Limerick (2 wins)	1887, 1896
Roscommon (2 wins)	1943, 1944
Donegal (1 win)	1992
Derry (1 win)	1993
There were no finals played in 1888.	

Thurles on 1 November to take steps for the formation of a Gaelic Association for the preservation and cultivation of our national pastimes, and for providing amusements for the Irish people during their leisure hours.' Maurice Davin was elected first president, Cusack, Wyse-Power and McKay were elected secretaries. Dr T.W. Croke, Archbishop of Cashel, became the Association's first patron. (Croke Park in Dublin, the headquarters of the organisation, is named in his honour.) Other patrons included Charles Stewart Parnell and Michael Davitt (see p. 54).

The GAA was nationalist in outlook. It imposed on its members a ban preventing them from playing specified non-Gaelic games. This ban has since been rescinded. Its rules continue to exclude from membership those who serve with British Crown Forces and it will not allow 'foreign games' to be played in its stadiums. These bans are a source of much controversy in Ireland today where the GAA has continued to prosper as the largest sporting body in the country. While professional games such as soccer continue to grow in popularity in Ireland, particularly after recent international successes, a self-preserving policy of banning foreign sports in GAA stadiums seems likely to continue.

The All-Ireland Finals, hurling and Gaelic football, take place in September every year at Croke Park in Dublin and are broadcast throughout the world to audiences in Britain, USA, Canada and Australia in particular. In the 1992/3 season there were 2800 registered GAA clubs in the island of Ireland, fielding 182,406 players of Gaelic Football and 96,894 hurlers. With 800,000 members and approximately 400,000 players in the GAA at home and abroad, it is a powerful national movement with an important social, cultural and economic role in Irish life.

Gaelic Football

Gaelic Football (Irish – 'Peil') is the most popular sport in Ireland, with approximately 250,000 players in 1992 (at senior, junior and minor levels, men and women).

The first record of Gaelic football is in the Statutes of Galway (1527), which allowed the playing of football but banned hurling. The earliest reported match took place at Slane, Co. Meath in 1712, when Meath played against neighbouring Co. Louth.

Basic Rules: The game is played by two teams of 15 with a round ball, slightly smaller than a soccer ball. The pitch should be 140–160 yards long and 84–100 yards wide. At either end of the pitch are goalposts.

Sending the ball over the crossbar and between the posts counts as one point. Sending the ball below the crossbar, between the posts and into the net is a goal and counts as three points. The ball may be passed with foot or fist but must not be thrown. The ball may be carried for only four steps without being bounced or played from foot to hand. The ball must be touched by the foot at least once between one bounce and the next. The ball can be played continuously between hand and foot if the four-step rule is observed. The game is supervised by a referee, two linesmen and four umpires.

Capacity crowds of 65,000 attend the All-Ireland Senior Football Final at Croke Park every September. All 32 counties of the island of Ireland compete in their provincial championships. The champions of each of the four provinces meet in the semi-finals. The winners of the final, as All-Ireland Senior Champions, receive the Sam Maguire Cup.

Since the first All-Ireland Senior Football Final in 1887, Kerry have been the most successful team, winning the cup 30 times. Dublin have won on 21 occasions – the rest fall far behind.

Only Kerry (twice) and Wexford have won in four successive years. The victors from 1991–3 – Down, Donegal and Derry – are all Ulster teams, the first three consecutive wins for the province.

The domination of Kerry and Dublin is all the more evident when their total All-Ireland Senior Football Final appearances are added up. Kerry were runners-up 16 times, thus making a total of 46 appearances. Dublin were runners-up 12 times – making a total of 33 appearances.

Fifteen counties have failed to win All-Ireland SFC titles: Antrim, Armagh, Carlow, Clare, Fermanagh, Kilkenny, Leitrim, Laois, Longford, Monaghan, Sligo, Tyrone, Waterford, Westmeath, Wicklow. (London were losers in five SFC finals. Teams made up of

Cork play Mayo at Gaelic Football, the most popular sport in Ireland with approximately 250,000 players nationwide. The modern game originated with the founding of the Gaelic Athletic Association in 1884, although a less organised version of the game was played as early as the 16th century.

London-Irish have played regularly in the GAA championships. The Irish population of London is larger than that of any county in Ireland other than Dublin.)

❧ **The highest attendance for an All-Ireland Senior Football Cup Final at Croke Park** was 90,556 at the 1961 Down v Offaly final.

Under the reduced capacity of the stadium, following the introduction of seating to the Cusack Stand in 1966, the highest attendance was 73,588 for the 1976 Dublin v Kerry final. A major redevelopment of Croke Park began after the 1993 All-Ireland SFC Final. When completed, the new capacity of the stadium will be 79,500.

❧ **Most appearances in an All-Ireland SFC Final:** Paudie O'Shea, Pat Spillane and Denis 'Ogie' Moran have each appeared in ten finals, playing in the same Kerry team. They were winners on eight occasions: 1975-6, 1978-82, 1984-6. John O'Keefe, Dan O'Keefe, Charlie Nelligan and Sean Walsh – all Kerry players – have won seven All-Ireland SFC medals.

❧ **The highest individual score in an All-Ireland SFC Final**, under the current 70-minute timescale, is 12 points by Jimmy Keaveney of Dublin in the 1977 final v Armagh, when he scored two goals and six points, and by Mike Sheehy of Kerry in the 1979 final v Dublin, with the same score.

International Series

Ireland and Australia have played four test series, each consisting of three matches, in which 'compromise rules' – a mixture of Gaelic Football and Australian Rules – are followed. It should be noted that GAA players are amateurs and Australian Rules players are professionals. The results are as follows:

Year	Venue	
1984	(Ireland)	Ireland 1 Australia 2
1986	(Australia)	Ireland 2 Australia 1
1987	(Ireland)	Ireland 1 Australia 2
1990	(Australia)	Ireland 2 Australia 1
Overall 6–6 in games and 2–2 in test series.		

Australian Rules Football

❧ **Jim Stynes** of Dublin began his career by playing Gaelic Football as a midfielder in the Dublin minor side which won the All-Ireland MFC in 1984. He emigrated to Australia, took up the 'Rules' game with Melbourne, and joined the senior team in 1987. Stynes has since progressed to become Melbourne's star player and in 1991 won two of the game's most prestigious awards, the Players Association Award and the Brownlow Medal. In the 'compromise rules' series he played for Australia in 1987 and for Ireland in 1990.

Women's Football

The Ladies Gaelic Football Association, Cumann Peile Gael na mBan, was founded in Haye's Hotel, Thurles, Co. Tipperary in 1974 by representatives from four counties, Offaly, Kerry, Tipperary and Galway. Since then, it has grown to rival camogie (a version of hurling for women) in popularity. There are 29 playing counties, including teams from London and Manchester, now playing in a Senior Football championship with a membership of approximately 25,000. Teams have recently been organised in Canada and the United States. The first All-Ireland Championship Senior Championship was held in 1989.

All-Ireland Senior Championship Football Winners – Women:
Kerry	–	1989, 1990, 1993
Waterford	–	1991, 1992

Hurling

Hurling is the oldest of Irish sports and has been played since pre-Christian times. It is the sport of the heroes of Irish mythology and it was included in the Tailteann Games (see p. 168). No standardised rules existed until the formation of the Gaelic Athletic Association in Thurles on 1 November 1884.

Hurling is the third most popular sport in Ireland. (As recently as 1986 it was second only to Gaelic football, but soccer has since overtaken hurling in popularity.) There are approximately 100,000 players at senior, junior and minor levels. Hurling is a male sport, women's hurling, camogie, is played to the same basic rules, but on a smaller pitch with smaller goals and smaller hurling sticks. There are 50,000 camogie players in the GAA.

Hurling is one of the fastest field games in the world. It is played with an ash stick or hurley, from 30¼–37 in (76.8–94 cm) long, with a broad curved end. The stick is used to hit and carry the ball, or sliotar, which weighs 3½–4½ oz. (99.22–127.57gm).

Basic Rules: The rules of hurling and Gaelic football are essentially the same. Hurling matches consist of two teams of 15 players. A goal, worth three points, can be scored by hitting the sliotar into the net, below the crossbar and between the posts. A single point is awarded for knocking the sliotar over the crossbar and between the posts. The sliotar must not be carried in the hand for more than four steps, but it may be carried indefinitely on the end of the hurley. The sliotar may be passed by hitting it with the hurley, the foot or the palm of the hand. It must not be thrown. There is no offside rule and consequently the ability to hit the sliotar for great distances is essential.

The game is supervised by one referee, two linesmen and four umpires. Capacity crowds of 65,000 people attend Croke Park every September to watch the All-Ireland Senior Hurling Final. All 32 counties compete in their provincial championships during the season. Each of the four provincial champions is drawn into a semi-final. The winners of the final are thus All-Ireland champions.

Since the first All-Ireland Senior Hurling Final (SHF) in 1887, Cork have won the most times with 27 victories. Kilkenny have won 25 and Tipperary 24. These counties have dominated hurling and continue to provide most of the best players. Of the provinces of Connacht and Ulster, only Galway have won the All-Ireland SHF.

Twenty of the 32 counties have failed to win an All-Ireland Senior Hurling Final.

Ten counties have failed to win either the Football or the Hurling titles: Antrim, Armagh, Carlow, Fermanagh, Leitrim, Longford, Monaghan, Sligo, Westmeath and Wicklow.

♣ **Highest individual score in a Senior Hurling Final**: Nicholas English of Tipperary scored 18 points (two goals and 12 points) in the 1989 final against Antrim. This was achieved in the 70 minutes currently designated for the hurling final. In the 60-minute final of 1928, Michael Ahearne of Cork scored 19 points (five goals and four points) against Galway.

♣ **Most appearances in a Senior Hurling Final:** Christy Ring of Cork (between 1941 and 1954), and John Doyle of Tipperary (between 1949 and 1965). Each appeared in 10 All-Ireland finals and each was on the winning team on 8 occasions.

♣ **Most All-Ireland Winners Medals:** Noel Skehan of Kilkenny won nine All-Ireland Senior Hurling winners medals between 1963 and 1983. He was a non-playing substitute for his first three finals.

♣ **The largest attendance at an All-Ireland Senior Hurling Final** in Croke Park was 84,856

when Cork beat Wexford in 1954. In 1956 a comparable 83,096 went to see Wexford defeat Cork. Since the capacity of the stand was reduced in 1966 with the introduction of more seating facilities, the highest attendance has been 71,384 at the Offaly v Galway match in 1981.

Dual Award Winners

Players who have won All-Ireland Senior medals in hurling and football:

Jack Lynch (Cork), ex-Taoiseach and leader of Fianna Fáil, is the **only player in the history of the GAA to win six All-Ireland medals in a row**, five in hurling: 1941, 1942, 1943, 1944, 1946; and one in football: 1945.

ALL-IRELAND SENIOR HURLING FINALS – ROLL OF HONOUR	
Cork (27 wins)	1890, 1892, 1893, 1894, 1902, 1903, 1919, 1926, 1928, 1929, 1931, 1941, 1942, 1943, 1944, 1946, 1952, 1953, 1954, 1966, 1970, 1976, 1977, 1978, 1984, 1986, 1990
Kilkenny (25 wins)	1904, 1905, 1907, 1909, 1911, 1912, 1913, 1922, 1932, 1933, 1935, 1939, 1947, 1957, 1963, 1967, 1969, 1972, 1974, 1975, 1979, 1982, 1983, 1992, 1993
Tipperary (24 wins)	1887, 1895, 1896, 1899, 1900, 1906, 1908, 1916, 1925, 1930, 1937, 1945, 1949, 1950, 1951, 1958, 1961, 1962, 1964, 1965, 1971, 1989, 1991
Limerick (7 wins)	1897, 1918, 1921, 1934, 1936, 1940, 1973
Dublin (6 wins)	1889, 1917, 1920, 1924, 1927, 1938
Wexford (5 wins)	1910, 1955, 1956, 1960, 1968
Galway (4 wins)	1923, 1980, 1987, 1988
Waterford (2 wins)	1948, 1959
Offaly (2 wins)	1981, 1985
Clare (1 win)	1914
Kerry (1 win)	1891
Laois (1 win)	1915
London (1 win)	1901
(Home champions: Cork)	

Ray Cummins (Cork)	Hurling 1971, 1972, 1977; Football 1971, 1973
Jimmy Barry Murphy (Cork)	Hurling 1976, 1977, 1978, 1983, 1986; Football 1973, 1974
Brian Murphy (Cork)	Hurling 1978, 1981; Football 1973, 1976
Liam Currans (Offaly)	Hurling 1981; Football 1982

Camogie

Women's hurling, camogie, has held an All-Ireland Senior Final at Croke Park since 1932. Dublin has been by far the most successful county with 26 wins. The roll of honour for All-Ireland Senior camogie is:

Dublin (26 wins):	1932, 1933, 1937, 1938, 1942, 1943, 1944, 1948, 1949, 1950, 1951, 1952, 1953, 1954, 1955, 1957, 1958, 1959, 1960, 1961, 1962, 1963, 1964, 1965, 1966, 1984
Cork (16 wins)	1934, 1935, 1936, 1939, 1940, 1941, 1970, 1971, 1972, 1973, 1978, 1980, 1982, 1983, 1992, 1993
Kilkenny (11 wins)	1974, 1976, 1977, 1981, 1985, 1986, 1987, 1988, 1989, 1990, 1991
Antrim (6 wins)	1945, 1946, 1947, 1956, 1967, 1979
Wexford (3 wins)	1968, 1969, 1975

SOCCER

Soccer is currently enjoying unprecedented popularity in Ireland following the successes of the Republic of Ireland team in recent years. It is now Ireland's second most popular sport after Gaelic football. There were 161,357 registered players in 8802 teams in the 1992/3 season. As recently as 1986, hurling had a significantly larger number of supporters and followers. However, since then, there has been an unprecedented 100% increase in the number of people playing organised soccer in the Republic of Ireland.

The League of Ireland is made up of part-time professional teams that attract only modest attendances. Professional players seek employment in foreign leagues, especially in England and Scotland. **In 1993 the Republic of Ireland team attained its highest ever world ranking at 6th.** The seeding of national sides is determined by the results achieved in international competition.

The Republic of Ireland national team was formed in 1921 and joined FIFA in 1923. The Republic of Ireland qualified for the final stages of the World Cup for the first time in Italy in 1990, when they were beaten 1–0 in the quarter-final by the host nation.

The Republic of Ireland team that played Italy in the quarter-final of the 1990 World Cup: Bonner; Morris; Staunton; McCarthy; Moran; McGrath; Houghton; Townsend; Sheedy; Quinn; Aldridge. Substitutes: Cascarino; Sheridan.

The Republic of Ireland team also qualified for the final stages of the 1994 World Cup in the USA, defeating Italy 1–0 in their first game. They reached the last 16, before being defeated 2–0 by Holland.

Northern Ireland fields its own national team and has qualified for three World Cup Final competitions. They reached the quarter-finals in Sweden 1958, and qualified for the second round in Spain 1982 and Mexico 1986.

The Northern Ireland team that played France in the quarter-final of the 1958 World Cup: Gregg; Keith; McMichael; Blanchflower; Cunningham; Cush; Bingham; Casey; Scott; McIlroy; McParland. (Result: France 4–0 N. Ireland.)

Leading players

♣ **George Best** was born in East Belfast in 1946. He was spotted at the age of 15 by Bob Bishop, a talent scout for Manchester United. Best made his debut in September 1963 against West Bromwich Albion. Within seven months he earned the first of his 31 international caps for Northern Ireland. He quickly became a sensation and attracted huge crowds wherever he played. He won League championship medals with Manchester United in 1965 and 1967 and scored in the team's 4–1 victory over Benfica at Wembley Stadium in the final of the 1968 European Cup. He was named English Footballer of the Year and was the First Division's top goalscorer in 1968. In a ten-year career, he scored 361 goals for Manchester United and 37 for Northern Ireland. He retired in 1973 after intense media pressure and alcoholism had undermined his performances. Despite his success, Northern Ireland never played in the World Cup during his time as a player, but Best's name is internationally known and is used as a common measure by which footballing skills are judged. The Brazilian Pele is on record as saying, with much modesty, that George Best was **the greatest footballer in the world.**

George Best, goal-scorer supreme for Manchester United and Northern Ireland (in whose colours he is shown here). In 1968 he was voted best Footballer of the Year in the English League and was the First Division's leading goalscorer.

☘ **Norman Whiteside,** born in Belfast in 1965, became **Britain's youngest ever international player** at the age of 17 years and 41 days on 17 June 1982, when he played for Northern Ireland v. Yugoslavia. At the same time he became the **youngest player ever to play in the World Cup finals.** He was also the **youngest player to score in the English FA Cup final** on 26 May 1983, when he played for Manchester United v. Brighton at 18 years and 19 days.

☘ **The Republic of Ireland's youngest international, James Holmes** (1953–), made his debut against Austria in Dublin on 30 May 1971 at 17 years and 200 days.

☘ **Pat Jennings** (1945–), born in Newry, Co. Down, goalkeeper for Northern Ireland was one of the world's best goalkeepers in his career 1964–86, during which he **earned a record 119 international caps**. He played league football in England with Watford (1963–4), Tottenham (1964–77) and Arsenal (1977–86). He was voted Footballer of the Year in 1973. With Tottenham he won an FA Cup winners' medal 1967, League Cup winners' medals 1971 and 1973, and UEFA Cup winners' medal 1972. He won his second FA Cup winners' medal with Arsenal in 1979.

Jennings made his last international appearance for Northern Ireland against Brazil in the final stages of the World Cup in Mexico, 12 June 1986 – his 41st birthday, **then the oldest player to play in the final stages of the World Cup.**

☘ **Robert Denis 'Danny' Blanchflower,** born in Belfast in 1926, was another outstanding footballer from Ulster. He played for Glentoran in the Irish League before signing for Barnsley in 1948. He moved to Aston Villa in 1951 and his career began to flourish, but it was with Tottenham Hotspur, which he joined in 1954 for a club record of £30,000, that his talents were fully recognised. He was captain of the Tottenham team that won the League and Cup double in 1961 (the first this century), the FA Cup in 1962 and the European Cup Winners' Cup in 1963. (Beating Atlético Madrid 5–1 in Rotterdam, Spurs became the first British club to lift a European trophy.) He was voted Britain's Footballer of the Year in 1958 and again in 1961, the only Irishman to be so honoured twice. He won 56 caps for Northern Ireland and captained the team to the quarter-finals of the 1958 World Cup. His career ended early after a leg injury in the 1963/64 season. He managed Chelsea FC for a brief spell and the Northern Ireland squad from 1976 to 1979.

Off the pitch, Blanchflower was admired as a leading critic of the £20 per week maximum wage and iniquitous retain and transfer system for footballers. As a graduate of St Andrews University and a newspaper columnist during his footballing career, he was in a position to expose eloquently and publicly the exploitation of professional footballers. He died on 9 December 1993.

☘ **Jackie Blanchflower,** brother of Danny, born in Belfast in 1933, played for Manchester United and Northern Ireland, but was badly injured in the Munich air crash of February 1958 and never played again. He won 12 caps for Northern Ireland and a League Champions medal with Manchester United in 1951/2.

♣ **Liam Brady** (1956–), born in Dublin, was one of Ireland's most outstanding footballers, winning 72 caps for the Republic of Ireland between 1974 and 1990. (By July 1994 the Irish goalkeeper **'Packie' Bonner** had amassed a record 77 caps and defender Kevin Moran had 71.) Brady played professional league football in England and Italy with Arsenal, Juventus, Sampdoria, Internazionale Milan, Ascoli and West Ham United. With Arsenal he won an FA Cup winners' medal in 1979 and a runners-up medal in the 1980 European Cup Winners Cup. He won two Italian League Championship medals with Juventus 1980/1 and 1981/2. (In 1982 he scored a vital penalty to win the title.) He was the Football Writers' Player of the Year in Britain in 1979. Brady was a brilliant playmaker and was famed for the accuracy of his passing.

♣ **Michael John 'Johnny' Giles** (1940–), born in Dublin, is one of the best footballers to have come from Ireland. At 17 he moved from the part-time Dublin team Home Farm to Manchester United, where he scored 13 goals in 114 matches and won an FA Cup medal in 1963. He joined Leeds United in 1963 and was the playmaster of the legendary Don Revie team. He scored 115 goals in 380 matches in 12 years at the club – an impressive total for a midfield player. He won two League Championship medals in 1965/6 and 1973/4 and was in the runners-up squad in four other seasons. He won his second FA Cup medal in 1972 and was on the losing side in three finals 1965, 1970 and

(above) *'Packie' Bonner of Co. Donegal, goal-keeper for Glasgow Celtic and Ireland. By July 1994 he had won a record 77 caps for the Republic of Ireland.*

(left) *Jack Charlton, manager of the Republic of Ireland team since 1986, was born in Northumberland and won a World Cup medal with the victorious English team in 1966. Following his success with the Irish team in the 1990 World Cup, he was given honorary citizenship of Ireland.*

1973, and thus holds a joint record of five English FA Cup Final appearances. He was also three times a runner-up with Leeds United in the European club competitions – the Fairs Cup (1967), the Cup Winners Cup (1973) and the European Cup (1975). His tally of 13 goals in European club competition remains an Irish record.

Giles later joined West Bromwich Albion as player-manager and steered them into Division One (now the Premier Division). Back in Dublin in 1978, he won an FAI Cup medal with Shamrock Rovers. He also played in the United States and Canada with Philadelphia and Vancouver. Giles won 60 caps for the Republic of Ireland 1959–79 and scored 5 international goals. He appears regularly as a commentator on RTE's soccer programmes.

✤ **Paul McGrath** was born in Ealing, London in 1959 to an Irish mother and a Nigerian father. He was raised in Dublin, where he played his early football. He moved from St Patrick's Athletic to Manchester United, where he played over 200 league and cup matches and won an FA Cup winners' medal in 1985. He has established himself as one of the best central defenders in Britain and currently plays for Aston Villa. He was first capped for the Republic of Ireland in 1985 and has since made over 60 appearances in defence and in midfield, scoring 6 international goals to date. He played a vital role in the Republic of Ireland's campaigns in the European Championships of 1988 and in the side which reached the quarter-finals of the World Cup in Italy in 1990. He won the Football Association of Ireland 'Player of the Year' award in 1990 and again in 1991. In 1993 he won the prestigious Professional Footballers' Association Player of the Year award in Britain.

✤ **Jack Charlton** (born 1935 in Ashington, Northumberland, England), manager of the Republic of Ireland team, is one of only six people who have been awarded honorary citizenship of Ireland*. Charlton, a member of the England team that won the 1966 World Cup, took up his post as Ireland's manager in February 1986 and has steered the national side to its best ever international rating. He was given honorary citizenship following the Irish team's jubilant homecoming after reaching the quarter-finals of the 1990 World Cup in Italy.

✤ **Roy Keane** (1971–), born in Cork, became **the most expensive player in British league football** in August 1993, when he was bought by Manchester United from Nottingham Forest for £3.75 million. Keane began his semi-professional career in the League of Ireland with Cobh Ramblers before signing with Nottingham Forest. He is currently a member of the Republic of Ireland squad.

✤ **William Ralph 'Dixie' Dean** (1907–80), one of the most prolific goalscorers in the history of professional football, finished his career in Ireland with Sligo Rovers, helping the club to the final of the Football Association of Ireland Cup in 1939. Dean, from Birkenhead in Lancashire, England, scored 379 goals in 437 league matches with Everton 1925–38. In the 1927/8 season, he scored 60 goals in 39 League matches – a record that still stands.

GOLF

✤ **Christy O'Connor**, born in Dublin in 1924, is the best golfer to come from Ireland. He never won the British Open, but finished in the top five seven times between 1958 and 1969, coming second in 1965. He twice won the Vardon Trophy for leading the Order of Merit in 1961 and 1962. He played in a record 10 consecutive Ryder Cup matches from 1955–73. He won the World Cup for Ireland in Mexico in 1958 with Harry Bradshaw. His major tournament wins include: Dunlop Masters 1956 and 1959, Professional Golfers Association (PGA) Match Play 1957, World Seniors 1976 and 1977.

✤ **Christy O'Connor Junior** (1948–), his nephew, was a Ryder Cup player in 1975 and again in 1989, when his win at the 18th hole in his match against Fred Couples won the tournament for Europe.

✤ **Arthur D'Arcy 'Bobby' Locke** (1917–87), born in Germiston, Transvaal, South Africa, was four times British Open Champion, 1949–50, 1952 and 1957. He was the son of an immigrant from Belfast.

✤ **Ronan Rafferty** (1964–) of Warrenpoint, Co. Down became **the youngest ever Walker Cup player** at 17 years, 8 months and 15 days at Cypress Point, California in 1981. In his professional career, Rafferty has been one of Ireland's most outstanding

* The other five honorary Irish citizens are: Chester Beatty; Tip and Mildred O'Neill (Tip O'Neill, who died in 1994, was speaker of the US Congress and a life-long lobbyist for Irish affairs in the US); Tiede and Elizabeth Herrema (Tiede Herrema, Dutch managing director of Ferenka Ltd, was kidnapped by republican paramilitaries who sought the release of Bridget Rose Dugdale, October–November 1975).

golfers and was a member of both Irish sides that won the Dunhill Cup 1988 and 1990. After coming 9th in 1986 and 1988 he was top in the Order of Merit placings in 1989 when he won the Italian Open, the Scandinavian Open and the Volvo Masters and played in the European Ryder Cup team. He is the only Irish player other than Christy O'Connor to win the Vardon Trophy.

Christy O'Connor Jnr plays a bunker shot at the British Open, Royal Birkdale in 1991. His uncle, Christy O'Connor Snr, appeared in a record 10 consecutive Ryder Cups between 1955 and 1975.

HORSE RACING

Horse-breeding and racing is a multi-million pound business in Ireland – over £90m per year is gambled on horses – and horse racing attracts over one million people to about 280 meets annually.

Horses were introduced into Ireland 2000 years ago by Stone Age farmers. These horses were cross-bred with the indigenous Connemara ponies and later with the chariot-pulling horses of the invading Celts. It is thought that many Spanish Arabian stallions survived the shipwrecks of the Spanish Armada off the west coast and were also cross-bred. Irish thoroughbreds have long been sought abroad. In the 18th and 19th centuries the French and Russian armies bought horses at Irish fairs for their cavalry corps. Napoleon's horse Marengo was allegedly bought in Ireland.

Horse racing has existed for as long as horses have been around and is described in the ancient legends of Ireland. **The first ever steeplechase** was held in Co. Cork in 1752 when two locals, O'Callaghan and Blake, raced from Buttevant to the steeple of Doneraile's St Leger Church about six miles away. (This race had probably been held for a number of years before it received its name in 1752.) **The first Irish Grand National was run in 1839 and the first Irish Derby in 1866.** In 1880 Henry Eyre Linde became **the first Irish winner of the English Grand National** and in 1907 Orby, owned by 'Boss' Croker* became the **first Irish horse to win the English Derby.**

The Irish National Stud was formed in 1945 to maintain good-quality bloodstock. The stud's museum displays the skeleton of **Arkle, the greatest Irish racehorse of this century.**

Horses

🍀 **The Byerley Turk** (c. 1680) was the first of three stallions from which all modern-day thoroughbreds are descended in the male line. When Buda was captured from the Turks in 1687, the horse was taken by Captain Byerley, who brought him to Ireland in 1689 to fight in the Battle of the Boyne. He was sent to stud in Durham and York in England.

🍀 **Eclipse** (1764–89), **the greatest racehorse of the 18th century,** was the great-great grandson of Darley Arabian, the second of the three stallions from which all modern thoroughbreds descend. Eclipse won all his 18 races, including eight walk-overs from opposition that recognised his unassailable supremacy. Eclipse was sold to **Dennis O'Kelly** (c.

* *Richard 'Boss' Croker (1841–1922) of Clonakilty, Co. Cork grew up in New York where he became alderman and head of Tammany Hall (New York Democratic Party and Irish-American power base). He was also Fire Commissioner and City Chamberlain. He made a fortune and returned to Ireland in 1907, living at Glencairn, Co. Dublin, now the residence of the British ambassador, until 1919. He returned to New York and died there.*

1720–87) of Ireland, who bought a half share for 650 guineas after two races and a year later the remaining share for a further 1100 guineas. Almost all the great horses of the 20th century trace back to Eclipse. His skeleton now stands in the National Horse Racing Museum in Newmarket.

Dennis O'Kelly came from an impoverished family in Ireland and emigrated to England as a young man. He secured his finances by marriage to a wealthy courtesan, Charlotte Hayes. Eclipse increased his fortune. He bet on the horse in its very first race and is famously reported to have declared, 'Eclipse first and the rest nowhere'. O'Kelly became a colonel in the Middlesex Militia and bought the estate of Cannons, near Edgware – now a suburb of London. Despite making his own fortune through gambling, O'Kelly stipulated in his will that his heir should forfeit £400 for every bet he made.

♣ **The greatest steeplechaser of all time, Arkle,** was foaled at Bryanstown, Co. Kildare in April 1957 and bred by Mary Baker in Co. Dublin. He won the Cheltenham Gold Cup three years in succession 1964–66. In his 1966 victory he was carrying three stones more than any other horse and still managed to win by 30 lengths. Other wins included the Irish Grand National 1964, Whitbread Gold Cup 1965, King George VI Chase 1965, Hennessy Gold Cup 1964–65 and the Leopardstown Chase 1964–66.

Arkle was bought by the Duchess of Westminster as a three-year-old and trained by Tom Dreaper. He broke a pedal bone in the King George VI Chase 1966 and was prematurely retired. His record in 35 races was: 1/3 on the flat, 4/6 at hurdles and 22/26 steeplechases where he came second twice and third twice – depite enormous handicaps. He won £78,824 in prize money, a record at the time. Arkle died on 31

The Byerley Turk – one of the three Arab stallions from which all modern thoroughbreds have descended in the male line – survived the Battle of the Boyne in 1690.

May 1970 and his skeleton is exhibited at the National Stud Museum in Kildare.

♣ **Mill House,** also foaled at Bryanstown, Co. Kildare in 1957, would have been a candidate for the best steeplechaser of all time, but for his contemporary and rival Arkle. He was bred by the Lawlors, near Naas, Co. Kildare and then sent to train with Syd Dale and Fulke Walwyn. From 1961 to 1968 he won 17 of his 36 races. From December 1962 to February 1964, he won six successive chases, including a defeat of Arkle in the 1963 Hennessy Gold Cup. In that race, Arkle gave him only 5lb weight – no other horse ever managed to beat Arkle with less than a 21lb advantage. Even then, it took a slip by Arkle to lose the lead. Mill House was second to Arkle in the Cheltenham Gold Cups of 1964 and 1965 and in their two other clashes. He died on 31 May 1970.

♣ **Captain Christy** (1967–77), bred by George Williams in West Cork, was another great steeplechaser. He won the King George VI Chase in 1974, by 30 lengths in 1975 and the Cheltenham Gold Cup in 1974. He was trained by Pat Taaffe (see p. 190) from 1972 and his wins record was: 6/15 over hurdles, 2/7 on the flat and 12/24 chases.

♣ **Cottage Rake** (1939–53), foaled in Fermoy, Co. Cork, was the second horse to win three successive Cheltenham Gold Cups 1948–50. On each occasion he was ridden by Aubrey Brabazon (see p. 189). Cottage Rake was the first of many great horses to be trained by Vincent O'Brien (see p. 191). Race wins record: 16/39 races 1945–53.

♣ **Dawn Run** (1978–86) was the first horse to win both the Champion Hurdle (1984) and the Gold Cup (1986) at Cheltenham. She was trained by Paddy Mullins at Goresbridge, Co. Kilkenny and had eight wins in nine races in 1983/4. Her race wins record is: 12/21 hurdles, 5/7 chases and 3/7 flat races. Her prize money set a new record for a jumper at £278,837. She was killed in a fall at Auteuil, France in June 1986.

♣ **Easter Hero** (1920–48) of Greenogue, Co. Dublin was twice winner of the Cheltenham Gold Cup by 20 lengths in 1929 and 1930. In a career lasting from 1925 to 1931 he won 20/40 races.

♣ **Golden Miller** (1927–57), of Stansted, Essex, was bred in Ireland by Laurence Geraghty. He was winner of the Cheltenham Gold Cup a record five times 1932–36 and, apart from L'Escargot, is the only horse to win the elusive double, as in 1934 he won the English Grand National in a record time of 9 min 20.4 sec. He won 29/55 races and was placed in a further 13.

♣ **L'Escargot** (1963–84), foaled in Mullingar, Co. Westmeath, was the only steeplechaser since Golden Miller to win the Cheltenham Gold Cup (1970 and 1971) and the English Grand National, in which on his fourth attempt, in 1975, he beat the favourite Red Rum. L'Escargot was bred in Mullingar by Barbara O'Neill and trained on the Curragh by Dan Moore.

♣ **Manifesto,** foaled near Navan, Co. Meath in 1888, was the best English Grand National horse before Red Rum. Coming fourth in 1895, he went on to win in 1897 carrying 11st 3lb and again in 1899 carrying 12st 7lb. In that 1899 victory he was carrying **a record maximum weight by a winner of the Grand National**, a record shared with three other horses: Cloister in 1893, Jerry M. in 1912 and Poethlyn in 1919. He was third in 1900 carrying 12st 13lb and again in 1902 and 1903.

♣ **Meld,** foaled in Ireland in 1952, was winner of the fillies' Triple Crown and Coronation Stakes in 1955. She only raced six times and won all but her first race. She died in 1983 and was **the oldest Triple Crown filly** at 31.

♣ **Monksfield** (1972–89), of Redthorn Stud, Co. Kildare, was rated the top National Hunt horse in Britain in 1978 and 1979, winning the Champion Hurdle in both years. In his hurdling career he won 49 races and was placed 2nd eleven times, 3rd ten times and 4th four times.

♣ **Nijinsky** (1967–92), born and bred in Canada, was trained in Ireland by Vincent O'Brien (see p. 191). In 1970 Nijinsky, ridden by Lester Piggott, won the British Triple Crown of 2000 Guineas, Derby and St Leger. He also won the Irish Derby and the King George VI and Queen Elizabeth Stakes. In his racing career he recorded 11 wins from 13 races and won £282,223.

♣ **Pretty Polly** (1901–31), born in Ireland, was winner of the fillies' Triple Crown (1000 Guineas, Oaks and St Leger) in 1904.

♣ **Prince Regent,** born in 1935, was Ireland's best horse during World War II but was unable to compete abroad. In 1946 he travelled to Cheltenham and won the Gold Cup by five lengths. He carried very heavy weights and still managed to win 20/49 career races, including the Irish Grand National in 1942.

❧ **Shergar** (1978–83?), bred by the Aga Khan and trained by Michael Stoute, owes his considerable fame as much to his mysterious fate as to his racing victories which included the Epsom Derby (by 10 lengths, **the greatest ever winning margin in the English Derby**), the Irish Derby and the King George VI and Queen Elizabeth Stakes. He was retired to the Aga Khan's stud at Ballymany, Co. Kildare and was kidnapped from there on 9 February 1983. He was never recovered and is presumed dead.

❧ **Sadler's Wells**, from the Coolmore Stud, near Fethard, Co. Tipperary, is **the world's most valuable stallion**. Breeding a mare from this horse has cost up to £200,000 for a semen sample of a few centilitres. Prices in horse breeding peaked in 1990 and have since dropped dramatically. Sadler's Wells is owned by a syndicate, divided into 41 shares, which were worth IR£1.5m in 1990.

❧ Sadler's Wells was sired by the Canadian stallion **Northern Dancer** (1961–90), the most successful stallion of all time. Northern Dancer was responsible for 634 foals, of which 143 were stakes winners. Breeders paid up to $1m for his services. His dam was Fairy Bridge, who was champion in Ireland in her first season.

Jockeys and Trainers

❧ **The oldest jockey in racing history** was **Harry Beasley** (1850–1939) of Kildare, who rode his last competitive race at Baldoyle Racecourse in Dublin on 10 June 1935 at the age of 85. Earlier in his career he won the 1891 English Grand National on Come Away and was runner-up on two other occasions. Other victories include 2 Irish Grand Nationals, 2 wins at the Grand Steeple in Auteuil, France, 6 Sefton Chases at Liverpool, 2 Grands Steeplechases de Paris and 6 Conyngham Cup races.

❧ **Aubrey Brabazon** (1920–) won three successive Cheltenham Gold Cup races on Cottage Rake 1948–50. He also won the Cheltenham Champion hurdle twice (on Hatton's Grace), 1949–50, thus completing a **unique double-double**. He won the Irish Oaks twice in succession, 1947–48 and the King George VI 1948.

❧ **Richard Dunwoody** (1964–) was born in Comber, Co. Down. His wins include the 1986 and 1994 Grand National, the 1986 Mackeson Gold Cup, the 1988 Cheltenham Gold Cup and the 1990 Champion Hurdle. He won the Ritz Club trophy for most successful jockey at the Cheltenham Festival in 1990. He won the King George VI twice on Desert Orchid and, to date, has ridden over 100 winners in five successive years to 1994, setting successive records for **the greatest prize money won in a season** – with £923,974 in 1991/2 and £1,088,320 in 1992/3, when he was champion jockey with 173 winners. His 1000th winner in Britain came on 30 January 1994.

❧ **Patrick Eddery** (1952–), of Blackrock, Co. Dublin, is the winner of 3 Epsom Derbys 1975/82/90, 2 English 2000 Guineas 1983/84, 2 Epsom Oaks 1974/79, 2 St Legers 1986/91, 4 Irish Derbys 1975/84/85/93, 2 Irish 2000 Guineas 1975/81, 2 Irish Oaks 1986/93, 4 Prix de l'Arc de Triomphes 1980/85/86/87 and 3 French Derbys 1983/88/90. He has been Champion Jockey in Britain nine times from 1974 to 1993. In 1990 he came close to an all-time record of season wins with a tally of 209, beating the 200 mark last reached by Gordon Richards in 1952.

❧ **Tommy Carberry** (1941–) rode the winner of the Cheltenham Gold Cup 3 times, in 1970 and 1971 on L'Escargot and in 1975 on Ten Up. In 1980 he came first on Tied Cottage, but was disqualified. He has ridden 12 Cheltenham National Hunt Festival winners and won the Grand National on L'Escargot in 1975, taking a magnificent double and beating the legendary Red Rum into second place. He was champion jockey in Ireland several times and won the Irish Grand National in 1975 and 1976 on Brown Lad.

❧ **Michael Kinane** (1959–), born in Co. Tipperary, has been Irish champion jockey nine times between 1984 and 1993. He has won the Irish 2000 Guineas twice, in 1982 and 1987, the Irish 1000 Guineas in 1988 and the Irish St Leger in 1989. International successes include: Prix de l'Abbaye 1985, Heinz '57' Phoenix Stakes 1983, Premio Paroli 1985, King George VI 1990, English 2000 Guineas 1990, Belmont Stakes 1990, Italian Derby 1992 and the English Derby 1993 on Commander-in-Chief.

❧ **Michael F. 'Mouse' Morris** (1951–), the son of Lord Killanin, President of the International Olympic Committee (see p. 171), is a successful National Hunt jockey and trainer. He has won three Cheltenham Chases as a jockey – the National Hunt in 1974 and the

Jonjo O'Neill of Castletownroche, Co. Cork rides Dawn Run in the Cheltenham Champion Hurdle in 1985. One of Ireland's most successful jockeys of all time, he set a record of 149 winning rides in a British National Hunt season in 1977–78.

Queen Mother Two-Mile Champion Chase in 1976 and 1977 – and has trained four Cheltenham Chase winners at Everardsgrange, Fethard, Co. Tipperary.

♣ **John Joseph 'Jonjo' O'Neill**, born in Castletownroche, Co. Cork in 1952, was Champion National Hunt jockey in Britain in the 1977/8 season, when he set the then **record of 149 winning rides in one British National Hunt Season.** He regained his title two years later in the 1979/80 season with 117 winners. His major wins include: 2 Cheltenham Gold Cups 1979 (Alverton) and 1986 (Dawn Run) and 2 Cheltenham Champion Hurdles in 1980 (Sea Pigeon) and 1983 (Dawn Run). He was **the first jockey to complete the Cheltenham Double.**

♣ **Christy Roche** (1950–), 'The Man from Bansha' (Bansha, Co. Tipperary), has been leading Irish flat jockey six times. He is famous for two spectacular victories – the 1984 Epsom Derby on the 14/1 outsider Secreto, beating the hot favourite El Gran Señor and, in 1990, the Epsom Oaks by 10 lengths on the 50/1 shot Jet Ski Lady.

♣ **Tommy Stack**, born in Co. Kerry in 1946, was Champion Jockey over fences in England 1974/5 and in 1976/7. He rode Red Rum to his historic third victory at the Aintree Grand National in 1977.

♣ **Walter Swinburn**, born in Oxford in 1961, is the son of top Irish jockey Wally Swinburn. He has won 7 English Classics (all races except the St Leger): the Derby 1981 and 1986, Epsom Oaks 1987, 2000 Guineas 1988 and 1000 Guineas 1989, 1992 and 1993. He has also won on 8 Irish Classic race winners: the 1000 Guineas in 1986 and 1992, 2000 Guineas 1989, Irish Derby 1983 and 1986 and Irish Oaks 1981, 1987 and 1989. Other wins include: 2 King George VI and Queen Elizabeth Stakes, 2 Coronation Stakes and the 1983 Prix de l'Arc de Triomphe.

♣ **Pat Taaffe** (1930–92), born in Rathcoole, Co. Dublin, rode a record four Cheltenham Gold Cup winners, including three in a row from 1964 to 1966 on the indomitable Arkle. His fourth victory was on Fort Leney in 1968. He rode 2 English Grand National winners (Quare Times in 1955 and Gay Trip in 1970) and 6 Irish Grand National winners 1954/55/59/61/64/66. On Arkle he rode to victory in the Whitbread Gold Cup, the Hennessy Gold Cup and the Leopardstown Chase twice. He rode five winners of the National Hunt Two-Mile-Champion Chases between 1960 and 1970 and holds **an Irish record of 28 Cheltenham Festival winners**.

As a trainer he produced the great Captain Christy, who won the Cheltenham Gold Cup in 1974.

Top Irish Trainers

❦ **Vincent O'Brien** (1917–) was born in Churchwild, Co. Cork. He was the leading jumps trainer in Britain 1952/3 and 1953/4. His horses won three English Grand Nationals in succession: Early Mist in 1953, Royal Tan in 1954 and Quare Times in 1955. He trained Cottage Rake, the horse which won the Cheltenham Gold cup three times 1948/49/50. His total tally of Cheltenham winners is 23. In flat racing he has trained a record 6 Irish Derby winners and a record 8 Irish St Leger winners as well as 4 Irish Oaks, 3 Irish 1000 Guineas and 5 Irish 2000 Guineas. He was top flat trainer in Britain in 1966 and 1977.

O'Brien's **total of 16 English classic winners is an Irish record** and places him 9th on the all-time list: 6 Epsom Derbys, 4 2000 Guineas, 1 1000 Guineas, 2 Epsom Oaks, 3 Doncaster St Legers. He also trained the winners of 3 Prix de l'Arc de Triomphe and 3 King George VI and Queen Elizabeth Stakes.

❦ **Thomas Dreaper** (1898–1975) of Ashbourne, Co. Meath trained an all-time record of 5 Cheltenham Gold Cup winners from his stable at Greenogue, Co. Dublin, including Prince Regent, who won three in a row 1964–6. His total of 25 Cheltenham winners is an Irish record. He trained the incomparable Arkle, who won 27 of his 35 starts, and a record 10 winners of the Irish Grand National including Royal Approach, who won an astonishing 7 in a row 1954–60.

❦ **Dermot Weld** (1948–), based at Roswell House Stables, is currently Ireland's leading trainer. In 1977 he became the first Irish trainer to have 100 winners

Joey Dunlop of Ballymoney, Co. Antrim, winner of a record five Formula One World TT Championships 1982–86. He has also won a record 15 Isle of Man TT races at 125 cc.

in a year. In 1991 he set a new record of 150 winners. His total continues to grow and has now exceeded 1900. He has trained horses that have won major stake races on three continents. In 1990 his horse Go and Go won the American Classic race and the Belmont Stakes, and in 1992 In a Tiff won the Italian Derby.

❦ On 2 November 1993 the Irish horse, Vintage Crop, ridden by Michael Kinane (see p. 189), trained by **Dermot Weld** and owned by Michael Smurfit (see p. 43), won the Melbourne Cup in Australia and collected the Australian $1.3 million (IR£620,000) prize money. No horse is ever recorded to have travelled so far to win a race. Dermot Weld has now brought winning horses to three continents.

Top Irish Races

Classics: Irish 2000 Guineas (1 mile), Irish 1000 Guineas (1 mile), Irish Derby (1 mile 4 furlongs), Irish Oaks (1 mile 4 furlongs), Irish St Leger (1 mile 6 furlongs) – all are run at the Curragh, Co. Kildare.

Flat Races: Champion Stakes (1 mile 2 furlongs, Leopardstown), Irish Lincolnshire Handicap (1 mile, Curragh), Irish Cambridgeshire Handicap (1 mile, Curragh), Irish Cesarewitch Handicap (2 miles, Curragh). Naas November Handicap (1 mile 4 furlongs, Naas), Leopardstown November Handicap (2 miles, Leopardstown).

Jump Races: Irish Grand National (3 miles 5 furlongs, Fairyhouse), Ladbroke Handicap Hurdle (2 miles, Leopardstown), Irish Champion Hurdle (2 miles, Leopardstown), Thyestes Handicap Chase (3 miles, Gowran Park), Harold Clarke Handicap Chase (3 miles, Leopardstown), Hennessy Irish Gold Cup (3 miles, Leopardstown), Galway Plate Steeplechase (2 miles 5 furlongs, Galway), Guinness Galway Hurdle (2 miles, Galway).

MOTOR CYCLING

❦ **William Joseph 'Joey' Dunlop,** born in Ballymoney, Co. Antrim in 1952, is **the most successful competitor at the Isle of Man Tourist Trophy races** and has won **a record five Formula One World TT Championships 1982–86** (coming 2nd in 1987, 1988 and 1990). In 1993 he won his 15th Isle of Man TT at 125cc, thus setting a new record. He also holds **the record for the fastest lap in the TT** – 118.48 mph (190.66 km/h). His brother Robert won the 125cc TT in 1989.

❦ **Stanley Woods**, born in Dublin in 1903, was the outstanding motorcycling champion of the 1920s and 1930s. He won ten TT victories on the Isle of Man at various levels between 1923 and 1939 and set numerous lap speed records. He was winner of 40 international events over this period, including 22 Grand Prix – all in 350cc or 500cc class races. He also excelled at speedway, hill climbs, trials, scrambling and long-distance events. At a jubilee celebration in 1957, 18 years after retiring, he set a TT course speed record of 86 mph. In 1990, at the age of 87, he lapped the Isle of Man course at over 80 mph. He ran a motor business in Pearse Street, Dublin and retired to Downpatrick. He died in 1993.

MOTOR RACING

❦ The greatest name in Irish motor sport is **Henry Segrave, the first person to hold the world land speed and water speed records simultaneously.**

Sir Henry O'Neill Dehane Segrave was born in Baltimore, Maryland, USA in 1896 to an Irish father and an American mother. At two years of age he came to live in Ireland and was brought up in Wicklow and at Belle Isle, near Portumna, Co. Galway. He was sent to England to be educated at Eton and returned to Ireland for summer holidays. He fought for the British Army and RAF in World War I and survived being shot down from 17,000 feet. After the war he made London his home and concentrated on motor racing. His career was outstanding. Of 49 races contested between 1917 and 1927, he won 31, including the French and San Sebastian Grand Prix. He was also three times a winner at Brooklands in England.

On the 9-mile stretch of Daytona Beach, Florida, USA on 29 March 1927, in front of 30,000 spectators, he set **a world landspeed record of 203.79 mph (327.95 km/h)** for the flying mile in a Sunbeam with twin aero-engines, each producing 400 hp. Special Dunlop tyres with a life of only 3.5 minutes were fitted to minimise resistance. He had set out to break the 200 mph barrier and on his first run reached 200.66 mph (322.92 km/h). On his return he reached 207 mph (333.12 km/h), thus averaging 203.79 mph (327.95 km/h) and shattering the previous world

The Gordon Bennett Cup Race was held in Ireland in July 1903 and ran from Athy, Co. Kildare to Phoenix Park in Dublin, where a new world landspeed record of 83.09 mph was set by the Belgian driver De Forest.

record by nearly 30 mph. The brakes of the Sunbeam failed on the second run and Segrave had to stop the car by driving through the shallow wash of the seashore.

In March 1929 Segrave returned to Daytona to set a new **world land speed record** after his 1927 mark had been exceeded. He travelled a flying mile in 15.5 seconds – 231.44 mph (372.46 km/h) – in his 23-litre Irving Napier *Golden Arrow*. He returned home to London as a national hero, was knighted and paraded through the streets of London with a naval and air force escort.

On Friday 13 June 1930, as winner of the 1929 International Championships of racing boats, he set out to break the world water speed record, which then stood at 92.52 mph (148.89 km/h). On Lake Windermere, he launched *Miss England II* and reached **a record speed of 98.76 mph (158.93 km/h).** Tragically, his boat hit a heavy branch in the water and capsized, fatally wounding him. His rescuers later reported his dying words to the world press, 'Have I got the record?' The Segrave Trophy was commissioned in his honour by Castrol in 1930.

❧ **Phoenix Park**, Dublin became **the world's fastest race track in 1937**, when the 100-mile race was won by Raymond Mays in an ERA, averaging a speed of 102.90 mph (165.6 km/h). Phoenix Park, with a circumference of 7 miles (11.26km) and encompassing 1760 acres (712.23 ha), is **the largest enclosed city park in Europe**.

❧ **The Gordon Bennett Cup Race** held in Ireland in July 1903, centred around Athy, Co. Kildare, was a 327-mile (526.24-km) race attended by the world's leading drivers. The Belgian race winner Jenatzy became **the first motorist to travel at a mile-a-minute/60mph.** On July 4, at Phoenix Park, his compatriot De Forest set a **new world landspeed record of 83.09 mph (133.72 km/h)** at the speed trials. This was also **the first time that an American motor racing team competed in Europe.** Many thousands of Dubliners attended and the excitement in the city prompted James Joyce (see p. 141) to write 'After the Race'.

❧ **Henry Ford** (see also p. 44), the Irish-American car producer, set a new **world landspeed record of 91.37 mph (147.04 km/h)** in 1904 in a Ford Arrow, on the frozen Lake St Clair in Michigan, USA.

❧ **Sir Algernon 'Algy' Lee Guinness** and **Kenhelm 'Bill' Lee Guinness**, two brothers from the famous Dublin brewing family, were successful Grand Prix drivers and land speed record holders. In October 1906 Algernon Guinness reached 112 mph (180.24 km/h) to set a new European speed record. In 1922 Bill Guinness set a new world land speed record of 133.75 mph (215.24 km/h) in a 350hp V-12 Sunbeam at Brooklands in England.

In the 1923 French Grand Prix, along with Henry Segrave and Albert Divo, Bill Guinness was a member of the winning British team in a British-built Sunbeam. Segrave and Guinness thus became **the first Irish (and British) winners of a grand prix and drivers of the first winning British car**.

❧ **John Watson**, born in Belfast in 1946, won the first of his five Formula One Grands Prix in Austria in 1976 for the American Penske team. In a highly successful career he came joint second in the 1982 World Championship, only five points behind the Swedish driver Keke Rosberg. In 1983 he made **the longest climb by any Grand Prix winner** at Long Beach, USA, when he came from 22nd place on the grid to win the race. In 1987 he came second in the World Endurance Championship.

❧ **Derek Daly,** born in Dublin in 1953, was a Formula One driver 1978–82 for Hesketh, Ensign, Tyrrell, March and Williams. He moved to US Indycar racing and finished 3rd in the Indianapolis 500. In 1988 he finished third in the Le Mans 24-hour race in France.

❧ **Eddie Jordan**, born in Dublin in 1948, took up team ownership and management in motor sport in 1981 after a career in Formula Two and Formula Three racing. Since then he has managed drivers such as Martin Brundle, Jean Alesi, Martin Donnelly and Johnny Herbert. He set up the Jordan team in the 1991 World Formula One Championships, earned 13 world championships points and finished overall 5th in the constructors' contest. Jordan is **the first Irish-based constructor in Formula One**.

RUGBY UNION

There are approximately 15,000 rugby players in 215 clubs in the Irish Rugby Football Union. International rugby is played by an all-Ireland team.

❧ **Lansdowne Road**, the headquarters of the Irish Rugby Football Union, is **the world's oldest international rugby ground**. The first international was played there on 11 March 1878. Its official capacity is now 50,000, and an attendance estimated at 53,000 has been recorded on a number of occasions.

🍀 Ireland has competed in the **Five Nations International Championship**, contested by Ireland, England, France, Wales and Scotland, since its foundation in 1884. (France joined the Championship in 1910.) Ireland has won the Championship 13 times, including the Grand Slam – won by defeating the other four teams in the International Championship – once, in 1948.

🍀 **The Triple Crown** is contested by the four home nations, excluding France, within the Five Nations Championship. Ireland has won the Triple Crown six times: 1894, 1899, 1948, 1949, 1982, 1985.

🍀 **Ireland reached the quarter-final of the Rugby World Cup** on 20 October 1991 and was defeated 18–19 by Australia at Lansdowne Road. Australia went on to win the Tournament.

🍀 **The greatest winning margin** for Ireland in international rugby is 60–0 v Romania in a friendly match in 1986.

🍀 **The greatest losing margin** for Ireland in international rugby is 6–59 v New Zealand in 1992.

Leading players and record holders

🍀 **Seamus Oliver 'Ollie' Campbell,** born in Dublin in 1954, was one of rugby's most consistent goal kickers, and a leading scorer for Ireland. He set an **Irish record of 217 points in 22 matches** 1976–84, although this was beaten in 1988 by **Michael Kiernan**. In 1982 Campbell scored 21 points – six penalties and a drop goal – against Scotland, **an Irish record for the number of points scored by an individual in an international**, to win the Triple Crown for Ireland. **The 52 points he scored in the 1983 Championship season remains an Irish record**.

🍀 The most exciting running back in Irish rugby and one of the best centres the game has seen, **Cameron Michael Gibson**, was born in Belfast in 1942. He played for Trinity College, Dublin, Cambridge University, North of Ireland FC and the Barbarians. He won 69 caps for Ireland between 1964 and 1979 and was, on retirement, the **world's most capped player. He and Willie John McBride are the only players to be chosen for five Lions tours.** Gibson is a Belfast solicitor by profession.

🍀 **Tom Kiernan**, born in Cork in 1939, won 54 caps for Ireland (the Irish record for a full back) and played in 5 tests with the British Lions. **He captained the Irish team a record 24 times** in his career 1960–73. His son **Michael Kiernan**, born in Cork in 1961, is **Ireland's top international points scorer** with 308 from 43 matches 1982–91, playing as a centre.

🍀 **Willie John McBride** (1940–), of Toomebridge, Co. Antrim, **holds the record, with Michael Gibson, of playing in five British Lions touring**

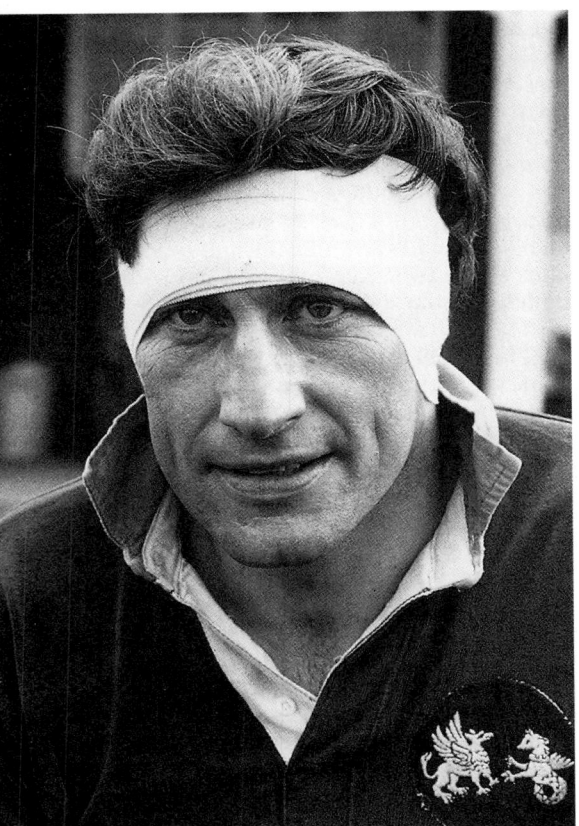

Towering lock-forward Willie John McBride played in five British Lions touring sides – a record he shares with fellow Irishman Michael Gibson. McBride won 63 caps for Ireland and 17 for the Lions.

sides. He made 80 international appearances, 63 for Ireland (12 as captain) and 17 for the Lions. He has coached the Irish team and was manager of the 1983 Lions tour to New Zealand.

♣ **Tony O'Reilly** (see also p. 42) was born in Dublin in 1926. As well as being Ireland's richest man, he won 28 caps for Ireland, 27 between 1955 and 1963, and one against England in 1970. His career span of 16 seasons of international rugby has only been matched by Michael Gibson in Ireland. O'Reilly's greatest achievement was to score 6 tries in the 10 test matches he played for the British Lions in South Africa (1955), Australia (1959) and New Zealand (1959). This remains **a Lions scoring record.**

♣ **The captain of the first All Blacks/New Zealand rugby team** was **Dave Gallaher** (1873–1917) of Ramelton, Co. Donegal. He emigrated at an early age and his family settled in Auckland. He led New Zealand in their first international, against Australia, in 1903 and then in their first tour of Britain and Ireland in 1905/6. He missed the games in Ireland through injury. He was killed in World War I at Passchendaele in 1917.

SNOOKER

♣ **Alex 'Hurricane' Higgins**, born in Belfast in 1949, was **World Professional Snooker Champion in 1972 and 1982.** He won his first world title at 23 and was, at the time, **the youngest ever winner**. His fast and exciting style of play always attracted crowds, although it was another ten years before he won his second world title. Other tournament successes include: British Gold Cup 1980, UK Open 1983, Benson & Hedges Masters 1978 and 1981, Irish Professional Championships 1983 and 1989 and Benson & Hedges Irish Masters 1989.

♣ **Dennis Taylor**, born in Coalisland, Co. Tyrone in 1949, **won the World Professional Championship in 1985.** In one of the most exciting finals ever, Taylor beat Steve Davis on the black in the last frame to win 18–17, in front of a TV audience of 18.5 million. Taylor was twice a semi-finalist in the World Championship in 1975 and 1977 and was runner-up to Terry Griffiths of Wales in the 1979 final. He was Irish Professional Champion in 1982 and from 1985 to 1987. Other titles include: the Rothmans Grand Prix in 1984 and the Benson & Hedges Masters in 1987.

♣ **Eugene Hughes** (1955–), born in Dún Laoghaire, Co. Dublin, was Irish Amateur Champion in 1976 and 1978. He turned professional in 1981 and peaked at a world ranking of 17.

♣ **Alex Higgins, Eugene Hughes** and **Dennis Taylor** combined as the Ireland team that won three successive World Cups 1985–87.

♣ **The youngest ever winner of the World Amateur Snooker Championships** is **Stephen O'Connor**, born in Ireland on 16 October 1972. O'Connor won the title in Colombo, Sri Lanka on 25 November 1990, at the age of 18 years and 40 days.

TENNIS

♣ **The world's first ladies' tennis championship** was held at Fitzwilton, Dublin in June 1879. The Irish ladies singles title was won by **Mary Isabella 'May' Langrishe** who thus became **the world's first national women's singles champion**.

♣ **Helena Bertha Grace 'Lena' Rice** (1866–1907), born at Marlhill, Newinn, Co. Tipperary, is the only Irish woman to have won the Wimbledon ladies singles title, which she achieved in 1890 by defeating Miss M. Jacks 6–4, 6–0 to win the £21 prize money. The previous year she had been beaten in the final by Blanche Hillyard. Later she had the distinction of becoming **the first woman line judge at Wimbledon**. She died suddenly at Marlhill on her 41st birthday.

♣ **The 1890 Wimbledon singles champion, James Willoughby Hamilton** (1864–1943), was born in Monasterevin, Co. Kildare, the first of several Irish champions in the 1890s.

♣ **The 1893 and 1894 Wimbledon singles champion, Dr Joshua Pim** (1869–1942), was born in Bray, Co. Wicklow. He defeated Wilfred Badeley, who had beaten him in the 1891 and 1892 finals. Pim was also doubles champion at Wimbledon in 1890 and 1893 with **Frank Owen Stoker** of Dublin. Stoker, who was the cousin of the author of Dracula (see p. 137), is **the only Wimbledon champion also to be awarded international caps at rugby** (5 for Ireland 1886–91).

♣ **The 1896 Wimbledon singles champion, Harold Sigerson Mahony** (1867–1905), born at

Dromore Castle, Co. Kerry, was also a winner of two silver and one bronze medal at the 1900 Olympic Games in Paris. He was beaten in the Wimbledon singles Challenge Round in 1897 and in the all-comers finals of 1893 and 1898. He was runner-up in the Wimbledon all-comers doubles finals of 1892 and 1903. (See also Olympic Games, p. 164.)

♣ **The 1912 Australian men's singles and doubles champion, James Cecil Parke** (1881–1946), of Clones, Co. Monaghan, was also an international rugby and golf player for Ireland. He won a silver medal in the Olympic doubles competition in London in 1908. At Wimbledon he was champion at mixed doubles with Ethel Larcombe in 1912 and 1914 and lost four times in the final of the all-comers men's doubles event, 1911–13 and 1920. (See also Olympic Games, p. 166.)

♣ **John Pius Boland** (see Olympic Games, p. 164) won two gold medals for tennis at the Olympic Games in Athens in 1896.

♣ **Mabel E. Cahill**, born in Ballyragget, Co. Kilkenny in 1863, is **the only Irish-born person to win a United States Championship.** She moved to New York in 1889 and won the US ladies singles title in 1891 and went on to win the doubles. In 1892 she made history by becoming **the first player in American tennis to win the Triple Crown:**

singles, mixed doubles (with Clarence Herbert), and the women's doubles (with Adeline McKinnan). She gave up competitive tennis the following year and in 1976 was placed in the **Tennis International Hall of Fame**.

WEIGHTLIFTING

♣ **The 1987 powerlift world champion in the 56kg class, Gerry McNamara,** was born in Limerick in 1963. He has won 11 All-Ireland titles between 52 and 60kg. He has also won three Senior European titles – in 1986 and 1987 in the 56kg class and in 1988 in the 60kg class. Since winning the world championship in 1987, he has come second in the world in the 60kg class in 1988 and 1990.

WRESTLING

♣ **Dan O'Mahony** of Ballydehob, Co. Cork won **the World Heavyweight Wrestling Championship** in 1934 by beating Ed Don George in Braves Field, Boston, USA, before a crowd of 50,000. A former soldier in the Irish Army, he emigrated to the US. He returned to Dalymount Park in Dublin in 1936 to defend his title successfully against Rube Wright. He introduced his own type of throw to the sport, now called the 'Irish Whip'.

the church

PATRON SAINTS OF IRELAND

🍀 **St Patrick:** All over the world St Patrick is recognised as the Patron Saint of Ireland. Less well known is the fact that he was not an Irishman, was not the first traditional saint of Ireland and nor was he the first to bring Christianity to Ireland.

The history of St Patrick and of Ireland in the fifth century remains largely unknown. In his writings, St Patrick says that he was from Roman Britain, the son of a deacon who lived in the village of Bannaven Taberniae, which has been variously located by scholars in Cumberland, the Severn Valley and Anglesey. Alternative claims have been legitimately made for the town of St Patrice, near Tours in France, where the cult of St Patrick is strong and predates his mission to Ireland c. AD 431. What is commonly accepted by all is that he was a Celt, but not a Gael, and that his name was Sucat, an old Roman title of nobility later changed to Patricius. It is also believed that, as described in his writings, he was abducted by Irish raiders at the age of 16 and brought to Ireland as a slave to herd sheep and cattle.

After six years of bondage, he escaped to his homeland but soon began to hear voices imploring him to return to Ireland. He never mentions in his writings where he studied for the church, but it is believed that it was in Auxerre, France or possibly at Tours. According to tradition, the Pope had appointed the bishop Palladius to Ireland in AD 431, but when St Patrick arrived later in the same year he found four bishops, excluding Palladius, already there: Ailbhe, Declan, Ciarán and Ibar. This indicates that a large number of Christians were practising in Ireland before Patrick's arrival. Over a period of 30 years Patrick had unprecedented success in making converts to Christianity. Ireland, it seems, was **the only country in Europe to embrace the new religion of Christianity without bloodshed or martyrdom**. It is to the success of his mission that St Patrick owes his fame.

The date and place of his death are uncertain, but tradition has it that he died at Saul, near Downpatrick,

Co. Down on 17 March c. AD 490. His name and that of Ireland have become inseparably linked and his feast day on 17 March is celebrated throughout the world.

The name 'Patrick' was relatively uncommon in Ireland before the end of the 17th century. The wider use of the name from that time has been attributed to the popularity of Patrick Sarsfield as much to St Patrick. (General Patrick Sarsfield, d. 1693, Earl of Lucan, fought in the service of James II against the Williamites at the siege of Limerick.)

🍀 **St Brigid** (c. AD 450–525) was possibly **the first and, so far, only female Christian bishop**. Little certain is known of her life and the various acts attributed to her belong to legend. She was most probably born at Faughart, near Dundalk in Co. Louth, and she founded a great religious house at Kildare. Brigid's life is recorded in the medieval hagiographies of monks, who described her importance in the Christianising of Celtic pagan customs and religious belief in Ireland.

Brigid and her followers enjoyed enormous power in the early Irish Church, a power that derived from a recognition of the sacredness of female fertility and the 'Mother Goddess' in a society that was reluctant to let go of many elements of its Celtic heritage.

The various *Lives of Brigid* describe her ordination as a bishop and, although some commentators are clearly uncomfortable with it, none deny it:

'The bishop being intoxicated with the grace of God there did not recognise what he was reciting from his book, for he consecrated Brigit with the orders of a bishop. "This virgin alone in Ireland," said Mel* [the bishop who ordained her], "will hold the episcopal ordination".'

Although there are those who reject the accounts of her actual consecration, Brigid clearly did perform the social duties of a bishop, mediated between rival factions and had the power to pardon criminals. The political significance of Brigid's position in ecclesiastical history is only now emerging.

St Brigid is venerated the world over. In England alone there are 19 dedications to her, including **the oldest place of Christian worship in London**, St Bride's in Fleet Street. (Fleet Street was traditionally an Irish ghetto until the Industrial Revolution.) Some scholars speculate that the word 'bride' passed into the English language based on an image of saintly womanhood represented by Brigid.

---

* Mel Colmcille Gibson, the Australian film star, is named after Mel.

In 1185 the Peace of Constance was ratified at St Brigid's Church, Fiesole in Italy, founded by the Irish saint Donato in the 9th century.

♣ **St Colmcille** (c. 521–597; feast day 9 June) of Gartan, Co. Donegal, also known as **St Columba of Iona**, was the great-grandson of the O'Neill chieftain who kidnapped St Patrick. Colmcille was the greatest scholar and leader of his day and was destined to become King of Ulster and probably King of Ireland had he not chosen a monastic life.

Colmcille had studied at the best monasteries in Ireland, at Moville, Clonard and Glasnevin, and acquired the bardic skills of poetry and music. He founded his first school at Derry and others at Kells, Durrow and Swords.

At the age of 42 he chose to visit Scotland to convert the Gaels of Ulster, who had settled in the remote western isles. This was to have a profound influence on Gaelic culture and Scottish ecclesiastical history. The demise of the Pictish kingdom coincided with the Christianising of Scotland and the rise of Gaelic culture. Within 200 years of Colmcille's mission the Picts had virtually disappeared from Scotland. Colmcille did not travel to Scotland to convert the Picts – this was more the work of his contemporary Moluag, also from Ulster, and other missionaries in subsequent years. Colmcille wanted to preach to his fellow Gaels in Scotland and to preserve the Gaelic culture, which was in danger of self-destruction. It was from Iona, however, that the greatest impetus for the conversion of Scotland and England came. (The monastery on Iona was founded by Colmcille in AD 563.) Colmcille carried out **the first Christian inauguration of a king**, when he consecrated Aidan as King of the Scots. His influence and reputation in Scotland was strong enough to survive the Reformation 1000 years later.

♣ **St Aidan** (d. 651; feast day 31 August) was the first bishop of Lindisfarne, Northumbria. In 633 Oswald became king of Northumberland and in 635 he allowed the monks of Iona, where he had lived in exile, to convert his kingdom to Christianity. (At Lindisfarne Aidan taught in Irish while the king acted as a translator.)

Although Augustine (d. c. 605) is called the Apostle of England, it is now recognised that it was the Irish monks who effectively converted England. Aidan was the first to make an impact in Northumbria, while his successors, Finian and Colman, both abbots of Lindisfarne, witnessed the spread of Christianity among the Anglo-Saxons in the south.

♣ **St Columbanus of Luxeuil** (c. 543–615; feast day 23 November) was born of a powerful Leinster family and educated at the famous school in Bangor, Co. Down. In 575 he arrived in France with 12 followers and, without any official authority, began denouncing bishops and royalty for their moral failings. That he was allowed to do this with little or no fear testifies to the strength of the Irish church in western Europe at this early stage. In fact, it was then widely believed that it was only a matter of time before the Irish Church took over from Rome as the head of Christendom. Columbanus put an end to these fears when he dedicated Ireland to the Universal Church and the Irish people to the papacy. Irish Catholic devotion to the papacy has endured, with few exceptions, to the present day.

Columbanus' mission in Europe was exceptionally

THE FIVE EARLIEST KNOWN IRISH SAINTS (Previous to St Patrick)

♣ **St Abban of Abingdon; feast day 13 May** Abingdon in Berkshire, England is said to have been founded in AD 165 by Abban, **the earliest known Irish saint.**

♣ **St Gunifort of Pavia; feast day 26 August:** Gunifort's relics continue to be venerated in Pavia, Italy, which later became a centre for Irish missionaries. Gunifort was martyred there c. AD 300.

♣ **St Mansuetus of Toul; feast day 24 September:** the first Bishop of Toul in France was appointed in AD 340 by the Pope. He was reputed to be from Ireland.

♣ **St Grimonia of Soissons, France; feast day 24 September:** Grimonia was martyred near Soissons in the 4th century. She was **Ireland's first woman martyr to be canonised.**

♣ **St Eliph of Toul, France; feast day 16 October:** this Irish monk was beheaded c. AD 362 with his brother and two sisters. Mount Eliph, near Toul, commemorates him, and his relics are now in Cologne, Germany.

successful. He and his disciples established over 100 monasteries, mostly in France and Switzerland. The most famous of these was St Gall in Switzerland, founded by his follower, Gall, and Bobbio in Italy, founded by Columbanus himself after he had been banished by King Theodoric II of Burgundy in 610. Bobbio, where Columbanus died, flourished as a centre of European learning for 12 centuries until it was closed by Napoleon in 1802. Numerous parishes in northern Italy are dedicated to him as are several international organisations, such as the Knights of Columbanus.

🍀 **The only Irish person to be offered the papacy** was reputedly **St Kilian of Aubigny** (feast day 13 November), not to be confused with his more famous namesake, St Kilian of Würzburg (see below). Kilian was a follower of St Fiacre of Meaux (see below), but set up his own mission in the 7th century AD at Aubigny, where he is the object of great veneration today. He declined to accept the papacy.

🍀 **St Kilian of Würzburg** (feast day 8 July) is believed to have been born near Cootehill, Co. Cavan. In 680 he arrived in Würzburg with two followers and converted Duke Gospert, who ruled the territory. St Kilian and his followers were later executed for questioning the marriage of the duke to the widow of his brother, but were publicly venerated as martyrs in 752.

🍀 **St Colman of Melk** (feast day 13 October): the Abbey of Melk, on the River Danube in Austria, was founded by the Irish monk Colman, who was martyred in 1012. The Abbey became a place of pilgrimage for people from all over Austria, Hungary and Bavaria. Colman (or Koloman as he is more commonly known) was himself a pilgrim to the Holy Land but was held back in Austria during a local war. He was tortured and hanged on suspicion of being a spy.

🍀 **St Fiacre** (feast day 30 August) arrived in the diocese of Meaux in about 626 and became one of the most hallowed of all saints in France. Three towns and 30 churches are named after him and he was special patron to St Vincent de Paul, who emulated his charity and compassion, Jacques-Bénigne Bossuet, Bishop of Meaux, and Cardinal Richelieu. The influence of these two latter figures over the French royal family was illustrated by the annual royal pilgrimages to the shrine of St Fiacre. His intercession was invoked by Louis XIII and Queen Anne of Austria to provide an heir. Louis XIV, the 'Sun King', was hailed as Fiacre's answer to their prayer. The village of Breuil is now on the site of St Fiacre. Fiacre is also remembered in Ireland at Graiguenamanagh, Co. Kilkenny and in Scotland at the church of St Fiacre, near St Ficker's Bay, close to Aberdeen. (When public transport first appeared in Paris, the horse-drawn cabs had their terminus at the Hôtel St Fiacre. A 'fiacre' became the French word for a 'cab' or a hired horse-drawn vehicle.)

🍀 **St Brendan the Navigator** (see p. 29).

🍀 **Marianus Scotus of Ratisbon** (d. 1088; feast day 9 February): Muiredach MacRobartaigh (MacGroarty) was born in Co. Donegal, a kinsman of the ruling O'Donnell clan. He left on a pilgrimage to Rome in 1067 but was persuaded to remain at a pilgrim's hostel in Ratisbon, Germany on the way. There the Abbess Emma, having seen his remarkable skill at writing manuscripts, encouraged him to dedicate himself to the local church of St Peter. In 1076 he was given charge of the church and founded the Abbey of St Peter. The success of the Abbey soon became famous and students came in large numbers from Ireland to work there. Within 100 years 12 abbeys altogether were granted the status of individual statehood. The Congregation of Abbeys consisted of St Peter's and St James' in Ratisbon, Würzburg, Nuremberg, Constance, St Mary's and St George's in Vienna, Erfurt, Oels, Kelheim, Memmingen and Schottenburg. These institutions were mostly staffed and funded from Ireland until 1515, when Scottish monks were admitted by Pope Leo X.

🍀 **St Gall, Patron Saint of Switzerland** (feast day 16 October): Gall was a companion of Columbanus (see p. 199) in Burgundy before their expulsion. They parted company and in 612 Gall set up an oratory in Switzerland. The site remained a centre for Irish missionaries for many centuries and is today the site of one of the great abbeys of Europe. The Swiss city and canton of St Gallen is named after him.

The Abbey of Sankt Gallen grew in status after the death of St Gall (c. 640). The 9th-century Irish scholar Moengal, considered the finest of his time, worked there and Tutilo (probably the Irish Tuathal, the great musical teacher) made the Abbey one of the main centres of Gregorian chant in the Middle Ages. The canton of St Gall joined the Swiss Confederation in 1454. The abbey was closed by Napoleon in 1805, but retained its treasures and continues to hold some of the finest Irish manuscripts in the world, including

the first Latin-German dictionary, written by an Irish monk in the 8th century.

✤ **St Fridolin of Sackingen** (feast day 6 March): St Fridolin established an abbey on the Rhine in the 6th century, where carved stones of Irish design can be seen today. He is widely venerated in Switzerland, Austria and Bavaria and, on his feast day, the inhabitants of Sackingen fly the flags of Germany, Switzerland and Ireland from their homes.

✤ **St Cathal of Taranto**, Italy (also known as Cathaldus in Latin, or Cataldo in Italian; feast day 10 May), was a bishop of Taranto in the 7th century and is one of the most popular saints in Italy. There is a town called St Cataldo in southern Italy and another in Sicily. His image adorns a pillar of the Basilica of the Nativity in Bethlehem. Cathal was a teacher in Lismore, Co. Waterford before he moved to Italy.

✤ **St Fergal** or **St Vergilius** (d. 784; feast day 27 November) left Ireland (where, according to the Annals of the Four Masters, he was Abbot of Aghaboe, Co. Laois) to teach at the court of Pepin the Short, the father of Charlemagne, before he was sent to Duke Otillo of Bavaria, who placed him in charge of the diocese of Salzburg. Fergal was appointed **the first archbishop of Salzburg** and after his death his church became a place of pilgrimage for people from all over Austria, northern Italy and Yugoslavia. (A statue of him stands in front of Salzburg Cathedral today.) Often called the Apostle of Carinthia, one Duke of Carinthia honoured him by issuing a coin embellished with his likeness. The reverse side portrayed a predecessor of Fergal's, called Rupert. According to tradition, Rupert was also from Ireland. His sister Erintrude is believed to have come with him to Carinthia, where she founded the convent at Nonnberg. (This convent was made famous in the film and play, *The Sound of Music*.)

Fergal came from a seafaring tribe in his native Waterford. Fergal independently arrived at the conclusion that the world was round, based on his seafaring experience. He wrote at length about the possibility of other human civilisations existing in the Antipodes. His ideas were condemned as heretical by many but were respected by Pope Zacharias, who consecrated him as Archbishop of Salzburg. It was several hundred years before his ideas were universally accepted.

✤ The remains of **St Valentine** (d. AD 270; feast day 14 February) are kept in Whitefriar Carmelite Church, Aungier Street, Dublin. Pope Gregory XVI gave the remains to Fr Spratt, the founder of the present church buildings, from the cemetery of St Hippolytus, Rome in 1835. St Valentine's feast-day is the Christianised celebration of the Roman love festival, Lupercalia. Valentine, a Roman martyr-priest, became the patron saint of lovers, but his feast was dropped from the liturgical calendar in 1969.

✤ St Ives, near Land's End, Cornwall at the southwest tip of England was reputedly named after an Irish nun, **St Eva** (feast day 3 February), who built her cell near the mouth of the River Hayle in the 5th century.

✤ **The first archbishop of Dublin** was **St Laurence O'Toole** (c. 1130–80; feast day 14 November). Born in Leinster of noble blood, he was sent to the monastery of Glendalough to be educated. In 1162 the clergy and people of Dublin chose him as their first archbishop. After the city fell to the invading Normans, led by Strongbow, Earl of Pembroke, in 1170, O'Toole helped to organise an army to retake it. The Irish, led by Roderic O'Connor, were routed in 1171. O'Toole, recognising that the Normans could not be defeated in battle, submitted to King Henry II, who arrived from Britain later that year to assert his authority. O'Toole persuaded Strongbow to build Christchurch Cathedral, which still stands today in Dublin's city centre. He strove constantly to keep the peace between the Normans and the native Irish, but incurred the anger of Henry II, who closed all Irish ports to him to prevent his return from a diplomatic mission in 1180. O'Toole followed Henry II to Normandy to seek permission to return home, but died in Eu, Normandy. He was canonised in 1226.

✤ **The last Catholic martyr to be executed at Tyburn in London, St Oliver Plunkett** (1625–81; feast day 1 July) was born at Loughcrew, Co. Meath. Educated at the Irish College in Rome 1647–54, he returned to take the archbishopric of Armagh in 1670. He reorganised his archdiocese with little interference for three years before he was forced to go into hiding for several years as the persecution of Catholics in Ireland intensified. After the Popish Plot – a supposed Catholic plot invented by Titus Oates – in London in 1678, an expulsion order was made against all Catholic clergy in Ireland. Plunkett was arrested in 1679 and charged with conspiring to bring about armed rebellion. He was transferred to Newgate Prison in London and, after months of delay, was subjected to a sham trial and found guilty of treason for complicity in the 'plot'. On 1 July 1681 he was hanged, drawn and quartered at Tyburn, the last religious martyr to die there. His head is preserved in St Peter's Church, Drogheda. He was beatified in 1920 and canonised in 1975, **the first Irish person to be made a saint since Laurence O'Toole** 749 years before.

OTHER RELIGIOUS FIGURES

♣ **Johannes Scotus Eriugena*** (c. 815–877?), born in Ireland, taught at the court school of Charles the Bald in Burgundy, France. Much of Eriugena's thinking lay outside mainstream European thought and his theories on predestination were dismissed as 'pultes Scotorum' – 'Irishman's porridge' – by the Council of Valence. He was the last Western scholar for many centuries who could read Greek. His Christian philosophy was overlaid with Neoplatonic and oriental ideas, and attempted to reconcile faith and reason. His translations of many works of the early Eastern Church provide an essential link with a past that would otherwise have been lost. At the request of Charles the Bald he translated into Latin the works of pseudo-Dionysus the Areopagite (Greek texts from which much of our knowledge of neoplatonic philosophy derives), which influenced the development of medieval mystical thought. *De Divisione,* his major work, was condemned in his own day and in later centuries as pantheistic. It was put on the Vatican's *Index of Prohibited Books* in 1685.

♣ **Johannes Duns Scotus** (c. 1265–1308) was probably born in Dun (Down) in Ulster. His name would then mean 'John the Irishman from Down' – although it is argued by some that he was born in Scotland. Duns Scotus was a brilliant scholastic philosopher, who rivalled St Thomas Aquinas as the greatest theologian of the Middle Ages. His writings gained many followers – named 'scotists' – and his

* *'Scotus' is the original word for Irishman. Scotland derives its name from the settlement of Irish people there. These were mostly invading Celtic tribes from Ulster who came between the 3rd and the 6th centuries* AD. *After that Christian monks came from Ireland to convert the pagan Picts of northern and central Scotland.*

'Eriugena' means 'born in Ireland'. 'Eriu' is an old form of 'Eire', Irish for Ireland. Literally translated, therefore, Johannes Scotus Eriugena means 'John the Irishman born in Ireland'.

It is said that Charles the Bald, always fond of a joke, once made a pun at Eriugena's expense by asking: 'What is the difference between an Irishman [Scotus in Latin] and a pig [sottus]?' Eriugena's reply was 'The table'.

St Oliver Plunkett, the last Catholic martyr to be executed at Tyburn, was a victim of Titus Oates' 'Popish Plot'. After 19 months in jail in Dublin and London, he was hanged, drawn and quartered at Tyburn on 1 July 1681.

arguments were part of standard Catholic theology until the Reformation.

He joined the Franciscan order and studied at Merton College, Oxford, where he held the chair of divinity from 1301. Consalvo, general of the Franciscans, recommended him to the University of Paris, then the centre of European learning. In Paris and then in Cologne he argued for the primacy of the will of the individual and was critical of the theological system of St Thomas Aquinas. He argued the doctrine of the Immaculate Conception with such skill that he earned the name 'Dr Subtilis' ('Subtle Doctor'). He wrote extensively, mostly on the Bible, Aristotle and the *Sentences* of Peter Lombard. The only complete edition of his works was produced by the Irish scholar Luke Wadding and was published in 12 volumes in Lyon in 1639.

Duns Scotus died in Cologne in 1308. His later followers were hostile to change and opposed the 'New Learning' of the Renaissance humanists. They were ridiculed as enemies of learning and the word 'duns' or 'dunce' hence derived its meaning.

🍀 **Chaplain-in-ordinary to Queen Victoria**, **Stopford Augustus Brooke** (1832–1916) was born in Glendoen, near Letterkenny in Co. Donegal. He published many volumes of sermons and criticism of Browning, Tennyson, Shakespeare and Milton. His *Primer of English Literature* (1876) sold half a million copies in his lifetime.

🍀 **Archbishop Thomas William Croke** (1824–1902), born in Ballyclough, Co. Cork and honoured in Dublin today by Croke Park Stadium (home of the Gaelic Athletic Association), is reputed to have fought at the barricades of Paris during the 1848 revolution. He was ordained in 1846 and in 1870 was theologian to the Bishop of Cloyne at the First Vatican Council. He was appointed Bishop of Auckland, New Zealand in the same year. In 1875 he returned to Ireland as Archbishop of Cashel and Emly and became a powerful figure in Irish politics at the end of the 19th century. He gave strong support to the Irish cultural revival movement, the GAA and to the Home Rule and Land League political alliance, incurring the wrath of the British political establishment. His huge popularity further consolidated the influence of the Catholic Church in the newly emerging independent state.

🍀 **The youngest Catholic archbishop in the world, Richard Joseph Downey** (1881–1953), born in Kilkenny, was appointed to Liverpool in 1928 at the age of 47. Downey was largely responsible for putting an end to sectarian tensions in Liverpool.

Downey is also remembered as a record-breaking weight-watcher: standing a mere 5ft 4in (1.63m) tall, he weighed a massive 18 stone (114kg) in 1932. Seven years of dieting and exercise later, he had reduced his weight to 9 stone (57kg). He was inundated by mail from people all over the world, asking how he achieved this.

🍀 **Henry Essex Edgeworth** (1745–1807), confessor to Madame Elizabeth of France and to Louis XVI at his execution on 21 January 1793, was born in Edgeworthstown, Co. Longford (see p. 103).

🍀 **Founder of the American Methodist Church, Philip Embury** (1728–1803) was born in Ballingrane, Co. Limerick, the son of refugees from the German Palatinate. He became a travelling preacher and helped to build the Methodist church at Court Matrix. He emigrated to the United States in 1760 and settled in New York, where he worked as a carpenter and a teacher. He took up preaching again and in 1768 built the First Methodist Church at John Street, New York, beginning a religious movement that became the now-nationwide Methodist Episcopal Church. He died in Washington County, New York.

🍀 **The founder of American Presbyterianism, the Reverend Francis Makemie** (c. 1658–1708) was born in Ramelton, Co. Donegal. He arrived in America in 1683, probably with his family. A wandering evangelist, he travelled throughout the American colonies and the West Indies, preaching and founding new churches. In 1706 he founded the Presbytery of Philadelphia, which became a unifying centre for churches scattered throughout Maryland, Pennsylvania, New York and Virginia. He was arrested in New York in 1707 and prosecuted for preaching without a licence. His subsequent acquittal was a formal recognition of Presbyterianism and was regarded as a great victory for religious tolerance in America.

🍀 **The founder of the Church of God, John Walker** (1768–1833), was born in Co. Roscommon. He was educated at Trinity College, Dublin, elected a fellow in 1791 and ordained a priest of the Church of Ireland. He left the church, having become convinced of the unchristian nature of many of its practices, and began lecturing around Dublin, where he set up his own congregation at Stafford Street. The congregation called itself the Church of God, but was more usually referred to as the Separatists or Walkerites. Walker moved to London in 1819 and published a number of works. In 1833 he was granted a pension of £600 per annum by Trinity College to make amends for his expulsion on leaving the church, but he died that same year in Dublin.

🍀 **The first Catholic Archbishop of New York City,** the Most Reverend **John Hughes** (1797–1864), was born in Annaloghlan, Co. Tyrone. He emigrated to the United States in 1817 and worked as a gardener in the seminary in Emmitsburg, Maryland, where he was eventually accepted as a student. He was ordained in 1826 and earned a reputation as a fierce defender of Catholicism. He was appointed bishop in

1842 and then archbishop in 1850, when New York was made an archdiocese to cater for the massive influx of Irish fleeing from The Famine.

Hughes was a supporter of the Union side in the Civil War and was sent to Europe by President Abraham Lincoln to promote the cause. He founded the college at Fordham, now the Jesuit University, and laid the foundation stone of St Patrick's Cathedral, New York in 1858.

✿ **The first Archbishop of Toronto** was **John Joseph Lynch** (1816–88) of Clones, Co. Monaghan. Lynch emigrated to Texas in 1846 and gradually moved up the hierarchical ladder of the Catholic Church. He moved to Niagara in 1856 and became bishop there in 1859. He was appointed first Archbishop of Toronto in 1870.

✿ **The First United States Cardinal, John McCloskey**, was born in Brooklyn, New York in 1810, the son of Irish immigrants. In 1847 he was appointed the first Bishop of Albany. He succeeded Archbishop John Hughes of New York in 1864 and became the first cardinal in 1875. He died in 1885.

✿ **The founder of the Order of Mercy, the largest religious congregation in the English-speaking world, Catherine McAuley** (1778–1841) was born in Dublin. Orphaned as a child, she inherited a large fortune from her foster-parents when they died. She used this to build a home for poor women and children in Lower Baggot Street, Dublin in 1827. With two friends, she entered the Presentation Convent, Dublin and in 1831 took vows of poverty, chastity and obedience. The Order of the Sisters of Mercy thus came into existence and was approved by Pope Gregory XVI on 24 March 1835. The order grew steadily, and houses were founded in England, Australia, New Zealand and the United States.

✿ **Archbishop of Melbourne, Daniel Mannix** (1864–1963), was born in Charleville, Co. Cork. He had a brilliant academic career at Maynooth College, Kildare, where he was appointed professor of mental and moral theology in 1891 and professor of theology in 1894. He was president of the college from 1903 until 1912, when he was sent as assistant to the Bishop of Melbourne, Australia. In 1917 he was made Archbishop of Melbourne and became one of Australia's most powerful public figures. He successfully led public opposition to conscription for overseas service in the Australian Army during World War I and was a vociferous supporter of Irish independence.

He was greeted by huge crowds on a visit to the US in 1920, but was intercepted at sea and arrested by the British Navy whilst on his way to Ireland. After landing in Cornwall he was forbidden to speak at centres of Irish population in Britain.

As Archbishop of Melbourne for 47 years he established 108 new parishes, over 150 primary schools, 17 high schools, 17 technical schools and the seminary, Corpus Christi College. His term of office marked an era of growing social and political influence for the Irish in Australia. He is buried in St Patrick's Cathedral, Melbourne.

✿ **Australia's first cardinal, Patrick Francis Moran** (1830–1911) of Leighlinbridge, Co. Carlow, went to Australia in 1884 as Archbishop of Sydney and became a cardinal the following year. He established many schools, churches and hospitals and advocated Home Rule for Ireland. He was a supporter of Australian federation.

✿ **Mother Mary Martin** (1892–1975), born in Glenageary, Dublin, founded **the Medical Missionaries of Mary** in May 1936 in Anua, Nigeria. The Medical Missionaries now run hospitals throughout Africa, the United States, Italy and Spain. Mary Martin received the Florence Nightingale Medal from the International Red Cross in 1963 and was elected as **the first female honorary member of the Royal College of Surgeons of Ireland** in 1966.

✿ **The founder of the Presentation Order, Honoria (Nano) Nagle** (1728–84), was born at Balgriffin, near Mallow, Co. Cork. She opened a school for the education of Catholics in Cork in 1754, although Catholic schools were illegal at the time. She founded a new order 'which excluded every exercise of charity which was not in favour of the poor' in Cork in 1777. The Presentation Order was recognised by Rome in 1791 and has since spread to England, the United States, Australia and India.

✿ **Mother Theresa of Calcutta, Agnes Gonxha Bojaxhiu** (1910–), was born an ethnic Albanian in Skopje, Macedonia (previously Yugoslavia). At the age of 12 she decided she wanted to become a missionary and, when she was old enough to leave home in 1928, joined the Sisters of Loretto in Dublin, where she was trained for the missions. For more than 50 years she has dedicated herself to the alleviation of poverty and the spread of the Catholic faith throughout the world. She received the Nobel Peace Prize in 1979.

ireland's area and population

AREA

REPUBLIC	27,136 sq mi	70,282 sq km
NORTHERN	5,642 sq mi	14,177 sq km
TOTAL	32,778 sq mi	84,459 sq km

(20th largest island on earth)

POPULATION

REPUBLIC (1991 census)	3,523,401

(Decrease of 14,924 on 1986 population. This is the first decrease since 1961).

NORTHERN (1991 census)	1,578,000

(Increase of 5000 on 1981 population)

TOTAL	5,101,401

Population by Province

Leinster	1,860,037
Munster	1,008,443
Connacht	422,909
Ulster (Republic)	232,012
Ulster (Northern Ireland)	1,578,000

Population of City Boroughs over 100,000

Dublin County and County Borough	1,024,429
Belfast City*	295,000
Cork City	127,024
Limerick City	109,816
Derry City	100,500

* If the outlying Borough Councils of Castlereagh, Newtownabbey and Lisburn are included, greater Belfast's population is 524,700.

Population density

REPUBLIC	130 persons/sq mile
NORTHERN	280 persons/sq mile

Birth Rate

REPUBLIC (1991)	15.0 live births/1000
NORTHERN (1990)	16.7 live births/1000

Death Rate

REPUBLIC (1991)	8.9 deaths/1000
NORTHERN (1990)	9.7 deaths/1000

Net Growth/Decrease

REPUBLIC	− 0.423% since 1986
NORTHERN	+ 2.9 since 1981

Irish Language Speakers

REPUBLIC (1991) 1,095,830 or 32.5% of the population. This is a combined figure of those who speak Irish only and those who speak Irish and English. The latter group is much larger as indicated by the survey. Although 2% speak Irish all the time, they are bi-lingual. There are now no adults left who cannot speak English.

NORTHERN (1991) 142,000 people in Northern Ireland claim to have some knowledge of Irish, of whom 79,000 claim to speak, read and write it fluently.

♣ Highest recorded population. The first reliable census to be made in Ireland in 1841 was also the highest population ever recorded when the island as a whole supported 8,175,124 inhabitants, an increase of 5.5% on 1831 and 172% on 1779. The 1841 census is a conservative estimate and it is likely that many people went uncounted. It is probable that nearly 9,000,000 were living in Ireland before the Famine struck in 1845.

❉ **Lowest recorded population.** The lowest recorded population of Ireland as a whole was 4,228,553 in the 1926 census. The Republic's population numbered 2,971,992, a decrease of 5.34% since 1911. Northern Ireland's population numbered 1,256,561, an increase of 0.5% since 1911.

❉ **The lowest population of the Republic of Ireland** was recorded in 1961 at 2,818,341.

❉ **The lowest population of Northern Ireland** was recorded in 1926 at 1,256,561. It is calculated that the population reached an all-time low of 1,243,000 in 1931, between the 1926 and 1937 census counts.

The De-population of Ireland (All 32 counties) 1831–1926

1831	7,767,401	1881	5,174,377
1841	8,175,124*	1891	4,704,750
1851	6,552,385*	1901	4,458,775
1861	5,798,564	1911	4,390,219
1871	5,412,377	1926	4,228,553
			all-time lowest.

* Rates of under-enumeration of up to 25% in 1841 and 10% in 1851 have been suggested. By 1845–46 it is probable that over 9,000,000 people were living in Ireland. This would suggest a population decrease of, at least, 2,500,000 in 5 years. It is estimated that 1,500,000 people died of famine and typhus between 1846–51, and that an additional 1,000,000 fled the country. The Great Famine was the worst catastrophe in Irish (and British) history and exceeded the Black Death and Yellow Fever pandemics of previous centuries in its ferocity.

By the 1840s most of the Irish population were completely dependent on the potato. Potato rot, *Phytophthora infestans*, was first reported in Ireland on 13 September 1845. Although it was widespread in Europe, its effects in Ireland were particularly devastating.

The pattern of massive emigration and flight from the land that began during the Famine lasted until the 1960s. Irish emigrants in these years were generally leaving small rural farms to live in the large cities of the English-speaking world. Population decrease was accompanied by lower marriage and birth rates and the virtual extinction of the Irish language.

Ireland's Population as a Percentage of Great Britain Under The Union

1841	Ireland's population = 31% of total of Great Britain and Ireland.*
1851	Ireland's population = 24% of total of GB and Ireland
1911	Ireland's population = 9.7% of total of GB and Ireland

* If the ratio of population between Ireland and Great Britain and Ireland had remained at the 1841 level of 31%, Ireland would today be home to 18.5 million people.

The de-population of Ireland is conversely illustrated by the statistics of immigration to the United States. Irish emigration to Britain was considered migration during the Union and statistics of the numbers entering Britain are often approximations.

ESTIMATED POPULATIONS OF THE IRISH DIASPORA

The number of people who have left Ireland in the last 150 years amounts to proportionally the largest movement of people in modern European history. Over 50% of those born in Ireland since the Famine (1846–49) have left the country. The population decreased steadily from 1845 to 1966. The subsequent 20 years saw a sharp increase in population and there was even a return migration of emigrants in the 1970s. However, between 1986 and 1991 renewed emigration and a drastically reduced birth rate led to a slight fall in population once again. Today there are in excess of sixty million people worldwide who claim Irish ancestry.

In the United States some 43–44 million people claim Irish ancestry. Although the huge migration from Ireland to the United States has slowed dramatically in recent years, a constant trickle still remains. Even today 1 million New Yorkers give Ireland as their only ancestral country.

In Canada (population 27.3 million) 4 million

people claim Irish ancestry. After the French and the English, the Irish have been the largest ethnic community in Canada for the last 100 years.

The Irish population of Britain is harder to define. A census of names in Britain would indicate that there are over 6 million people of Irish heritage in Britain today, amounting to 1.2 million families, or nearly 11% of the population. The Irish-born (Republic only) population of Britain in the 1991 census was 592,020 (a 12% drop on 1961) or 1.05% of the population. This accounted for 14.7% of all British residents born outside Britain.

In Australia 25% of the population of 17.3 million is estimated to be Irish or of Irish descent, while the figure for New Zealand (population 3.4 million) is 15%. The bulk of the Irish arrived in the 19th century. Of these, one in eight were transported convicts.

The ethnic Irish population of Argentina (population 32.4 million) is estimated at 300,000. Of all the Latin American countries Argentina has the largest ethnic Irish community. The first Irish settlers in South America were exiles from Ireland and their descendants who worked in the service of the Spanish from the 17th century. Among the British invasion force of 1806–08 were many Irishmen who deserted the Royal Navy and stayed behind. During the 19th century Irish settlers and the Argentine government actively encouraged Irish men and women to come to

Argentina to supply the need for cheap labour for the fast-growing meat and wool industries. Emigrants came from a distinct geographical area that encompasses large parts of counties Westmeath, Wexford and Longford. This was a result of recruitment by earlier settlers from the same area. Virtually the entire town of Ballymore and environs in Co. Westmeath emigrated to Buenos Aires in the 1860s. In 1878 Buenos Aires had an Irish population of 25,000.

In France 400,000 Irishmen fought in the French Army during the War of the Spanish Succession (1701–13), the War of the Austrian Succession (1740–48), the Seven Years War (1756–63) and the Revolutionary and Napoleonic Wars (1792–1815). Most of these soldiers stayed on the continent and were widely dispersed and rapidly assimilated. A huge number of them died in battle, but many were accompanied by their families. Thus a significant, if displaced, dispersed and disorganised Irish community existed in continental Europe for some time.

An eviction scene in rural Ireland during the Famine. With the failure of the potato crop 1845–49 Irish cottiers had neither the strength nor the money to work their land and pay their rent. Thousands were evicted and starved to death on the roadsides.

a superlative map of Ireland

See pages 210–12 for full descriptions of the sites listed below

1. Highest point Carrantuohill together with Beenkeragh and Caher both over 3000 ft. **2.** Mount Brandon. **3.** Lugnaquilla. **4.** Galtymore. **5.** Highest point in N. Ireland – Slieve Donard. **6.** Longest river – The Shannon. **7.** Largest Lake – Lough Neagh. **8.** Lough Corrib. **9.** Lough Erne. **10.** Lough Ree. **11.** Highest waterfall – Powerscourt. **12.** Highest cliffs – Croaghan.

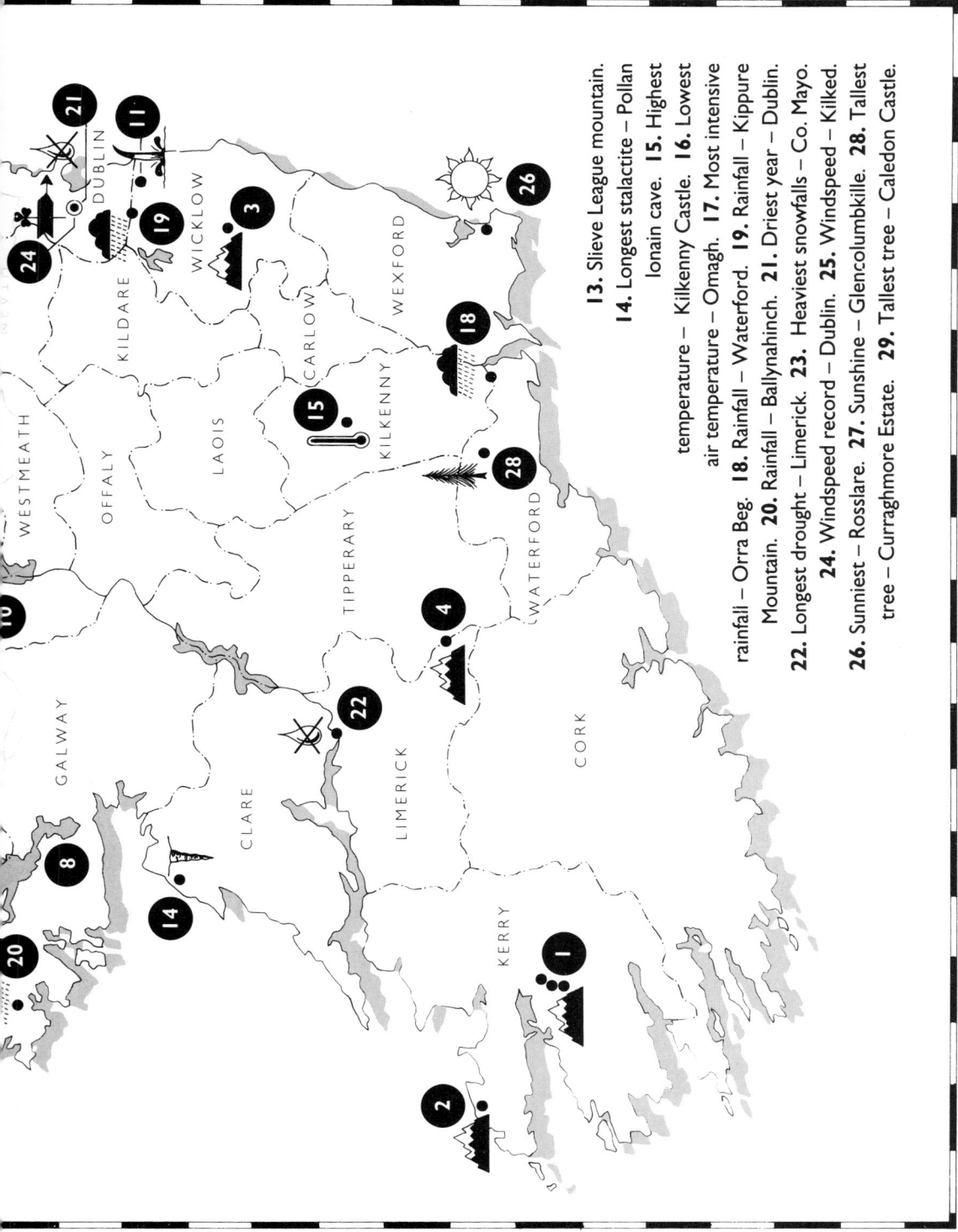

13. Slieve League mountain.
14. Longest stalactite – Pollan
    lonain cave. 15. Highest
    temperature – Kilkenny Castle. 16. Lowest
    air temperature – Omagh. 17. Most intensive
    rainfall – Orra Beg. 18. Rainfall – Waterford. 19. Rainfall – Kippure
    Mountain. 20. Rainfall – Ballynahinch. 21. Driest year – Dublin.
22. Longest drought – Limerick. 23. Heaviest snowfalls – Co. Mayo.
24. Windspeed record – Dublin. 25. Windspeed – Kilked.
26. Sunniest – Rosslare. 27. Sunshine – Glencolumbkille. 28. Tallest
    tree – Curraghmore Estate. 29. Tallest tree – Caledon Castle.

ireland's natural superlatives

❀ **Highest point** – The highest mountain on the island of Ireland is Carrantuohill in the MacGillycuddy's Reeks, Co. Kerry at 3414ft (1041m)

Five other peaks exceed 3000ft (915m):
Beenkeragh, a peak north of Carrantuohill – 3314ft (1011m)
Caher, a peak south-west of Carrantuohill – 3200ft (976m)
Mount Brandon, also in Kerry but part of the Dingle Peninsula – 3127ft (954m)
Lugnaquilla, the highest peak in the Wicklow hills is 45km south of Dublin and reaches a height of 3039ft (927m)
Galtymore, on the Tipperary/Limerick border is 3018ft (920m) high.

❀ **The highest point in Northern Ireland** is Slieve Donard, the tallest of the Mourne Mountains in Co. Down at 2789 ft (850 m).

❀ **Lowest point** – No point on the island is below sea level.

❀ **Longest river** – The Shannon is the longest river in Ireland. It rises 258 ft (79m) above sea level in Co. Cavan and flows 240 miles (386 km), including a 56 mile (90 km) estuary, to Loop Head and the Atlantic Ocean. The Shannon is longer than any river in the British Isles.

❀ **Largest lake** – The largest lake in Ireland is Lough Neagh (also the largest in the British Isles). It is bordered by all the counties of Northern Ireland excluding Fermanagh, is 18 miles (29 km) long and 11 miles (17.7 km) wide. It encompasses an area of 147.39 miles sq (381.73 km sq). Its deepest point is 102ft (31m) and it is 48ft (14.6m) above sea level.

Lough Corrib in Counties Galway and Mayo covers an area of 65.62 sq miles (170 sq km).

Lough Erne in Co. Fermanagh covers an area of 54 sq miles (140 sq km).

Lough Ree, north of Athlone town encompasses 38.6 sq miles (100 sq km).

Approximately one third of the area of County Fermanagh is water.

❀ **Highest waterfall** – The highest waterfall in Ireland is the Powerscourt Waterfall, 350ft (106m), on the River Dargle in Co. Wicklow.

❀ **Highest cliffs** – The highest cliffs in Ireland rise 2192ft (668m) sheer above the sea at Croaghan on the north coast of Achill Island, Co. Mayo. These are the highest cliffs in north-west Europe.

❀ Slieve League mountain, in south-west Co. Donegal rises 1971ft (601m) sheer above the Atlantic ocean.

❀ **Longest stalactite** – The longest free-hanging stalactite known is one of 20 ft 4in (6.2m) in the Pollan Ionain cave in Co. Clare. Stalactites supported artificially or by cave walls can grow longer.

❀ **Earthquakes** – No earthquake with its epicentre in Ireland has ever been recorded instrumentally. A shock, reported in August 1734, caused damage to 100 houses and five churches. More recently, the highest instrumentally recorded quake in Great Britain (on land) which hit North Wales on 19 July 1984 and measured 5.4 on the Richter Scale, was felt on the east coast of Ireland and caused minor structural damage. Statistically, Ireland is the safest place in the world to avoid earthquakes.

CLIMATE

Ireland enjoys a temperate, maritime climate. Although the country lies between 51.5 and 55 degrees north, the temperature is kept mild by the Gulf Stream. Ireland is on the same latitude as the Canadian tundra, which is frozen over for most of the year. Were the Gulf Stream to change its course, Ireland would be plunged into a mini ice-age.

The North Atlantic dictates the climate. Temperatures are equable and seasonal changes are gradual and prolonged. The air is moist and precipitation is generally caused by the movement of Atlantic frontal systems from the west. Strong winds are frequent,

A view of the Lakes of Killarney, Co. Kerry, with MacGillycuddy's Reeks (Ireland's highest mountains) in the background. Carrantuohill, the tallest of all, rises to 3414 ft. Co. Kerry has three other peaks exceeding 3000 ft.

especially during winter when the temperature difference between the equator and the north pole is at its greatest. This causes extra turbulence in the atmosphere and Ireland lies in the path of many of the resulting depressions.

🌸 **Temperature** – highest recorded. The highest shade temperature ever recorded in Ireland since records began in 1881 was 92°F/33.3°C at Kilkenny Castle on 26 June 1887.

🌸 **Lowest recorded**. The lowest air temperature ever recorded in Ireland was −2.92°F/−19.4°C at Omagh, Co. Tyrone on 23 January 1881.

🌸 **Rainfall** – The most intense fall of rain recorded in Ireland occurred in Orra Beg, Co. Antrim on 1 August 1980 when 3.82in (97mm) of rain fell in just 45 minutes. On 26 August 1949, 1.5in (38mm) of rain fell in 12 minutes at Waterford.

The storm of 25/26 August 1986 set new precipitation records nationwide. Kippure Mountain, Co. Wicklow (754 m) recorded a fall of 10.63in (270mm) in a 24 hour period.

The number of days on which rain falls in Ireland is generally high in comparison with other countries. Ballynahinch, Co. Galway recorded rainfall on 309 days in the calendar year 1923 – the most rainy days in one year recorded in Ireland and Britain.

🌸 **The driest year** on record was 1887 when a mere 14in (356.6mm) of rain fell in Dublin.

🌸 **The longest drought** recorded lasted from 3 April to 10 May 1938 at Mulgrave Street weather station in Limerick.

🌸 **Snowfall – The heaviest snowfalls** recorded in Ireland occurred in 1917. On 25/26 January, the south and west experienced a storm that deposited 23.6in (0.6m) over much of the south and west of the country while drifts of 177.5in (4.5m) were observed in Co. Mayo. 1 April of the same year saw even more severe falls with snow covering the country to depths of 51.2in (1.3m) with 118.2in (3.0m) drifts.

♣ **Windspeed** – The most damaging storm in Irish history occurred on 6/7 January 1839. Windspeeds on 'The Night of the Big Wind' cannot accurately be judged, but accounts of the death and destruction caused across Ireland, Wales, northern England and southern Scotland, together with records of atmospheric pressure and temperature recordings, would suggest that winds in excess of 100 knots were experienced. Up to 25% of all buildings in Dublin were partially or wholly destroyed.

A severe storm which passed over Ireland on 11/12 January 1974 produced a gust of 108 knots at Kilkeel, Co. Down, the highest ever recorded for a station at sea level in Ireland.

♣ **Sunshine** – The southeast corner is the sunniest area of Ireland. In 1959, Rosslare experienced the sunniest year on record with 1996.4 hours. A monthly total of more than 250 hours is extremely rare. However, Valentia Observatory recorded 308.2 hours of sunshine in July 1955.

Glencolumbkille, Co. Donegal experienced a mere 6.4 hours in the month of January 1974.

An aerial view of the River Shannon at Athlone. The Shannon is the longest river in Ireland – and the British Isles – flowing 240 miles from source to mouth.

select
bibliography

Australian Encyclopedia (Sydney, 1958)

Boylan, Henry, *Dictionary of Irish Biography* (Dublin, Gill & Macmillan, 1988, second edition)

Brady, A. and Cleeve, B., *A Biographical Dictionary of Irish Writers* (Dublin, Lilliput, 1985)

Briggs, Asa, *Dictionary of 20th Century World Biography* (Oxford University Press, 1992)

Byrne, Art, and McMahon, Seán, *Lives, 113 Great Irishwomen and Irishmen* (Dublin, Poolbeg, 1990)

Byrne, Art, and McMahon, Seán, *Great Northerners* (Dublin, Poolbeg, 1991)

Buchanan, Ian, *The Guinness Book of British Olympians* (London, 1991)

Callahan, Bob, *The Big Book of American Irish Culture* (New York, Viking, 1987)

Chambers, John, *101 Irish Lives* (Dublin, Gill & Macmillan, 1992)

Coakley, Davis, *The Irish School of Medicine* (Dublin, Townhouse, 1988)

Cooper, Brian, *The Irish American Almanac and Green Pages* (New York, Harper & Row, 1990)

Deane, Seamus, *The Field Day Anthology of Irish Literature* (Derry, Field Day Publications 1991)

De Breffny, Brian, *Ireland: A Cultural Encyclopaedia* (London, Thames & Hudson, 1993)

De Courcy Ireland, John, *Ireland and the Irish in Maritime History* (Dún Laoghaire, Glendale Press, 1986)

Dictionary of American Biography (New York, 1978–84)

Dictionary of National Biography (London, 1890–1980)

Dictionary of Scientific Biography (New York, 1976)

Doherty, Richard, *Irish Generals* (Belfast, Appletree Press, 1993)

Dublin Corporation Public Libraries, *Some Eminent Dubliners* (Dublin, 1988)

Dungan, Myles, *Distant Drums, Irish Soldiers in Foreign Armies* (Belfast, Appletree Press, 1993)

Encyclopaedia of Canada (Toronto, 1935)

Gleeson, John, *The Book of Irish Lists and Trivia* (Dublin, Gill & Macmillan, 1989)

Gleeson, John, *Fyffes Dictionary of Irish Sporting Greats* (Dublin, Etta Place Publishers, 1993)

Griffin, William D., *The Book of Irish Americans* (New York, Times Books, 1990)

Guiney, David, *Gold, Silver, Bronze* (Dublin, Sportsworld Productions, 1993)

Hayes, Richard, *Biographical Dictionary of Irishmen in France* (Dublin, 1949)

Hennessy, Maurice, *The Wild Geese: the Irish Soldier in Exile* (London, Sidgwick & Jackson, 1973)

Hickey, D.J., and Doherty, J.E., *A Dictionary of Irish History 1800–1980* (Dublin, Gill & Macmillan, 1980)

Hickey, D.J., and Doherty, J.E., *A Chronology of Irish History since 1500* (Dublin, Gill & Macmillan, 1989)

Killanin, Lord, and Duignan, Michael V., *The Shell Guide to Ireland*, 1989 edition (Dublin, Gill & Macmillan)

Magnusson, Magnus (ed.), *Chambers Biographical Dictionary* (Edinburgh, 1990)

Matthews, Peter; Buchanan, Ian; and Mallon, B., *The Guinness International Who's Who of Sport* (London, 1993)

Mollan, Charles; Davis, William; Finucane, Brendan, *Some People and Places in Irish Science and Technology* (Dublin, Royal Irish Academy, 1985)

Montague, Patrick, *The Saints and Martyrs of Ireland* (Buckinghamshire, Colin Smyth, 1981)

Myler, Patrick, *The Fighting Irish* (Dingle, Brandon Books, 1987)

Naughton, Lindie, and Watterson, Johnny, *Irish Olympians* (Dublin, Blackwater Press, 1992)

Newman, Kate, *Dictionary of Ulster Biography* (Belfast, Institute of Irish Studies, 1993)

Shannon, William V., *The American Irish* (University of Massachusetts, 1989)

Shepherd, S., and Morley, B., *Reader's Digest/AA Illustrated Guide to Ireland* (London, Reader's Digest, 1992)

Smith, Raymond, *The Sunday Independent/ACC Bank Complete Handbook of Gaelic Games* (Dublin, Sporting Books Publishers, 1993)

Swords, Liam, *The Green Cockade: the Irish in the French Revolution 1789-1815* (Dún Laoghaire, Glendale, 1989)

Whelehen, T.P., *The Irish Wines of Bordeaux* (Dublin, Vine Press, 1990)

index

Picture Acknowledgements

The Publishers wish to thank the following for permission to reproduce pictures in this book:

Allsport UK Ltd
Ann Ronan Picture Library
Archives Snark
The Associated Press Ltd
Barnardo's Photographic Archive
Bord Failte – Irish Tourist Board
Hulton-Deutsch Collection Ltd
Image Select
London Features International Ltd
Mary Evans/Fawcett Library
Mary Evans Picture Library
Popperfoto
The Press Association Ltd